Popcorn Romance

Tomoko Taniguchi
Writer and Artist

CPM®
MANGA
New York, New York

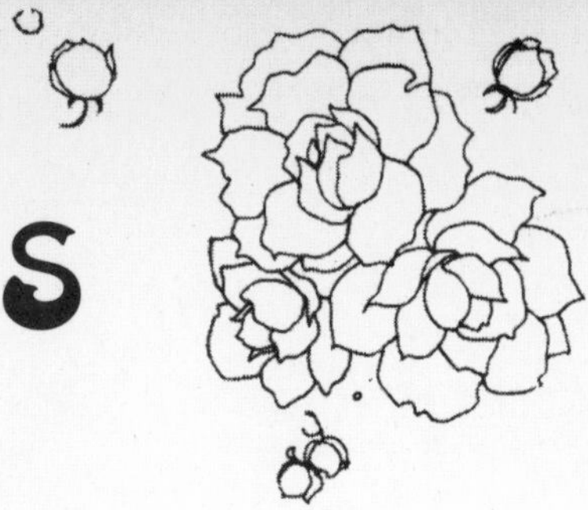

CONTENTS

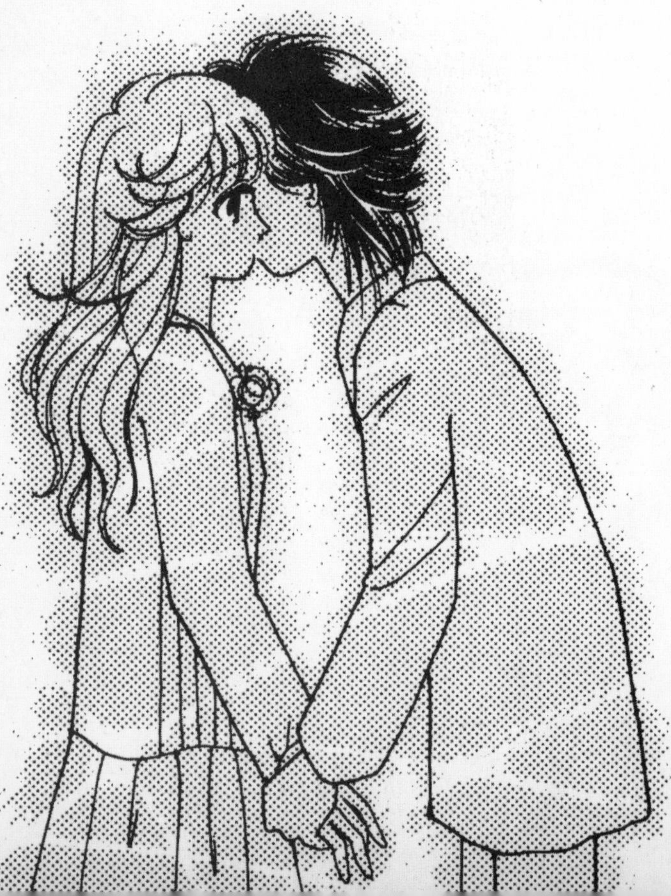

CHARACTER PROFILES

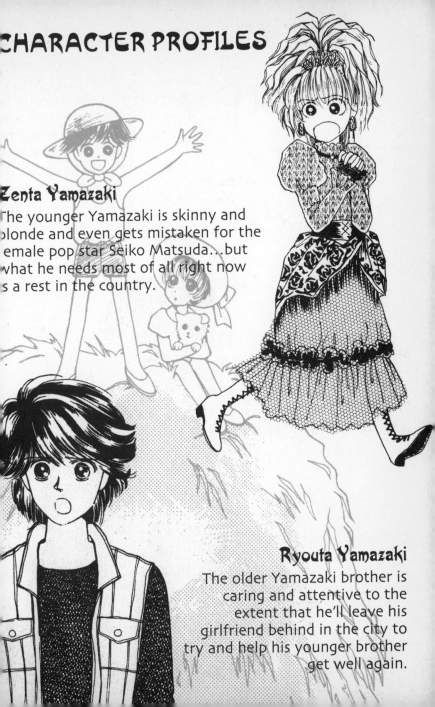

Zenta Yamazaki

The younger Yamazaki is skinny and blonde and even gets mistaken for the female pop star Seiko Matsuda...but what he needs most of all right now is a rest in the country.

Ryouta Yamazaki

The older Yamazaki brother is caring and attentive to the extent that he'll leave his girlfriend behind in the city to try and help his younger brother get well again.

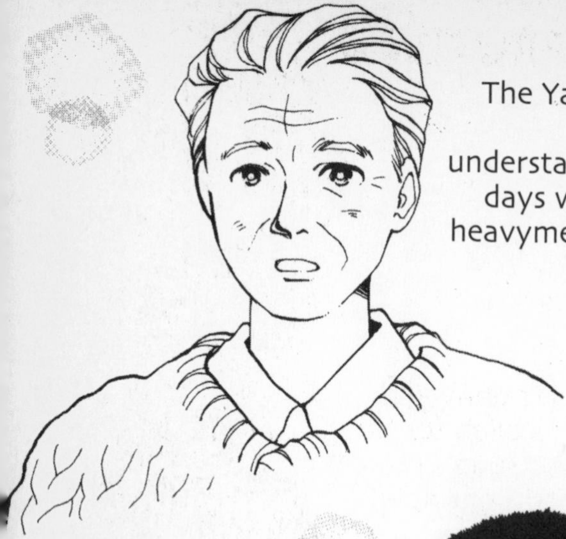

Grandpa Yamazak

The Yamazaki's old crotchet grandpa just doesn' understand the teenagers thes days with their long hair an heavymetal music. How will h deal with his tw rocker grandsons

Shima Obata

Ryouta's girlfriend is patient and kind...but how long can a young girl wait for romance?

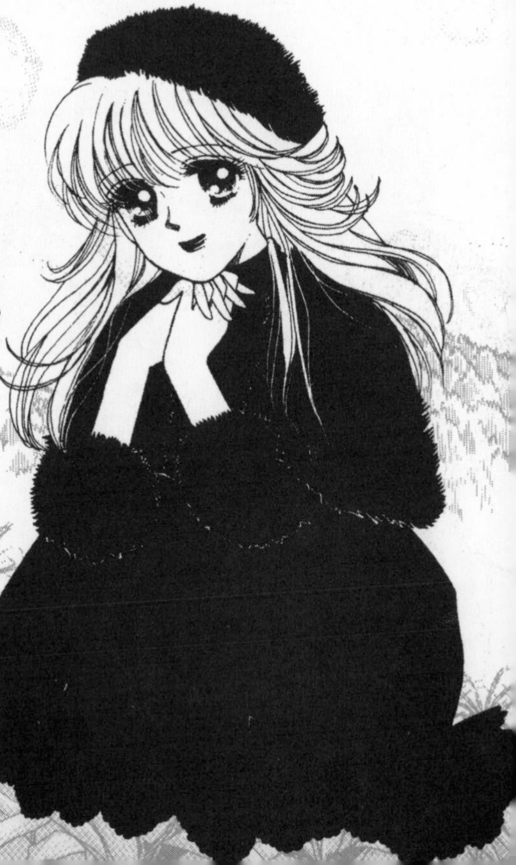

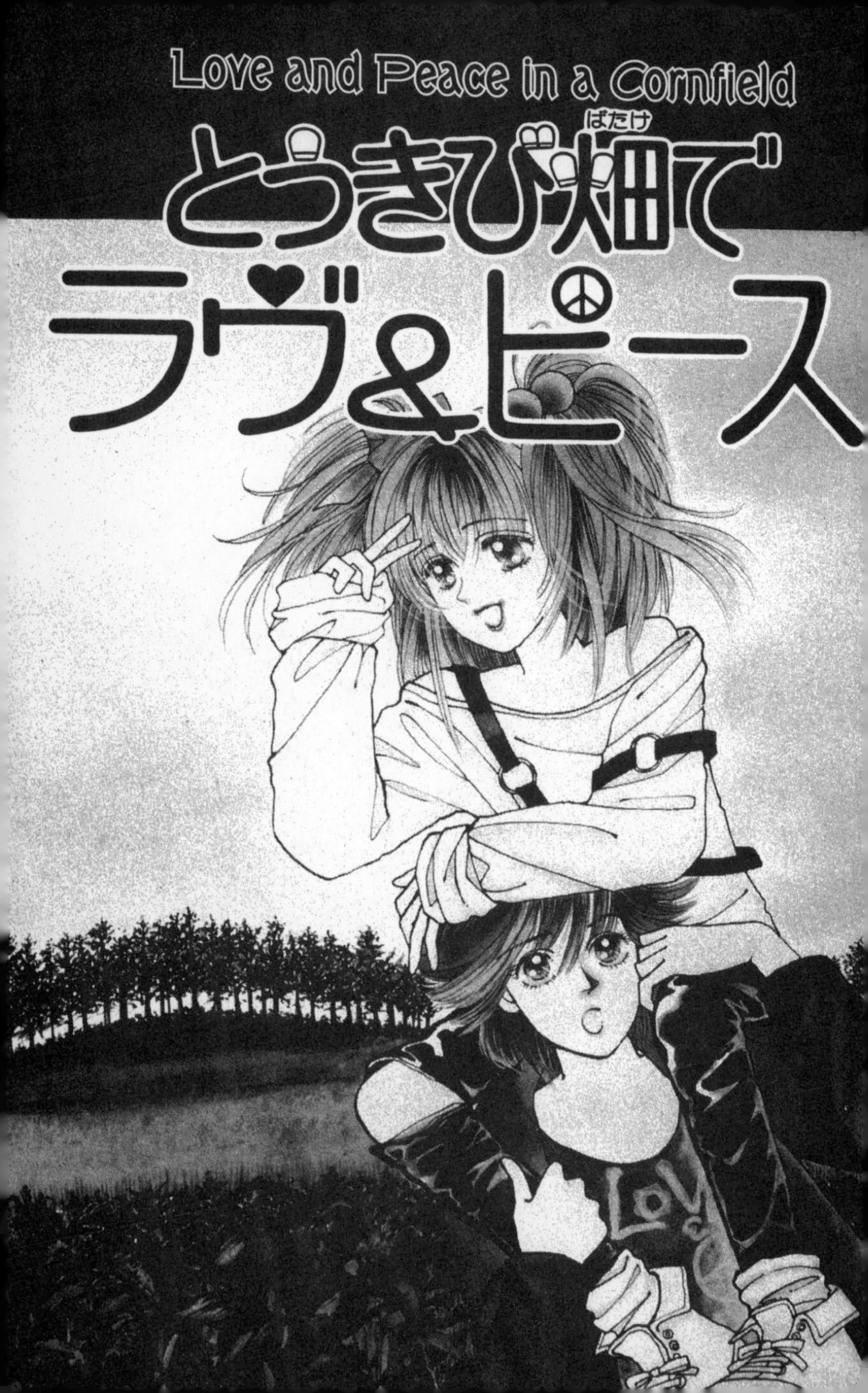
Love and Peace in a Cornfield
とうきび畑で
ラヴ&ピース

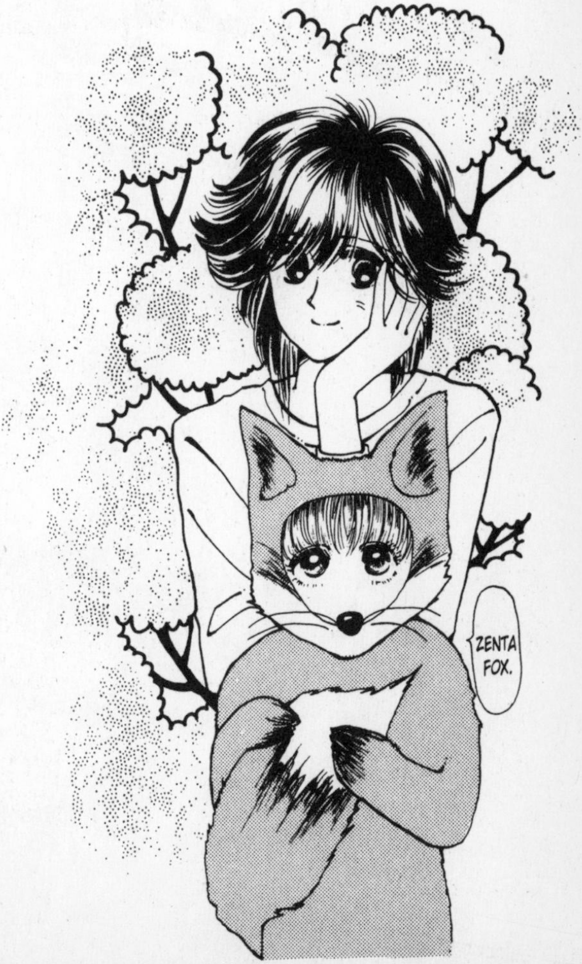
ZENTA FOX.

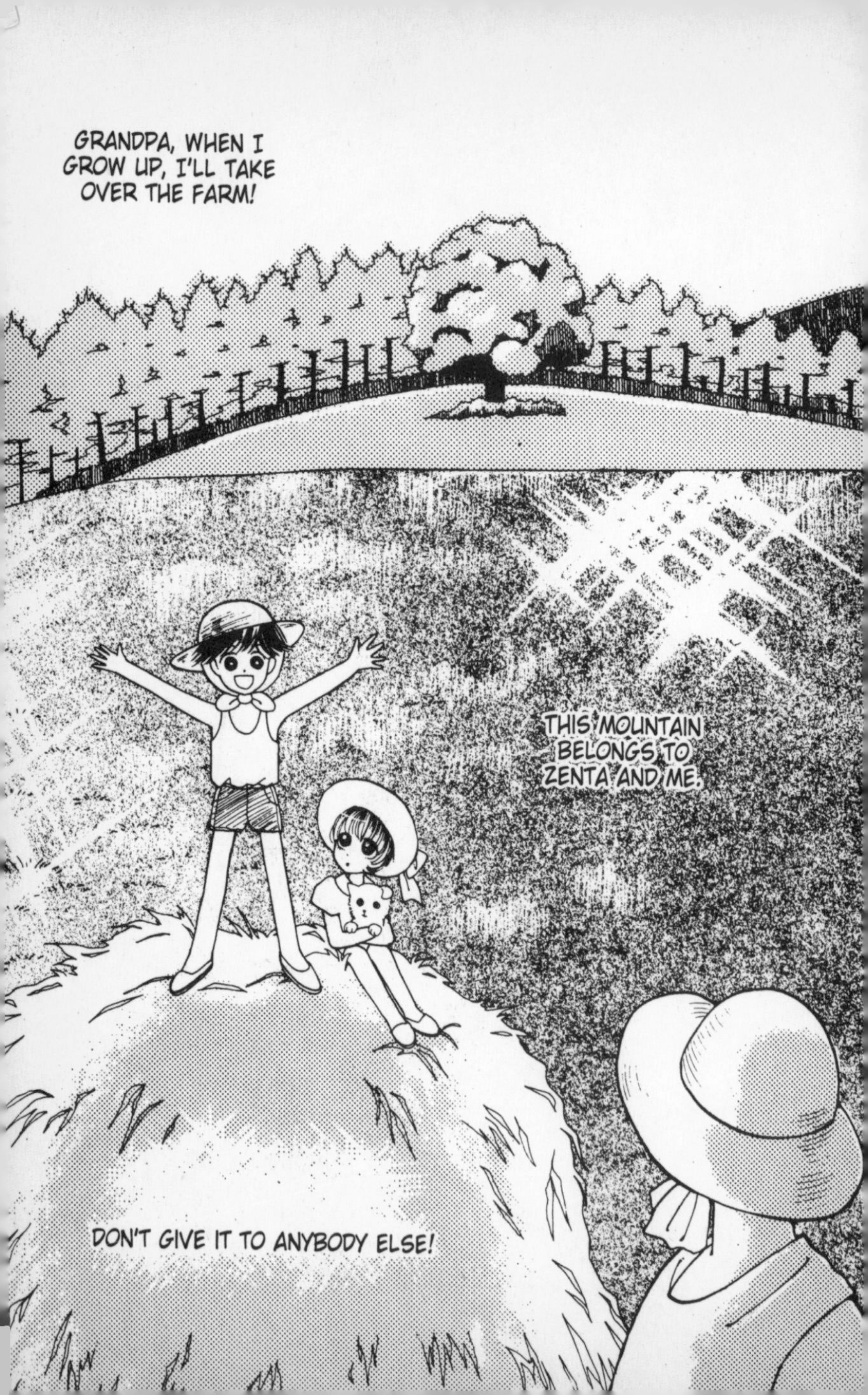
GRANDPA, WHEN I GROW UP, I'LL TAKE OVER THE FARM!
THIS MOUNTAIN BELONGS TO ZENTA AND ME.
DON'T GIVE IT TO ANYBODY ELSE!

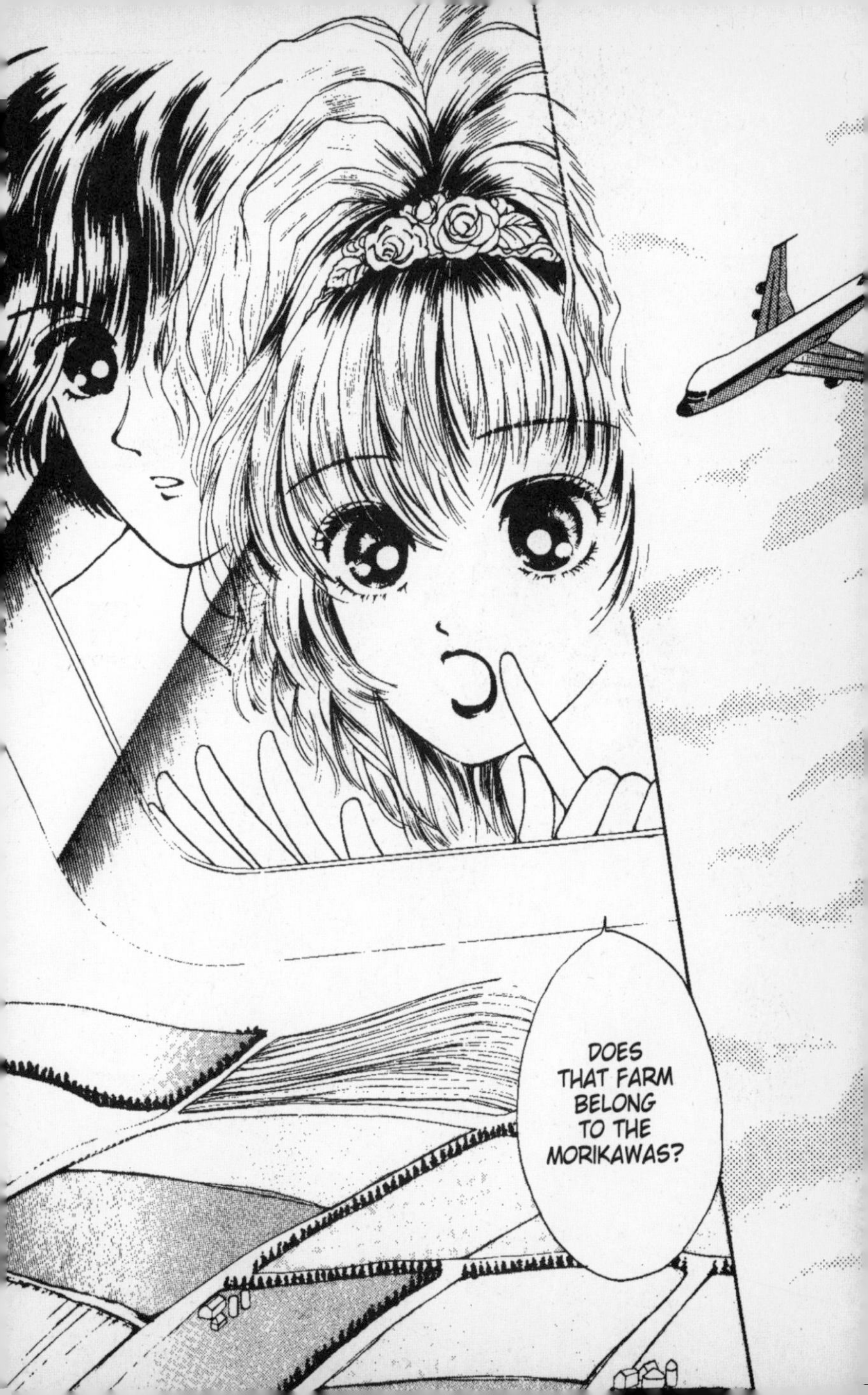
DOES THAT FARM BELONG TO THE MORIKAWAS?

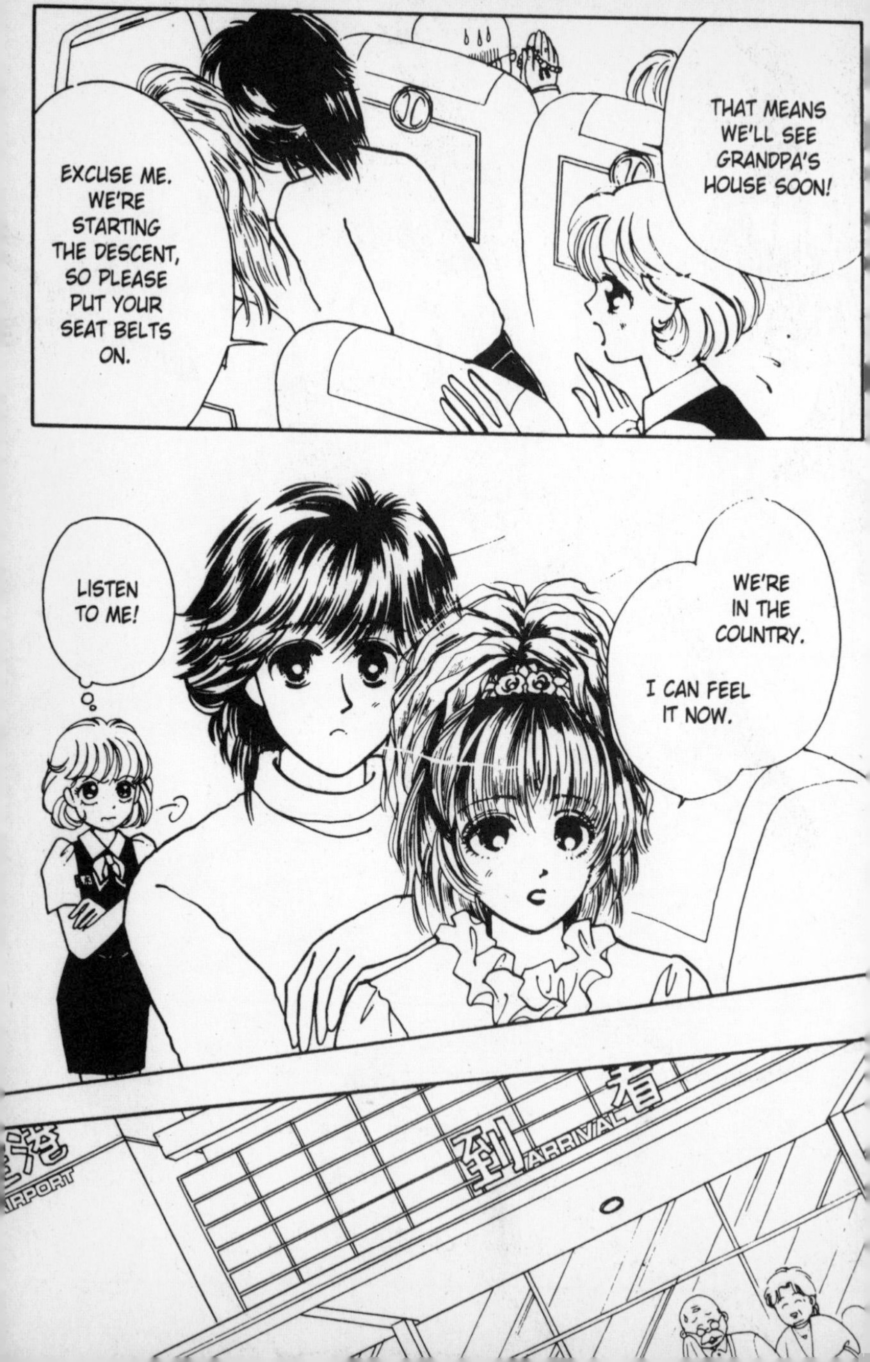
THAT MEANS WE'LL SEE GRANDPA'S HOUSE SOON!
EXCUSE ME. WE'RE STARTING THE DESCENT, SO PLEASE PUT YOUR SEAT BELTS ON.
WE'RE IN THE COUNTRY.
I CAN FEEL IT NOW.
LISTEN TO ME!
到着
ARRIVAL

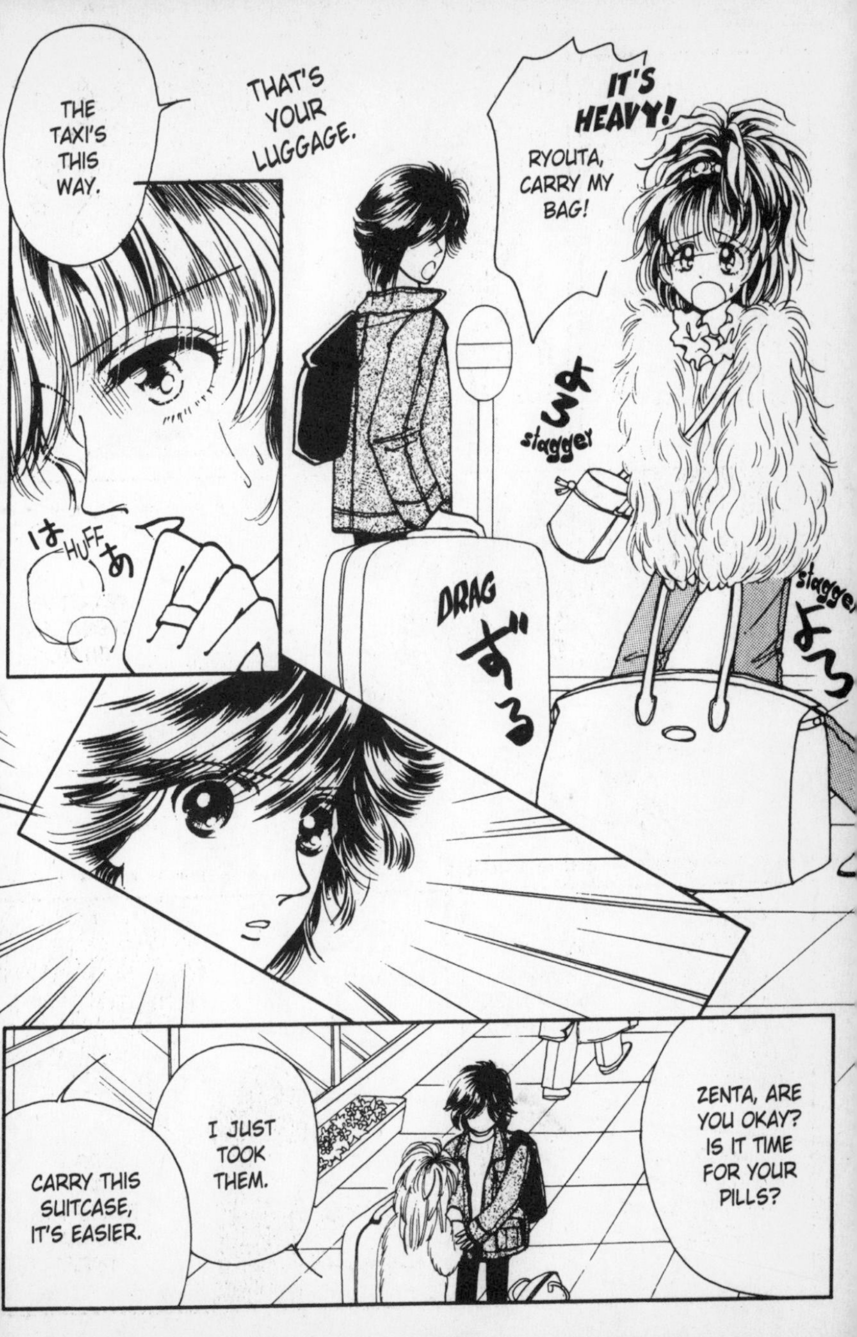
IT'S HEAVY!
RYOUTA, CARRY MY BAG!
stagger よろ
stagger よろ
THAT'S YOUR LUGGAGE.
DRAG ずる
THE TAXI'S THIS WAY.
HUFF はあ
ZENTA, ARE YOU OKAY? IS IT TIME FOR YOUR PILLS?
I JUST TOOK THEM.
CARRY THIS SUITCASE, IT'S EASIER.

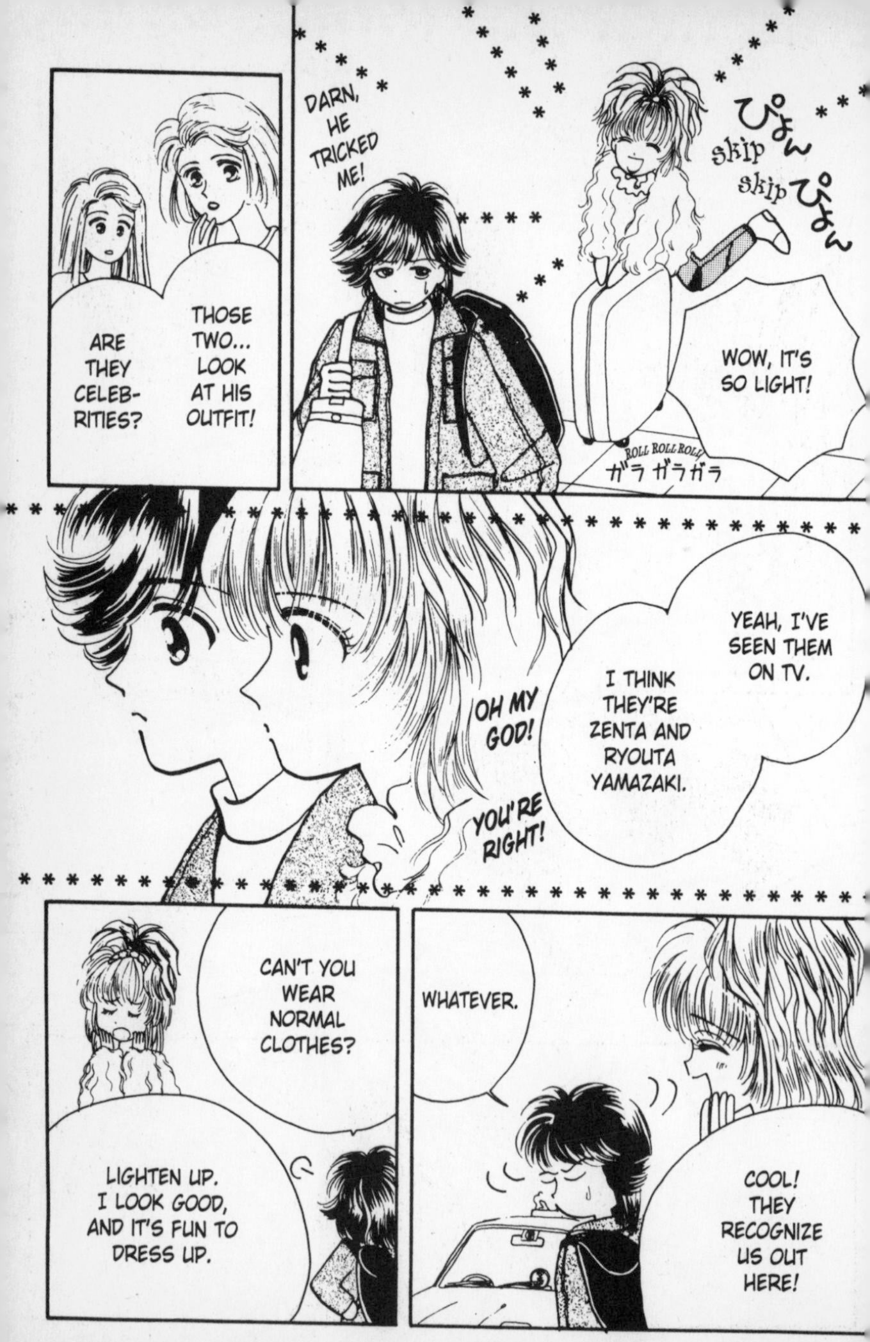

ぴょん skip skip ぴょん
WOW, IT'S SO LIGHT!
DARN, HE TRICKED ME!
ROLL ROLL ROLL ガラガラガラ
THOSE TWO... LOOK AT HIS OUTFIT!
ARE THEY CELEBRITIES?
YEAH, I'VE SEEN THEM ON TV.
I THINK THEY'RE ZENTA AND RYOUTA YAMAZAKI.
OH MY GOD!
YOU'RE RIGHT!
COOL! THEY RECOGNIZE US OUT HERE!
WHATEVER.
CAN'T YOU WEAR NORMAL CLOTHES?
LIGHTEN UP. I LOOK GOOD, AND IT'S FUN TO DRESS UP.

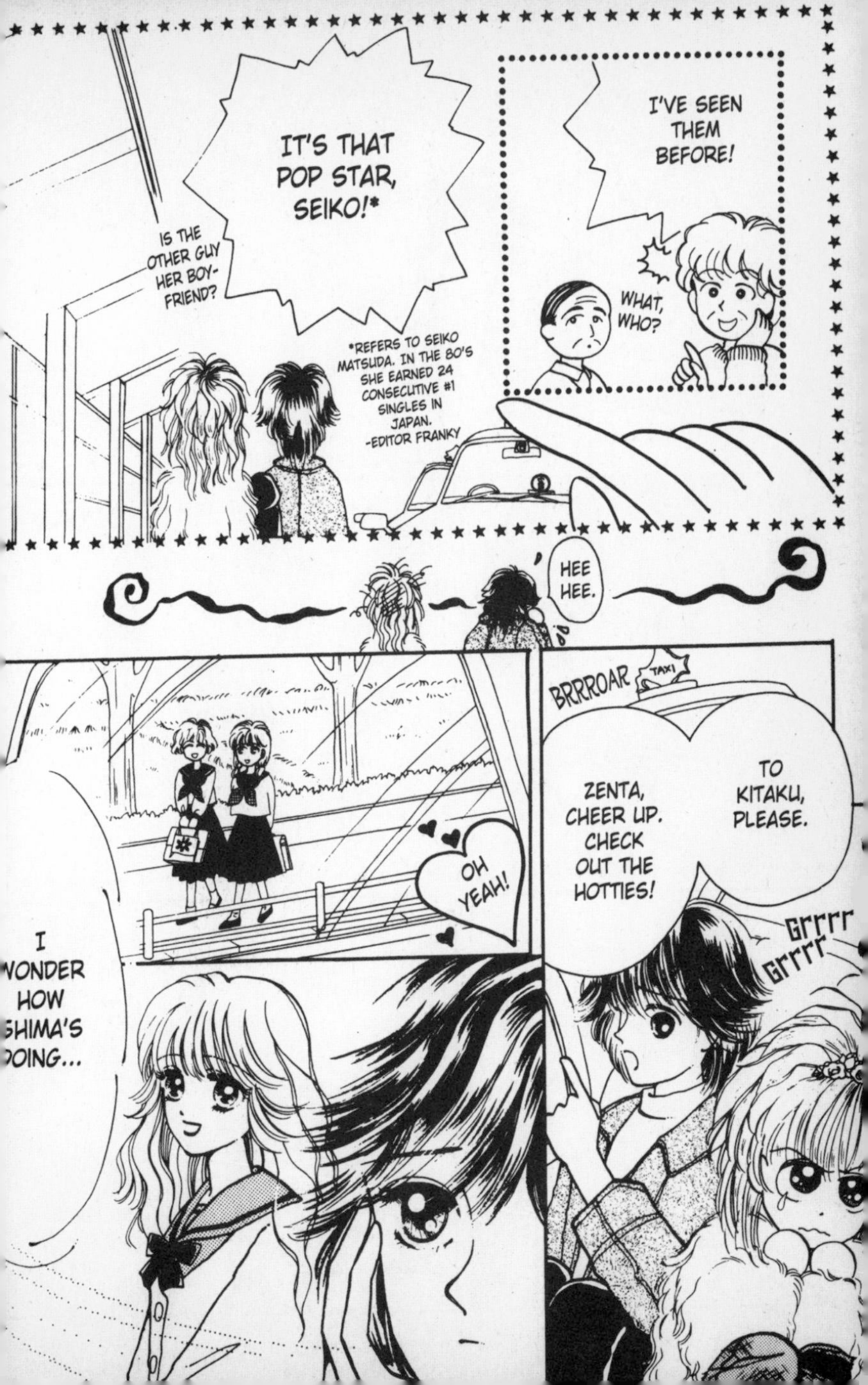
I'VE SEEN THEM BEFORE!
WHAT, WHO?
IT'S THAT POP STAR, SEIKO!*
IS THE OTHER GUY HER BOY-FRIEND?
*REFERS TO SEIKO MATSUDA. IN THE 80'S SHE EARNED 24 CONSECUTIVE #1 SINGLES IN JAPAN. -EDITOR FRANKY
HEE HEE.
BRRROAR
TAXI
TO KITAKU, PLEASE.
ZENTA, CHEER UP. CHECK OUT THE HOTTIES!
Grrrr Grrrr
OH YEAH!
I WONDER HOW SHIMA'S DOING...

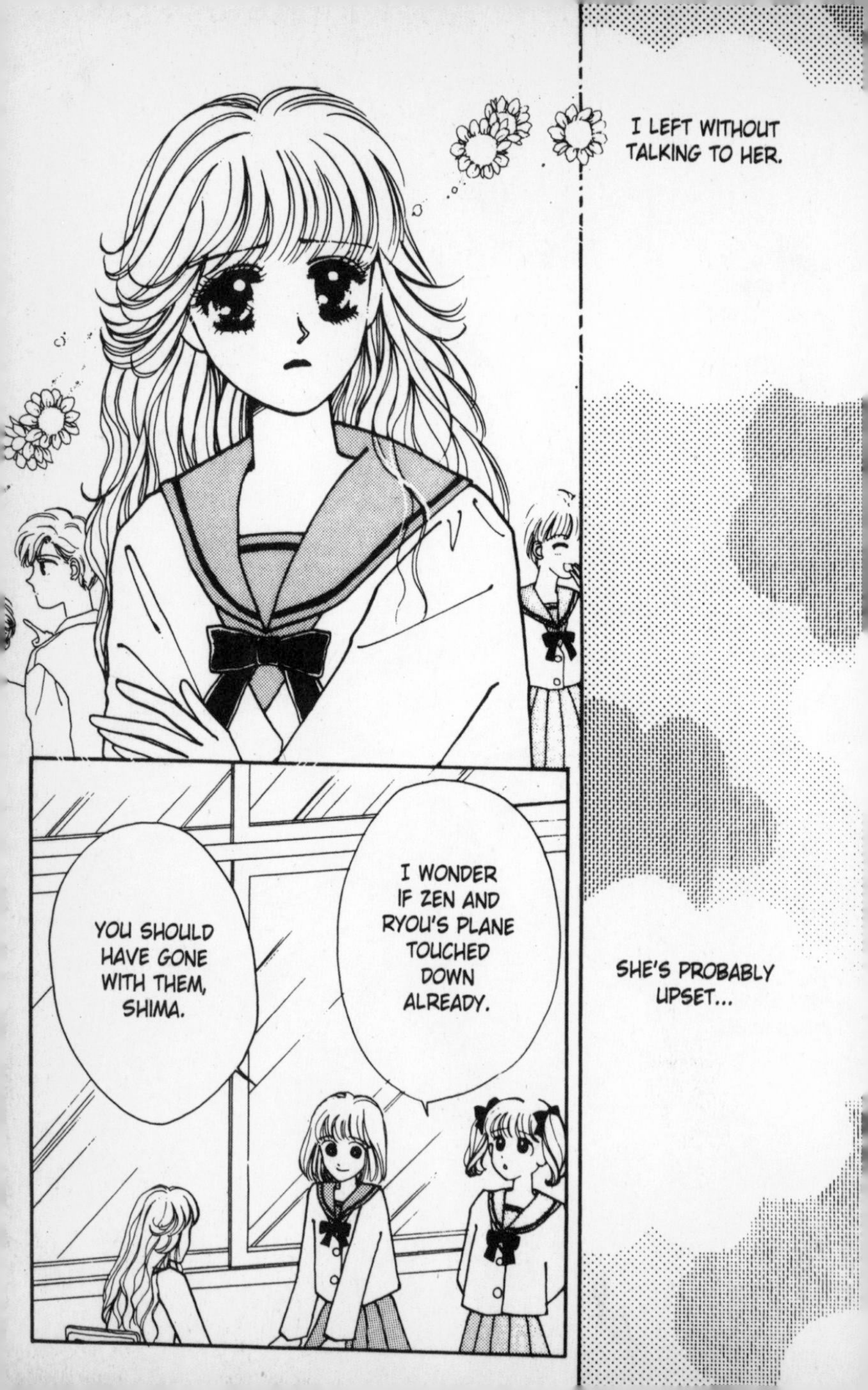
I LEFT WITHOUT TALKING TO HER.
SHE'S PROBABLY UPSET...
I WONDER IF ZEN AND RYOU'S PLANE TOUCHED DOWN ALREADY.
YOU SHOULD HAVE GONE WITH THEM, SHIMA.

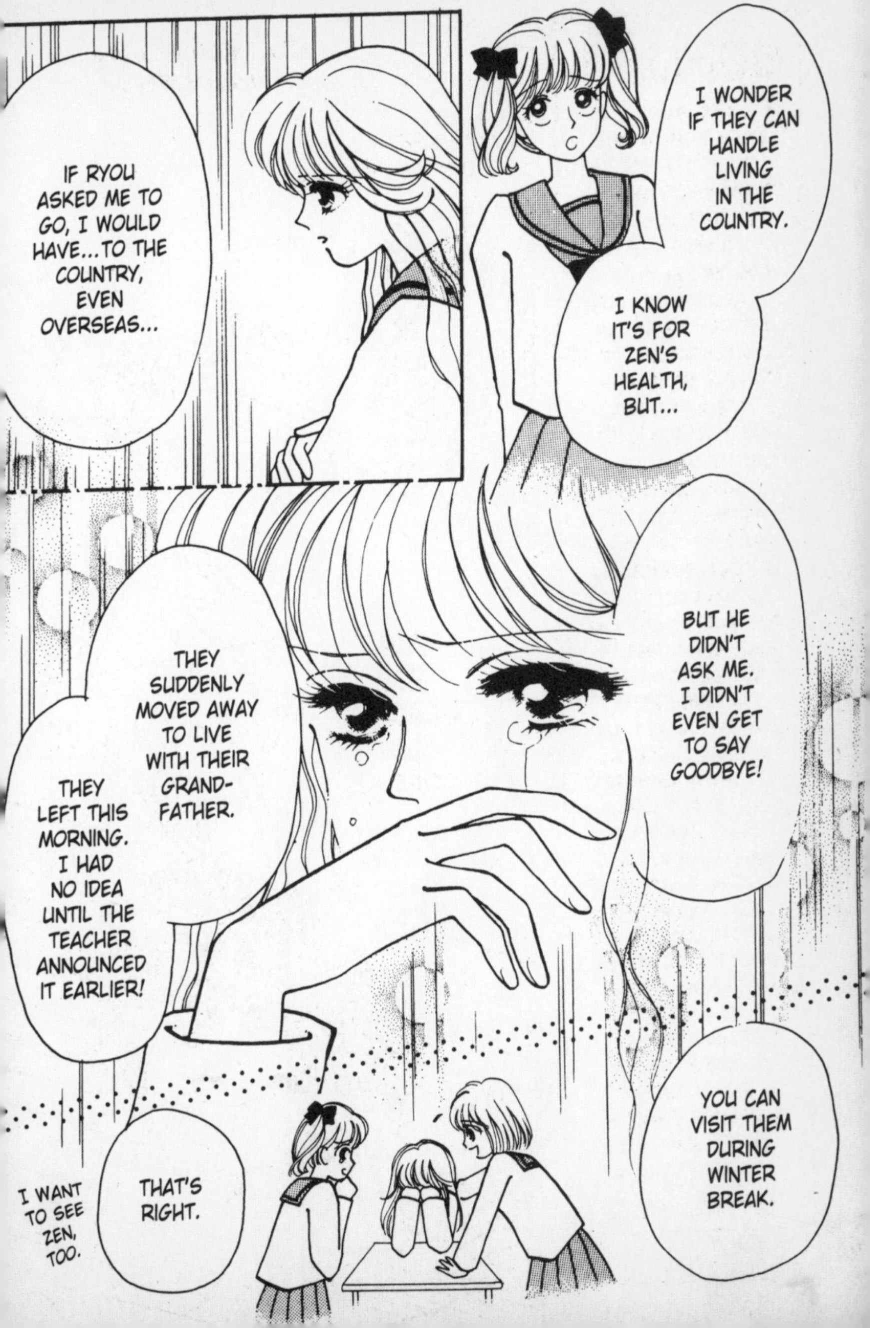
I WONDER IF THEY CAN HANDLE LIVING IN THE COUNTRY.
I KNOW IT'S FOR ZEN'S HEALTH, BUT...
IF RYOU ASKED ME TO GO, I WOULD HAVE...TO THE COUNTRY, EVEN OVERSEAS...
BUT HE DIDN'T ASK ME. I DIDN'T EVEN GET TO SAY GOODBYE!
THEY SUDDENLY MOVED AWAY TO LIVE WITH THEIR GRAND-FATHER.
THEY LEFT THIS MORNING. I HAD NO IDEA UNTIL THE TEACHER ANNOUNCED IT EARLIER!
YOU CAN VISIT THEM DURING WINTER BREAK.
THAT'S RIGHT.
I WANT TO SEE ZEN, TOO.

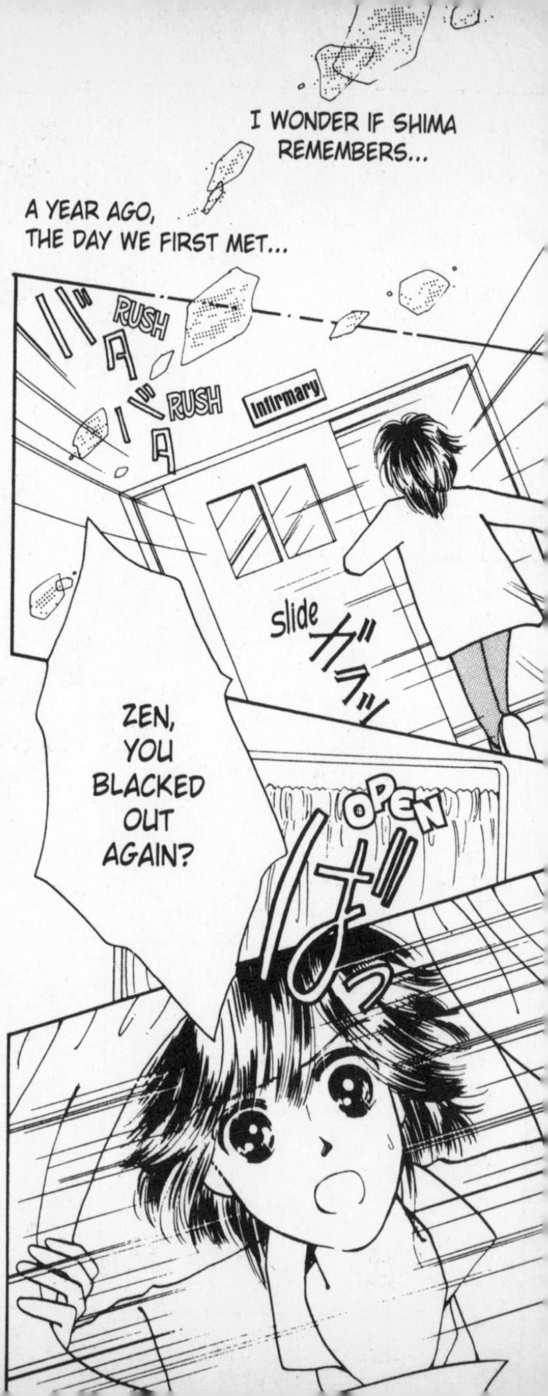
I WONDER IF SHIMA REMEMBERS...
A YEAR AGO, THE DAY WE FIRST MET...
RUSH
RUSH
Infirmary
slide
ZEN, YOU BLACKED OUT AGAIN?
OPEN

BONUS 1.

♥ WOOHOO! MY SEVENTH MANGA! I WANT TO SAY THANK YOU TO ALL MY READERS, NEW AND OLD ALIKE! I'M SORRY I HAVEN'T BEEN ABLE TO RESPOND TO YOUR LETTERS. THANK YOU TO EVERYONE THAT WROTE ME, SAYING "IT'S MY SECOND LETTER" AND "I'LL WRITE AGAIN." PLEASE WAIT FOR ME, I PROMISE TO WRITE BACK (IF THE FIRST ♡ LETTER IS MEMORABLE, ALL THE BETTER!) THIS STORY, "LOVE AND PEACE IN A CORNFIELD" WAS BASED ON MY OLD FAMILY HOME. I AM ORIGINALLY FROM HOKKAIDO. HIKARIYA BOOKS IN ABASHIRI HAS SIGNED COPIES OF MY COMICS FOR SALE, SO IF YOU LIVE NEARBY, PLEASE ASK FOR THEM AT THE STORE! ANYWAY, A GOLF COURSE WILL BE ♥ REPLACING MY OLD FAMILY FARM. IT'S REALLY TRAGIC, BECAUSE I WAS SO PROUD THAT MY GRANDPA OWNED A LARGE FARM AND A MOUNTAIN...

CONTINUED ON P.62

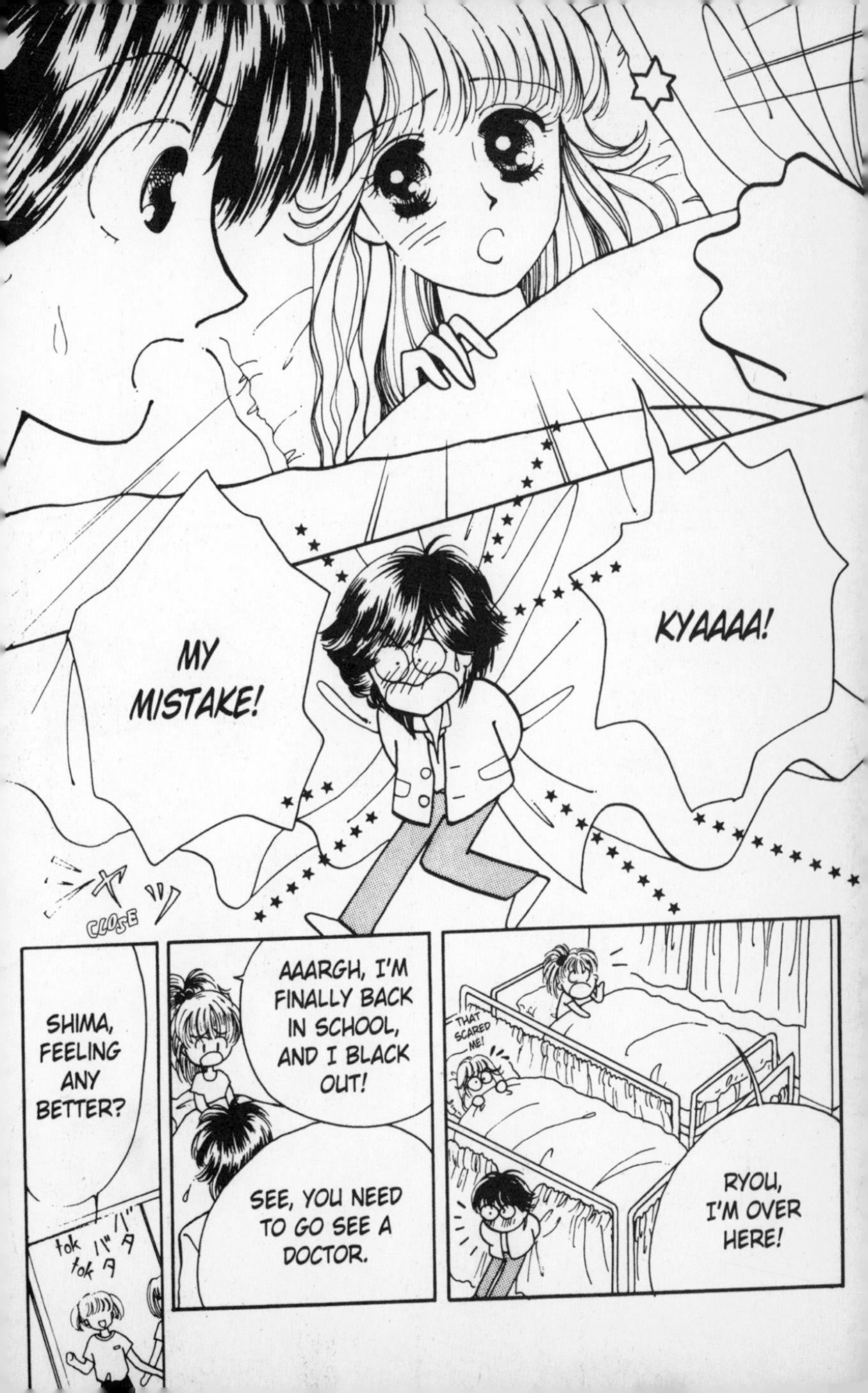
KYAAAA!
MY MISTAKE!
CLOSE
RYOU, I'M OVER HERE!
THAT SCARED ME!
AAARGH, I'M FINALLY BACK IN SCHOOL, AND I BLACK OUT!
SEE, YOU NEED TO GO SEE A DOCTOR.
SHIMA, FEELING ANY BETTER?
tok tok
バタバタ

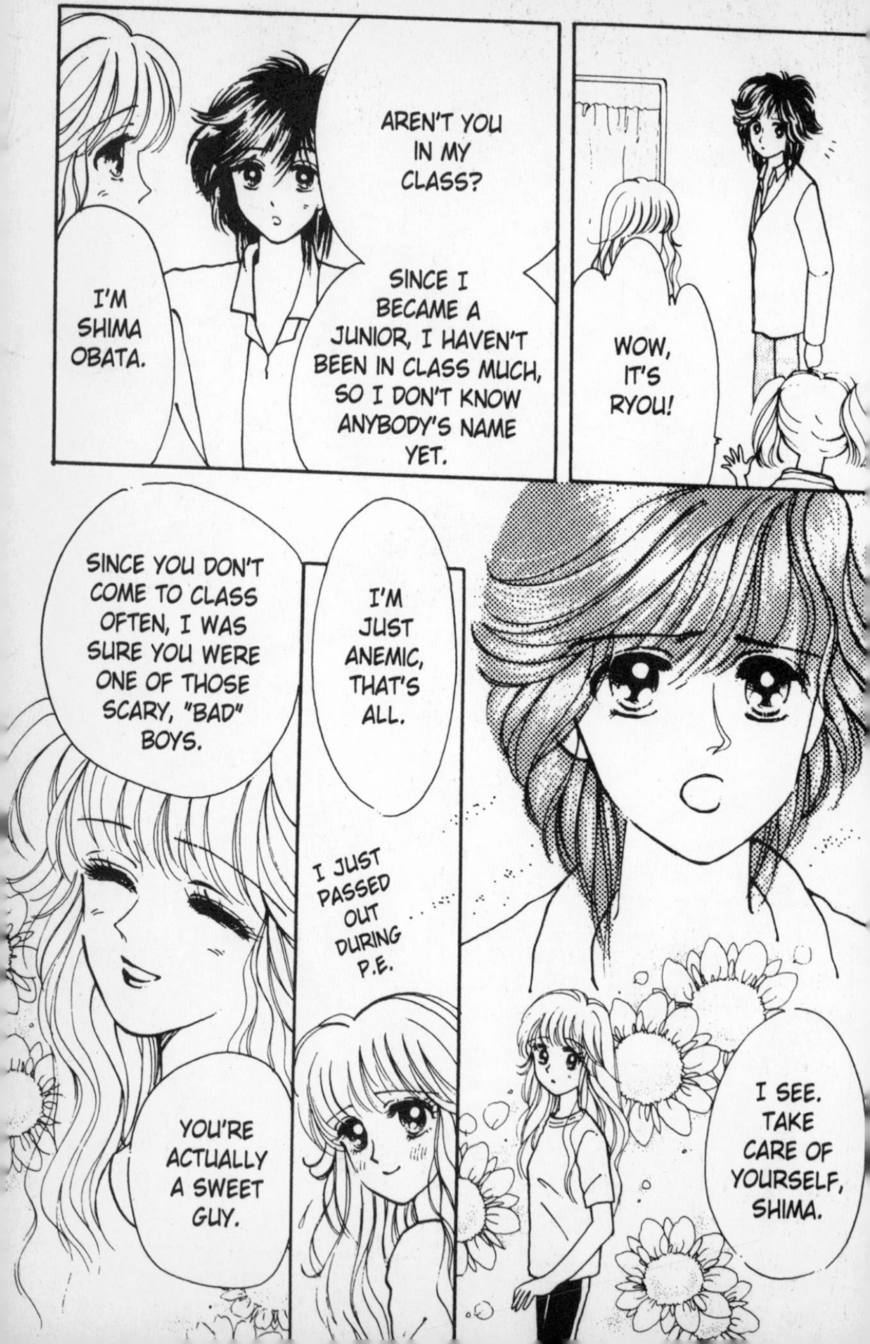
AREN'T YOU IN MY CLASS?
I'M SHIMA OBATA.
SINCE I BECAME A JUNIOR, I HAVEN'T BEEN IN CLASS MUCH, SO I DON'T KNOW ANYBODY'S NAME YET.
WOW, IT'S RYOU!
SINCE YOU DON'T COME TO CLASS OFTEN, I WAS SURE YOU WERE ONE OF THOSE SCARY, "BAD" BOYS.
I'M JUST ANEMIC, THAT'S ALL.
I JUST PASSED OUT DURING P.E.
I SEE. TAKE CARE OF YOURSELF, SHIMA.
YOU'RE ACTUALLY A SWEET GUY.

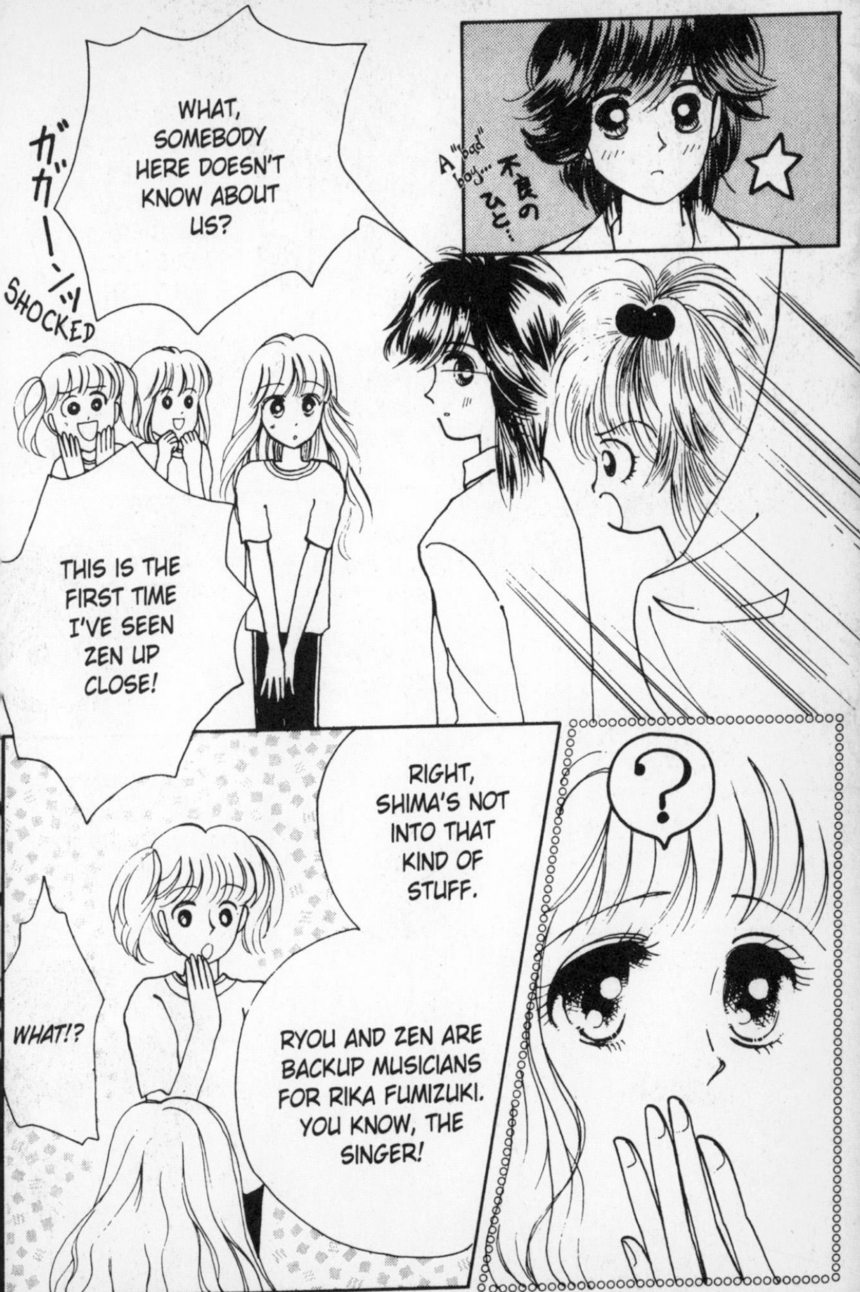
A "bad" boy...
不良のひと…
WHAT, SOMEBODY HERE DOESN'T KNOW ABOUT US?
ガガーンッ
SHOCKED
THIS IS THE FIRST TIME I'VE SEEN ZEN UP CLOSE!
?
RIGHT, SHIMA'S NOT INTO THAT KIND OF STUFF.
WHAT!?
RYOU AND ZEN ARE BACKUP MUSICIANS FOR RIKA FUMIZUKI. YOU KNOW, THE SINGER!

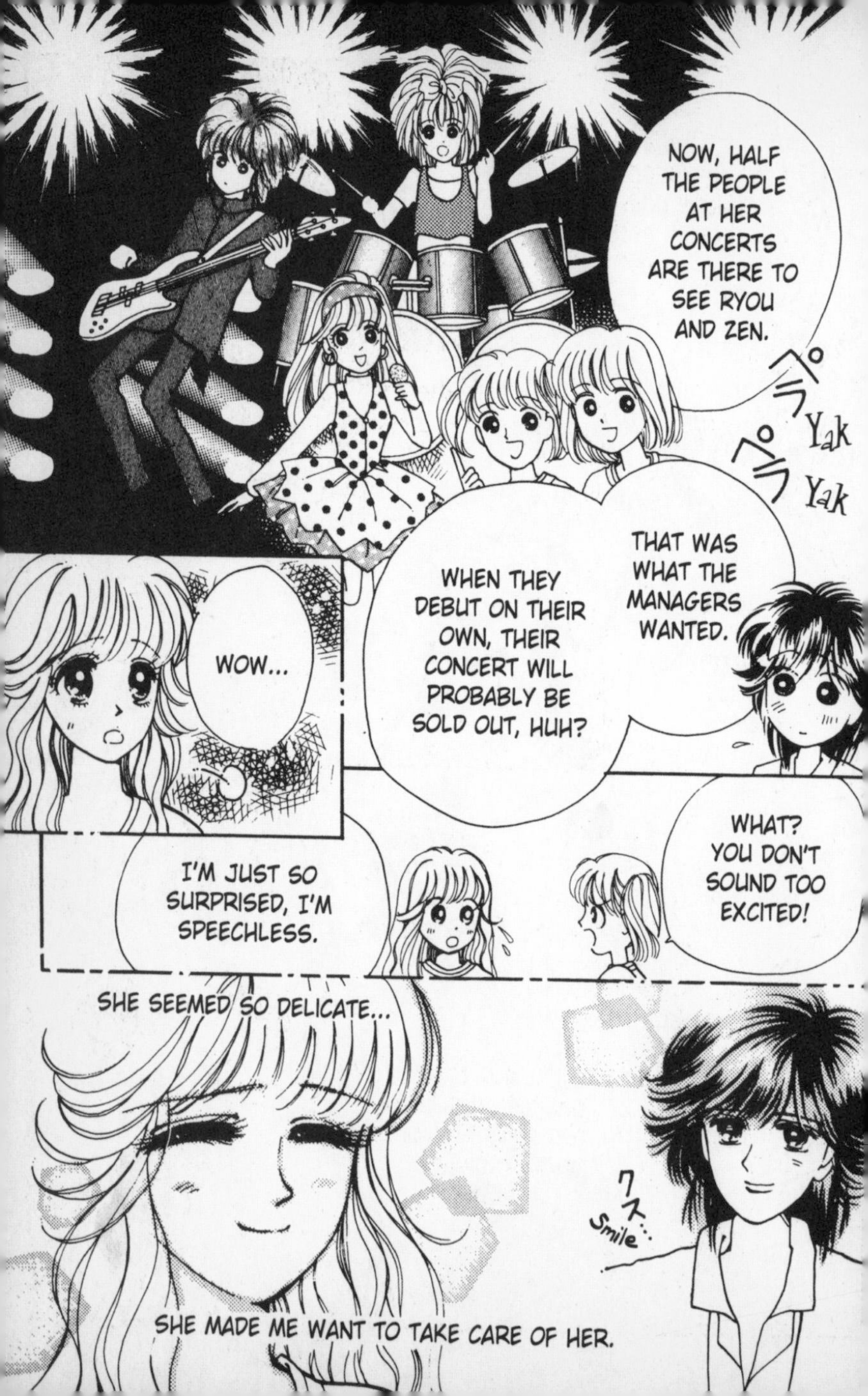
NOW, HALF THE PEOPLE AT HER CONCERTS ARE THERE TO SEE RYOU AND ZEN.
ペラ Yak
ペラ Yak
THAT WAS WHAT THE MANAGERS WANTED.
WHEN THEY DEBUT ON THEIR OWN, THEIR CONCERT WILL PROBABLY BE SOLD OUT, HUH?
WOW...
WHAT? YOU DON'T SOUND TOO EXCITED!
I'M JUST SO SURPRISED, I'M SPEECHLESS.
SHE SEEMED SO DELICATE...
クス... Smile
SHE MADE ME WANT TO TAKE CARE OF HER.

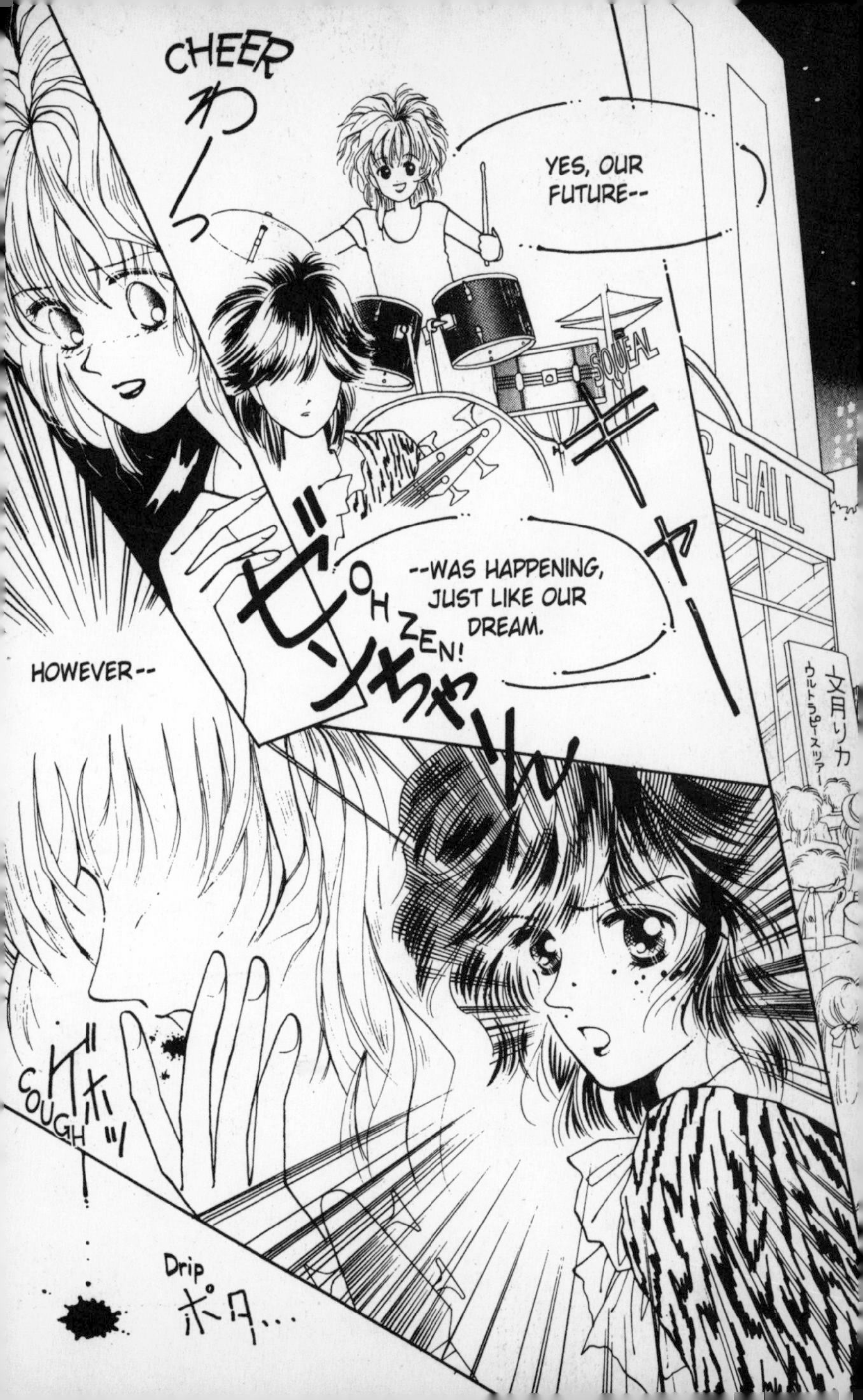
YES, OUR FUTURE--
--WAS HAPPENING, JUST LIKE OUR DREAM.
SQUEAL
キャー
OH ZEN!
ゼンちゃん
HALL
文月リカ
ウルトラピースツアー
CHEER
わーっ
HOWEVER--
COUGH
ゲホッ
Drip
ポタ...

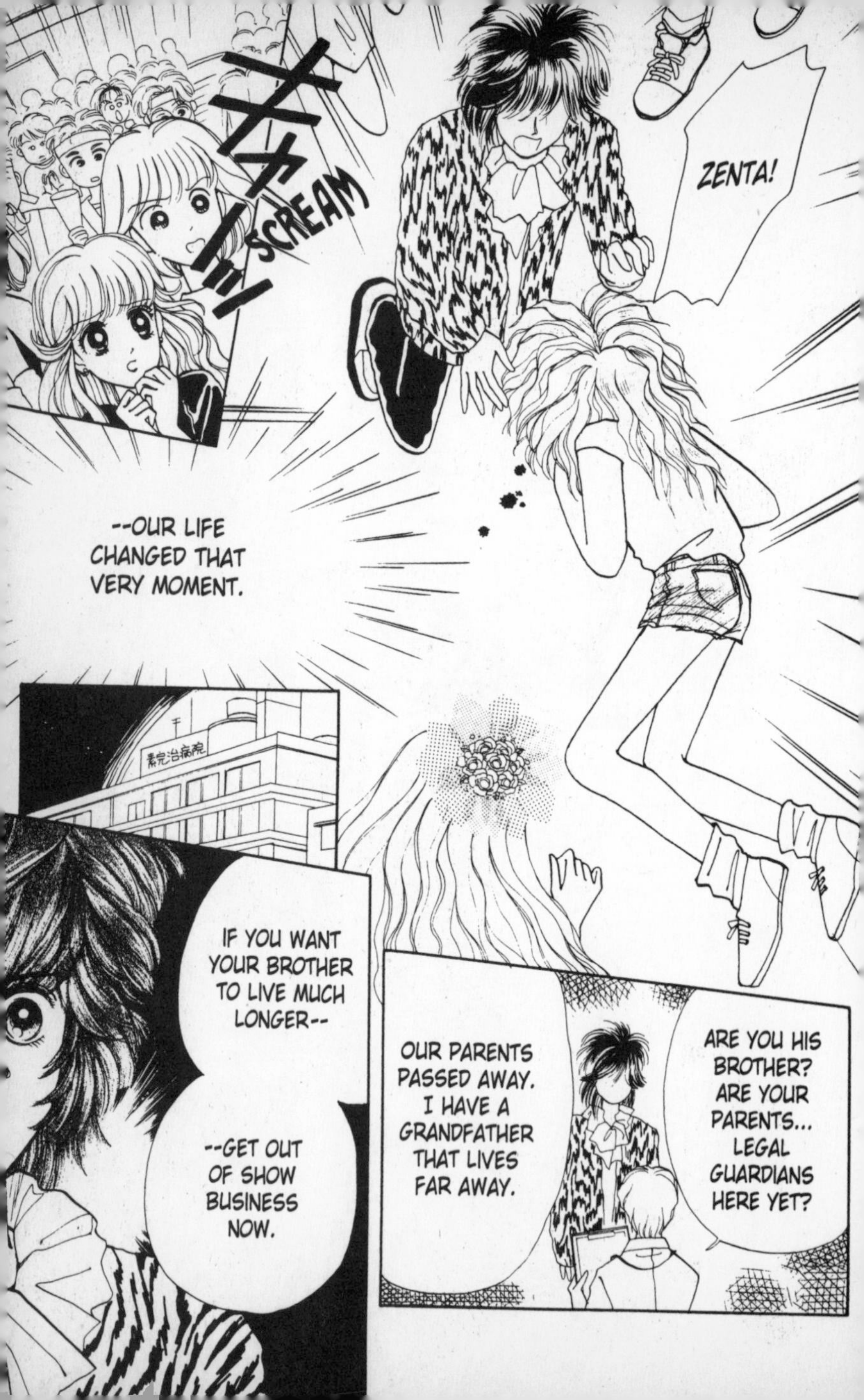
ZENTA!
SCREAM
--OUR LIFE CHANGED THAT VERY MOMENT.
ARE YOU HIS BROTHER? ARE YOUR PARENTS... LEGAL GUARDIANS HERE YET?
OUR PARENTS PASSED AWAY. I HAVE A GRANDFATHER THAT LIVES FAR AWAY.
IF YOU WANT YOUR BROTHER TO LIVE MUCH LONGER--
--GET OUT OF SHOW BUSINESS NOW.

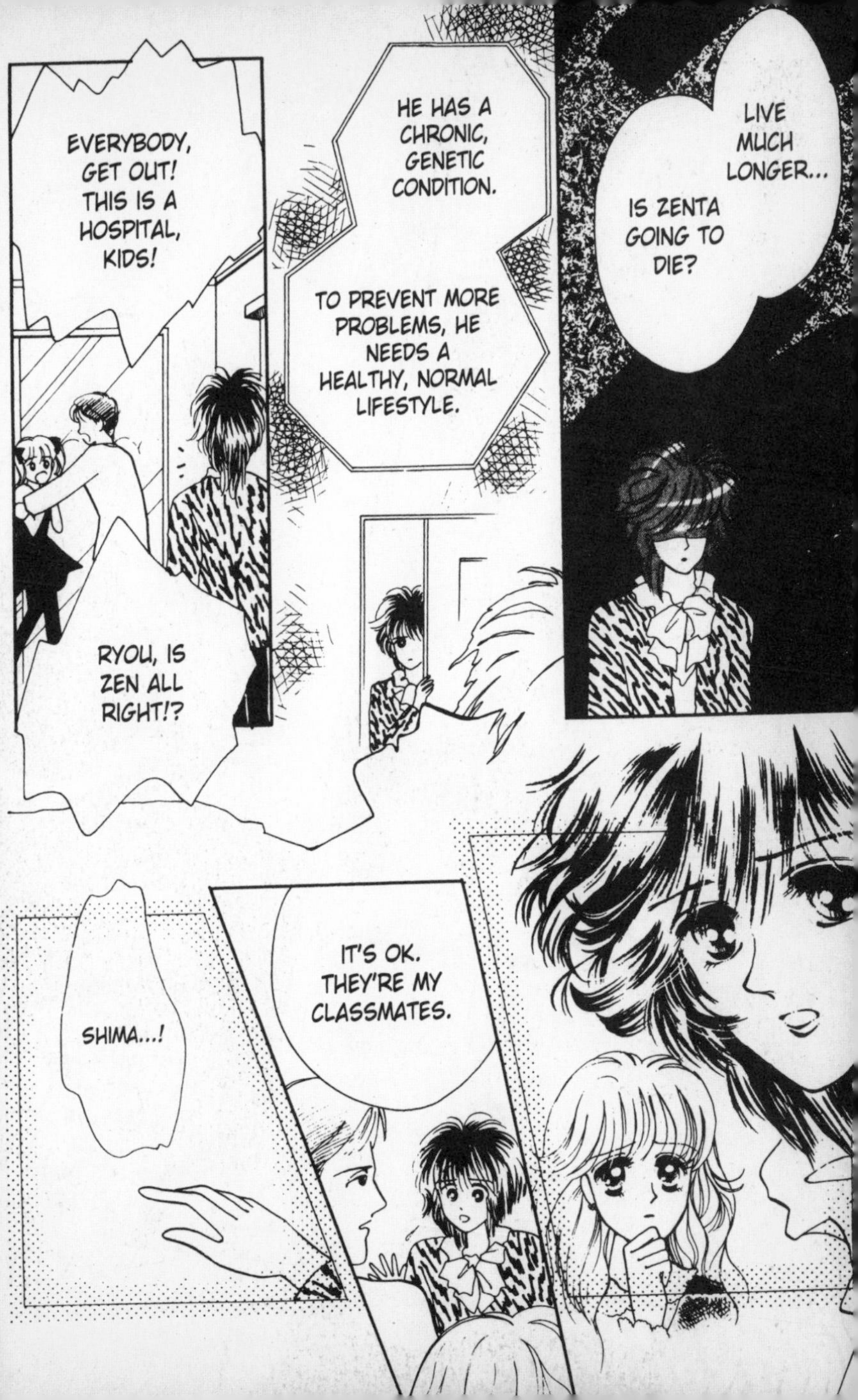
LIVE MUCH LONGER...
IS ZENTA GOING TO DIE?
HE HAS A CHRONIC, GENETIC CONDITION.
TO PREVENT MORE PROBLEMS, HE NEEDS A HEALTHY, NORMAL LIFESTYLE.
EVERYBODY, GET OUT! THIS IS A HOSPITAL, KIDS!
RYOU, IS ZEN ALL RIGHT!?
IT'S OK. THEY'RE MY CLASSMATES.
SHIMA...!

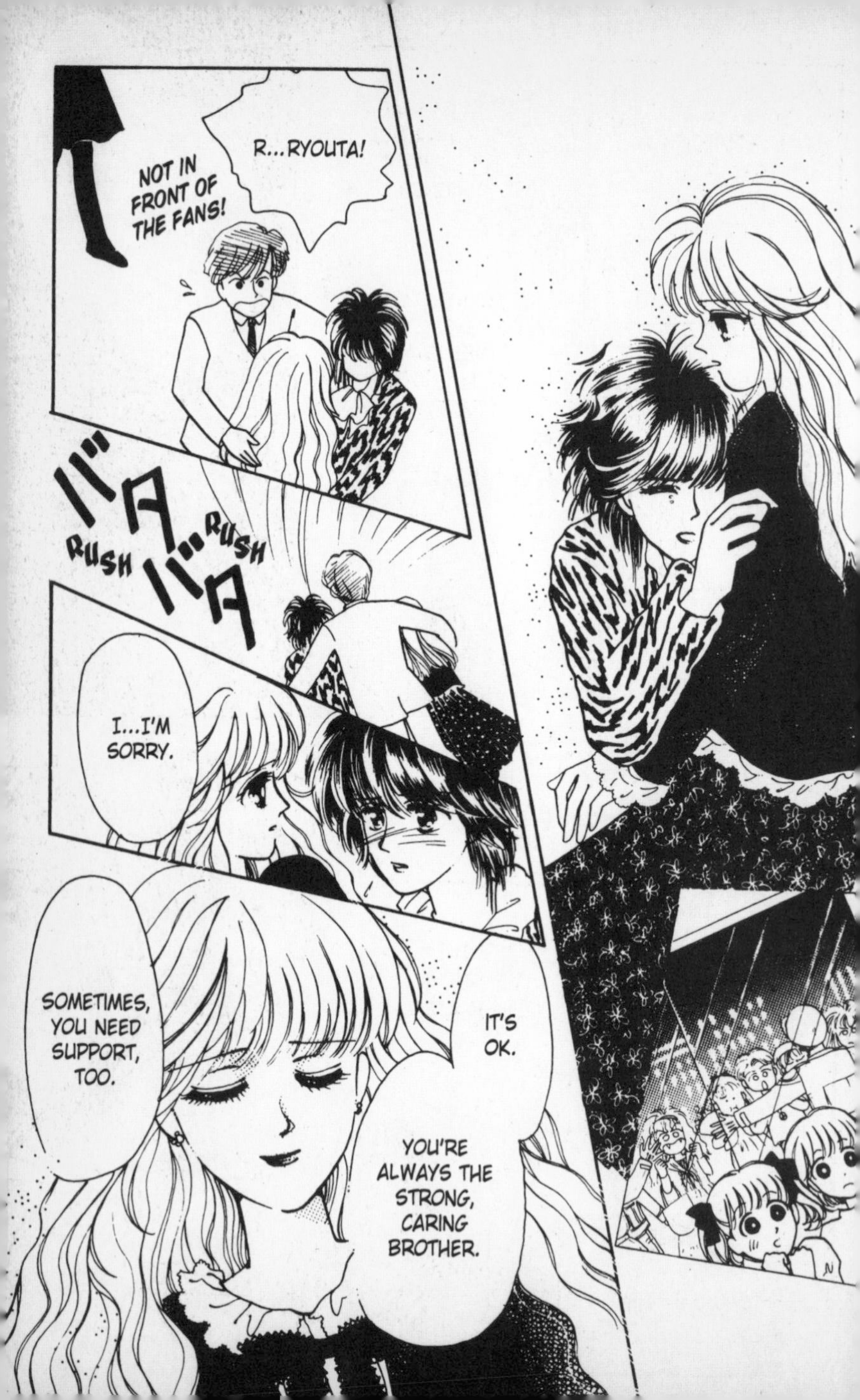
R...RYOUTA!
NOT IN FRONT OF THE FANS!
バタ
RUSH...RUSH
バタ
I...I'M SORRY.
IT'S OK.
YOU'RE ALWAYS THE STRONG, CARING BROTHER.
SOMETIMES, YOU NEED SUPPORT, TOO.

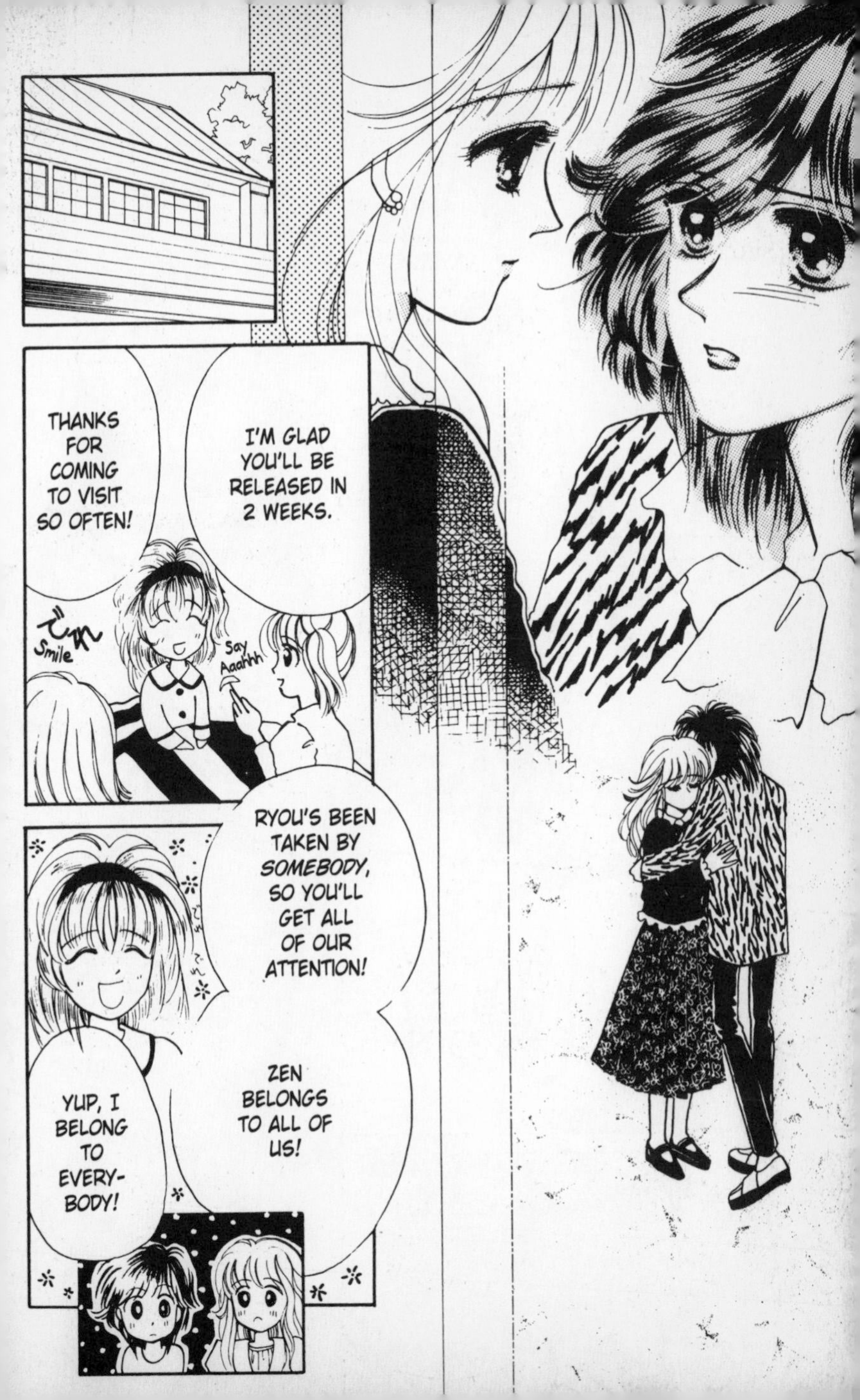
I'M GLAD YOU'LL BE RELEASED IN 2 WEEKS.
THANKS FOR COMING TO VISIT SO OFTEN!
Say Aaahhh
Smile
RYOU'S BEEN TAKEN BY SOMEBODY, SO YOU'LL GET ALL OF OUR ATTENTION!
ZEN BELONGS TO ALL OF US!
YUP, I BELONG TO EVERY-BODY!

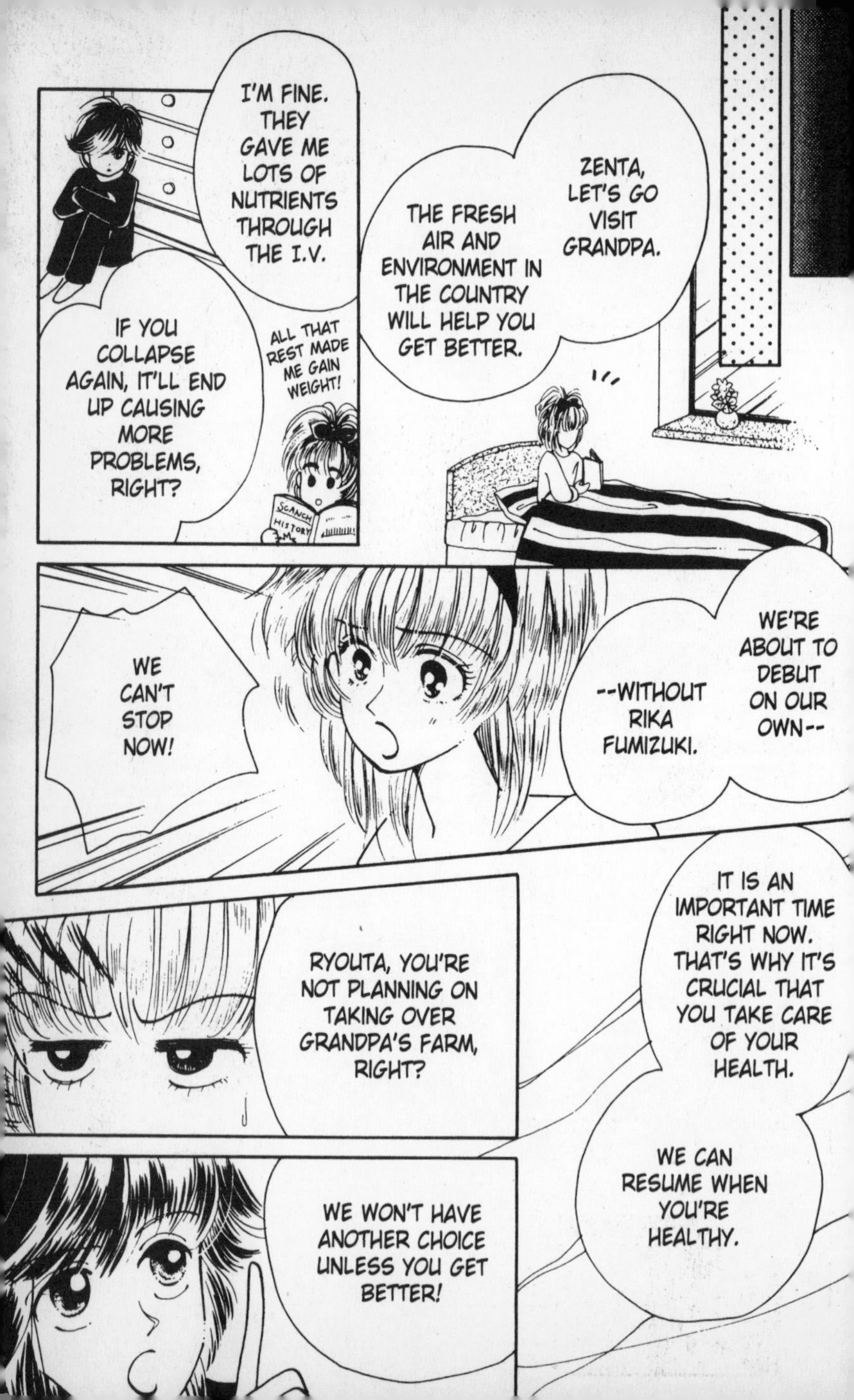
ZENTA, LET'S GO VISIT GRANDPA.
THE FRESH AIR AND ENVIRONMENT IN THE COUNTRY WILL HELP YOU GET BETTER.
I'M FINE. THEY GAVE ME LOTS OF NUTRIENTS THROUGH THE I.V.
ALL THAT REST MADE ME GAIN WEIGHT!
IF YOU COLLAPSE AGAIN, IT'LL END UP CAUSING MORE PROBLEMS, RIGHT?
SCANCH HISTORY
WE'RE ABOUT TO DEBUT ON OUR OWN--
--WITHOUT RIKA FUMIZUKI.
WE CAN'T STOP NOW!
IT IS AN IMPORTANT TIME RIGHT NOW. THAT'S WHY IT'S CRUCIAL THAT YOU TAKE CARE OF YOUR HEALTH.
RYOUTA, YOU'RE NOT PLANNING ON TAKING OVER GRANDPA'S FARM, RIGHT?
WE CAN RESUME WHEN YOU'RE HEALTHY.
WE WON'T HAVE ANOTHER CHOICE UNLESS YOU GET BETTER!

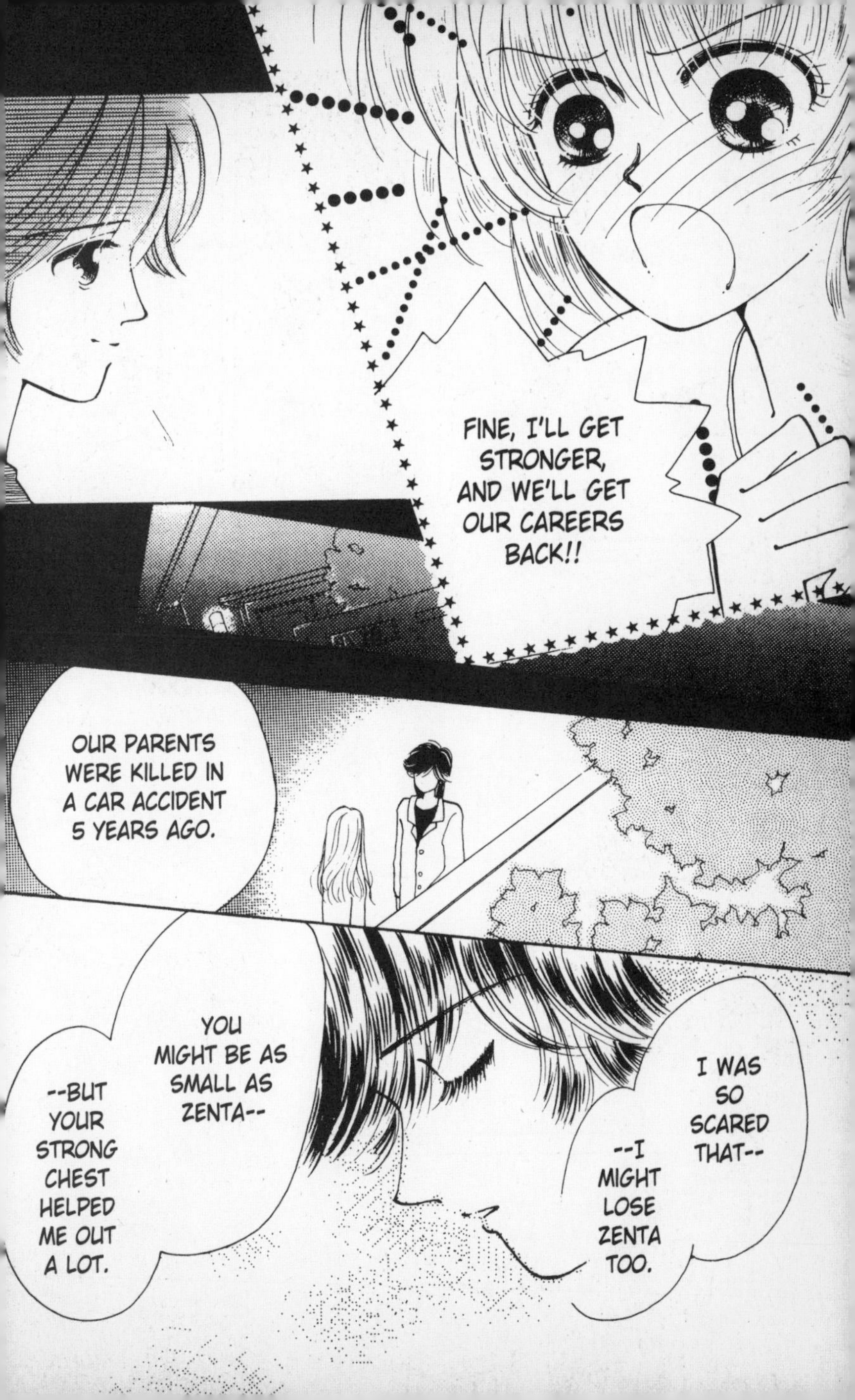
FINE, I'LL GET STRONGER, AND WE'LL GET OUR CAREERS BACK!!
OUR PARENTS WERE KILLED IN A CAR ACCIDENT 5 YEARS AGO.
I WAS SO SCARED THAT--
--I MIGHT LOSE ZENTA TOO.
YOU MIGHT BE AS SMALL AS ZENTA--
--BUT YOUR STRONG CHEST HELPED ME OUT A LOT.

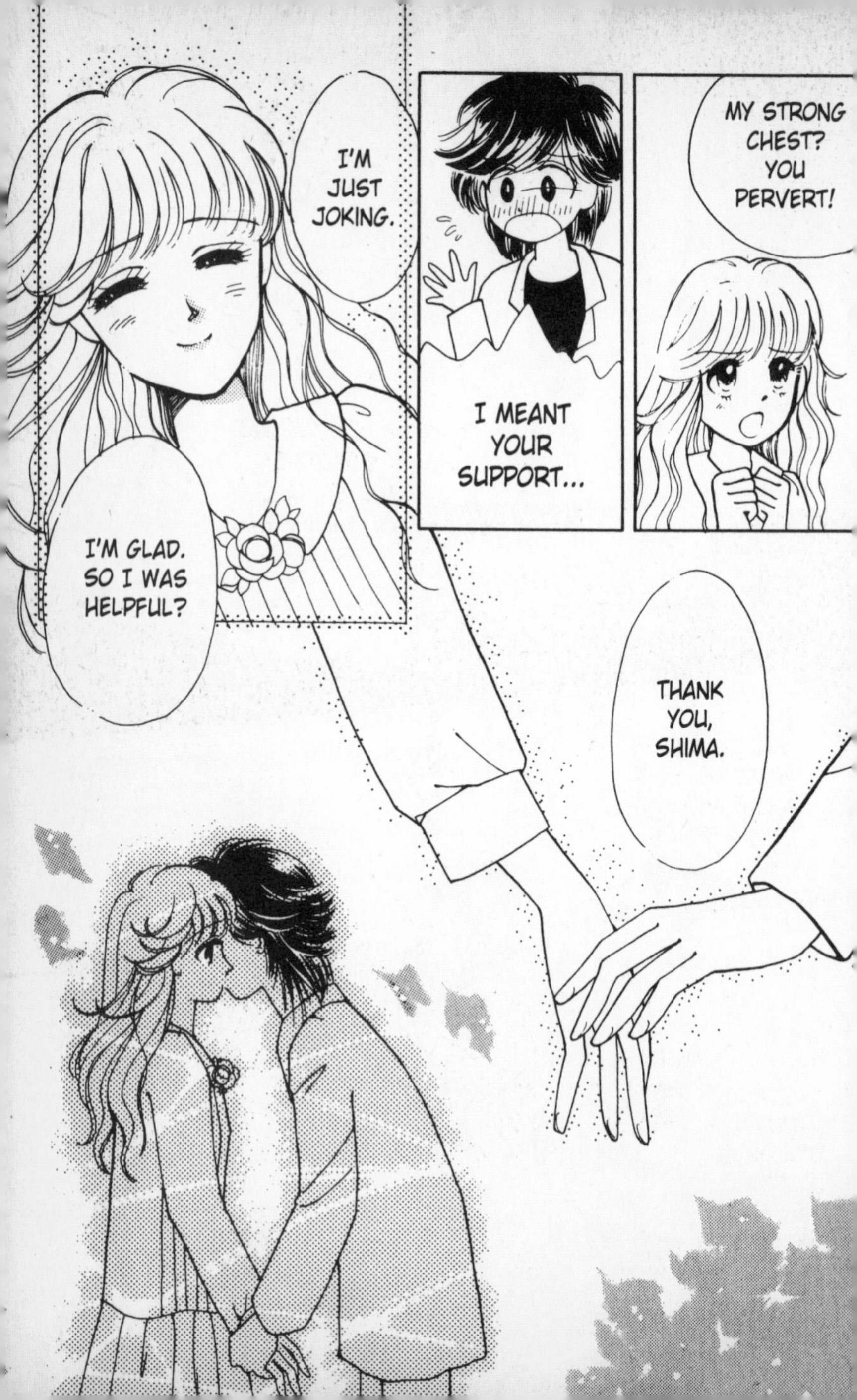
MY STRONG CHEST? YOU PERVERT!
I MEANT YOUR SUPPORT...
I'M JUST JOKING.
I'M GLAD. SO I WAS HELPFUL?
THANK YOU, SHIMA.

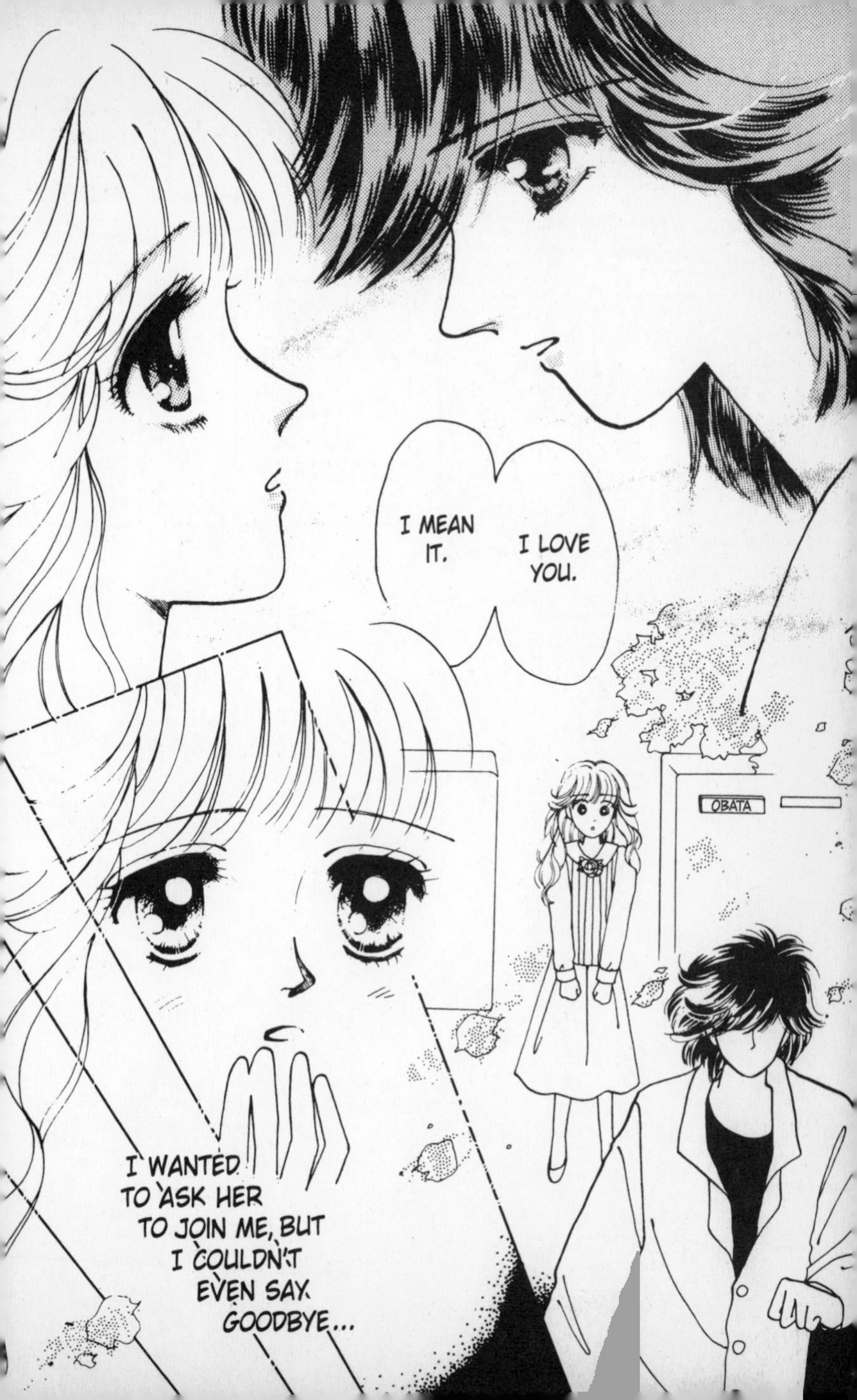
I MEAN IT. I LOVE YOU.
OBATA
I WANTED TO ASK HER TO JOIN ME, BUT I COULDN'T EVEN SAY GOODBYE...

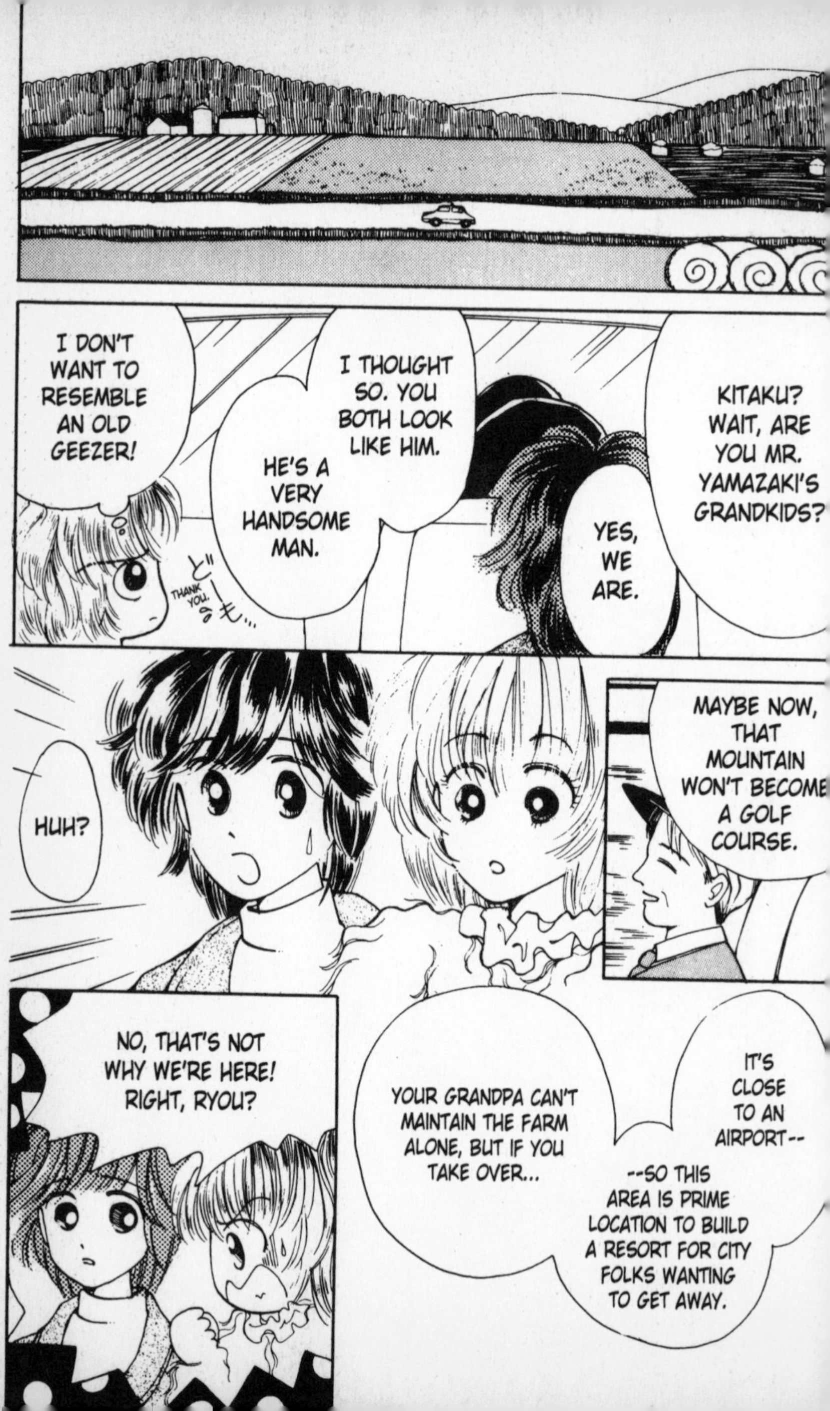
KITAKU? WAIT, ARE YOU MR. YAMAZAKI'S GRANDKIDS?
YES, WE ARE.
I THOUGHT SO. YOU BOTH LOOK LIKE HIM.
HE'S A VERY HANDSOME MAN.
どーも…
THANK YOU.
I DON'T WANT TO RESEMBLE AN OLD GEEZER!
MAYBE NOW, THAT MOUNTAIN WON'T BECOME A GOLF COURSE.
HUH?
IT'S CLOSE TO AN AIRPORT--
--SO THIS AREA IS PRIME LOCATION TO BUILD A RESORT FOR CITY FOLKS WANTING TO GET AWAY.
YOUR GRANDPA CAN'T MAINTAIN THE FARM ALONE, BUT IF YOU TAKE OVER...
NO, THAT'S NOT WHY WE'RE HERE! RIGHT, RYOU?

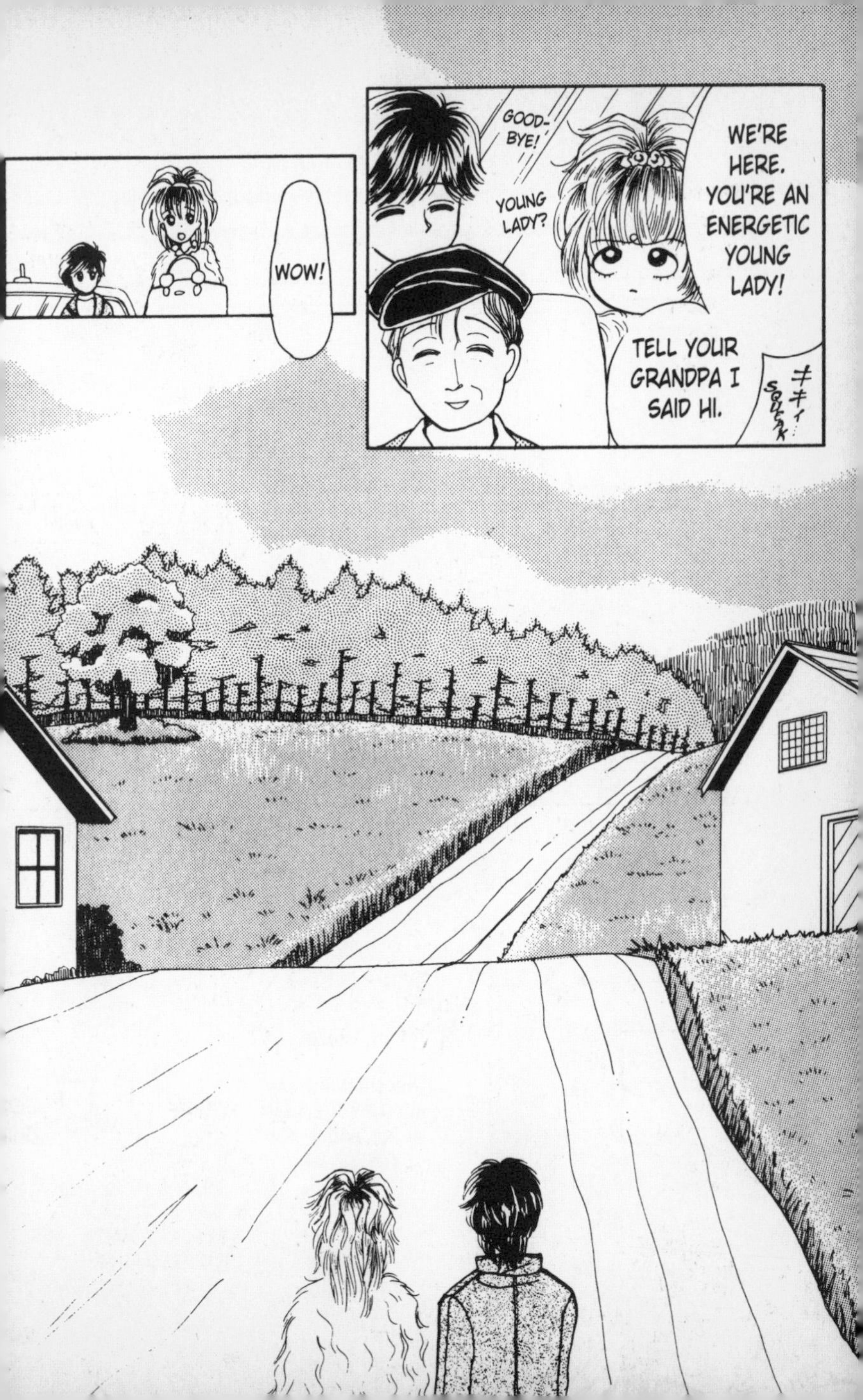
WE'RE HERE. YOU'RE AN ENERGETIC YOUNG LADY!
YOUNG LADY?
TELL YOUR GRANDPA I SAID HI.
キキィ… SQUEAK
GOOD-BYE!
WOW!

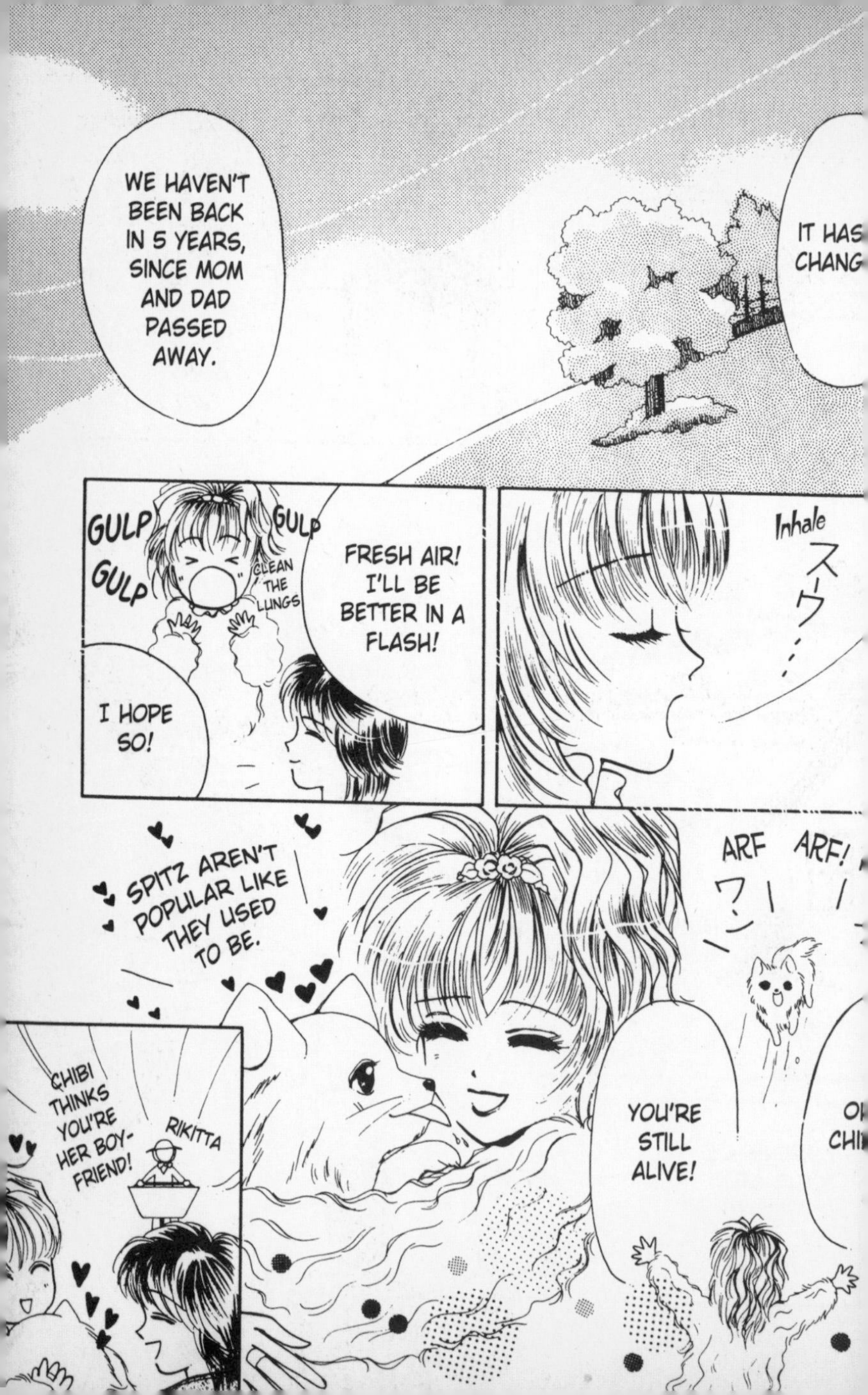
IT HAS CHANG
WE HAVEN'T BEEN BACK IN 5 YEARS, SINCE MOM AND DAD PASSED AWAY.
Inhale
スウ・・・
FRESH AIR! I'LL BE BETTER IN A FLASH!
GULP
GULP
GULP
CLEAN THE LUNGS
I HOPE SO!
O CHI
ARF ARF!
ワン
YOU'RE STILL ALIVE!
SPITZ AREN'T POPULAR LIKE THEY USED TO BE.
RIKITTA
CHIBI THINKS YOU'RE HER BOY-FRIEND!

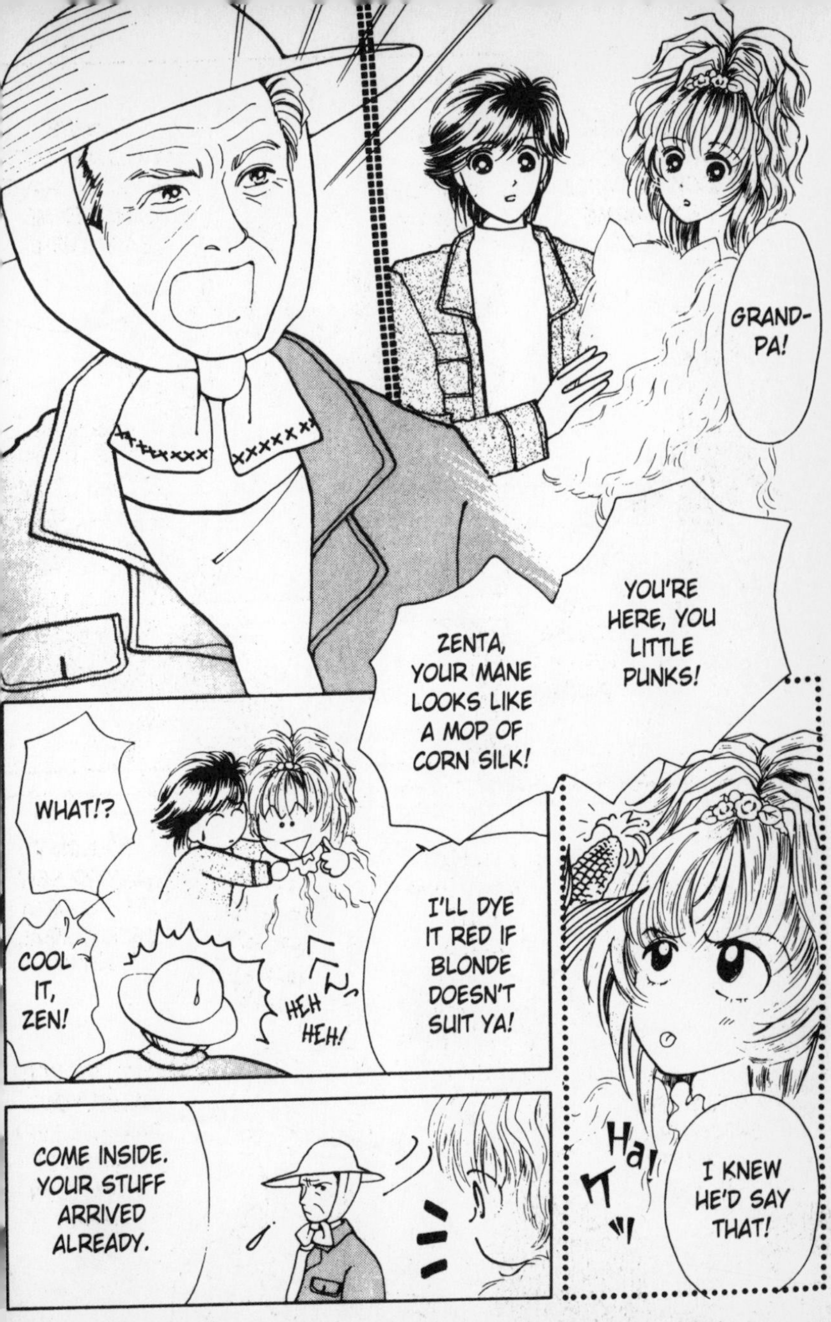
GRAND-PA!
YOU'RE HERE, YOU LITTLE PUNKS!
ZENTA, YOUR MANE LOOKS LIKE A MOP OF CORN SILK!
Ha! ha!
I KNEW HE'D SAY THAT!
I'LL DYE IT RED IF BLONDE DOESN'T SUIT YA!
HEH HEH!
WHAT!?
COOL IT, ZEN!
COME INSIDE. YOUR STUFF ARRIVED ALREADY.

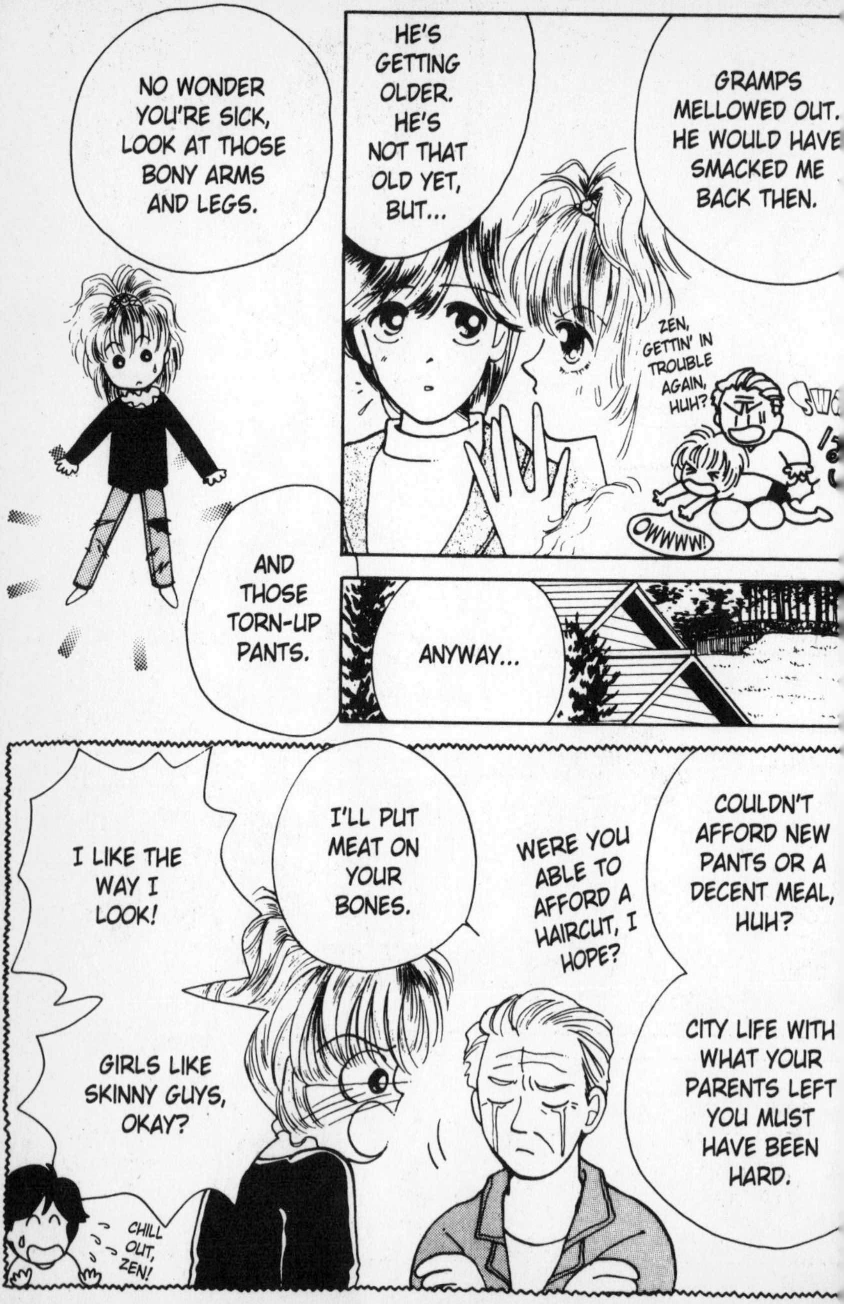
GRAMPS MELLOWED OUT. HE WOULD HAVE SMACKED ME BACK THEN.
HE'S GETTING OLDER. HE'S NOT THAT OLD YET, BUT...
ZEN, GETTIN' IN TROUBLE AGAIN, HUH?
OWWWW!
ANYWAY...
NO WONDER YOU'RE SICK, LOOK AT THOSE BONY ARMS AND LEGS.
AND THOSE TORN-UP PANTS.
COULDN'T AFFORD NEW PANTS OR A DECENT MEAL, HUH?
CITY LIFE WITH WHAT YOUR PARENTS LEFT YOU MUST HAVE BEEN HARD.
WERE YOU ABLE TO AFFORD A HAIRCUT, I HOPE?
I'LL PUT MEAT ON YOUR BONES.
I LIKE THE WAY I LOOK!
GIRLS LIKE SKINNY GUYS, OKAY?
CHILL OUT, ZEN!

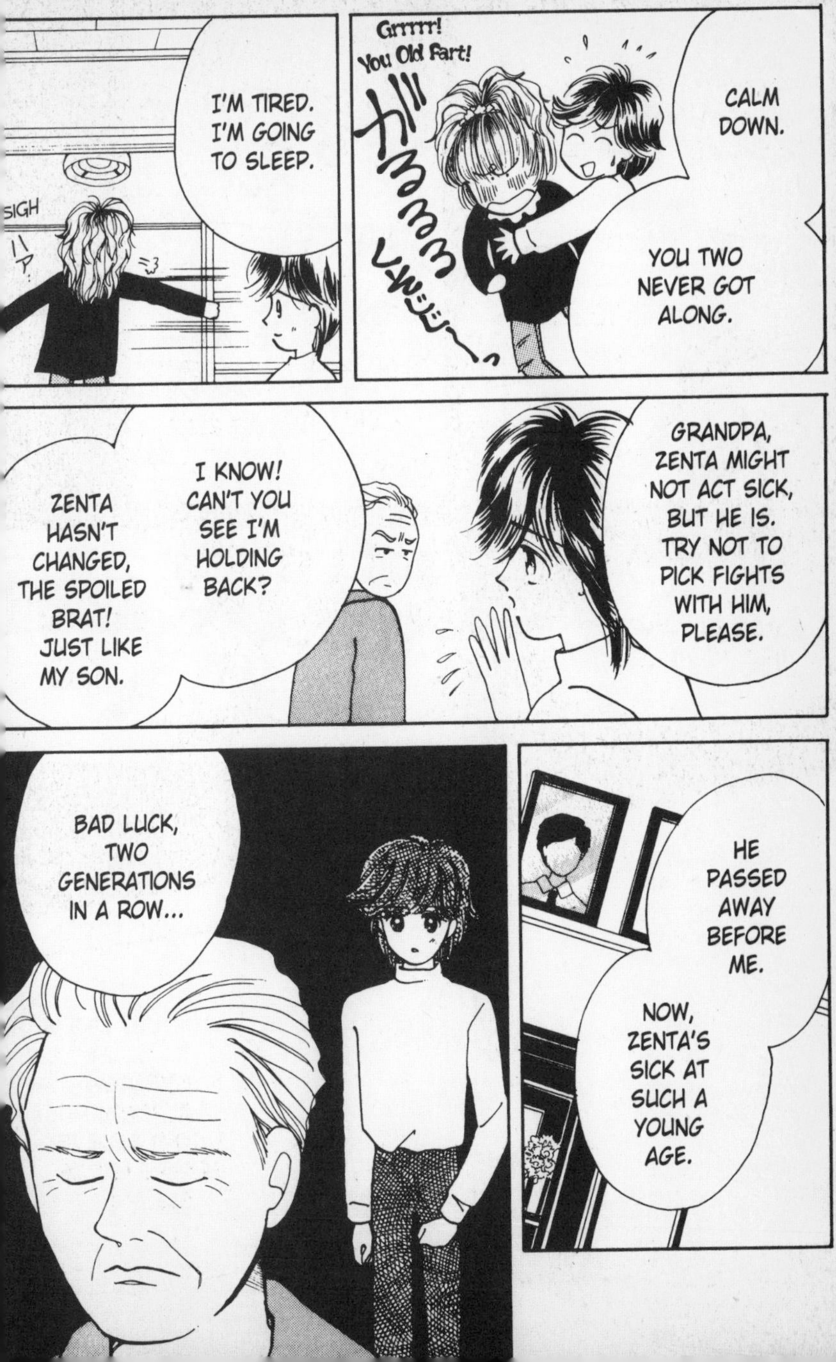
CALM DOWN.
Grrrrr! You Old Fart!
YOU TWO NEVER GOT ALONG.
I'M TIRED. I'M GOING TO SLEEP.
SIGH
GRANDPA, ZENTA MIGHT NOT ACT SICK, BUT HE IS. TRY NOT TO PICK FIGHTS WITH HIM, PLEASE.
I KNOW! CAN'T YOU SEE I'M HOLDING BACK?
ZENTA HASN'T CHANGED, THE SPOILED BRAT! JUST LIKE MY SON.
HE PASSED AWAY BEFORE ME.
NOW, ZENTA'S SICK AT SUCH A YOUNG AGE.
BAD LUCK, TWO GENERATIONS IN A ROW...

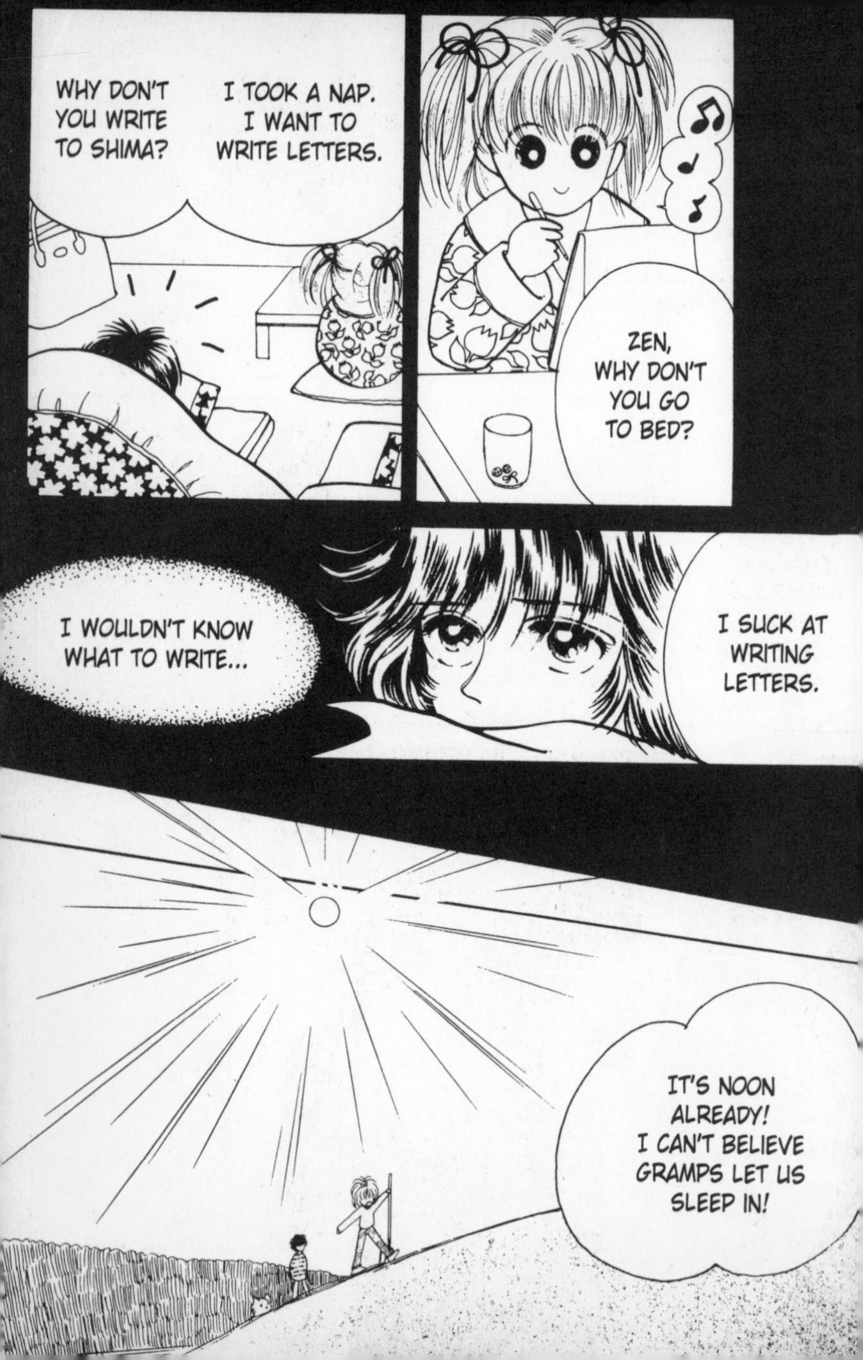
ZEN, WHY DON'T YOU GO TO BED?
I TOOK A NAP. I WANT TO WRITE LETTERS.
WHY DON'T YOU WRITE TO SHIMA?
I SUCK AT WRITING LETTERS.
I WOULDN'T KNOW WHAT TO WRITE...
IT'S NOON ALREADY! I CAN'T BELIEVE GRAMPS LET US SLEEP IN!

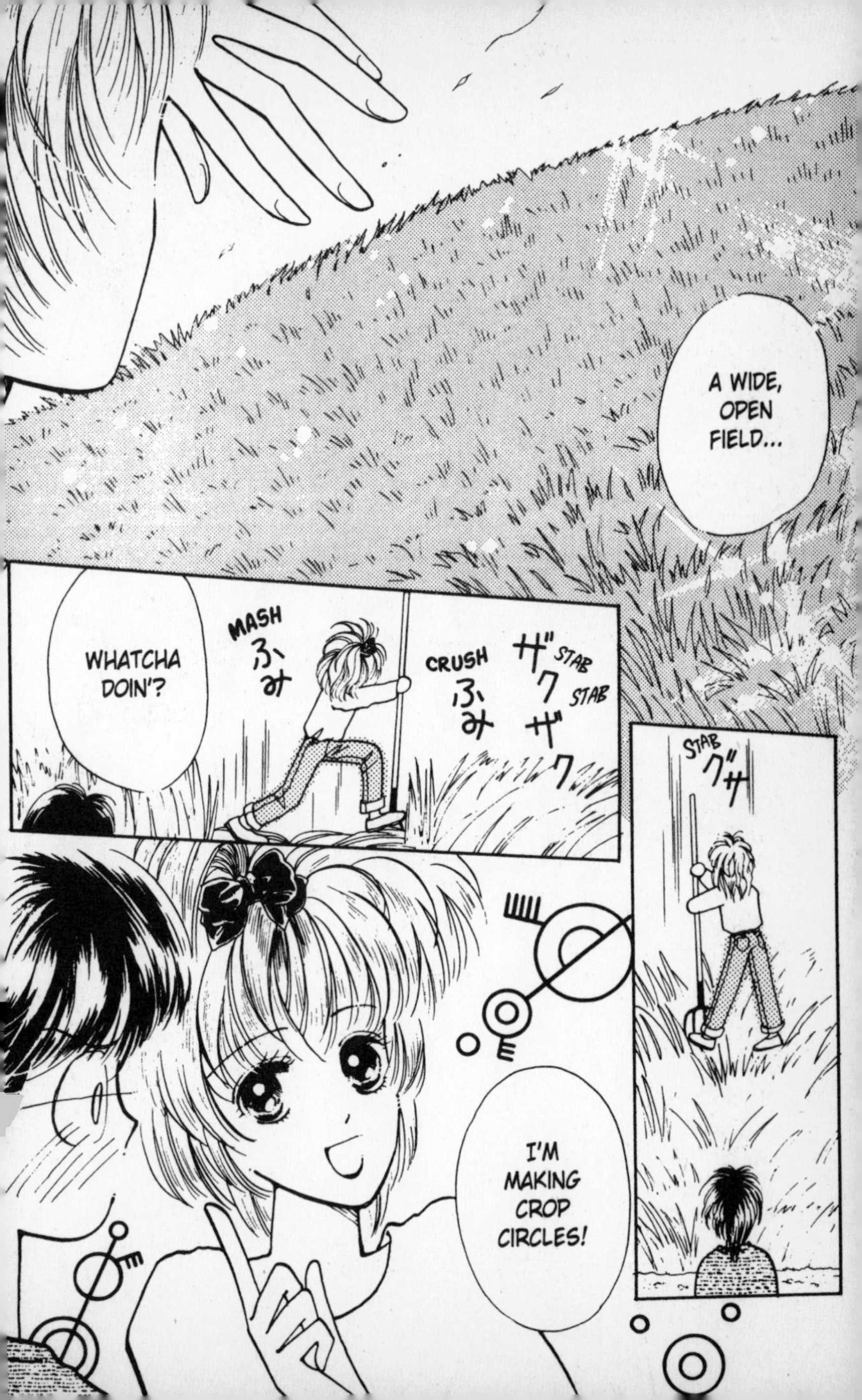
A WIDE, OPEN FIELD...
WHATCHA DOIN'?
MASH
ふみ
CRUSH
ふみ
STAB
ザク
STAB
ザク
STAB
グザ
I'M MAKING CROP CIRCLES!

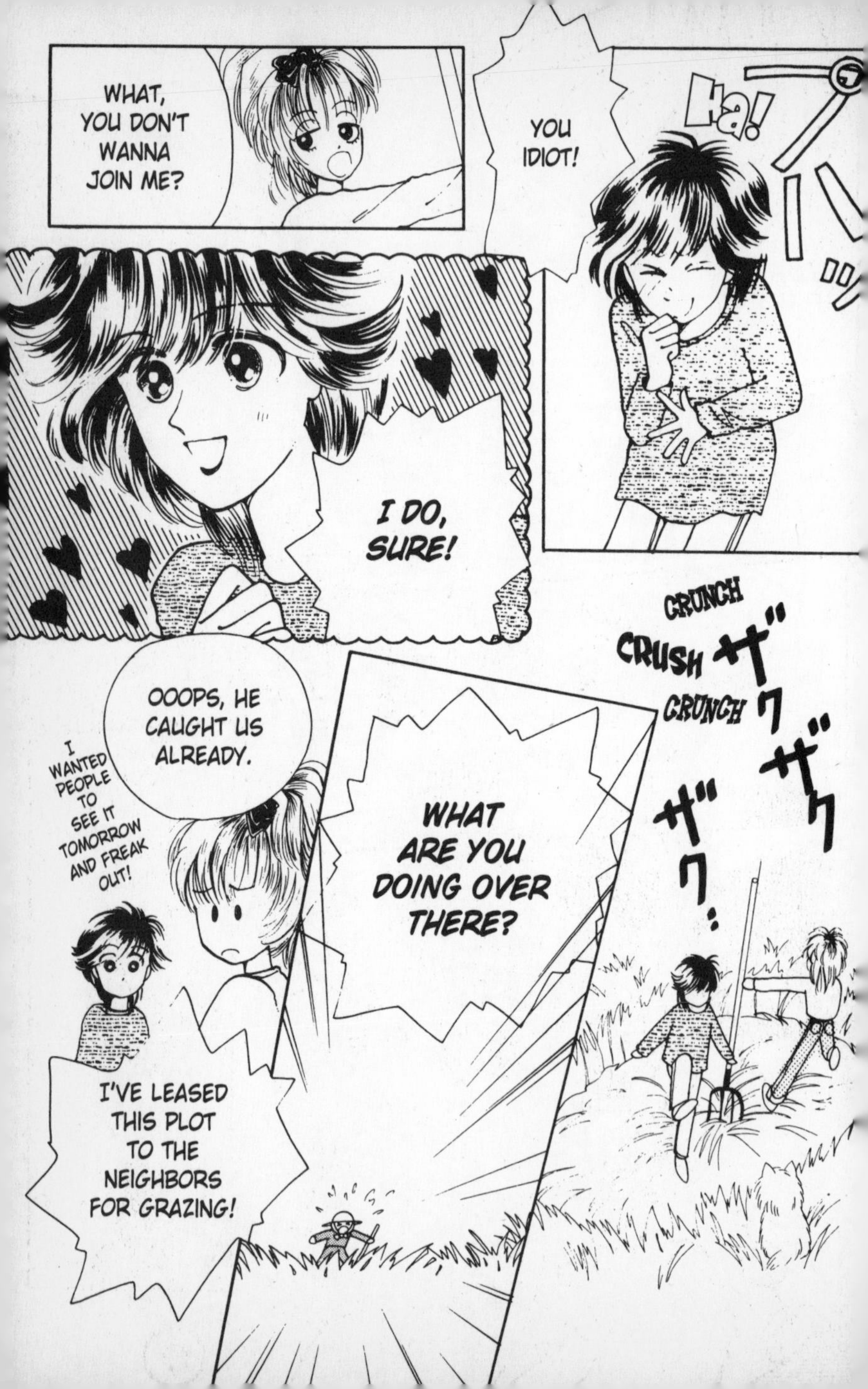
YOU IDIOT!
Ha!
アハハッ
WHAT, YOU DON'T WANNA JOIN ME?
I DO, SURE!
CRUNCH
CRUSH
CRUNCH
ザクザクザク
WHAT ARE YOU DOING OVER THERE?
I'VE LEASED THIS PLOT TO THE NEIGHBORS FOR GRAZING!
OOOPS, HE CAUGHT US ALREADY.
I WANTED PEOPLE TO SEE IT TOMORROW AND FREAK OUT!

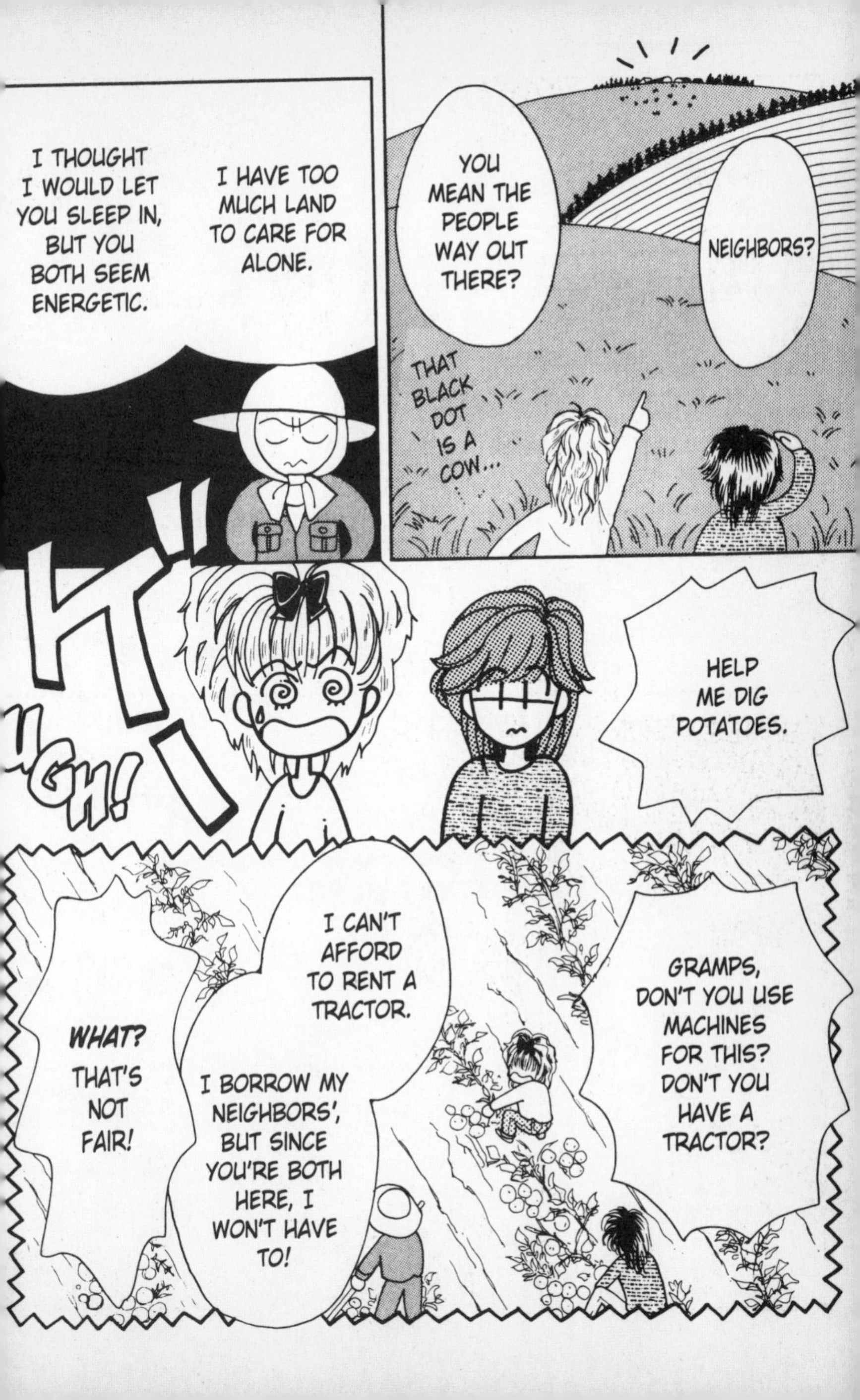

NEIGHBORS?
YOU MEAN THE PEOPLE WAY OUT THERE?
THAT BLACK DOT IS A COW...
I THOUGHT I WOULD LET YOU SLEEP IN, BUT YOU BOTH SEEM ENERGETIC.
I HAVE TOO MUCH LAND TO CARE FOR ALONE.
HELP ME DIG POTATOES.
UGH!
GRAMPS, DON'T YOU USE MACHINES FOR THIS? DON'T YOU HAVE A TRACTOR?
I CAN'T AFFORD TO RENT A TRACTOR.
I BORROW MY NEIGHBORS', BUT SINCE YOU'RE BOTH HERE, I WON'T HAVE TO!
WHAT? THAT'S NOT FAIR!

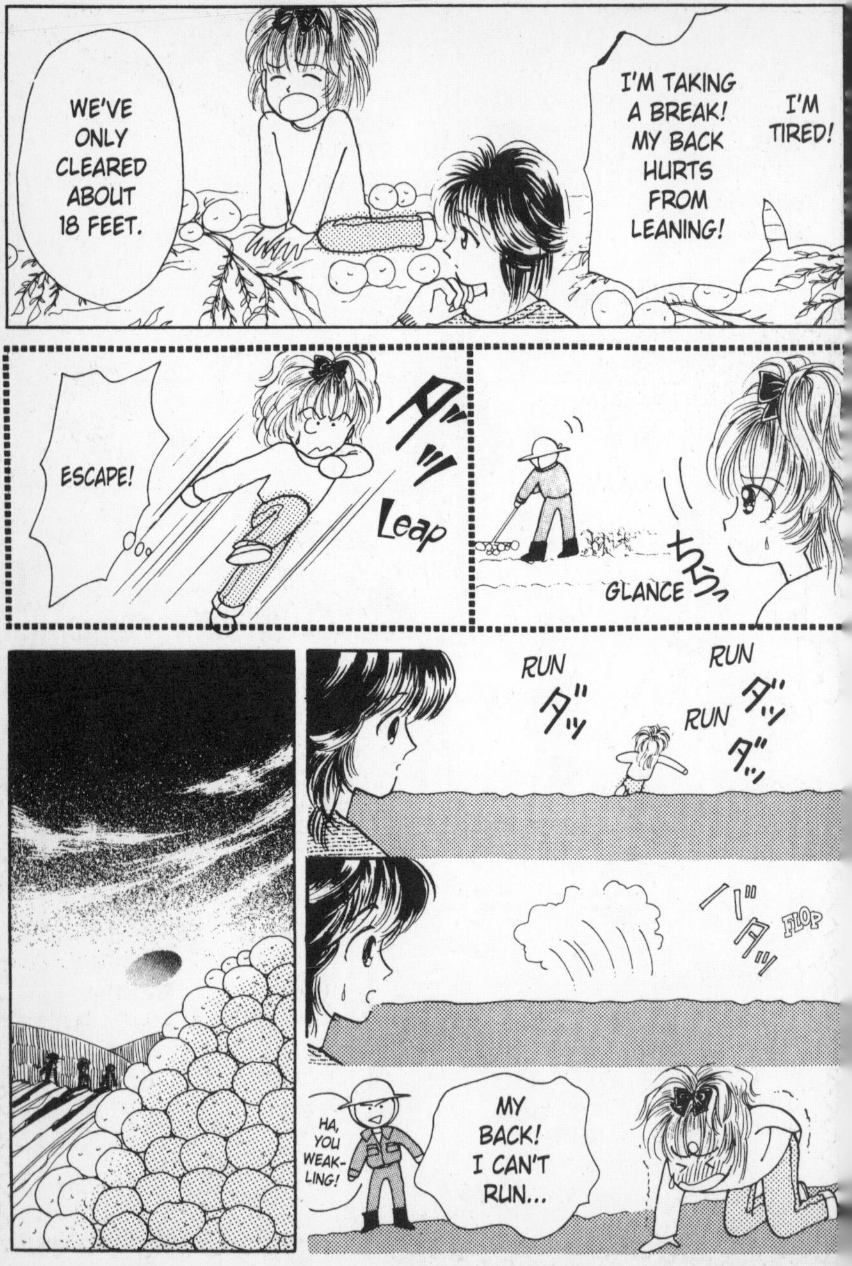
I'M TIRED!
I'M TAKING A BREAK! MY BACK HURTS FROM LEANING!
WE'VE ONLY CLEARED ABOUT 18 FEET.
ちらっ
GLANCE
ダッ
Leap
ESCAPE!
RUN
ダッ
RUN
ダッ
RUN
ダッ
バタッ
FLOP
MY BACK! I CAN'T RUN...
HA, YOU WEAK-LING!

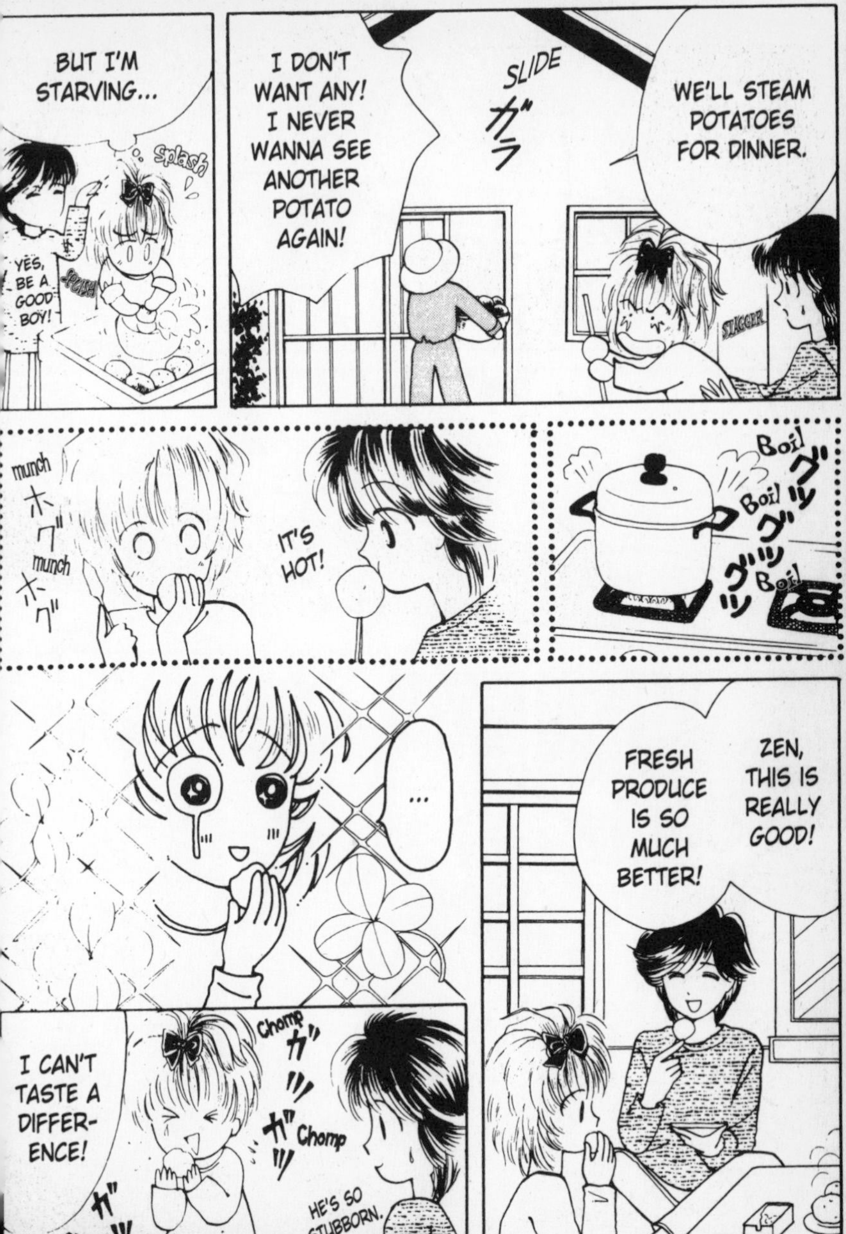
WE'LL STEAM POTATOES FOR DINNER.
STAGGRR
SLIDE
ガラ
I DON'T WANT ANY! I NEVER WANNA SEE ANOTHER POTATO AGAIN!
BUT I'M STARVING...
Splash
YES, BE A GOOD BOY!
SPLASH
Boil
Boil
Boil
グツグツグツ
IT'S HOT!
munch
ホグ
munch
ホグ
ZEN, THIS IS REALLY GOOD!
FRESH PRODUCE IS SO MUCH BETTER!
...
Chomp
ガッ
Chomp
ガッ
I CAN'T TASTE A DIFFER-ENCE!
Chomp
ガッ
HE'S SO STUBBORN.

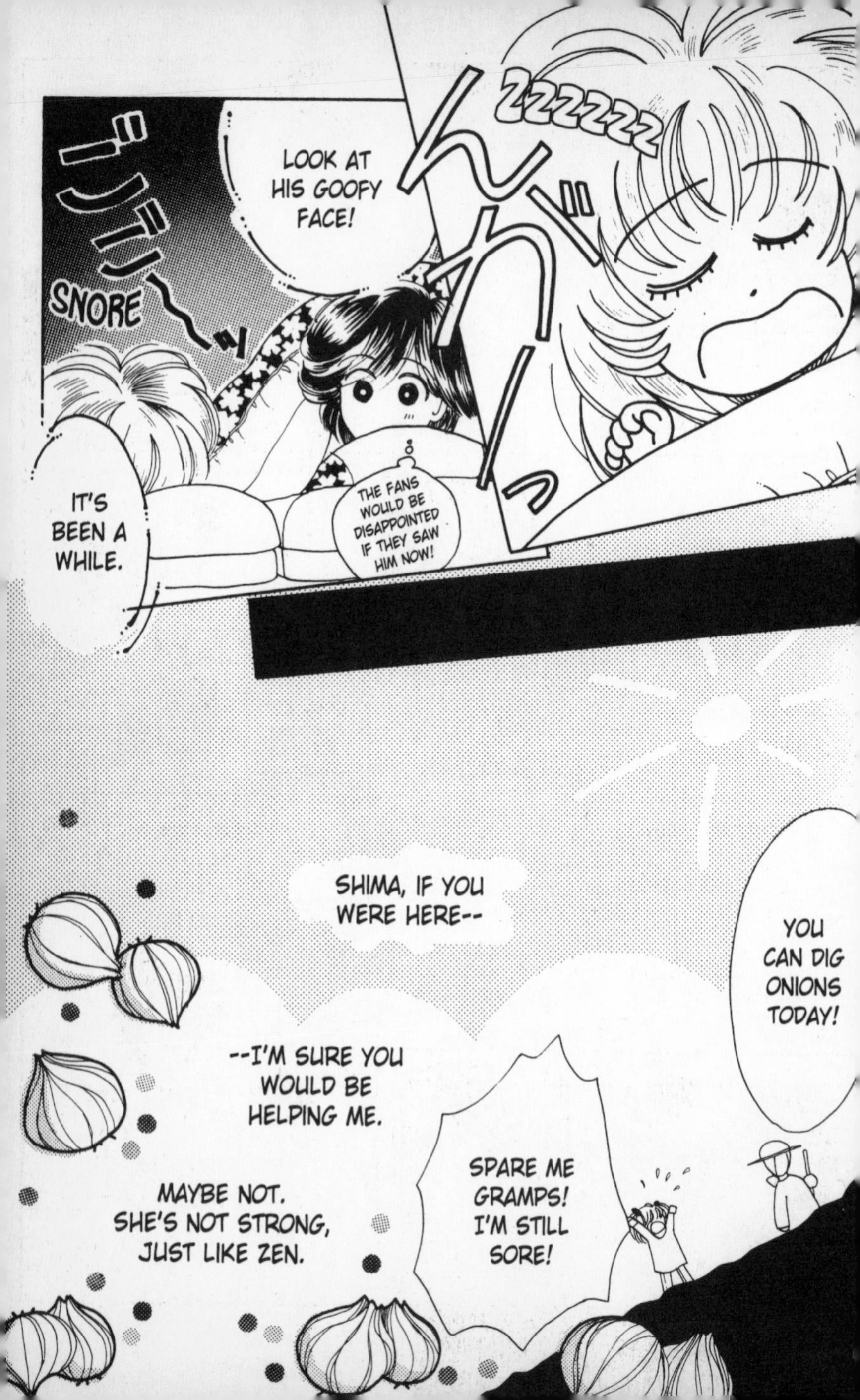
ZZZZZZ
LOOK AT HIS GOOFY FACE!
SNORE
IT'S BEEN A WHILE.
THE FANS WOULD BE DISAPPOINTED IF THEY SAW HIM NOW!
YOU CAN DIG ONIONS TODAY!
SHIMA, IF YOU WERE HERE--
--I'M SURE YOU WOULD BE HELPING ME.
SPARE ME GRAMPS! I'M STILL SORE!
MAYBE NOT. SHE'S NOT STRONG, JUST LIKE ZEN.

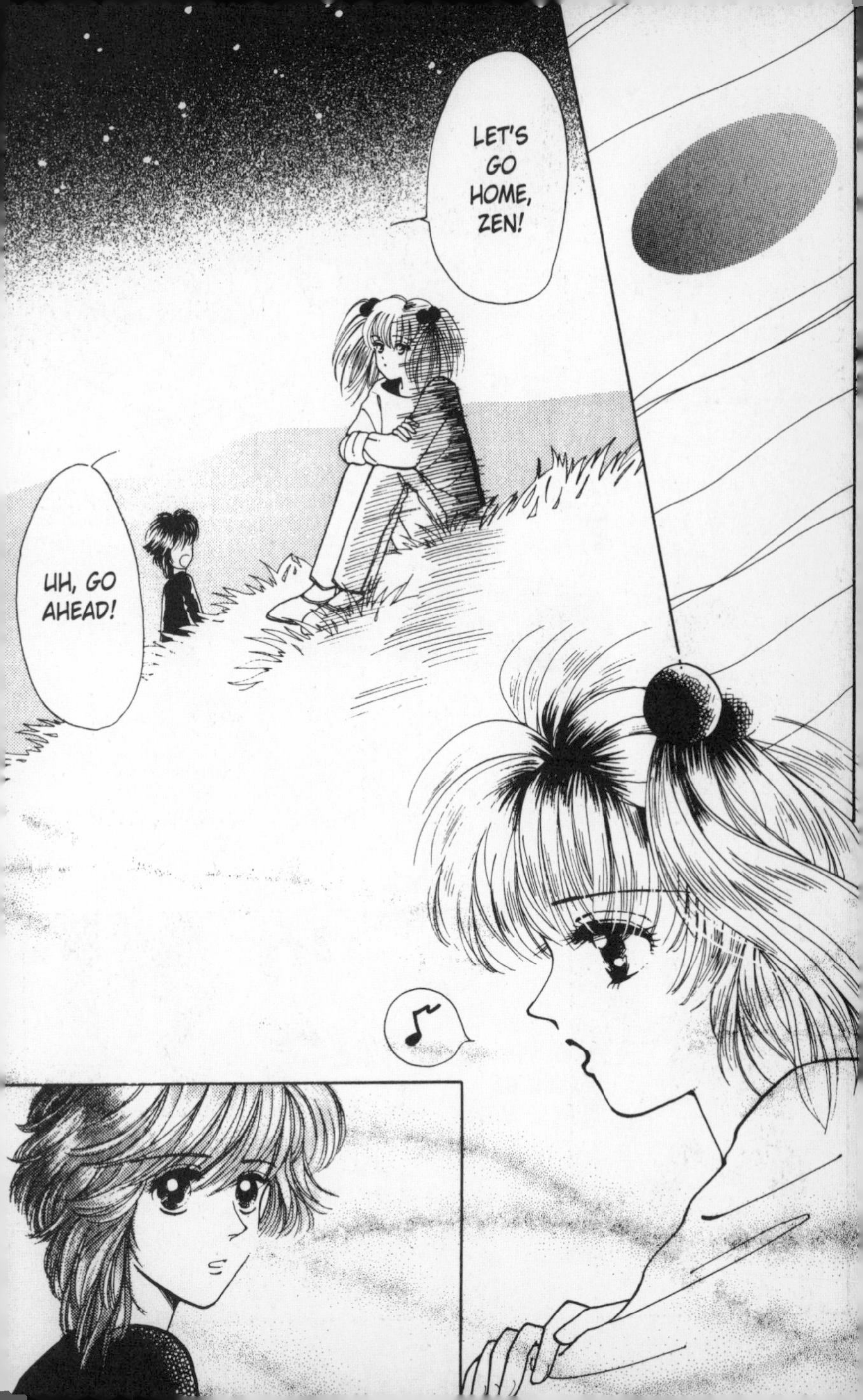
LET'S GO HOME, ZEN!
UH, GO AHEAD!

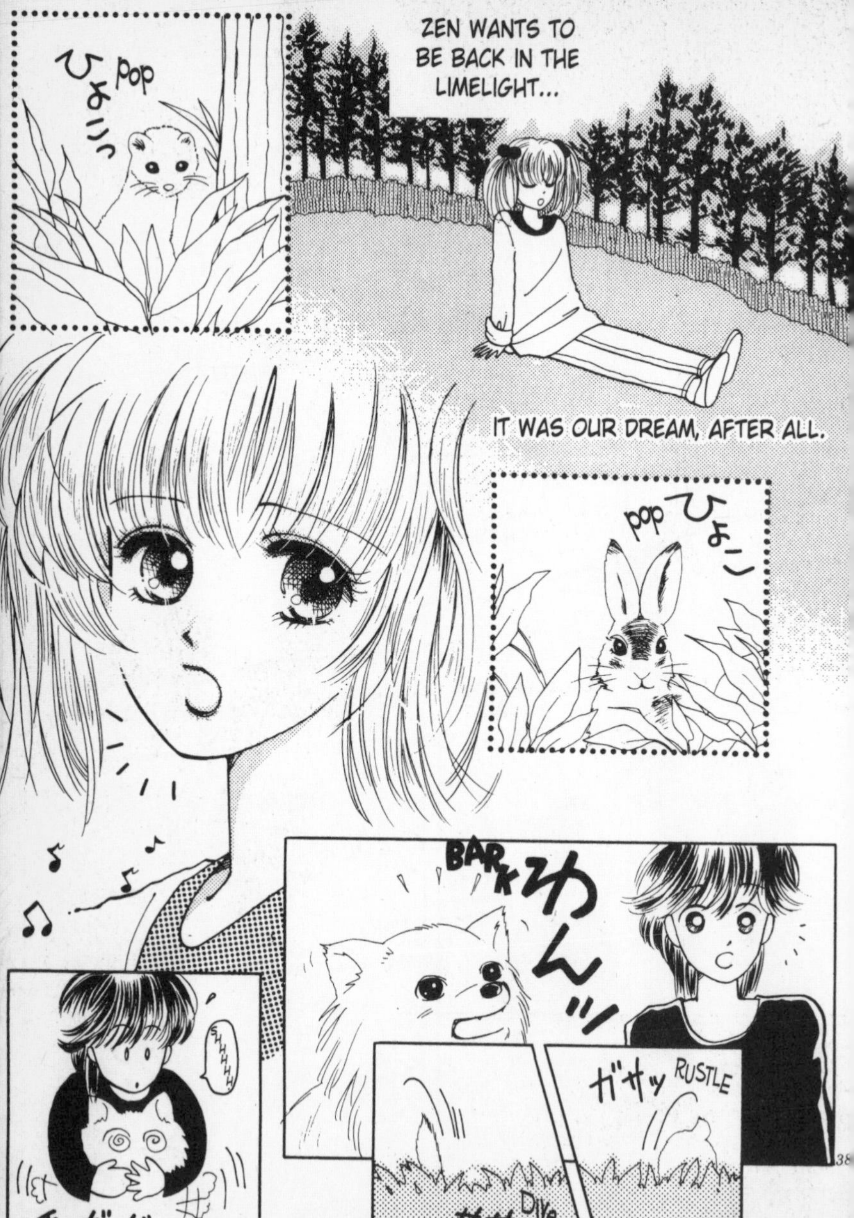

ZEN WANTS TO BE BACK IN THE LIMELIGHT...
ひょこっ pop
IT WAS OUR DREAM, AFTER ALL.
pop ひょこっ
BARK わんッ
ガサッ RUSTLE
ササッ Dive
SHHHHH
モガガ SMOTHER

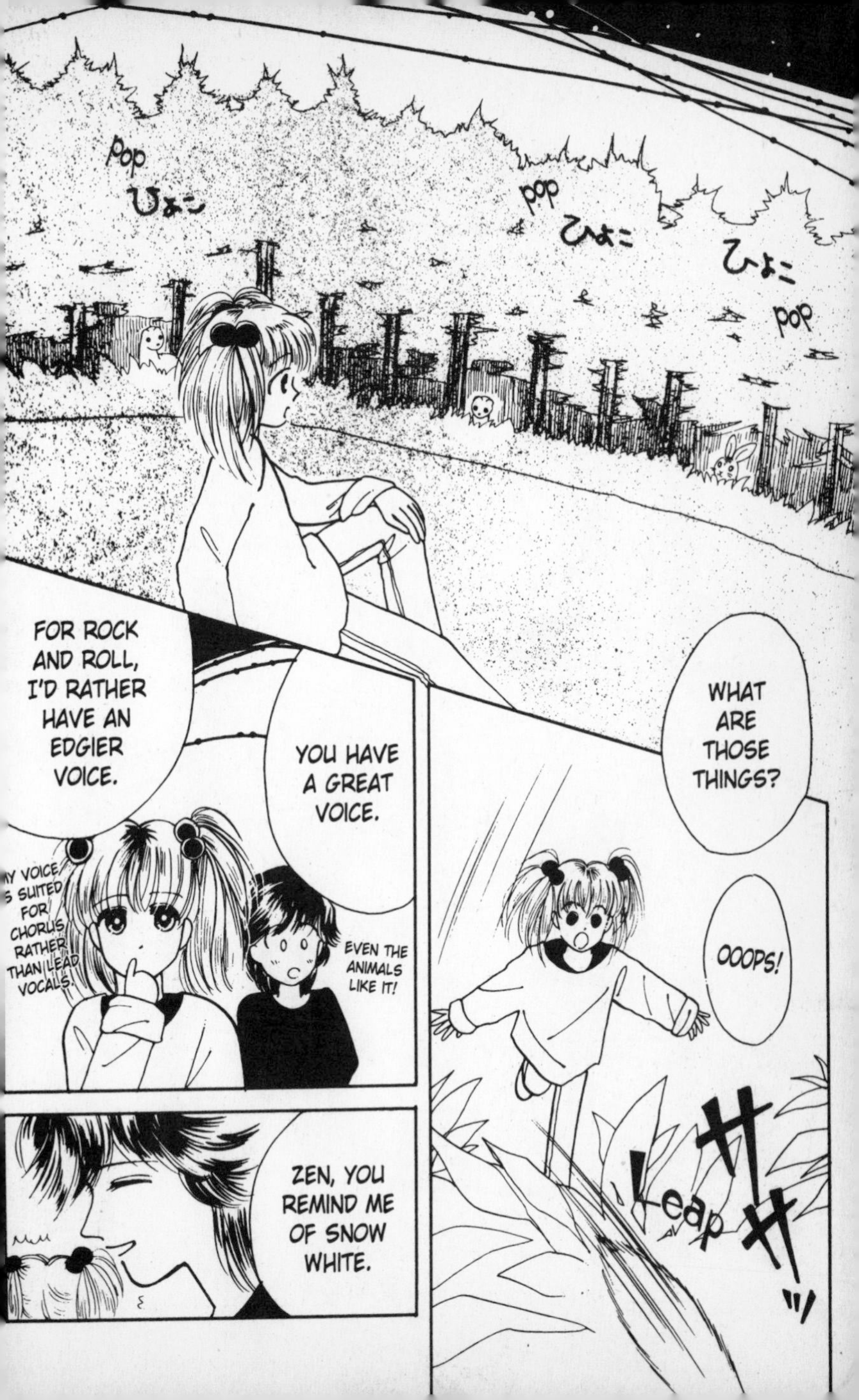
pop
ひょこ
pop
ひょこ
ひょこ
pop
WHAT ARE THOSE THINGS?
OOOPS!
Leap
YOU HAVE A GREAT VOICE.
FOR ROCK AND ROLL, I'D RATHER HAVE AN EDGIER VOICE.
EVEN THE ANIMALS LIKE IT!
MY VOICE IS SUITED FOR CHORUS RATHER THAN LEAD VOCALS.
ZEN, YOU REMIND ME OF SNOW WHITE.

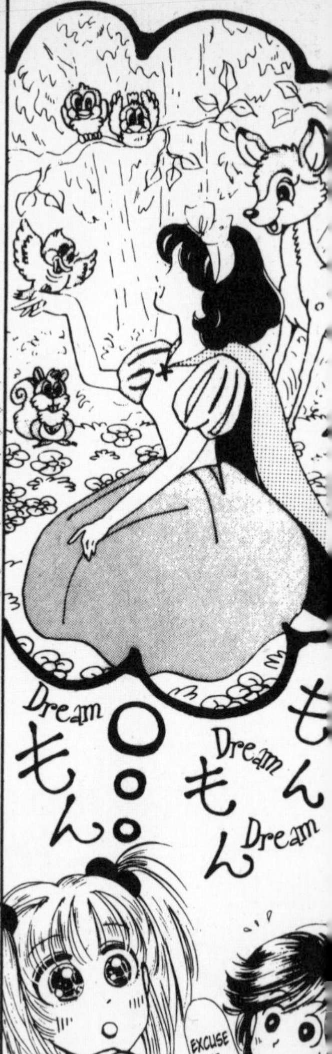
Dream もん
Dream もん
Dream もん
EXCUSE ME...

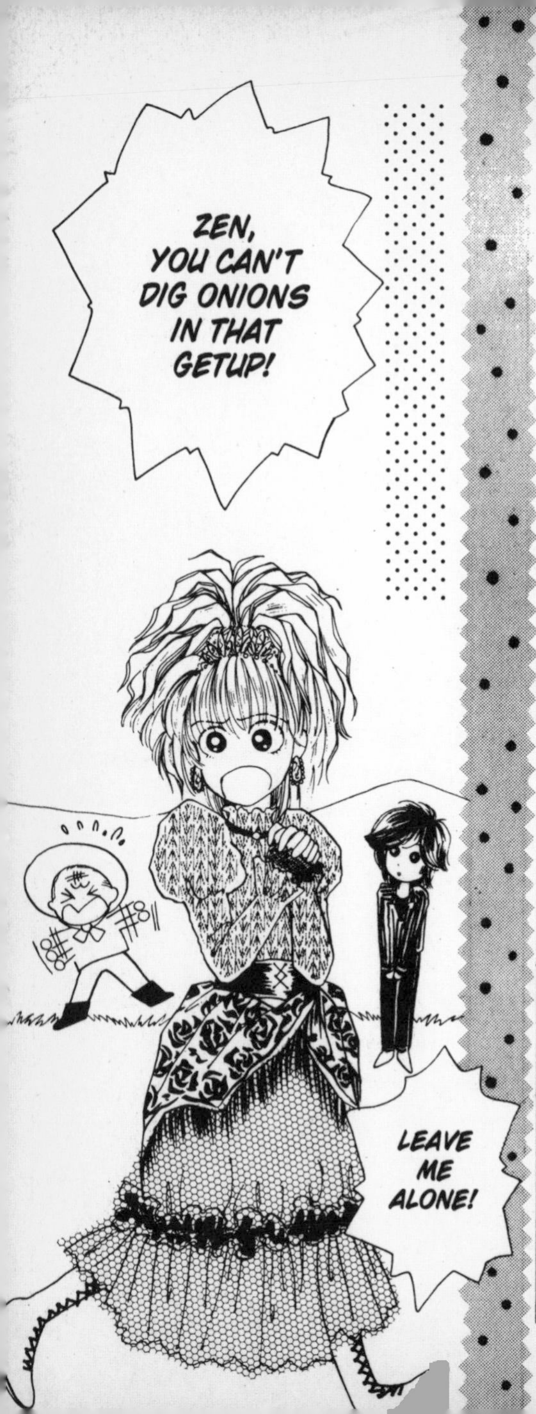
ZEN, YOU CAN'T DIG ONIONS IN THAT GETUP!
LEAVE ME ALONE!

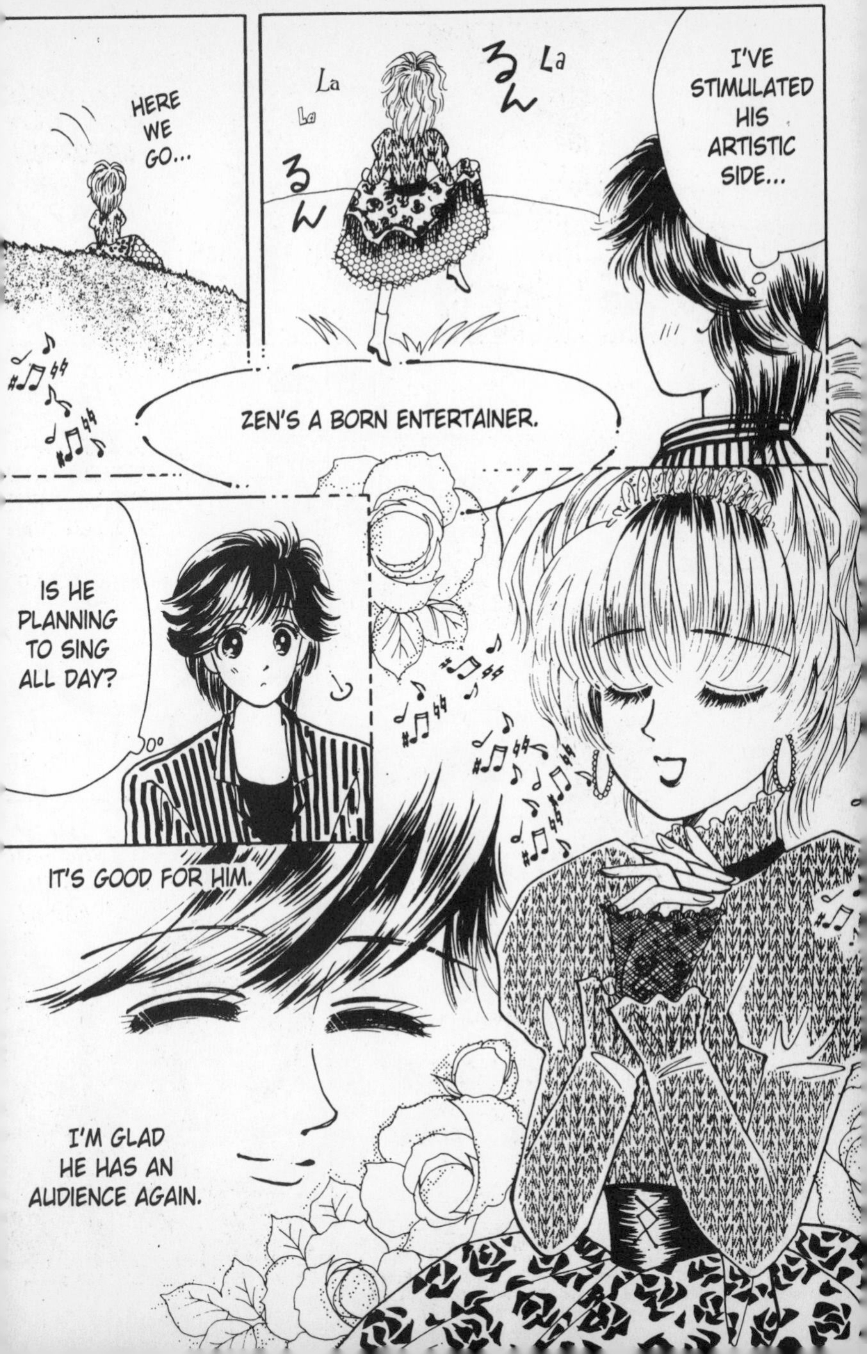
I'VE STIMULATED HIS ARTISTIC SIDE...
るん
La
La
La
るん
HERE WE GO...
ZEN'S A BORN ENTERTAINER.
IS HE PLANNING TO SING ALL DAY?
IT'S GOOD FOR HIM.
I'M GLAD HE HAS AN AUDIENCE AGAIN.

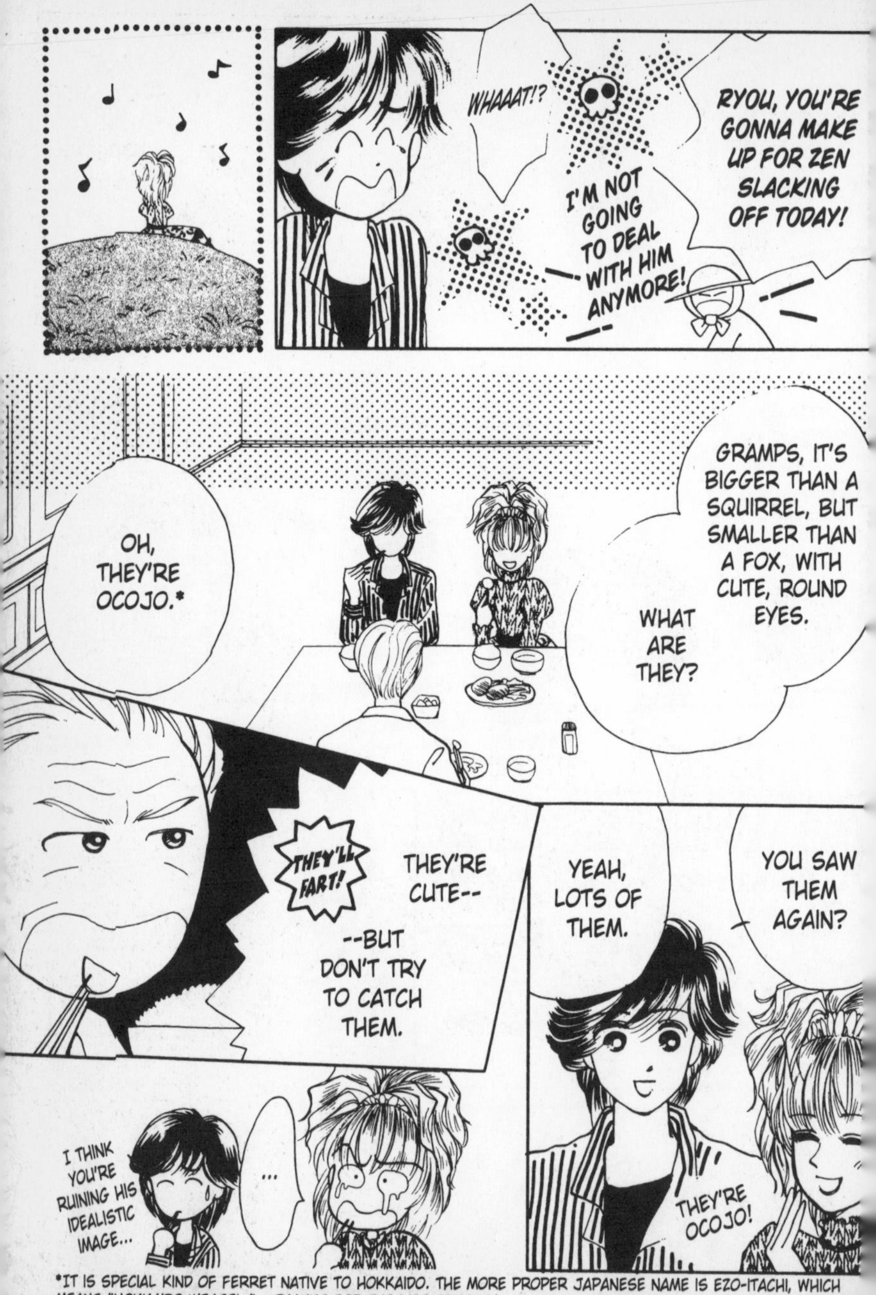
RYOU, YOU'RE GONNA MAKE UP FOR ZEN SLACKING OFF TODAY!
I'M NOT GOING TO DEAL WITH HIM ANYMORE!
WHAAAT!?
GRAMPS, IT'S BIGGER THAN A SQUIRREL, BUT SMALLER THAN A FOX, WITH CUTE, ROUND EYES.
WHAT ARE THEY?
OH, THEY'RE OCOJO.*
YOU SAW THEM AGAIN?
YEAH, LOTS OF THEM.
THEY'RE OCOJO!
THEY'RE CUTE--
--BUT DON'T TRY TO CATCH THEM.
THEY'LL FART!
...
I THINK YOU'RE RUINING HIS IDEALISTIC IMAGE...

*IT IS SPECIAL KIND OF FERRET NATIVE TO HOKKAIDO. THE MORE PROPER JAPANESE NAME IS EZO-ITACHI, WHICH MEANS "HOKKAIDO WEASEL." -THANKS FOR THE INFO TOMOKO!-

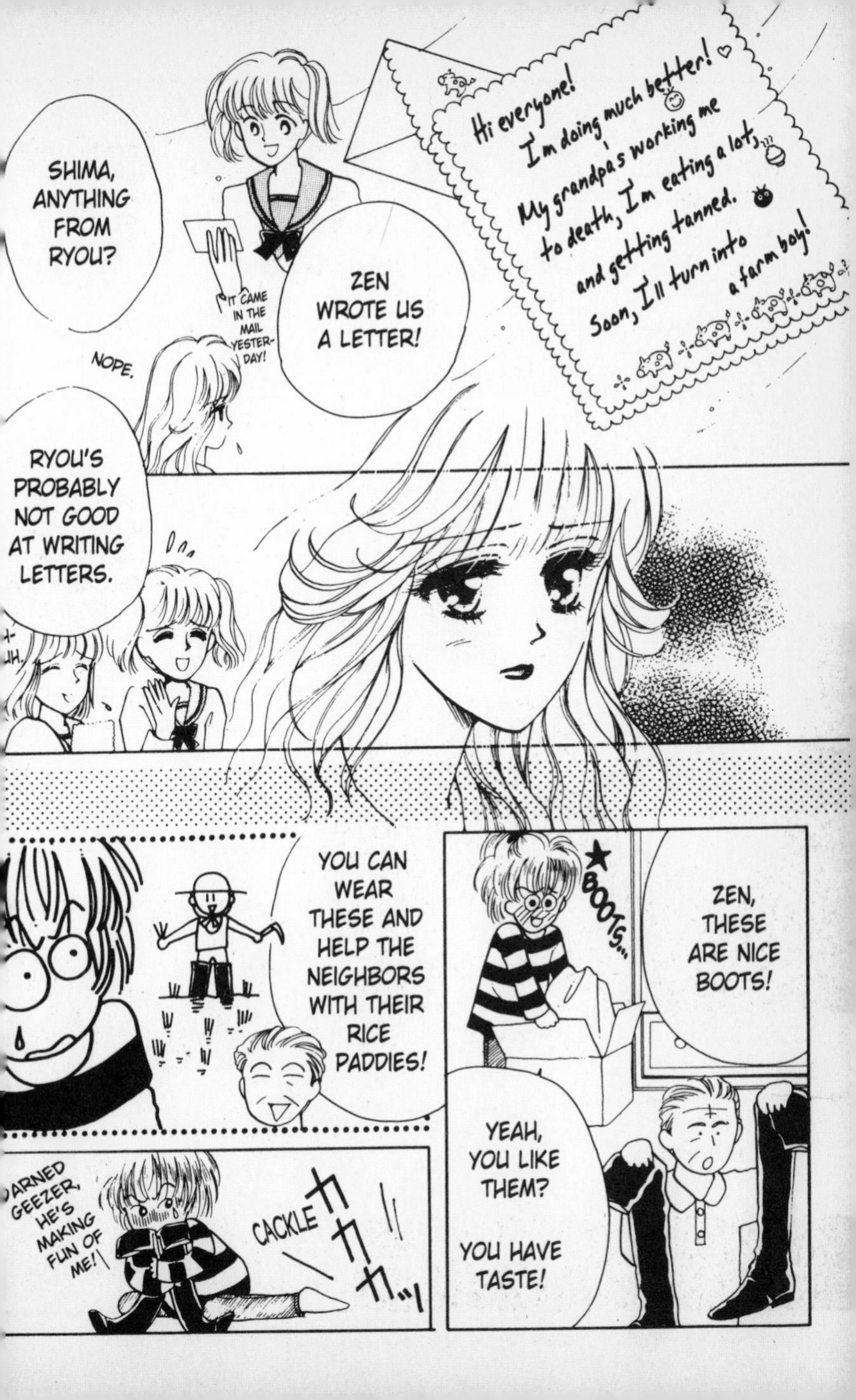
Hi everyone! I'm doing much better! My grandpa's working me to death, I'm eating a lot, and getting tanned. Soon, I'll turn into a farm boy!
ZEN WROTE US A LETTER!
IT CAME IN THE MAIL YESTERDAY!
SHIMA, ANYTHING FROM RYOU?
NOPE.
RYOU'S PROBABLY NOT GOOD AT WRITING LETTERS.
ZEN, THESE ARE NICE BOOTS!
★BOOTS...
YEAH, YOU LIKE THEM?
YOU HAVE TASTE!
YOU CAN WEAR THESE AND HELP THE NEIGHBORS WITH THEIR RICE PADDIES!
ARNED GEEZER, HE'S MAKING FUN OF ME!
CACKLE

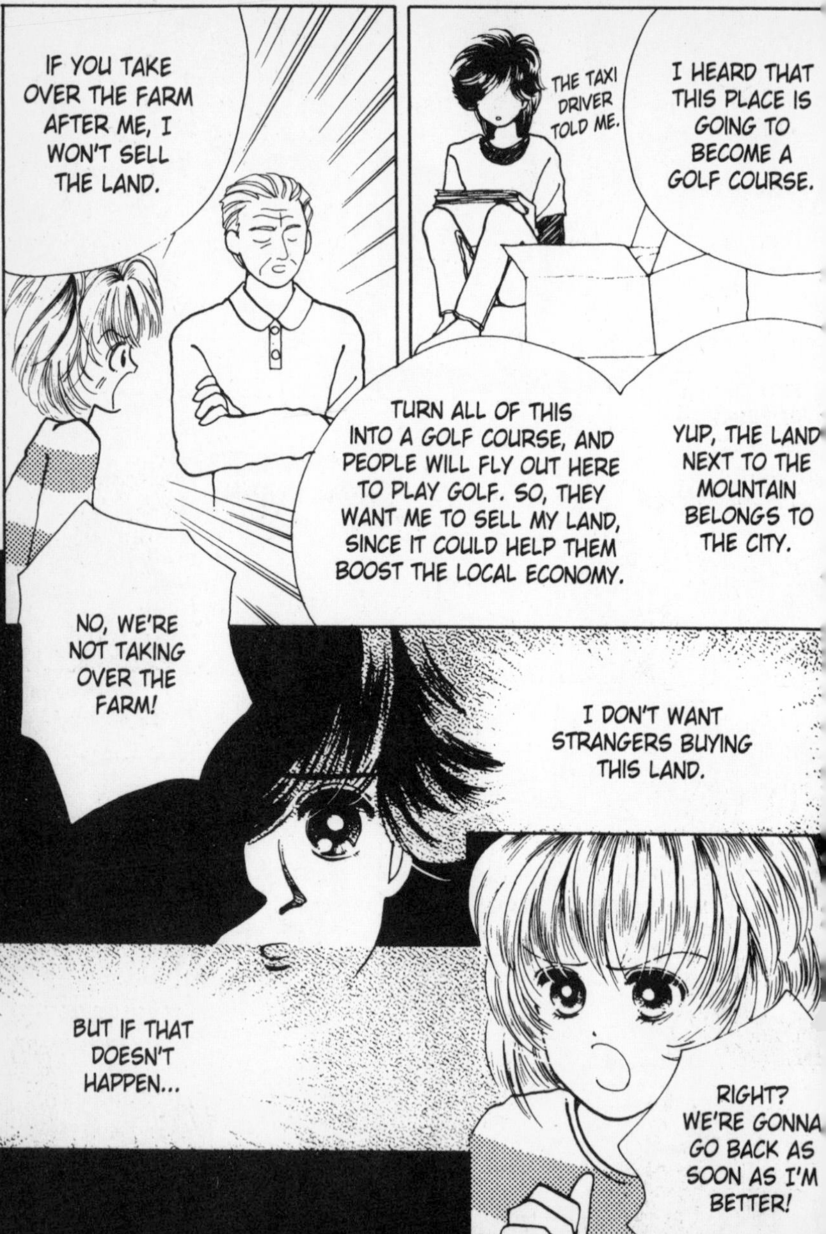
I HEARD THAT THIS PLACE IS GOING TO BECOME A GOLF COURSE.
THE TAXI DRIVER TOLD ME.
YUP, THE LAND NEXT TO THE MOUNTAIN BELONGS TO THE CITY.
TURN ALL OF THIS INTO A GOLF COURSE, AND PEOPLE WILL FLY OUT HERE TO PLAY GOLF. SO, THEY WANT ME TO SELL MY LAND, SINCE IT COULD HELP THEM BOOST THE LOCAL ECONOMY.
IF YOU TAKE OVER THE FARM AFTER ME, I WON'T SELL THE LAND.
NO, WE'RE NOT TAKING OVER THE FARM!
RIGHT? WE'RE GONNA GO BACK AS SOON AS I'M BETTER!
I DON'T WANT STRANGERS BUYING THIS LAND.
BUT IF THAT DOESN'T HAPPEN...

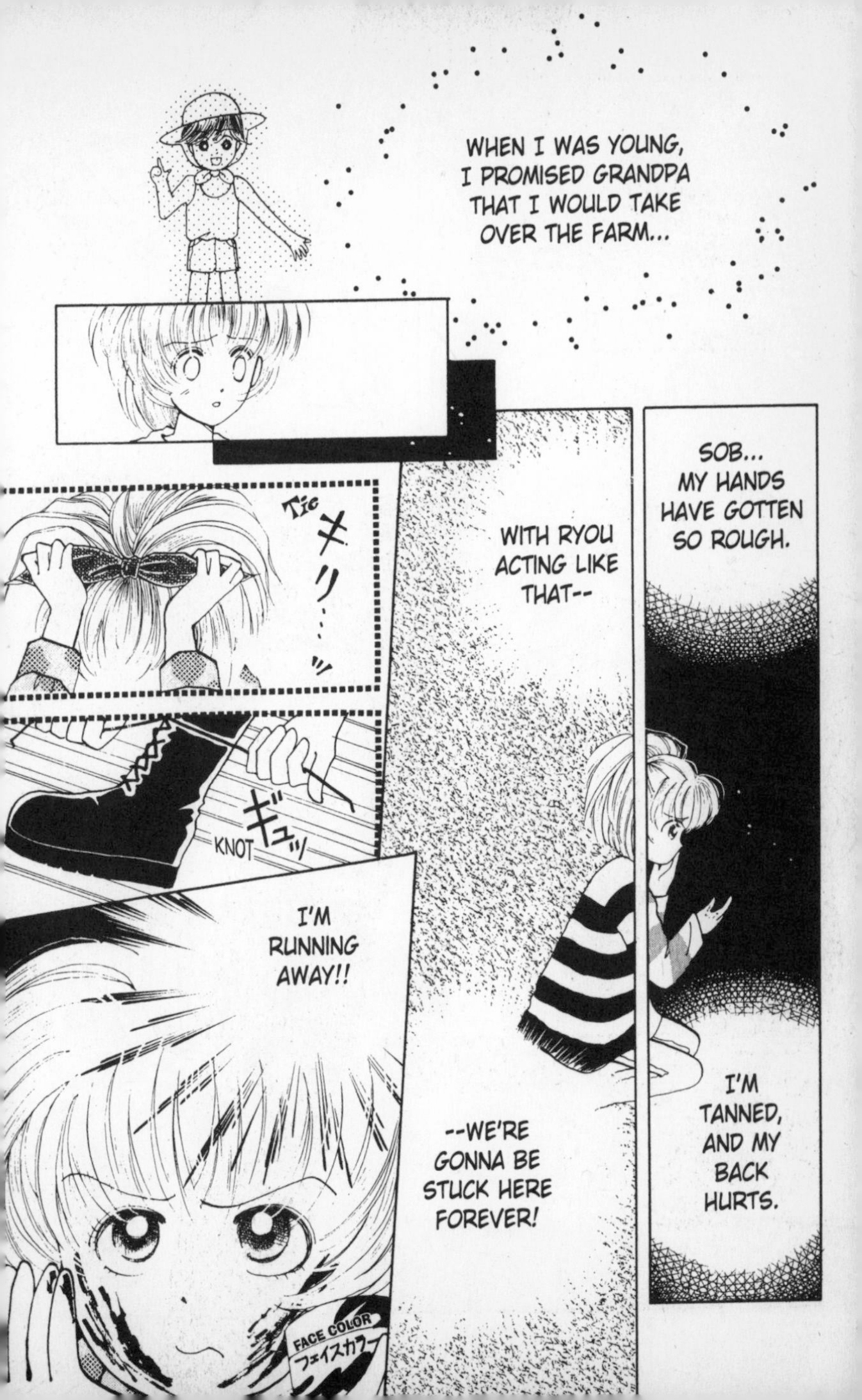
WHEN I WAS YOUNG, I PROMISED GRANDPA THAT I WOULD TAKE OVER THE FARM...
SOB... MY HANDS HAVE GOTTEN SO ROUGH.
I'M TANNED, AND MY BACK HURTS.
WITH RYOU ACTING LIKE THAT--
--WE'RE GONNA BE STUCK HERE FOREVER!
Tic
キリ…ッ
KNOT
ギュッ
I'M RUNNING AWAY!!
FACE COLOR
フェイスカラー

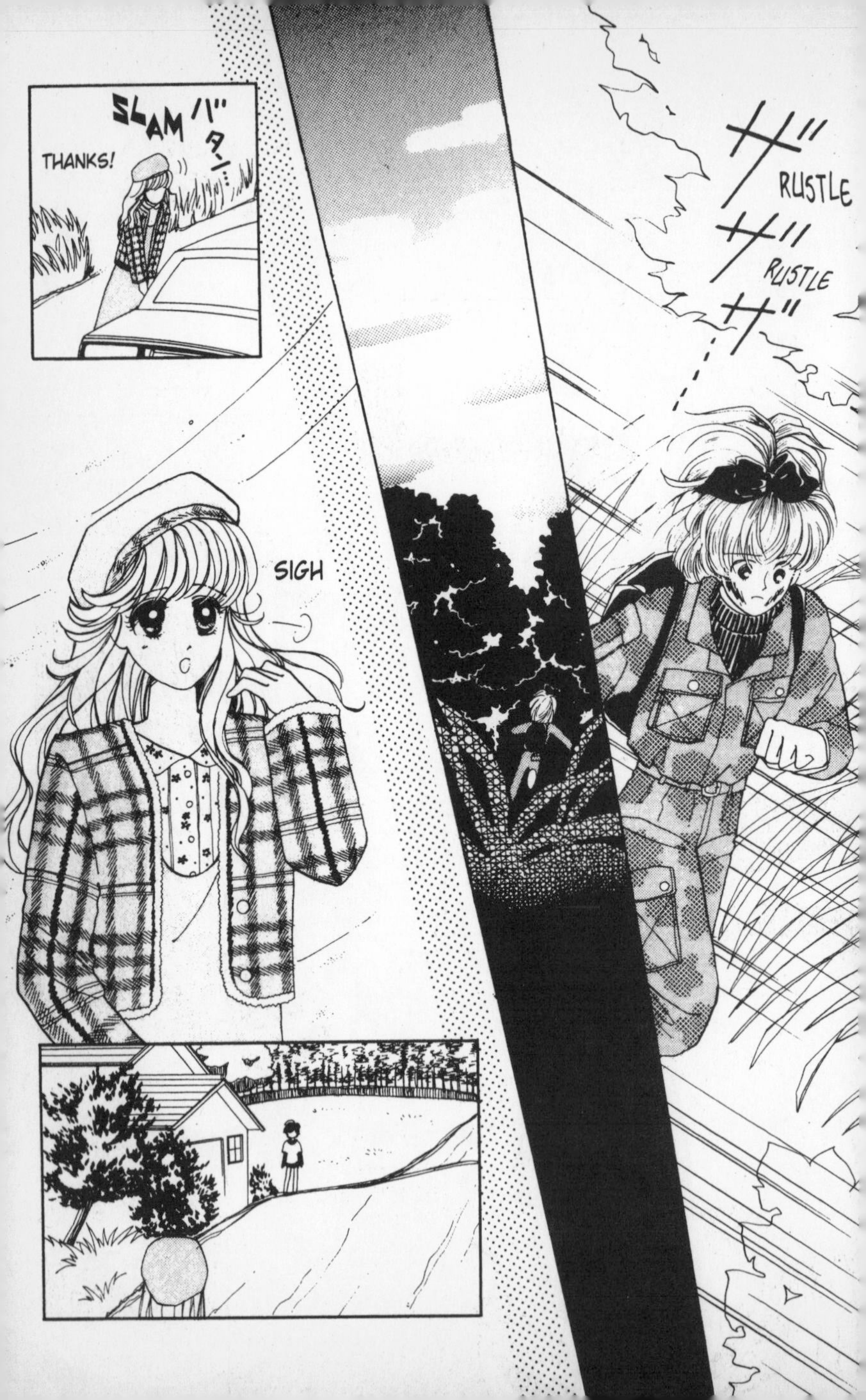

ザ
RUSTLE
ザ
RUSTLE
ザ
SLAM
バターン…
THANKS!
SIGH

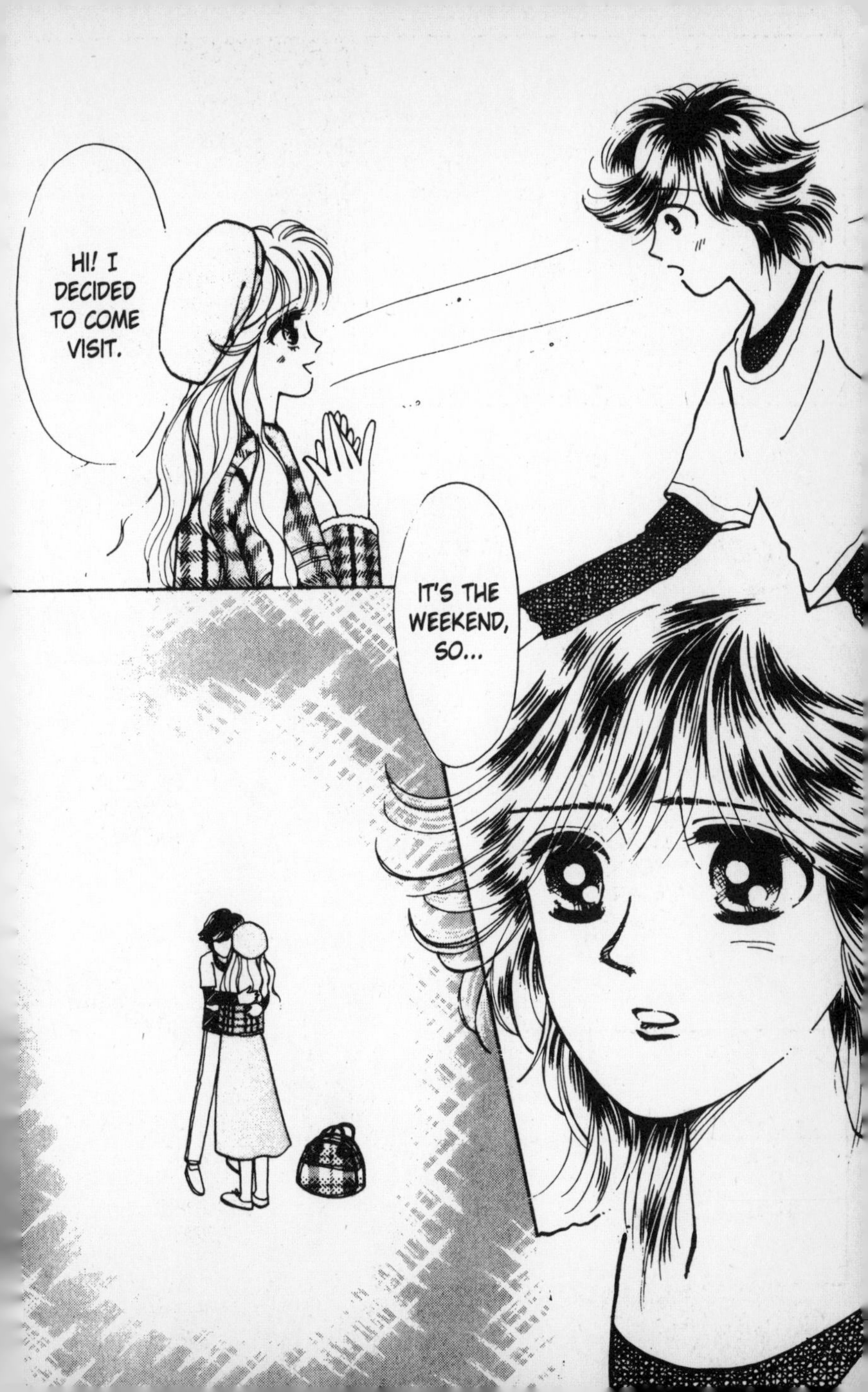
HI! I DECIDED TO COME VISIT.
IT'S THE WEEKEND, SO...

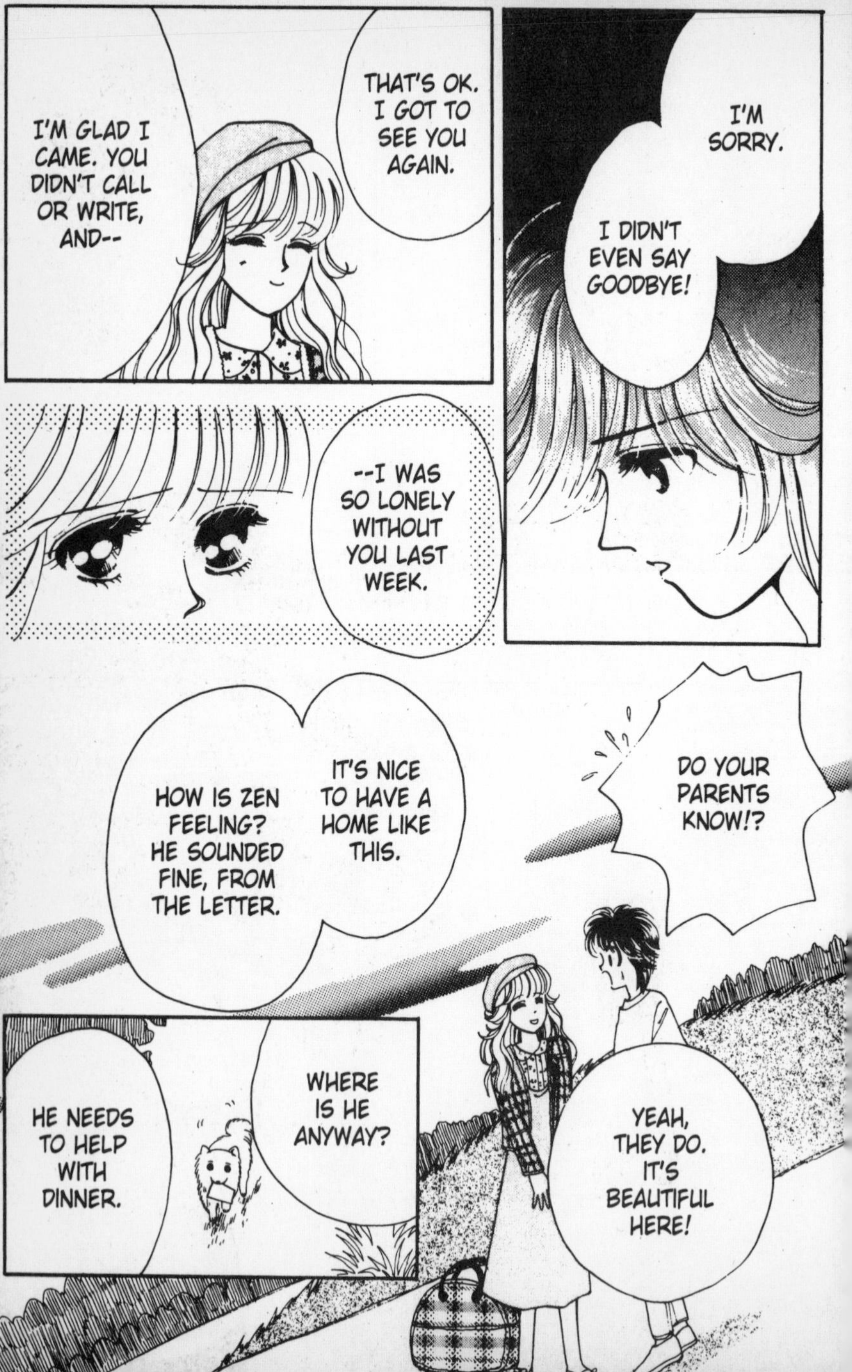
I'M SORRY.
I DIDN'T EVEN SAY GOODBYE!
THAT'S OK. I GOT TO SEE YOU AGAIN.
I'M GLAD I CAME. YOU DIDN'T CALL OR WRITE, AND--
--I WAS SO LONELY WITHOUT YOU LAST WEEK.
DO YOUR PARENTS KNOW!?
YEAH, THEY DO. IT'S BEAUTIFUL HERE!
IT'S NICE TO HAVE A HOME LIKE THIS.
HOW IS ZEN FEELING? HE SOUNDED FINE, FROM THE LETTER.
WHERE IS HE ANYWAY?
HE NEEDS TO HELP WITH DINNER.

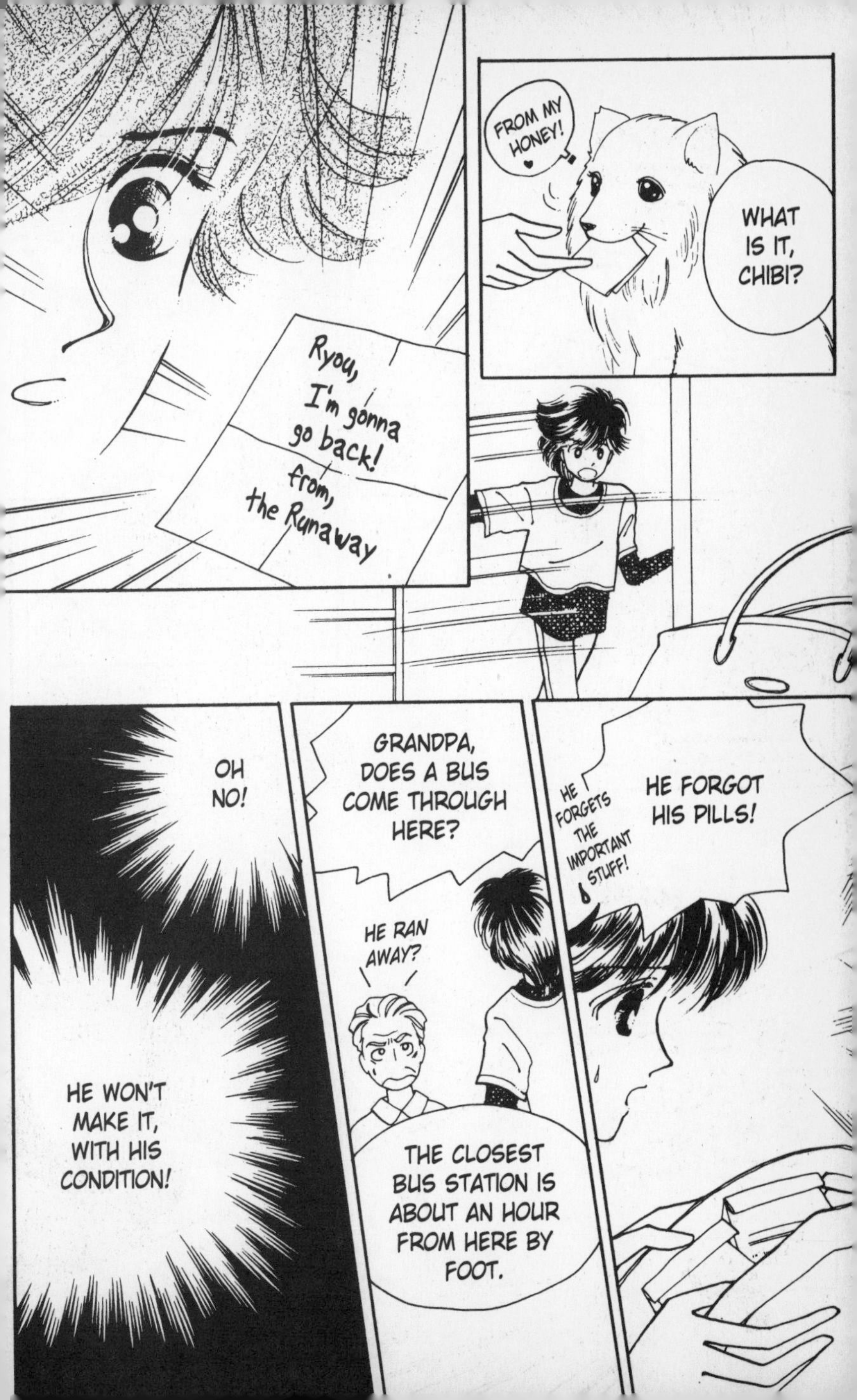
WHAT IS IT, CHIBI?
FROM MY HONEY!
Ryou, I'm gonna go back! from, the Runaway
HE FORGOT HIS PILLS!
HE FORGETS THE IMPORTANT STUFF!
GRANDPA, DOES A BUS COME THROUGH HERE?
HE RAN AWAY?
THE CLOSEST BUS STATION IS ABOUT AN HOUR FROM HERE BY FOOT.
OH NO!
HE WON'T MAKE IT, WITH HIS CONDITION!

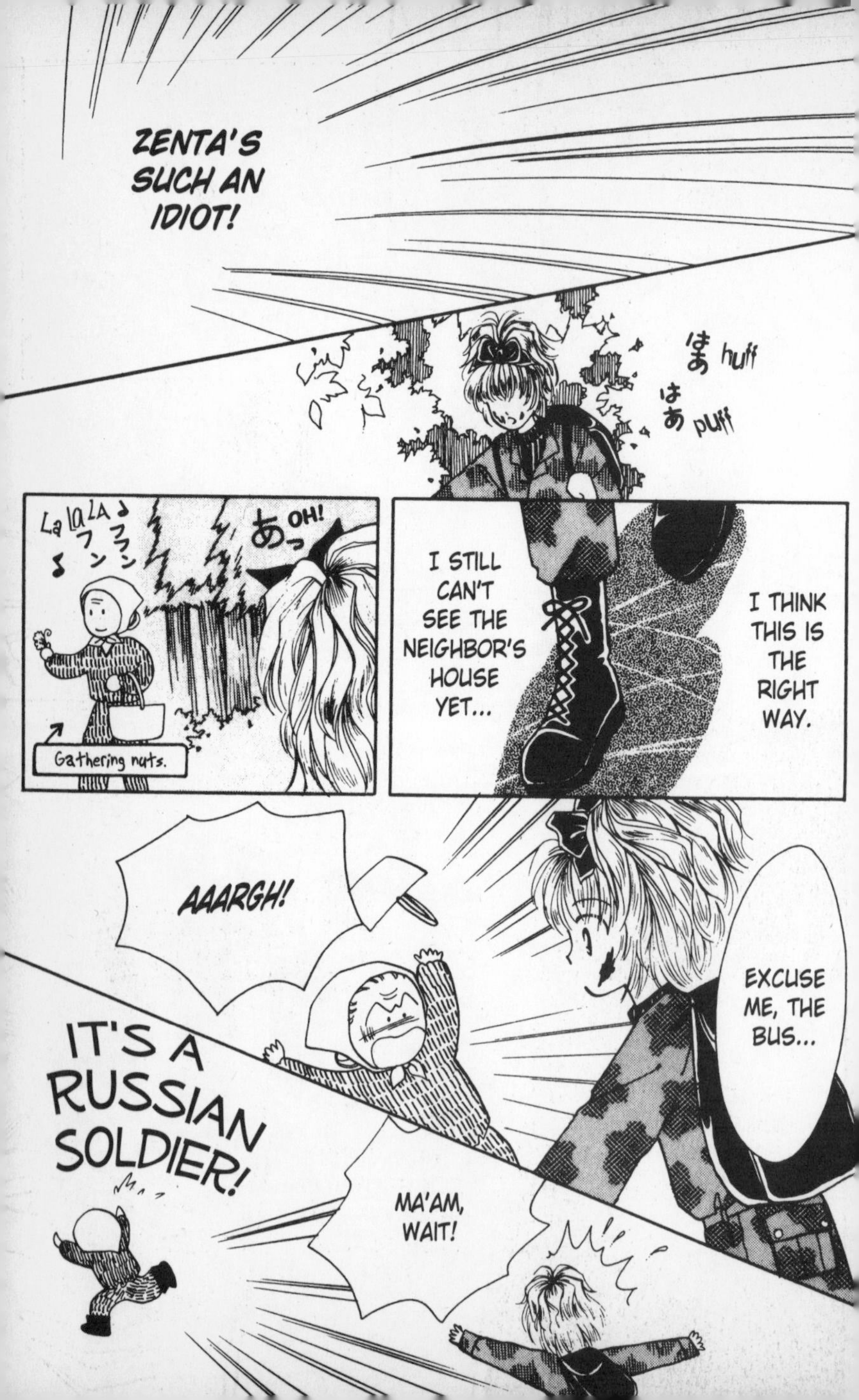
ZENTA'S SUCH AN IDIOT!
はあ huff
はあ puff
I THINK THIS IS THE RIGHT WAY.
I STILL CAN'T SEE THE NEIGHBOR'S HOUSE YET...
あっ OH!
La La LA
フンフン
Gathering nuts.
EXCUSE ME, THE BUS...
AAARGH!
IT'S A RUSSIAN SOLDIER!
MA'AM, WAIT!

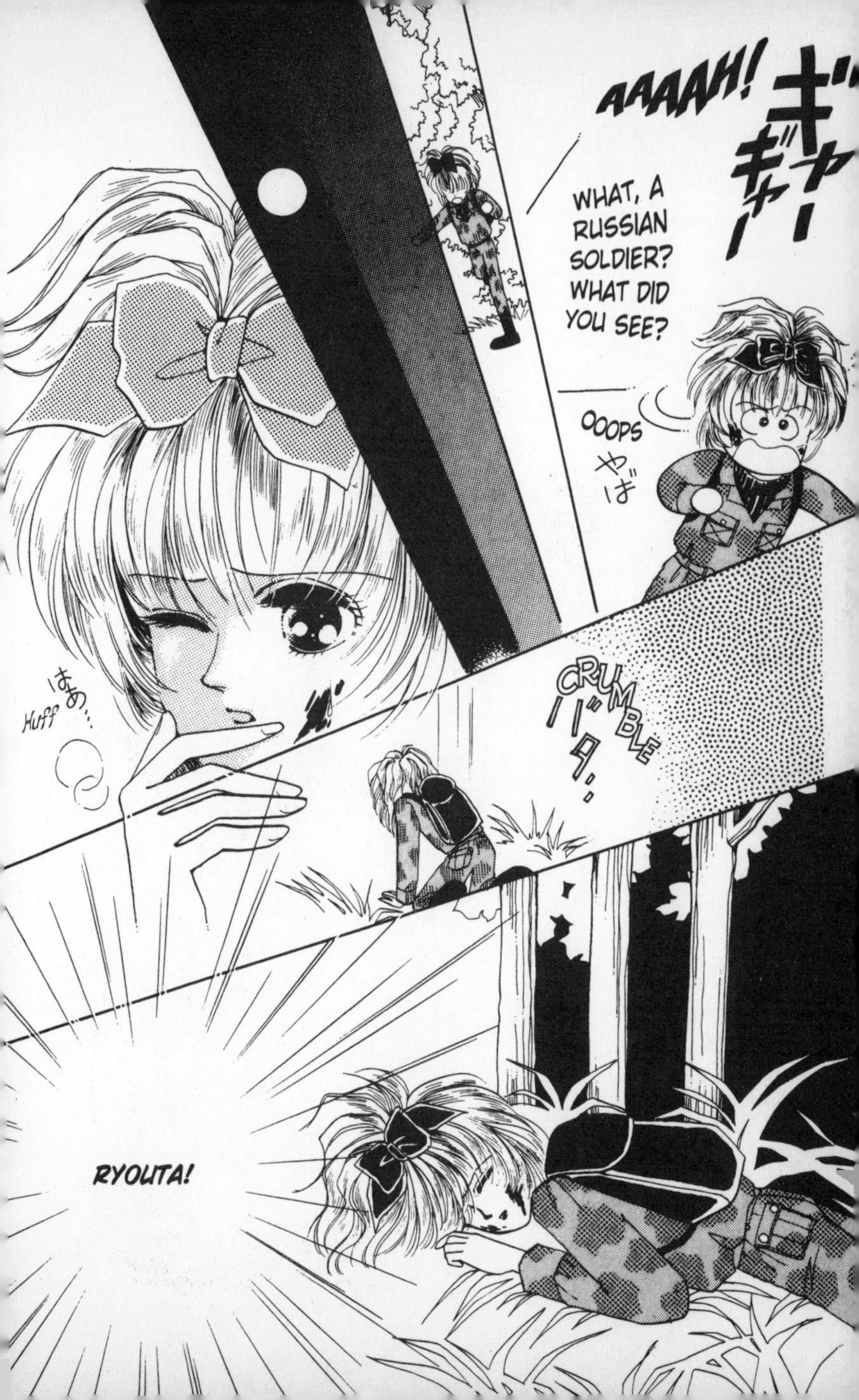
AAAAH!
ギャーギャー
WHAT, A RUSSIAN SOLDIER? WHAT DID YOU SEE?
OOOPS
やば
Huff
はあ…
CRUMBLE
バタ
RYOUTA!

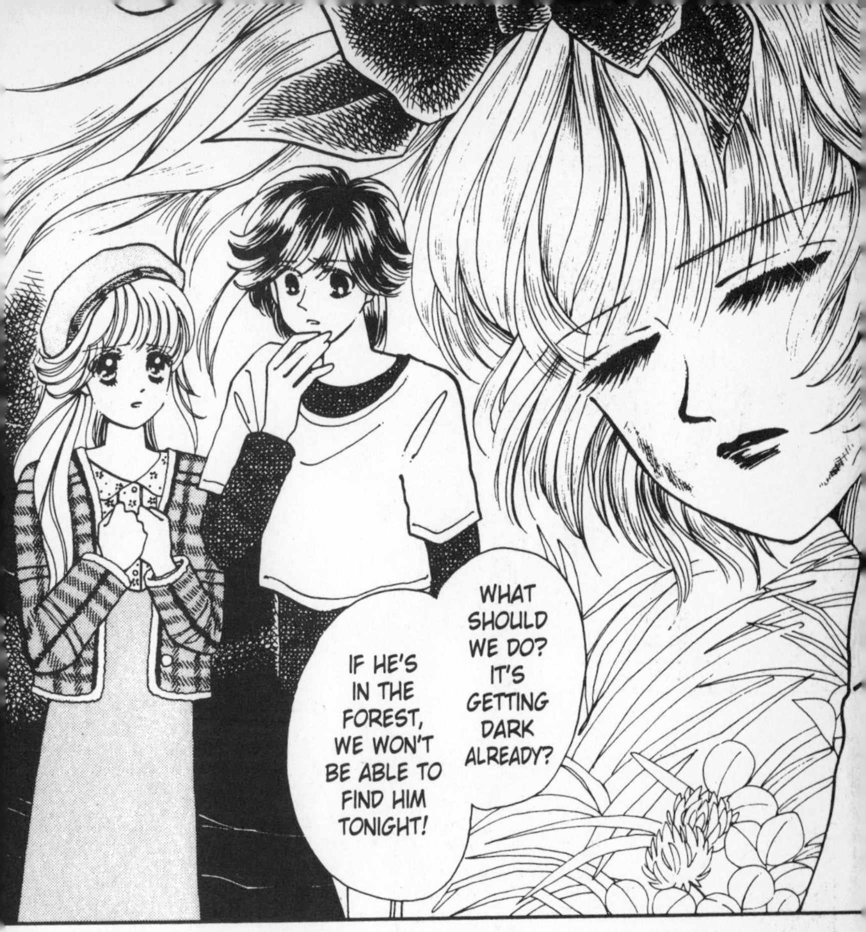
WHAT SHOULD WE DO? IT'S GETTING DARK ALREADY?
IF HE'S IN THE FOREST, WE WON'T BE ABLE TO FIND HIM TONIGHT!

BONUS 2. WHEN I WAS LITTLE, THERE WERE HORSES AND COWS ON THE FARM. I LIKED BIG ANIMALS, SO I WANTED TO GET CLOSE ENOUGH TO PET THEM. AS SOON AS I GOT CLOSE ENOUGH, THEY WOULD RUN AWAY! SO I WOULD SLOWLY CREEP UP TO THEM AGAIN (LAUGH). IF YOU SAY "BEE BEE" FOR COWS AND "PO PO" FOR HORSES, THEY'RE SUPPOSED TO COME TO YOU. I FIGURED THEY WOULDN'T COME NEAR ME, SO I CALLED OUT, FROM FAR AWAY, "BEE BEE." I WAS SHOCKED WHEN THREE OR FOUR COWS CAME RUNNING OVER! ALSO, A WHILE BACK, THE SPITZ WAS A POPULAR BREED. IF YOU HAVE ONE, I'D LOVE TO HEAR FROM YOU!

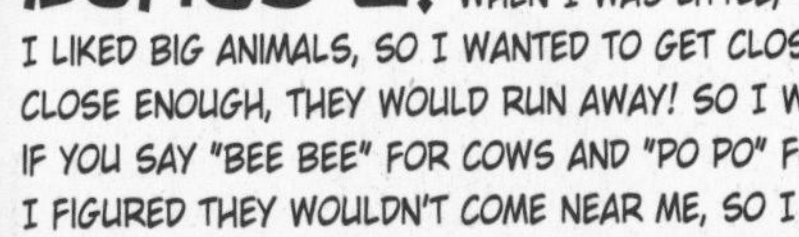
grass
Bee bee
Little me
Moo
Moo
Moo
Waaah!

CHIBI, MY GRANDFATHER'S SPITZ, ♡ WAS MY FAVORITE, BUT CHIBI PASSED AWAY ABOUT 10 YEARS AGO.

I HAVEN'T HAD DREAMS ABOUT HER SINCE SHE PASSED AWAY...CONTINUED ON P. 67.

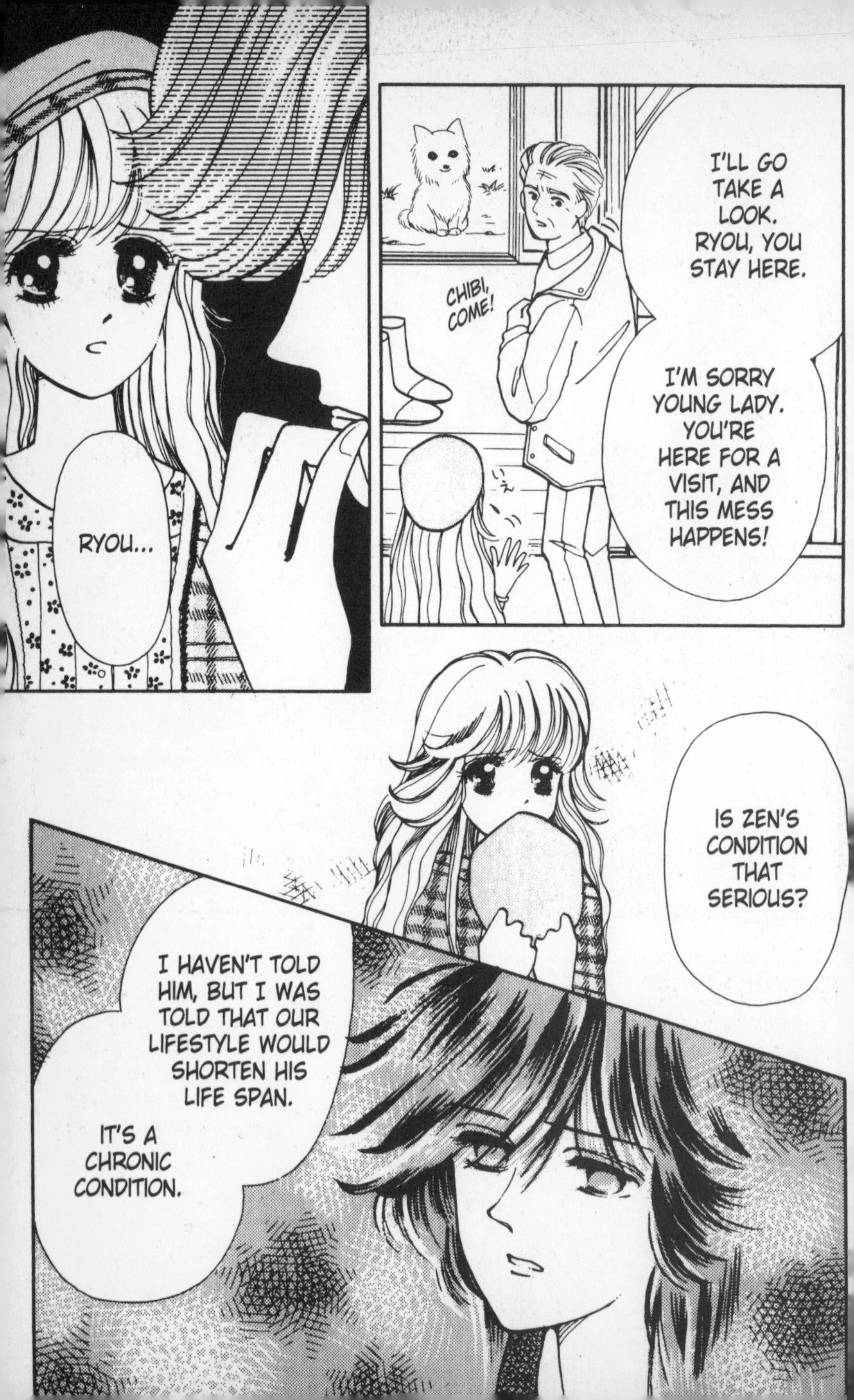

I'LL GO TAKE A LOOK. RYOU, YOU STAY HERE.
CHIBI, COME!
I'M SORRY YOUNG LADY. YOU'RE HERE FOR A VISIT, AND THIS MESS HAPPENS!
いぇ
RYOU...
IS ZEN'S CONDITION THAT SERIOUS?
I HAVEN'T TOLD HIM, BUT I WAS TOLD THAT OUR LIFESTYLE WOULD SHORTEN HIS LIFE SPAN.
IT'S A CHRONIC CONDITION.

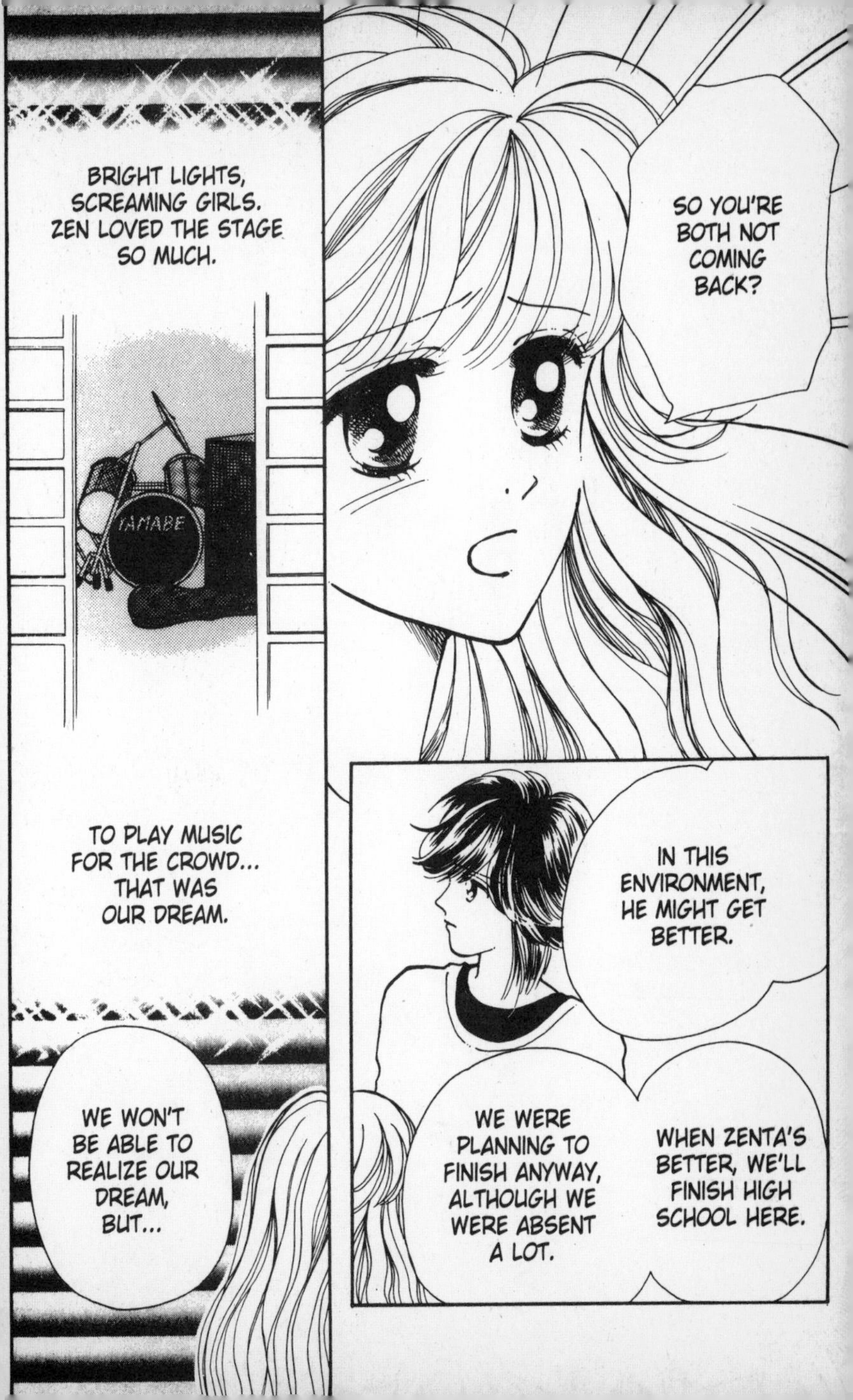
SO YOU'RE BOTH NOT COMING BACK?
IN THIS ENVIRONMENT, HE MIGHT GET BETTER.
WHEN ZENTA'S BETTER, WE'LL FINISH HIGH SCHOOL HERE.
WE WERE PLANNING TO FINISH ANYWAY, ALTHOUGH WE WERE ABSENT A LOT.
BRIGHT LIGHTS, SCREAMING GIRLS. ZEN LOVED THE STAGE SO MUCH.
YAMABE
TO PLAY MUSIC FOR THE CROWD... THAT WAS OUR DREAM.
WE WON'T BE ABLE TO REALIZE OUR DREAM, BUT...

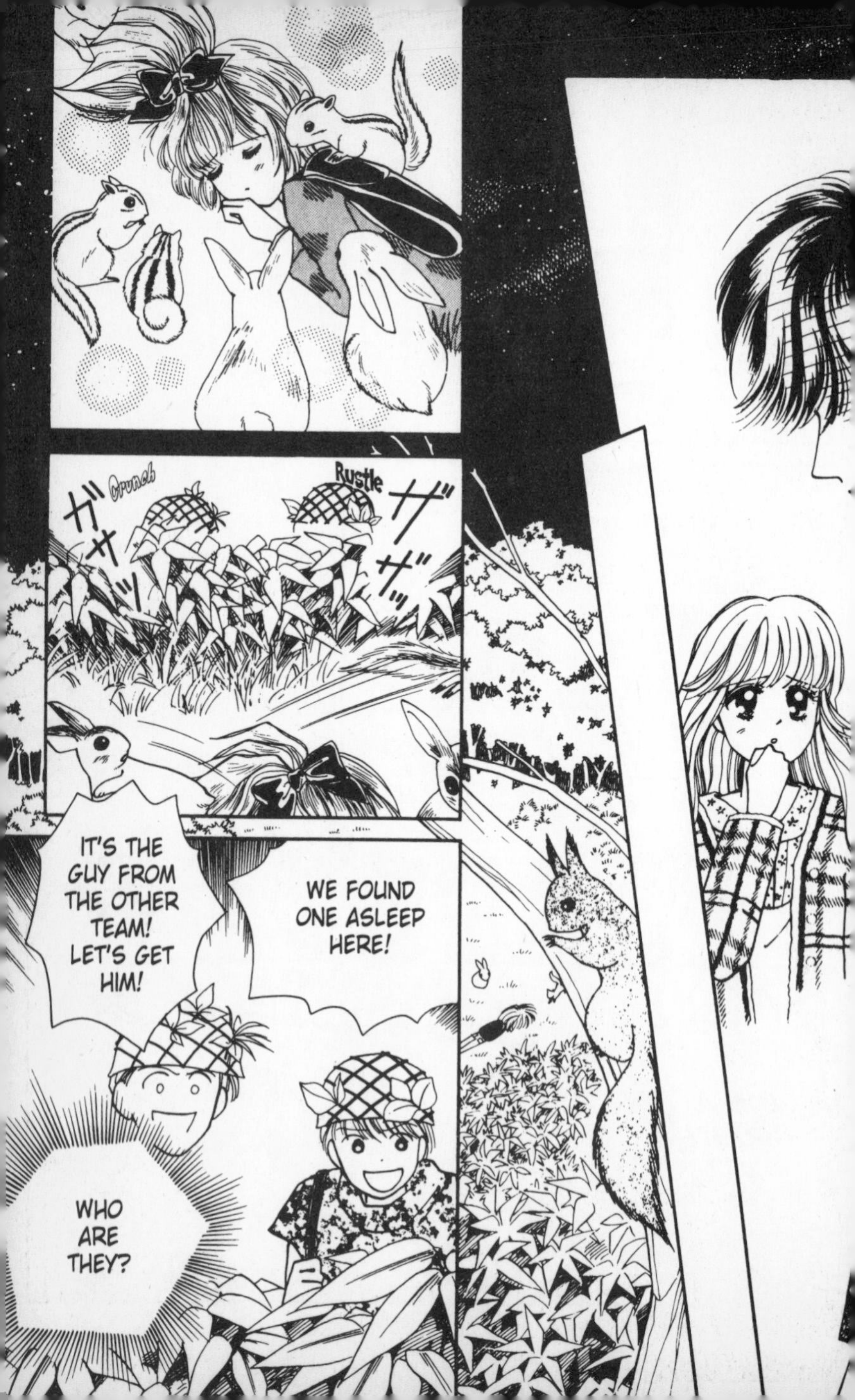
Rustle
ザザッ
Crunch
ガサッ
WE FOUND ONE ASLEEP HERE!
IT'S THE GUY FROM THE OTHER TEAM! LET'S GET HIM!
WHO ARE THEY?

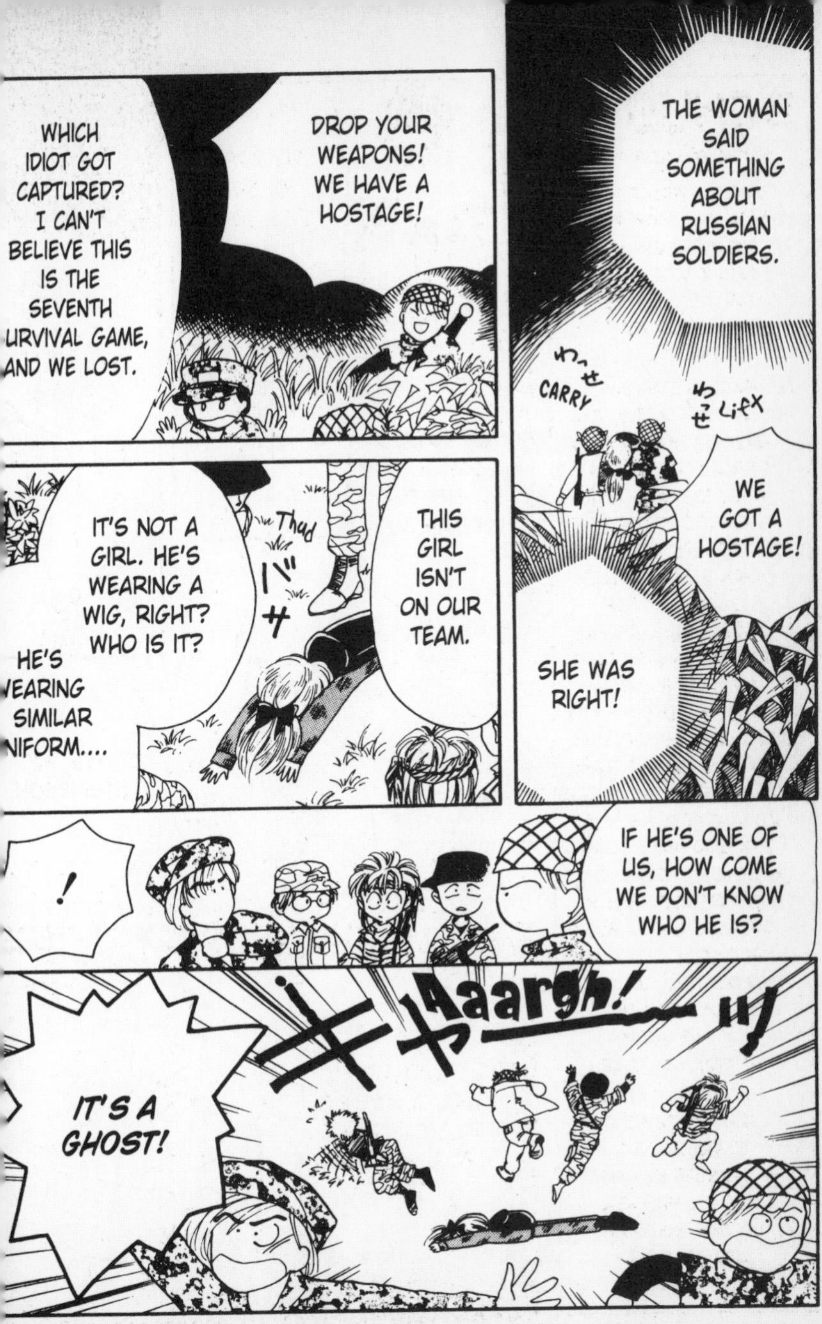

THE WOMAN SAID SOMETHING ABOUT RUSSIAN SOLDIERS.
わっせ
CARRY
わっせ
LIFT
WE GOT A HOSTAGE!
SHE WAS RIGHT!
DROP YOUR WEAPONS! WE HAVE A HOSTAGE!
WHICH IDIOT GOT CAPTURED? I CAN'T BELIEVE THIS IS THE SEVENTH URVIVAL GAME, AND WE LOST.
THIS GIRL ISN'T ON OUR TEAM.
バサ
Thud
IT'S NOT A GIRL. HE'S WEARING A WIG, RIGHT? WHO IS IT?
HE'S VEARING SIMILAR NIFORM....
IF HE'S ONE OF US, HOW COME WE DON'T KNOW WHO HE IS?
!
キャー
Aaargh!
IT'S A GHOST!

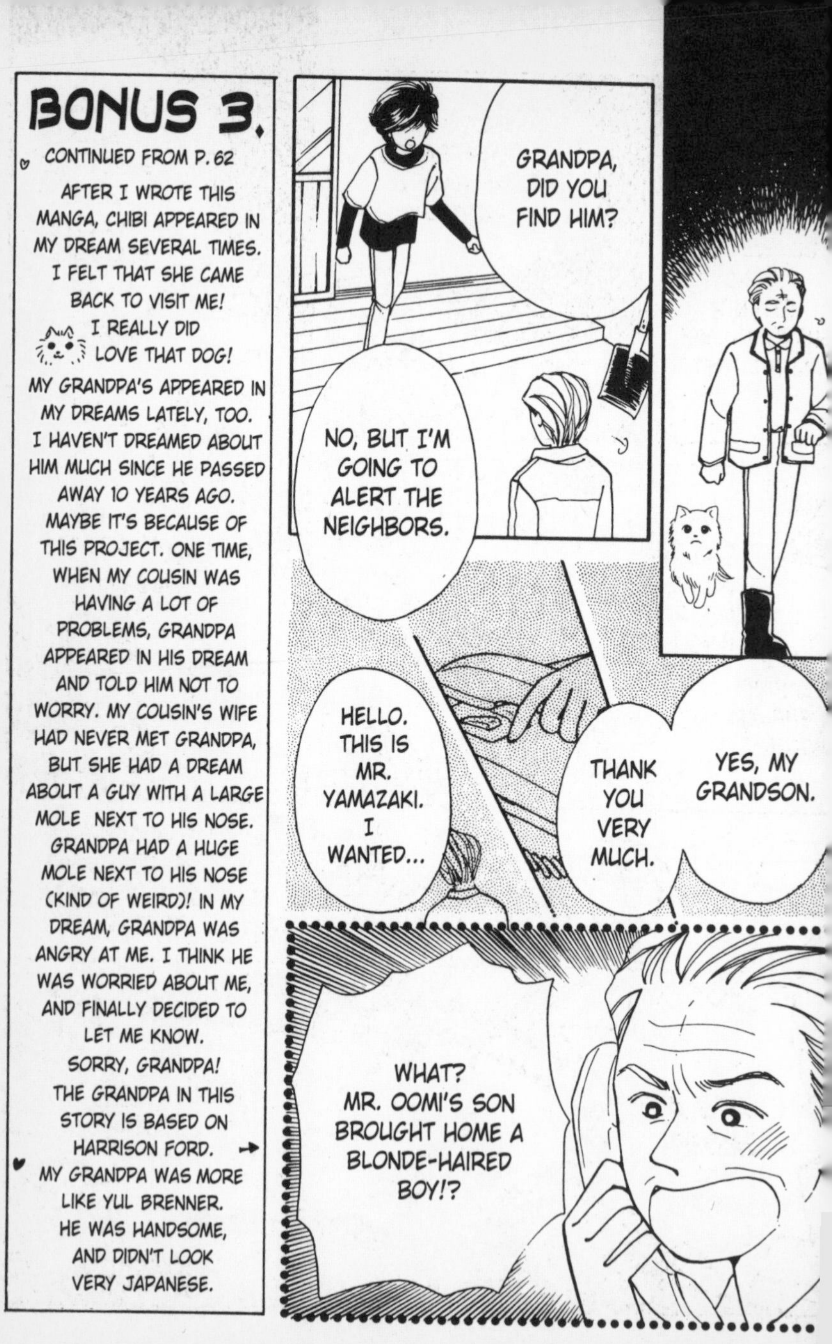
GRANDPA, DID YOU FIND HIM?
NO, BUT I'M GOING TO ALERT THE NEIGHBORS.
YES, MY GRANDSON.
THANK YOU VERY MUCH.
HELLO. THIS IS MR. YAMAZAKI. I WANTED...
WHAT? MR. OOMI'S SON BROUGHT HOME A BLONDE-HAIRED BOY!?

BONUS 3.

CONTINUED FROM P. 62

AFTER I WROTE THIS MANGA, CHIBI APPEARED IN MY DREAM SEVERAL TIMES. I FELT THAT SHE CAME BACK TO VISIT ME!

I REALLY DID LOVE THAT DOG!

MY GRANDPA'S APPEARED IN MY DREAMS LATELY, TOO. I HAVEN'T DREAMED ABOUT HIM MUCH SINCE HE PASSED AWAY 10 YEARS AGO. MAYBE IT'S BECAUSE OF THIS PROJECT. ONE TIME, WHEN MY COUSIN WAS HAVING A LOT OF PROBLEMS, GRANDPA APPEARED IN HIS DREAM AND TOLD HIM NOT TO WORRY. MY COUSIN'S WIFE HAD NEVER MET GRANDPA, BUT SHE HAD A DREAM ABOUT A GUY WITH A LARGE MOLE NEXT TO HIS NOSE. GRANDPA HAD A HUGE MOLE NEXT TO HIS NOSE (KIND OF WEIRD)! IN MY DREAM, GRANDPA WAS ANGRY AT ME. I THINK HE WAS WORRIED ABOUT ME, AND FINALLY DECIDED TO LET ME KNOW.

SORRY, GRANDPA!

THE GRANDPA IN THIS STORY IS BASED ON HARRISON FORD. →

MY GRANDPA WAS MORE LIKE YUL BRENNER. HE WAS HANDSOME, AND DIDN'T LOOK VERY JAPANESE.

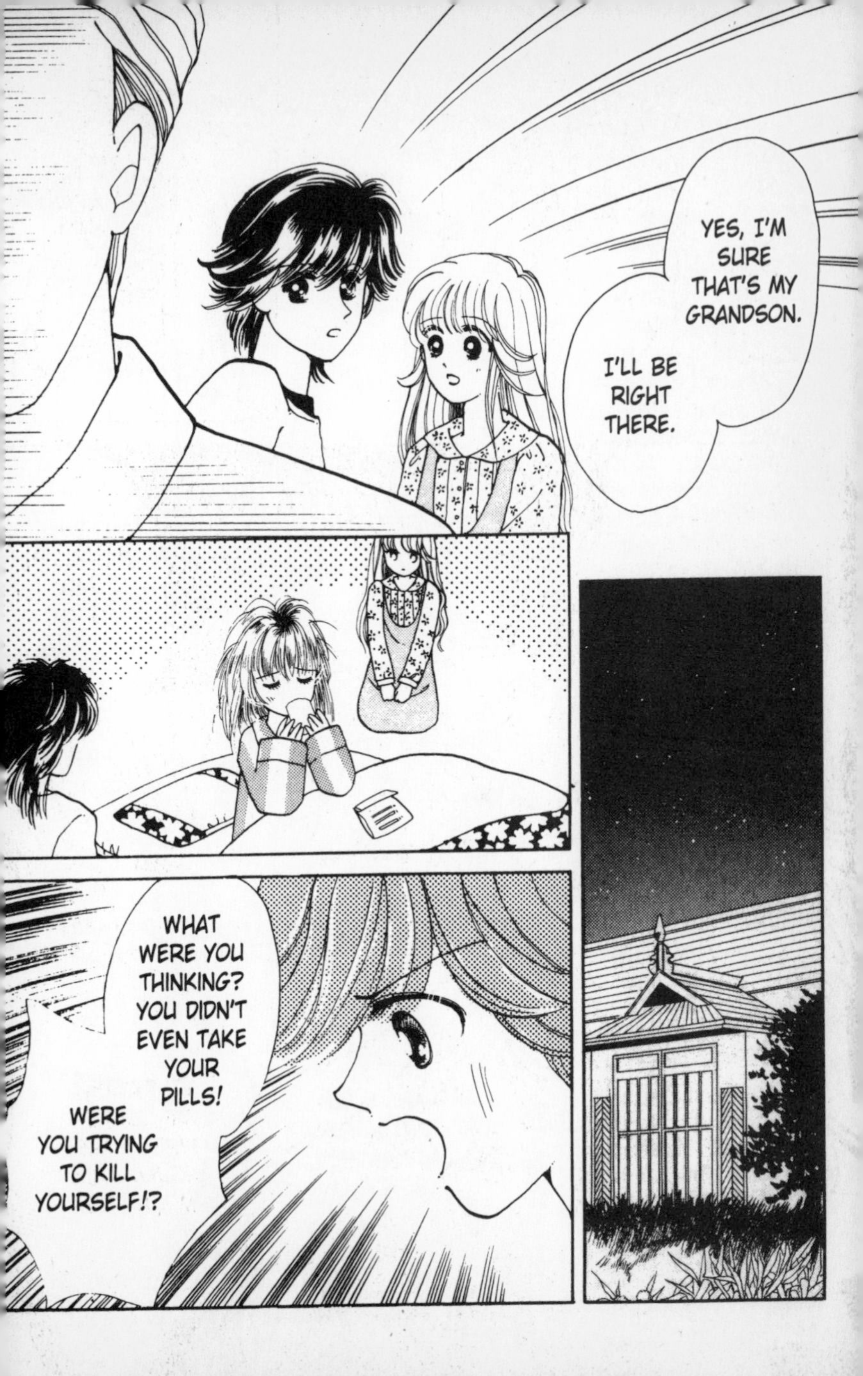
YES, I'M SURE THAT'S MY GRANDSON.
I'LL BE RIGHT THERE.
WHAT WERE YOU THINKING? YOU DIDN'T EVEN TAKE YOUR PILLS!
WERE YOU TRYING TO KILL YOURSELF!?

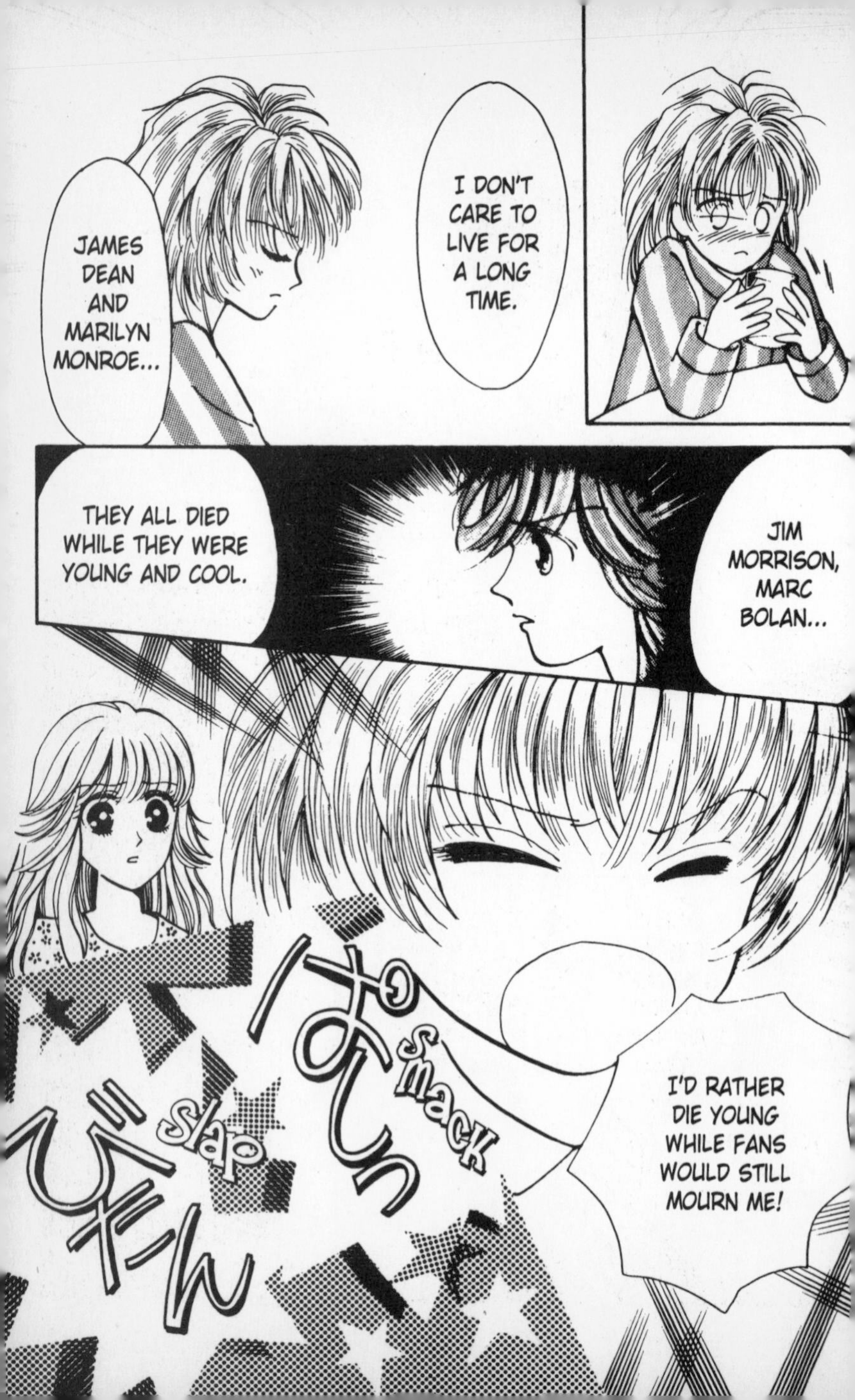

I DON'T CARE TO LIVE FOR A LONG TIME.
JAMES DEAN AND MARILYN MONROE...
JIM MORRISON, MARC BOLAN...
THEY ALL DIED WHILE THEY WERE YOUNG AND COOL.
I'D RATHER DIE YOUNG WHILE FANS WOULD STILL MOURN ME!
smack
slap

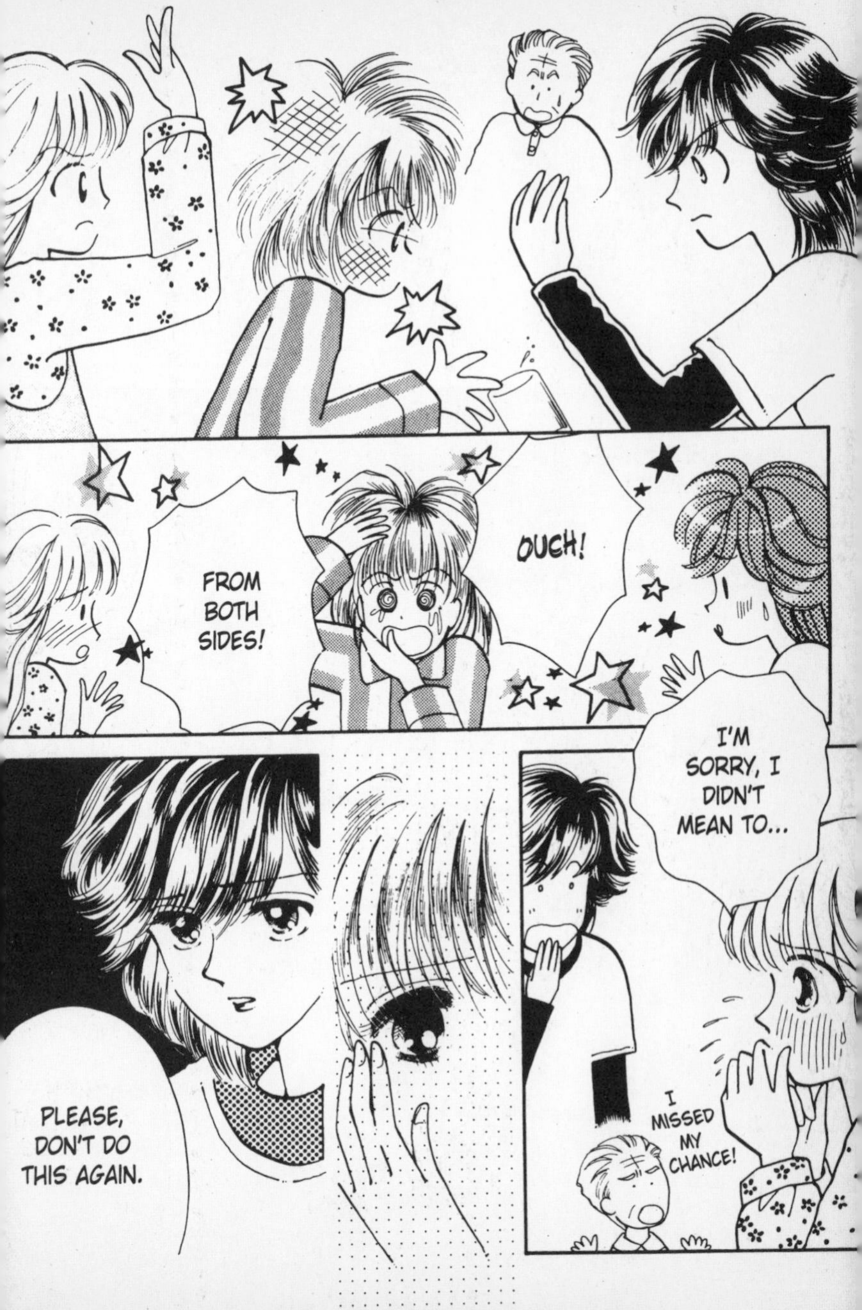
OUCH!
FROM BOTH SIDES!
I'M SORRY, I DIDN'T MEAN TO...
I MISSED MY CHANCE!
PLEASE, DON'T DO THIS AGAIN.

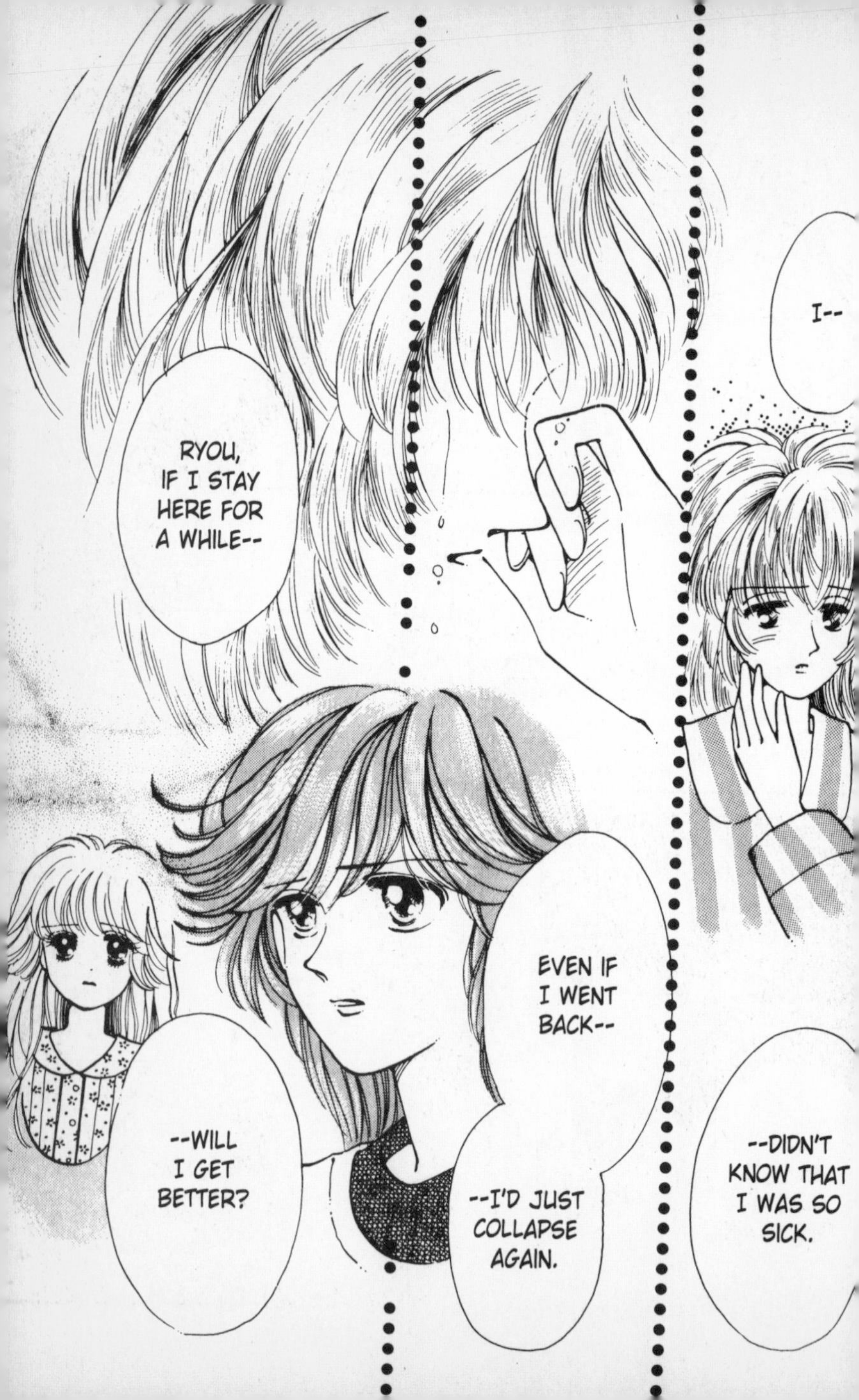
I--
--DIDN'T KNOW THAT I WAS SO SICK.
EVEN IF I WENT BACK--
--I'D JUST COLLAPSE AGAIN.
RYOU, IF I STAY HERE FOR A WHILE--
--WILL I GET BETTER?

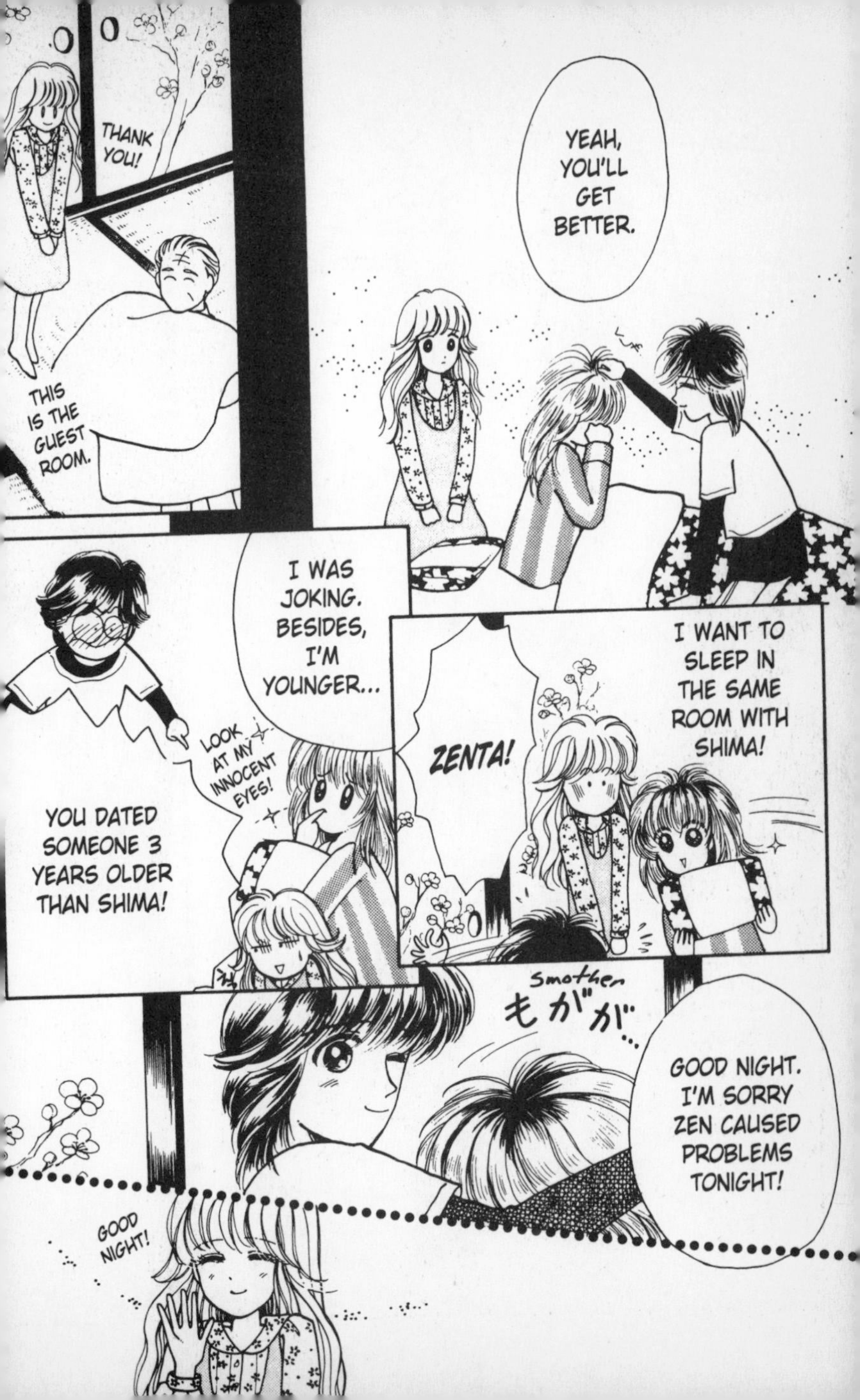
YEAH, YOU'LL GET BETTER.
THANK YOU!
THIS IS THE GUEST ROOM.
I WANT TO SLEEP IN THE SAME ROOM WITH SHIMA!
ZENTA!
I WAS JOKING. BESIDES, I'M YOUNGER...
LOOK AT MY INNOCENT EYES!
YOU DATED SOMEONE 3 YEARS OLDER THAN SHIMA!
Smother もがが...
GOOD NIGHT. I'M SORRY ZEN CAUSED PROBLEMS TONIGHT!
GOOD NIGHT!

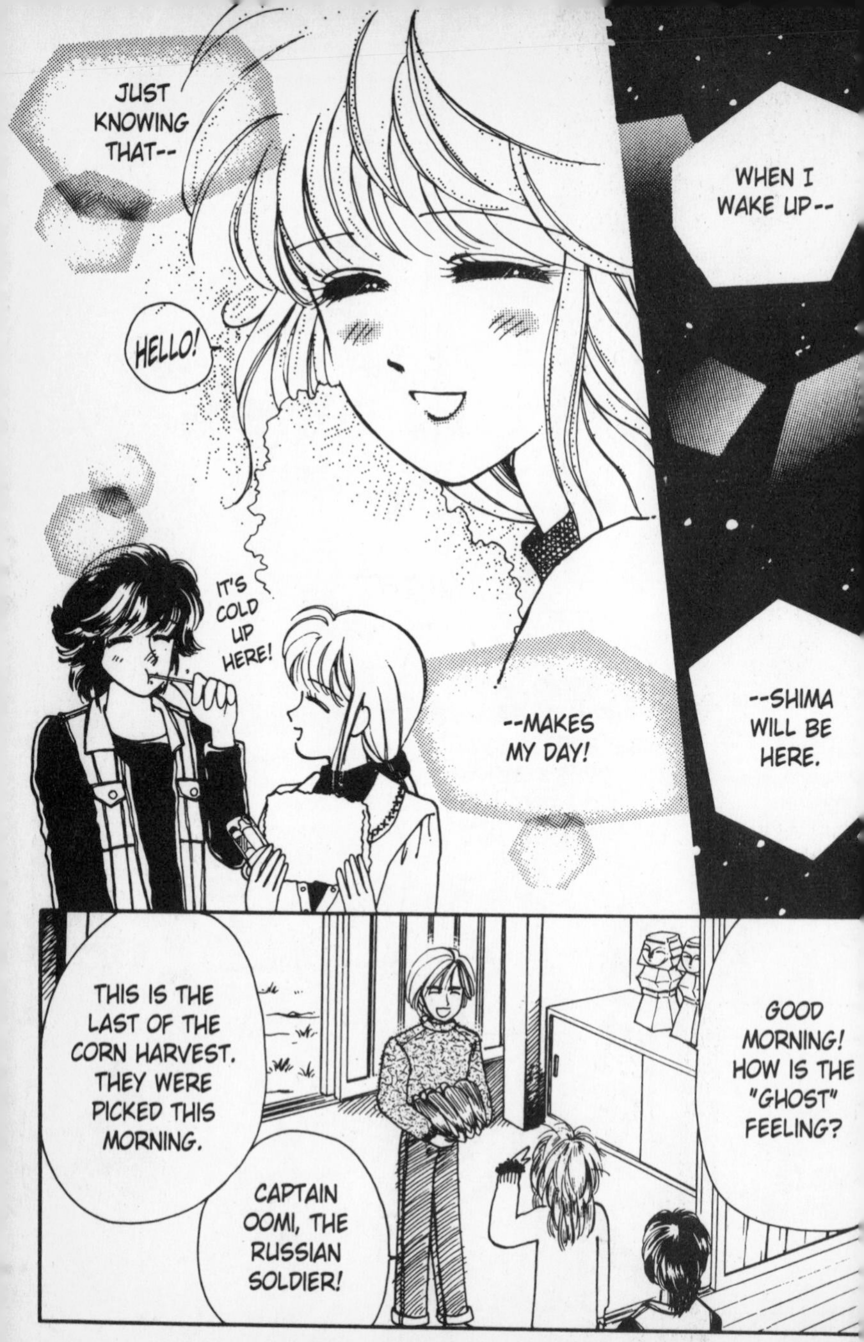
WHEN I WAKE UP--
--SHIMA WILL BE HERE.
JUST KNOWING THAT--
HELLO!
IT'S COLD UP HERE!
--MAKES MY DAY!
GOOD MORNING! HOW IS THE "GHOST" FEELING?
THIS IS THE LAST OF THE CORN HARVEST. THEY WERE PICKED THIS MORNING.
CAPTAIN OOMI, THE RUSSIAN SOLDIER!

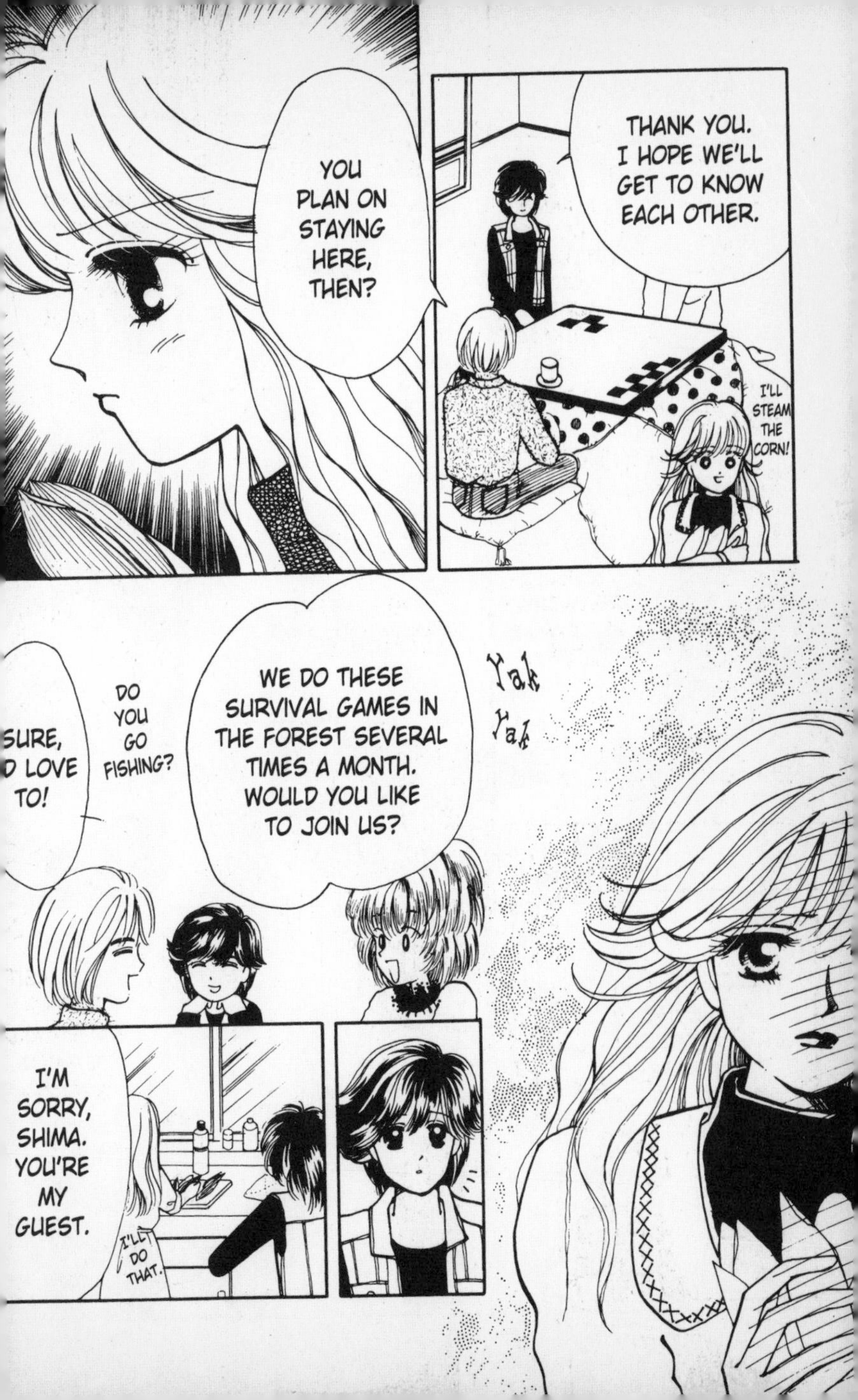
THANK YOU. I HOPE WE'LL GET TO KNOW EACH OTHER.
I'LL STEAM THE CORN!
YOU PLAN ON STAYING HERE, THEN?
Yak Yak
WE DO THESE SURVIVAL GAMES IN THE FOREST SEVERAL TIMES A MONTH. WOULD YOU LIKE TO JOIN US?
DO YOU GO FISHING?
SURE, D LOVE TO!
I'M SORRY, SHIMA. YOU'RE MY GUEST.
I'LL DO THAT.

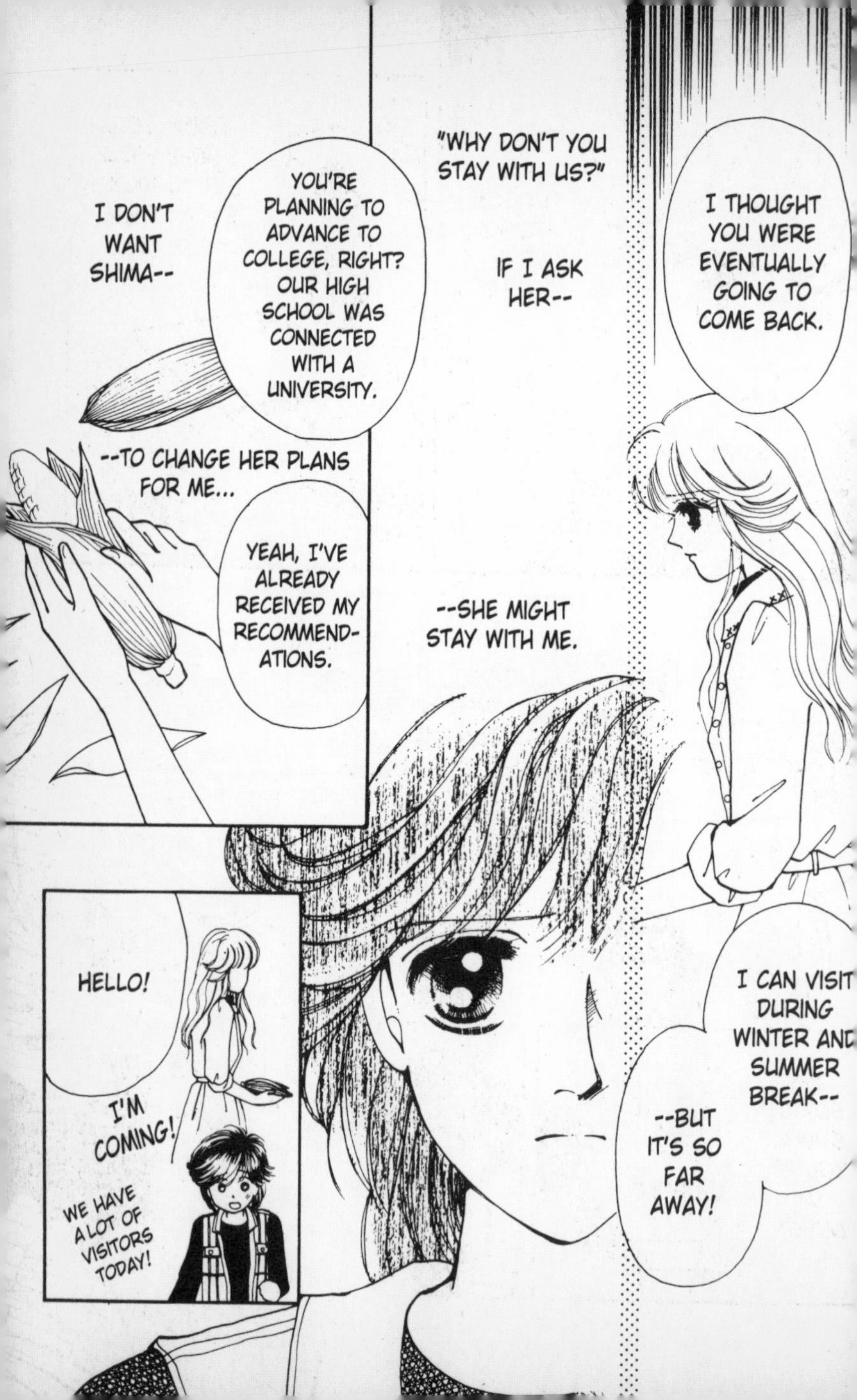
I THOUGHT YOU WERE EVENTUALLY GOING TO COME BACK.
"WHY DON'T YOU STAY WITH US?"
IF I ASK HER--
--SHE MIGHT STAY WITH ME.
YOU'RE PLANNING TO ADVANCE TO COLLEGE, RIGHT? OUR HIGH SCHOOL WAS CONNECTED WITH A UNIVERSITY.
I DON'T WANT SHIMA--
--TO CHANGE HER PLANS FOR ME...
YEAH, I'VE ALREADY RECEIVED MY RECOMMENDATIONS.
I CAN VISIT DURING WINTER AND SUMMER BREAK--
--BUT IT'S SO FAR AWAY!
HELLO!
I'M COMING!
WE HAVE A LOT OF VISITORS TODAY!

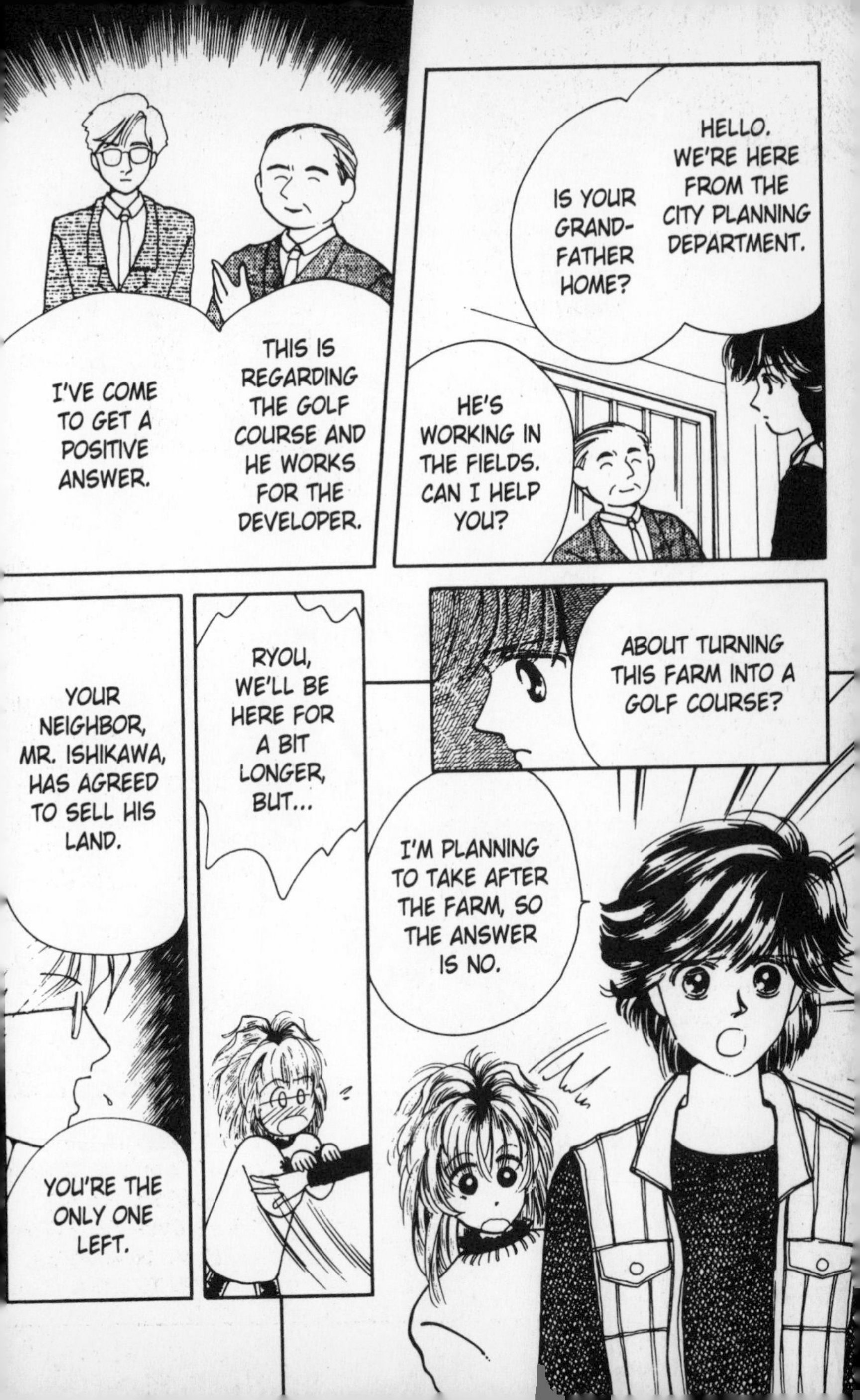
HELLO. WE'RE HERE FROM THE CITY PLANNING DEPARTMENT.
IS YOUR GRAND-FATHER HOME?
HE'S WORKING IN THE FIELDS. CAN I HELP YOU?
THIS IS REGARDING THE GOLF COURSE AND HE WORKS FOR THE DEVELOPER.
I'VE COME TO GET A POSITIVE ANSWER.
ABOUT TURNING THIS FARM INTO A GOLF COURSE?
I'M PLANNING TO TAKE AFTER THE FARM, SO THE ANSWER IS NO.
RYOU, WE'LL BE HERE FOR A BIT LONGER, BUT...
YOUR NEIGHBOR, MR. ISHIKAWA, HAS AGREED TO SELL HIS LAND.
YOU'RE THE ONLY ONE LEFT.

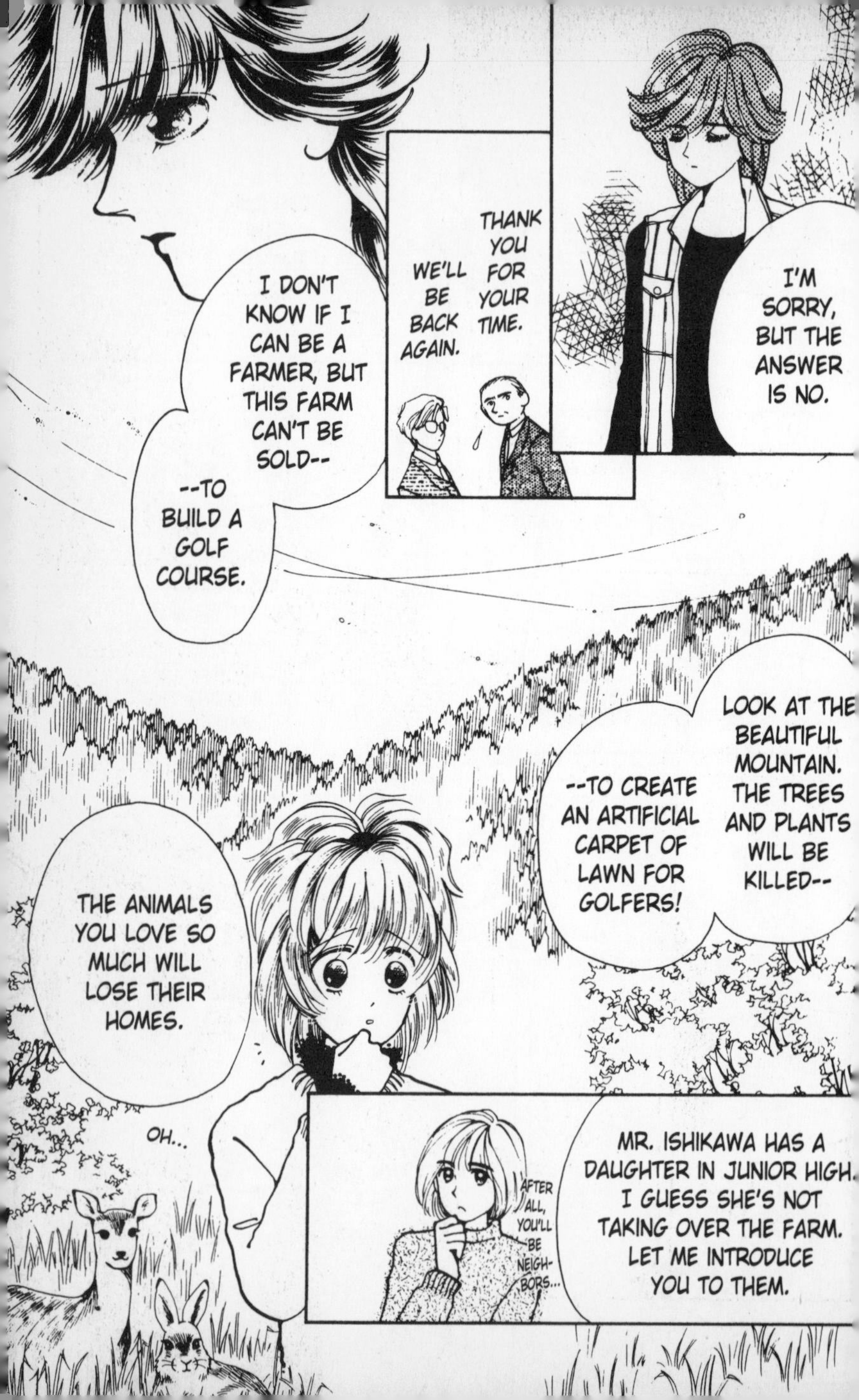
I'M SORRY, BUT THE ANSWER IS NO.
THANK YOU FOR YOUR TIME.
WE'LL BE BACK AGAIN.
I DON'T KNOW IF I CAN BE A FARMER, BUT THIS FARM CAN'T BE SOLD--
--TO BUILD A GOLF COURSE.
LOOK AT THE BEAUTIFUL MOUNTAIN. THE TREES AND PLANTS WILL BE KILLED--
--TO CREATE AN ARTIFICIAL CARPET OF LAWN FOR GOLFERS!
THE ANIMALS YOU LOVE SO MUCH WILL LOSE THEIR HOMES.
OH...
MR. ISHIKAWA HAS A DAUGHTER IN JUNIOR HIGH. I GUESS SHE'S NOT TAKING OVER THE FARM. LET ME INTRODUCE YOU TO THEM.
AFTER ALL, YOU'LL BE NEIGH-BORS...

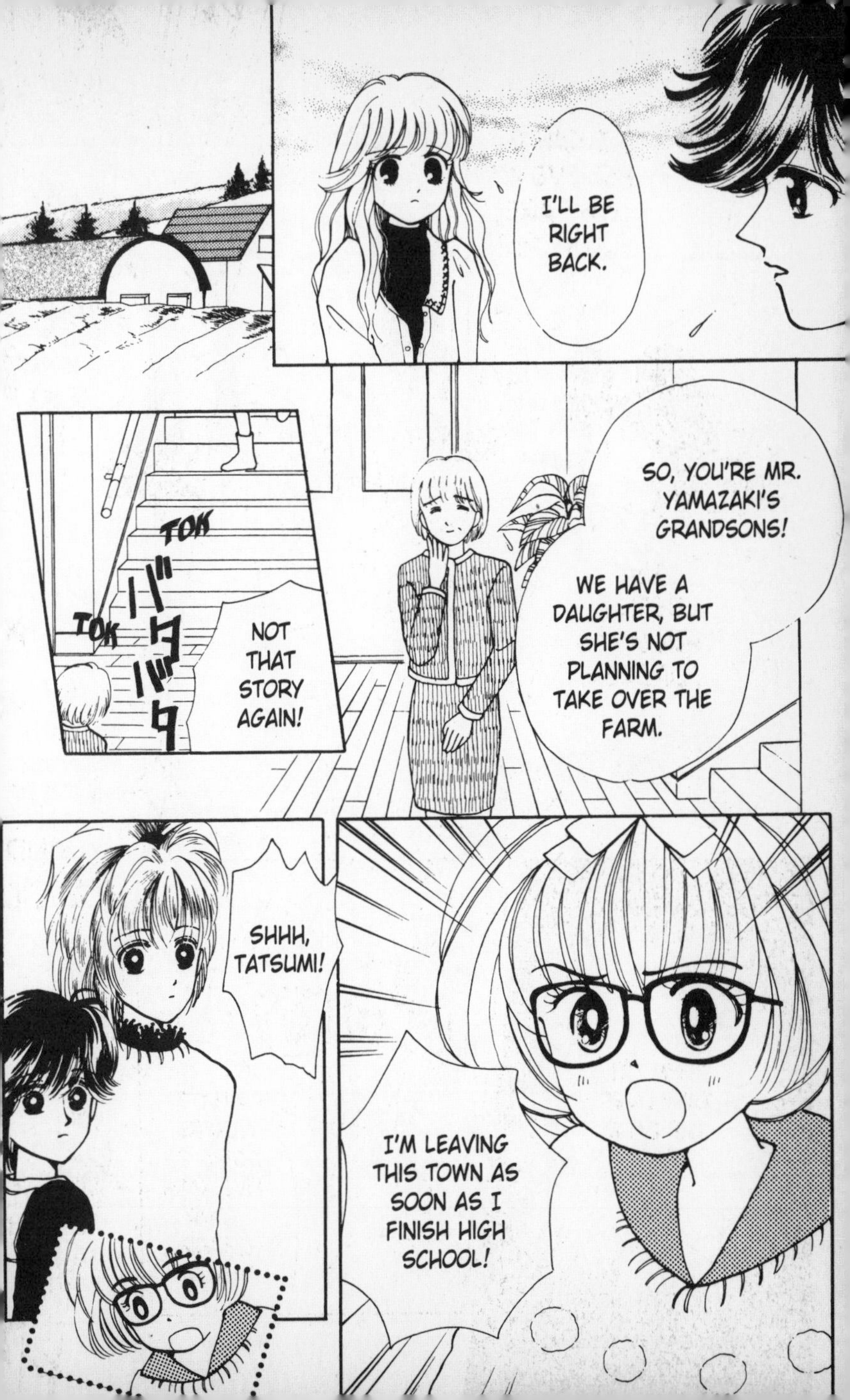
I'LL BE RIGHT BACK.
SO, YOU'RE MR. YAMAZAKI'S GRANDSONS!
WE HAVE A DAUGHTER, BUT SHE'S NOT PLANNING TO TAKE OVER THE FARM.
TOK
バタバタ
TOK
NOT THAT STORY AGAIN!
I'M LEAVING THIS TOWN AS SOON AS I FINISH HIGH SCHOOL!
SHHH, TATSUMI!

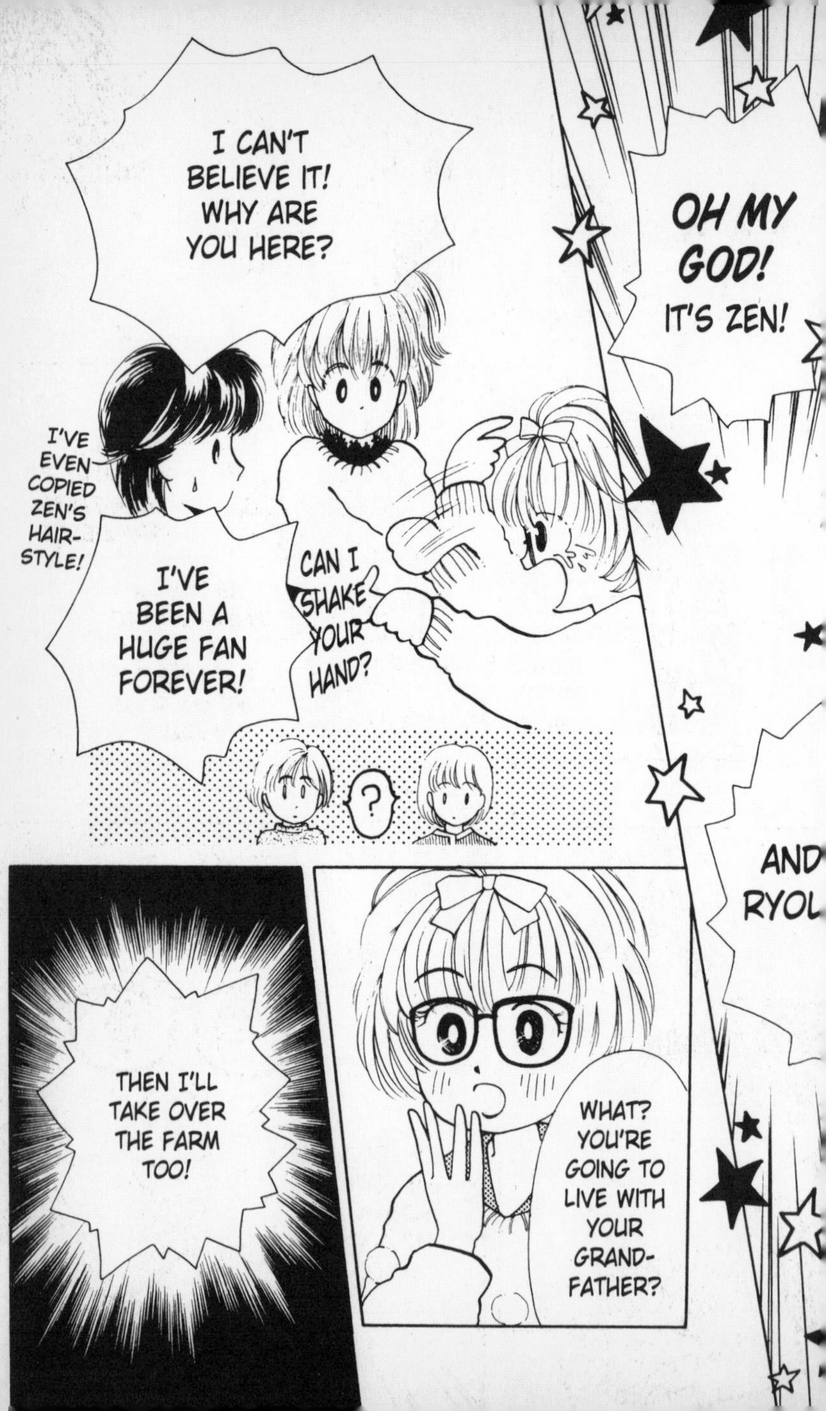
OH MY GOD!
IT'S ZEN!
AND
I CAN'T BELIEVE IT! WHY ARE YOU HERE?
CAN I SHAKE YOUR HAND?
I'VE BEEN A HUGE FAN FOREVER!
I'VE EVEN COPIED ZEN'S HAIR-STYLE!
?
WHAT? YOU'RE GOING TO LIVE WITH YOUR GRAND-FATHER?
THEN I'LL TAKE OVER THE FARM TOO!

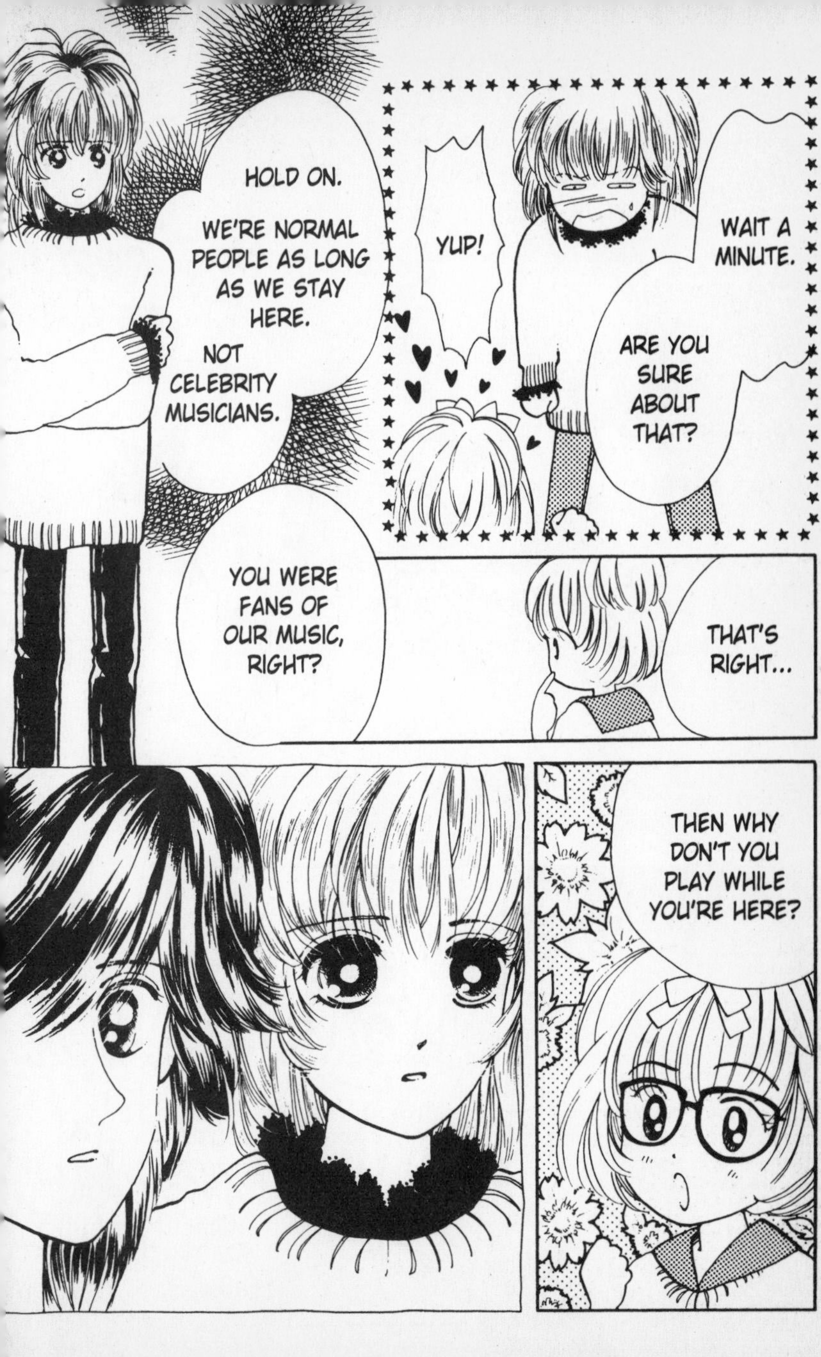
WAIT A MINUTE.
ARE YOU SURE ABOUT THAT?
YUP!
THAT'S RIGHT...
HOLD ON.
WE'RE NORMAL PEOPLE AS LONG AS WE STAY HERE.
NOT CELEBRITY MUSICIANS.
YOU WERE FANS OF OUR MUSIC, RIGHT?
THEN WHY DON'T YOU PLAY WHILE YOU'RE HERE?

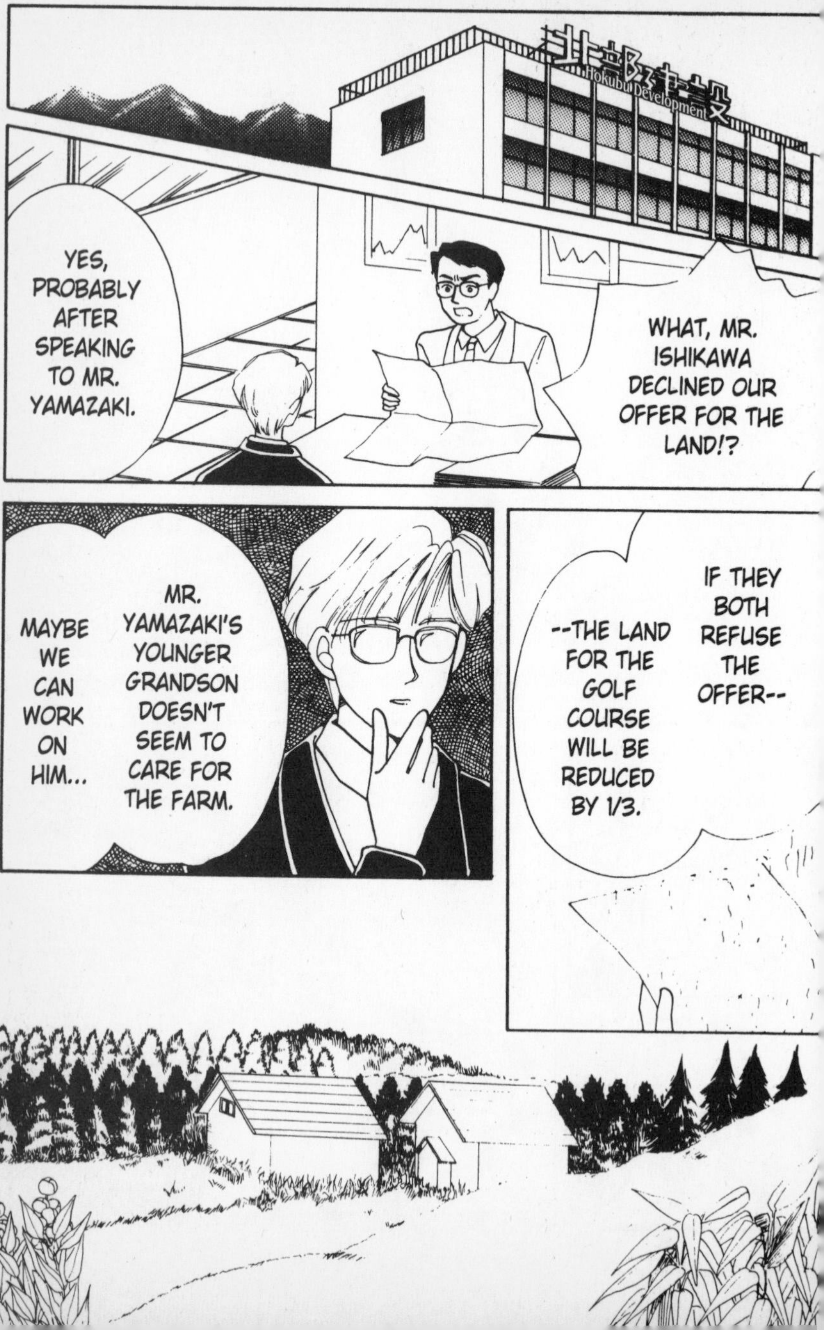
Hokubu Development
WHAT, MR. ISHIKAWA DECLINED OUR OFFER FOR THE LAND!?
YES, PROBABLY AFTER SPEAKING TO MR. YAMAZAKI.
IF THEY BOTH REFUSE THE OFFER--
--THE LAND FOR THE GOLF COURSE WILL BE REDUCED BY 1/3.
MR. YAMAZAKI'S YOUNGER GRANDSON DOESN'T SEEM TO CARE FOR THE FARM.
MAYBE WE CAN WORK ON HIM...

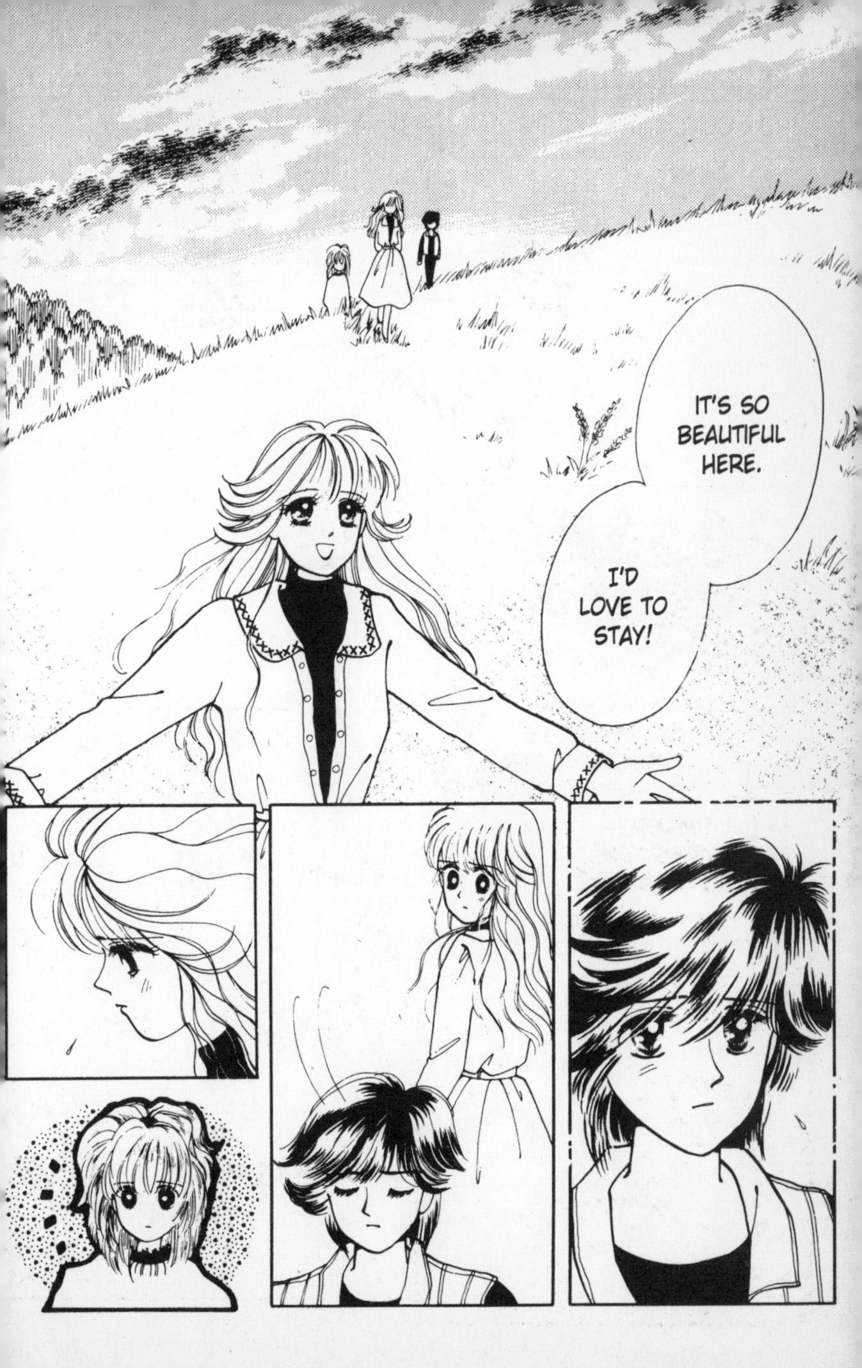
IT'S SO BEAUTIFUL HERE.
I'D LOVE TO STAY!

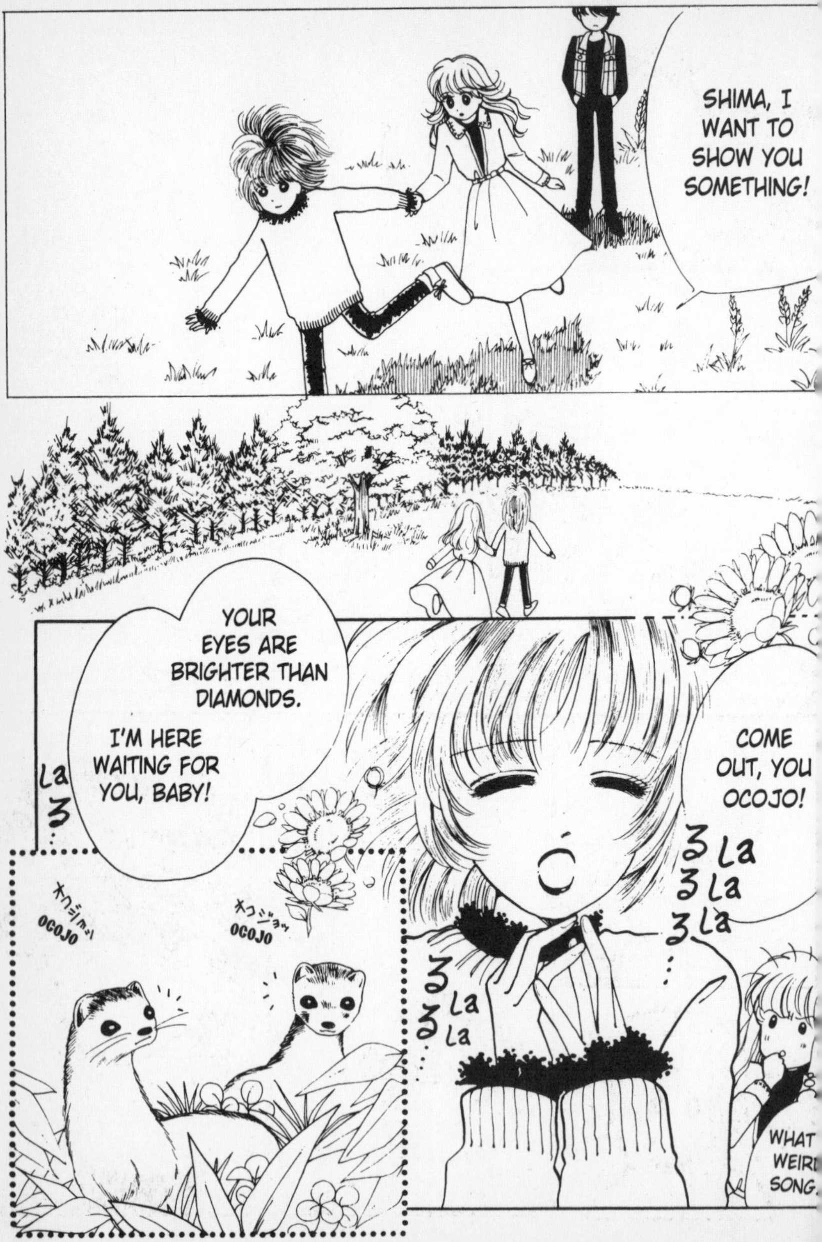
SHIMA, I WANT TO SHOW YOU SOMETHING!
COME OUT, YOU OCOJO!
る la る la る la
る la る la
WHAT WEIRD SONG.
YOUR EYES ARE BRIGHTER THAN DIAMONDS.
I'M HERE WAITING FOR YOU, BABY!
la る
オコジョッ OCOJO
オコジョッ OCOJO

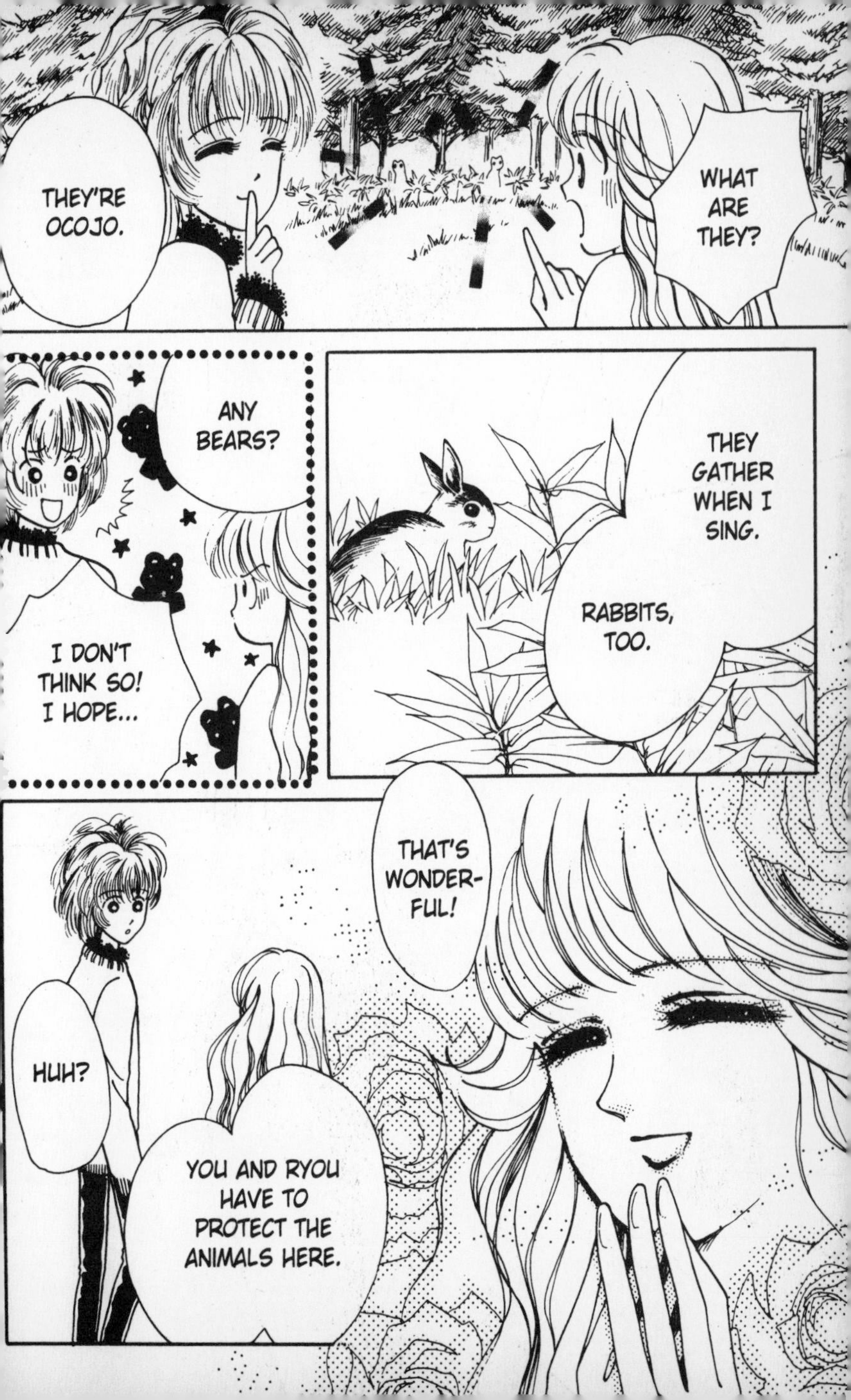
WHAT ARE THEY?
THEY'RE OCOJO.
THEY GATHER WHEN I SING.
RABBITS, TOO.
ANY BEARS?
I DON'T THINK SO! I HOPE...
THAT'S WONDER-FUL!
YOU AND RYOU HAVE TO PROTECT THE ANIMALS HERE.
HUH?

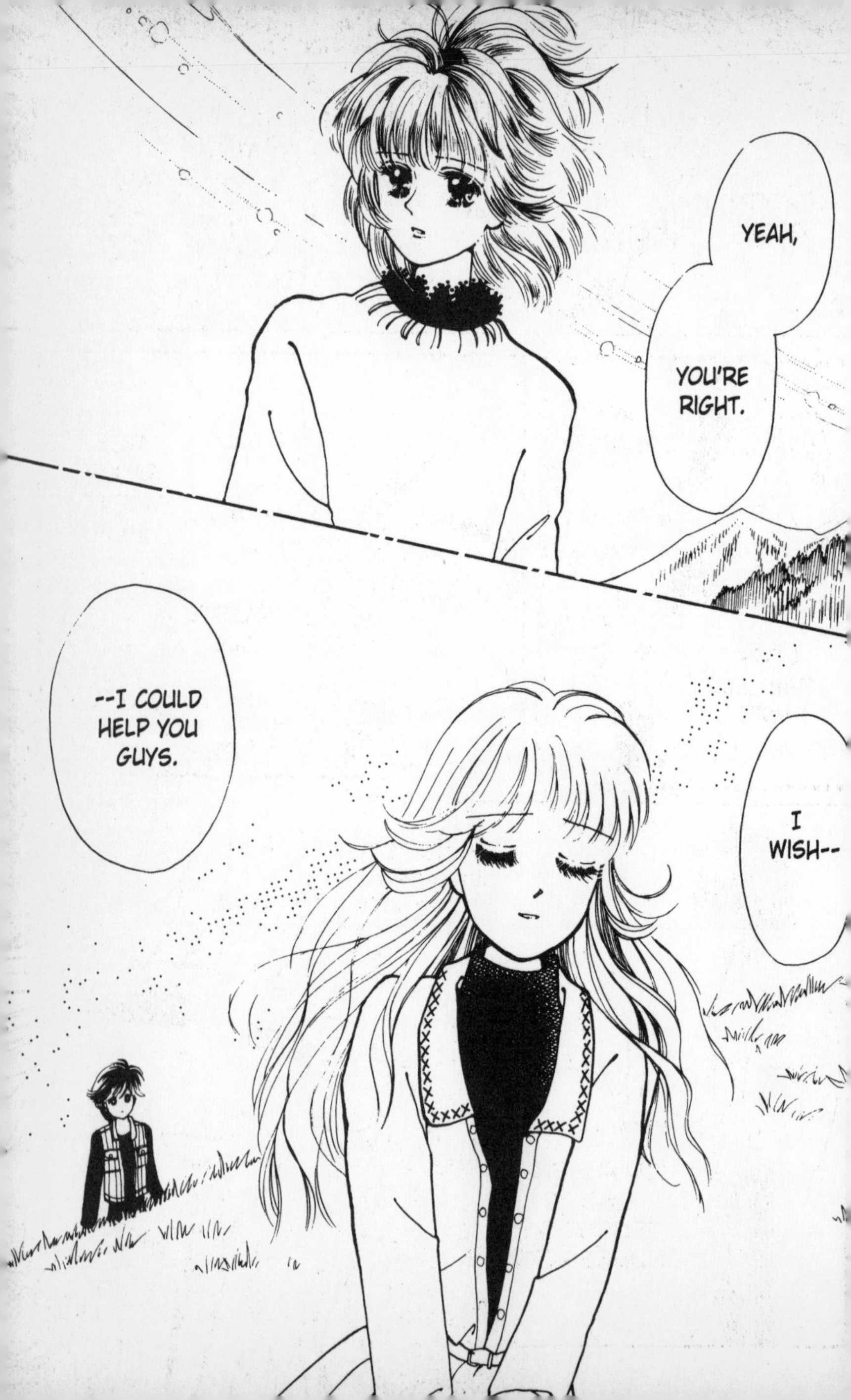
YEAH,
YOU'RE RIGHT.
I WISH--
--I COULD HELP YOU GUYS.

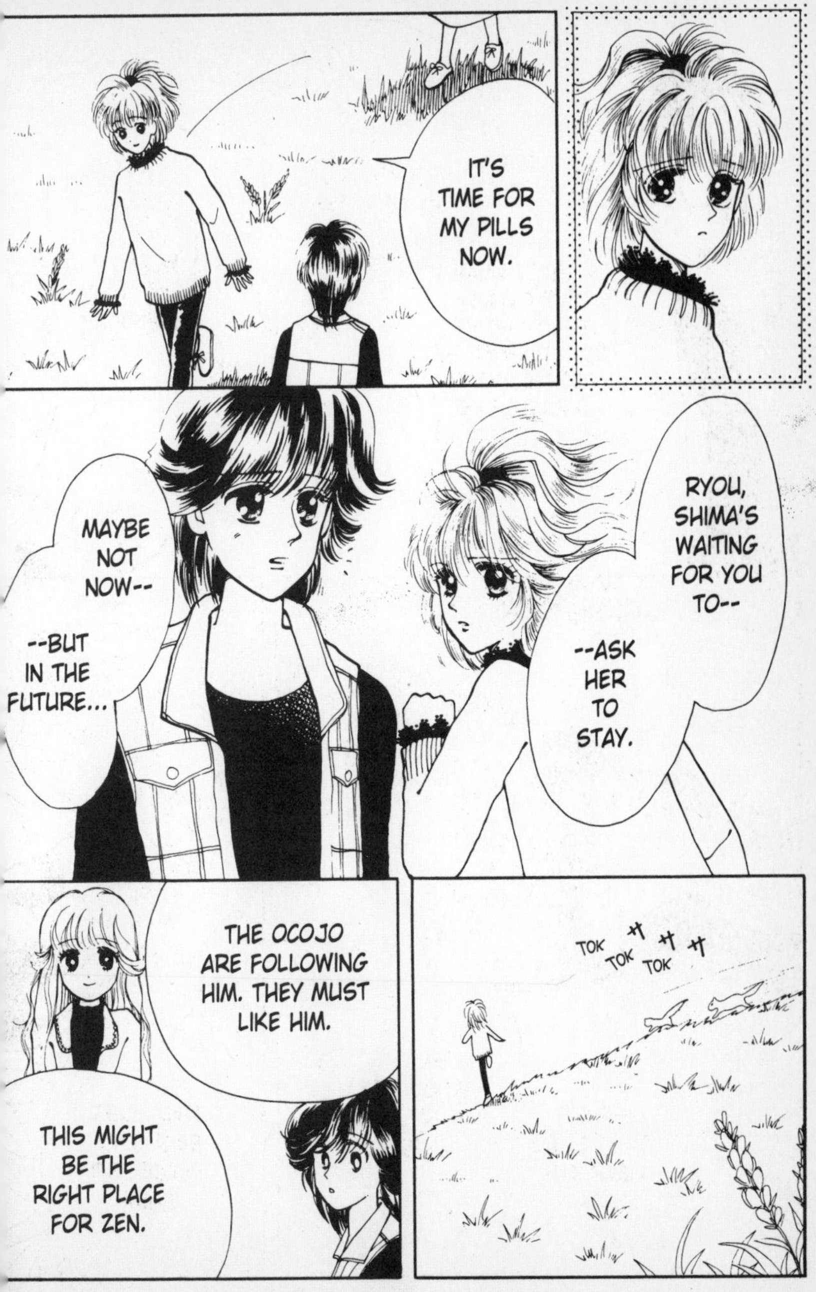
IT'S TIME FOR MY PILLS NOW.
RYOU, SHIMA'S WAITING FOR YOU TO--
--ASK HER TO STAY.
MAYBE NOT NOW--
--BUT IN THE FUTURE...
TOK TOK TOK
THE OCOJO ARE FOLLOWING HIM. THEY MUST LIKE HIM.
THIS MIGHT BE THE RIGHT PLACE FOR ZEN.

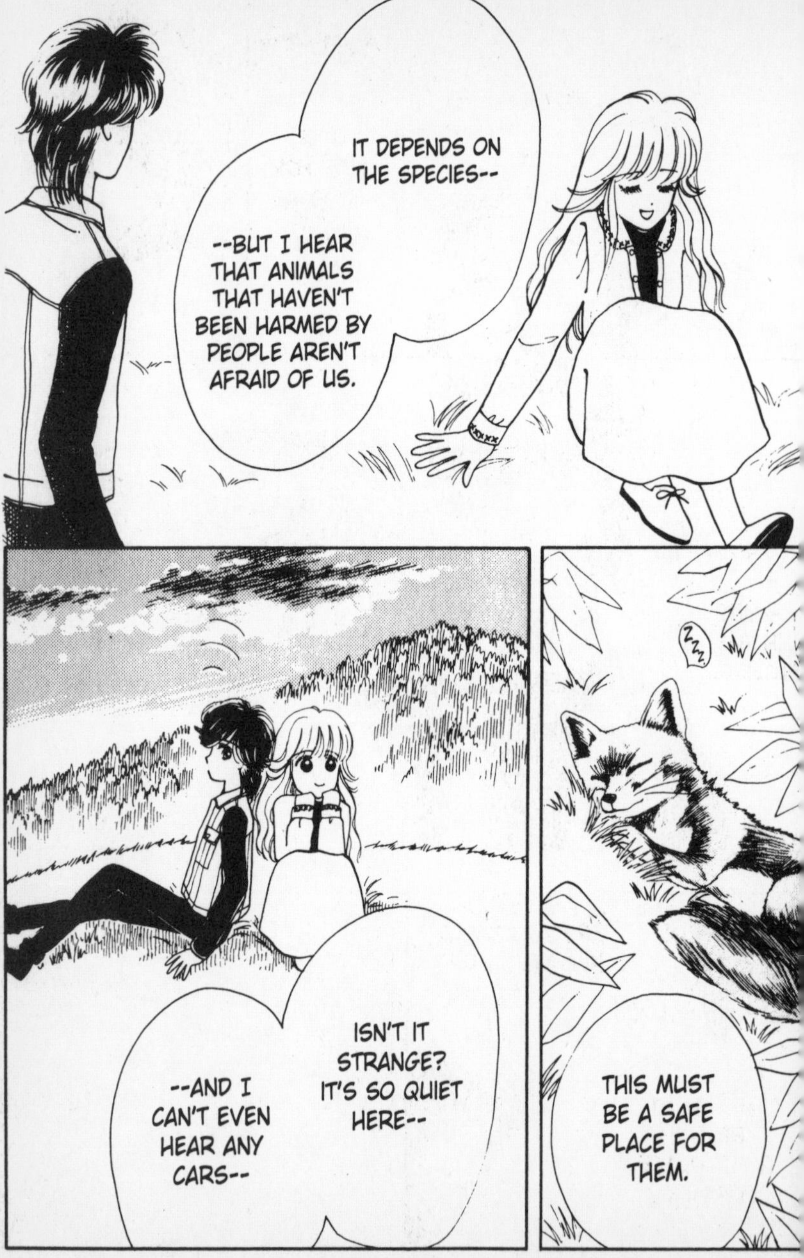
IT DEPENDS ON THE SPECIES--
--BUT I HEAR THAT ANIMALS THAT HAVEN'T BEEN HARMED BY PEOPLE AREN'T AFRAID OF US.
ZZZ
THIS MUST BE A SAFE PLACE FOR THEM.
ISN'T IT STRANGE? IT'S SO QUIET HERE--
--AND I CAN'T EVEN HEAR ANY CARS--

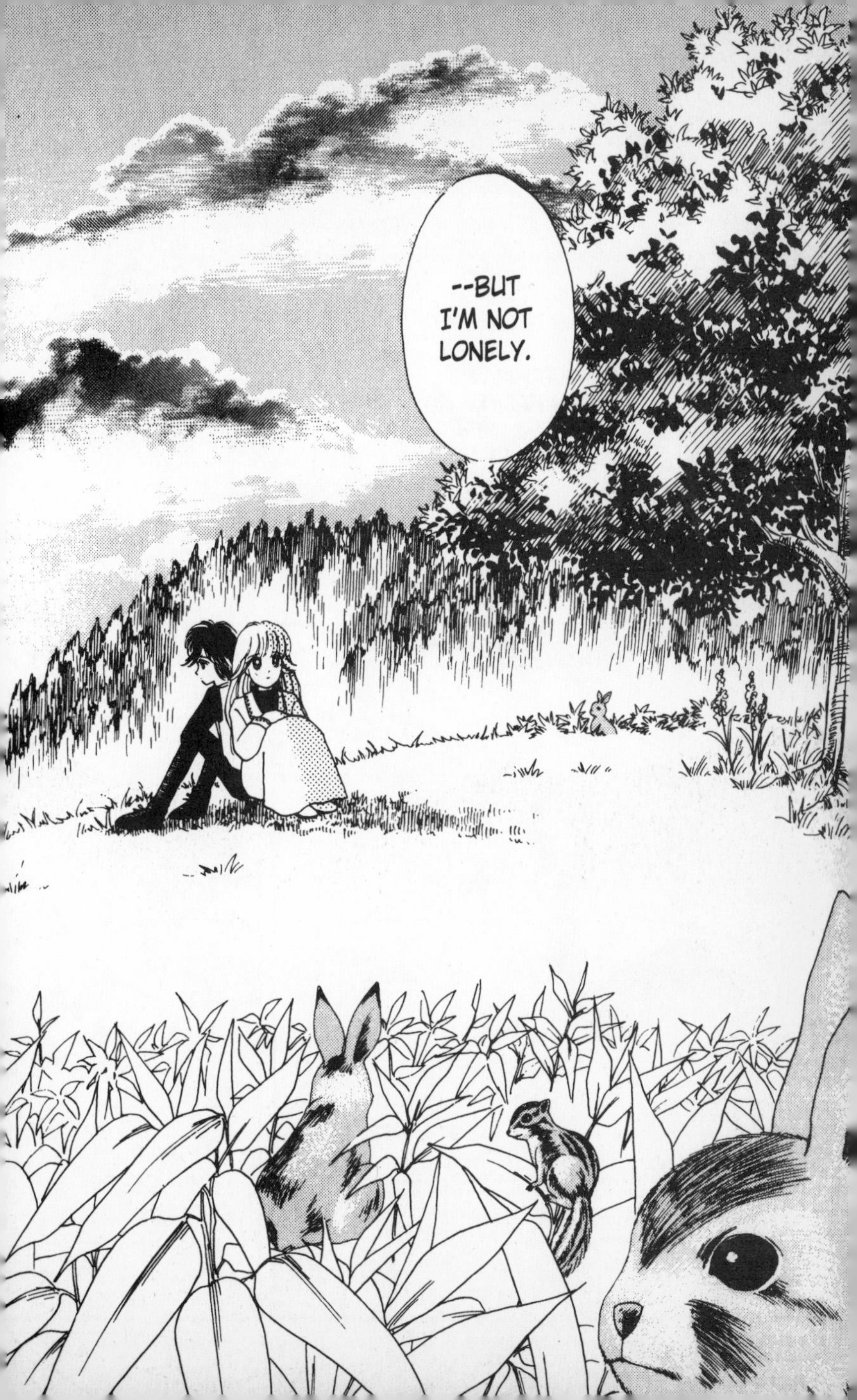
--BUT I'M NOT LONELY.

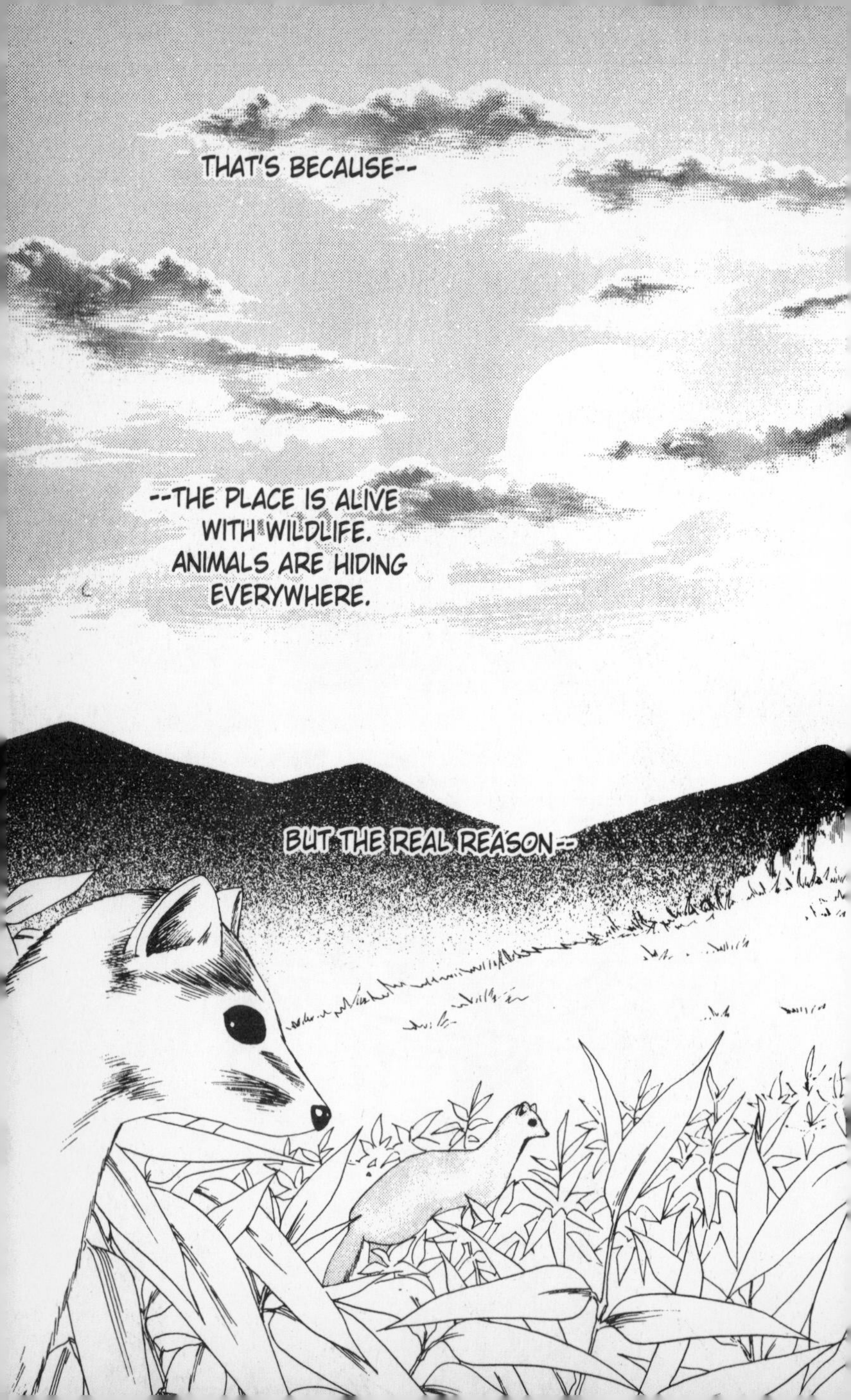
THAT'S BECAUSE--
--THE PLACE IS ALIVE WITH WILDLIFE. ANIMALS ARE HIDING EVERYWHERE.
BUT THE REAL REASON--

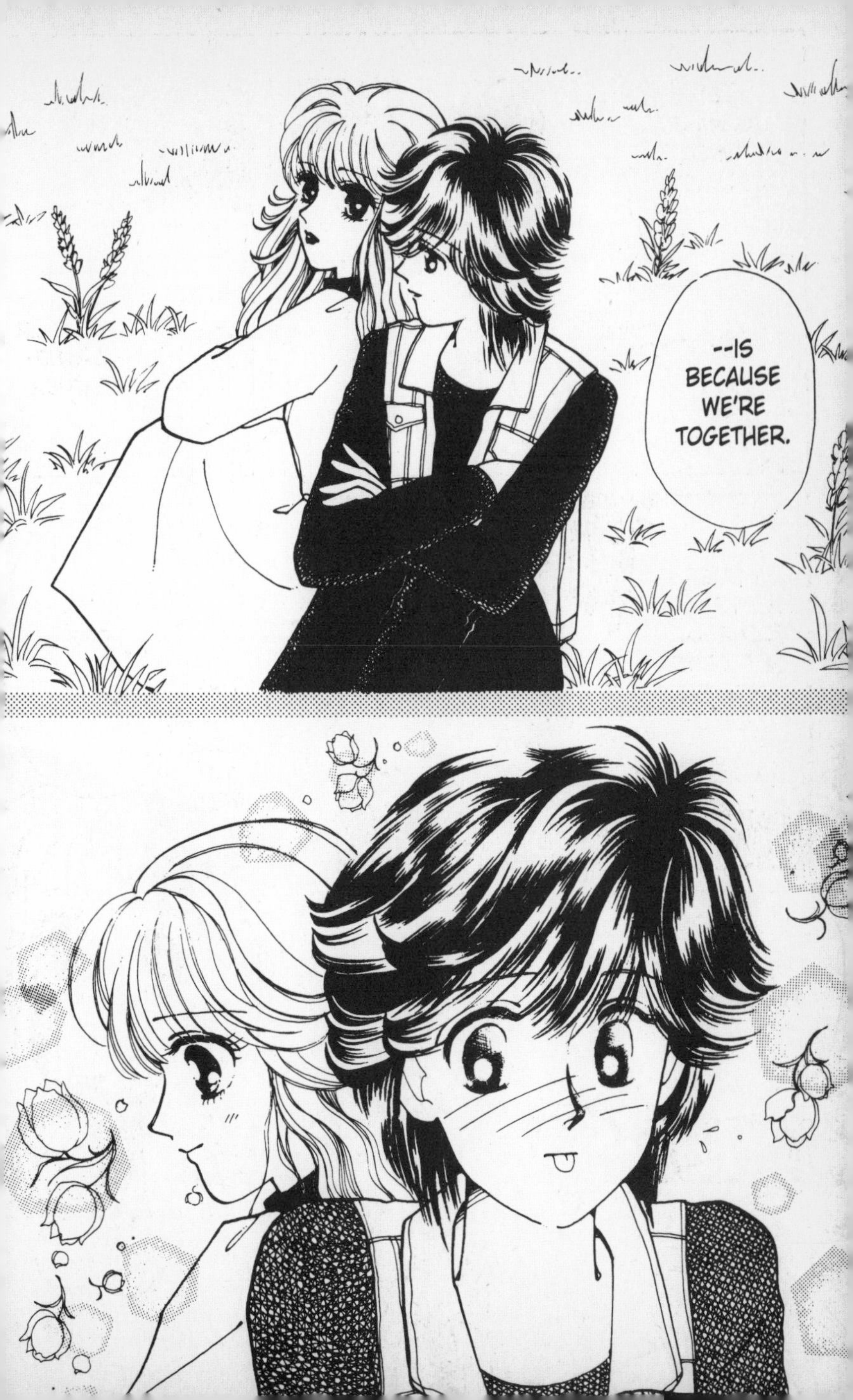
--IS BECAUSE WE'RE TOGETHER.

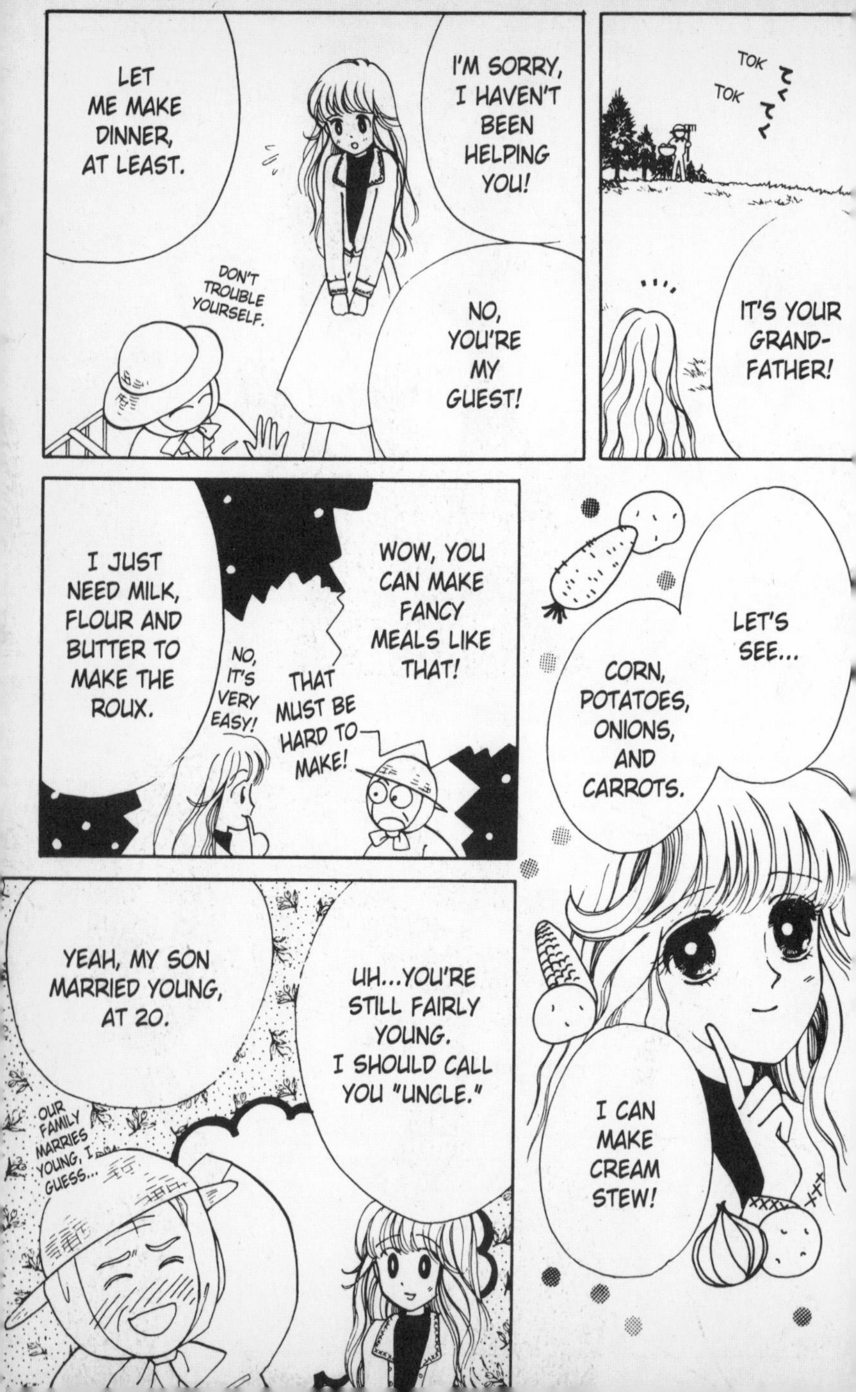
TOK TOK
...
IT'S YOUR GRANDFATHER!
I'M SORRY, I HAVEN'T BEEN HELPING YOU!
NO, YOU'RE MY GUEST!
DON'T TROUBLE YOURSELF.
LET ME MAKE DINNER, AT LEAST.
LET'S SEE...
CORN, POTATOES, ONIONS, AND CARROTS.
I CAN MAKE CREAM STEW!
WOW, YOU CAN MAKE FANCY MEALS LIKE THAT!
THAT MUST BE HARD TO MAKE!
NO, IT'S VERY EASY!
I JUST NEED MILK, FLOUR AND BUTTER TO MAKE THE ROUX.
UH...YOU'RE STILL FAIRLY YOUNG. I SHOULD CALL YOU "UNCLE."
YEAH, MY SON MARRIED YOUNG, AT 20.
OUR FAMILY MARRIES YOUNG, I GUESS...

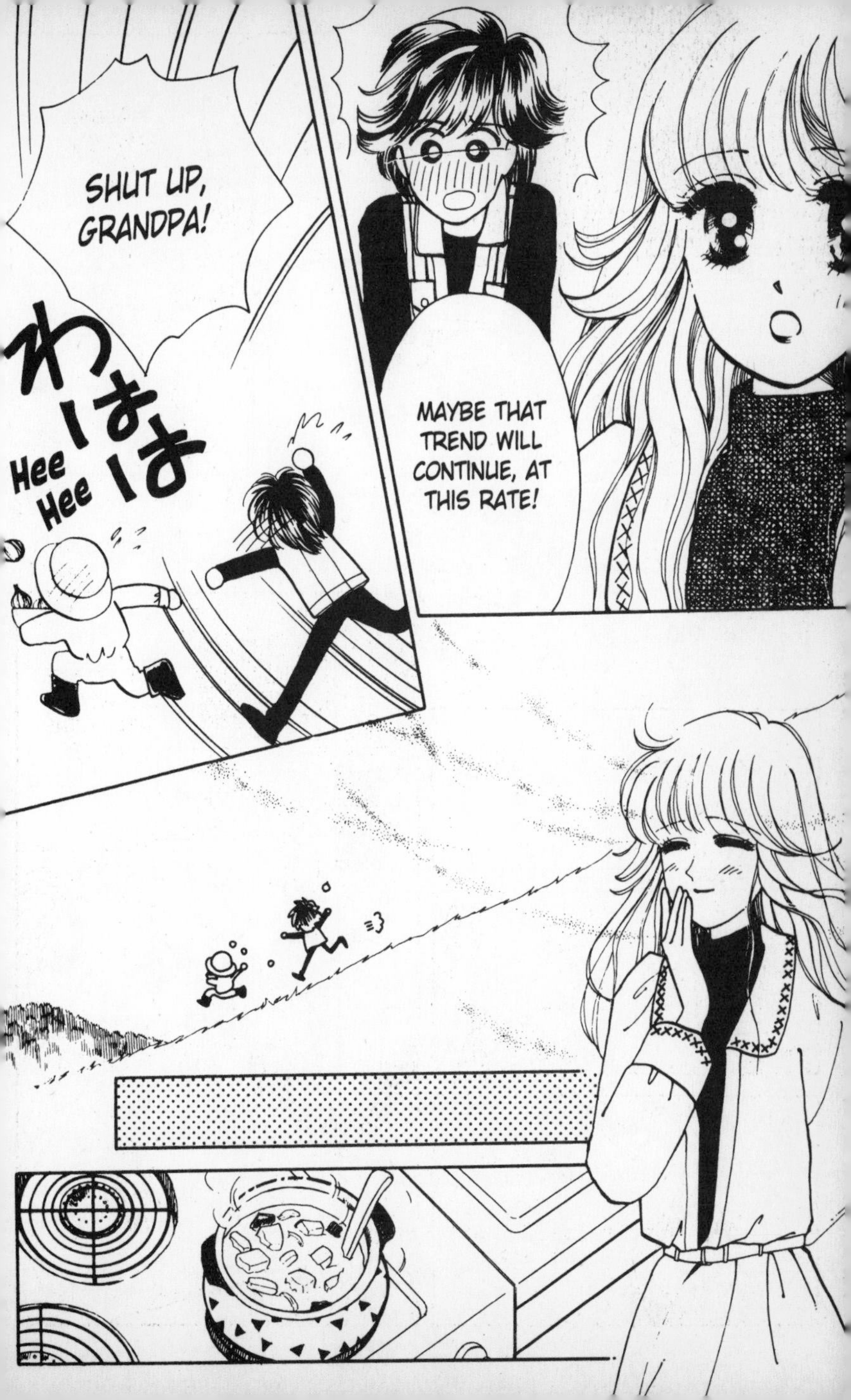
MAYBE THAT TREND WILL CONTINUE, AT THIS RATE!
SHUT UP, GRANDPA!
わはは
Hee Hee

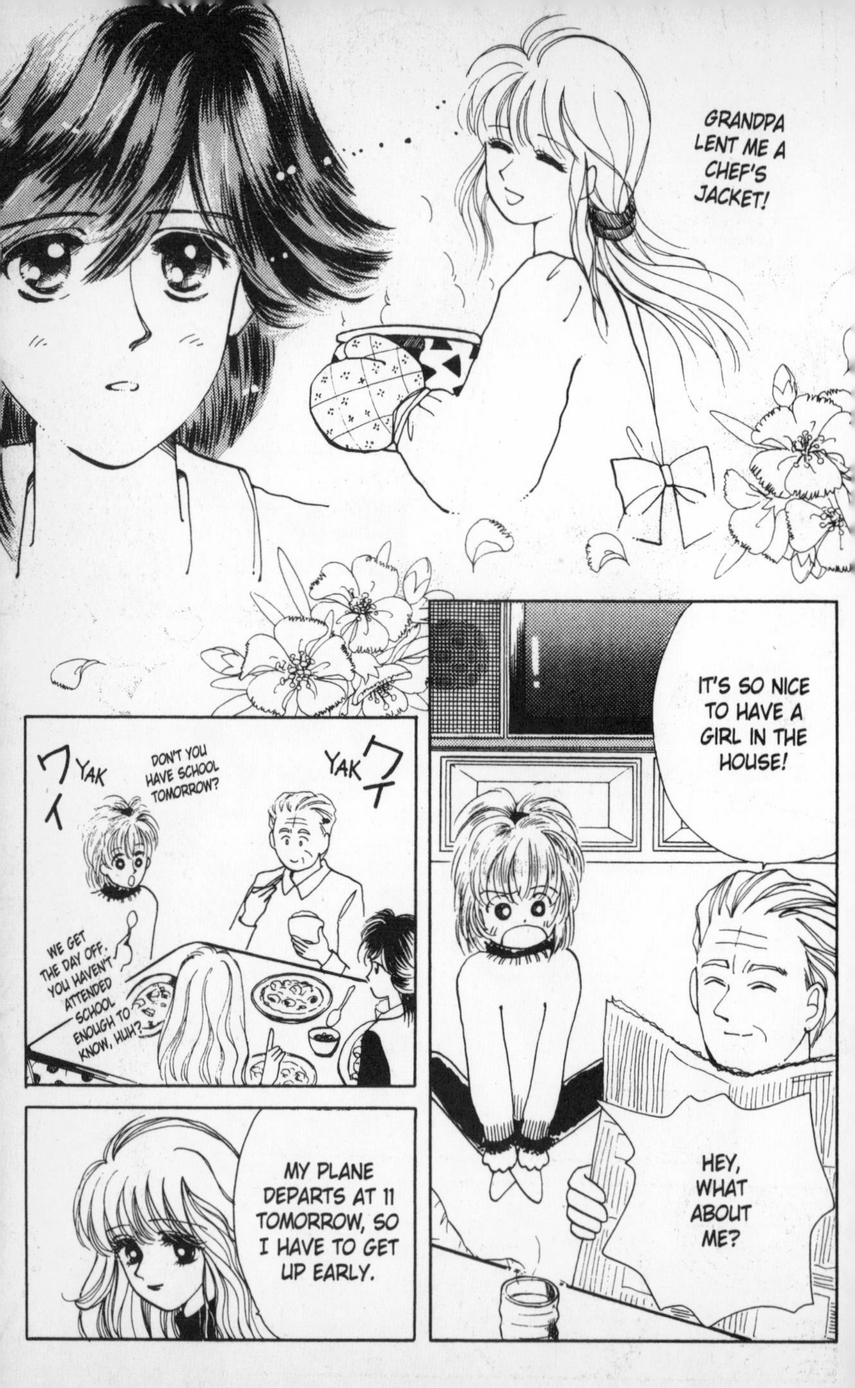
GRANDPA LENT ME A CHEF'S JACKET!
IT'S SO NICE TO HAVE A GIRL IN THE HOUSE!
HEY, WHAT ABOUT ME?
ワイ YAK
DON'T YOU HAVE SCHOOL TOMORROW?
ワイ YAK
WE GET THE DAY OFF. YOU HAVEN'T ATTENDED SCHOOL ENOUGH TO KNOW, HUH?
MY PLANE DEPARTS AT 11 TOMORROW, SO I HAVE TO GET UP EARLY.

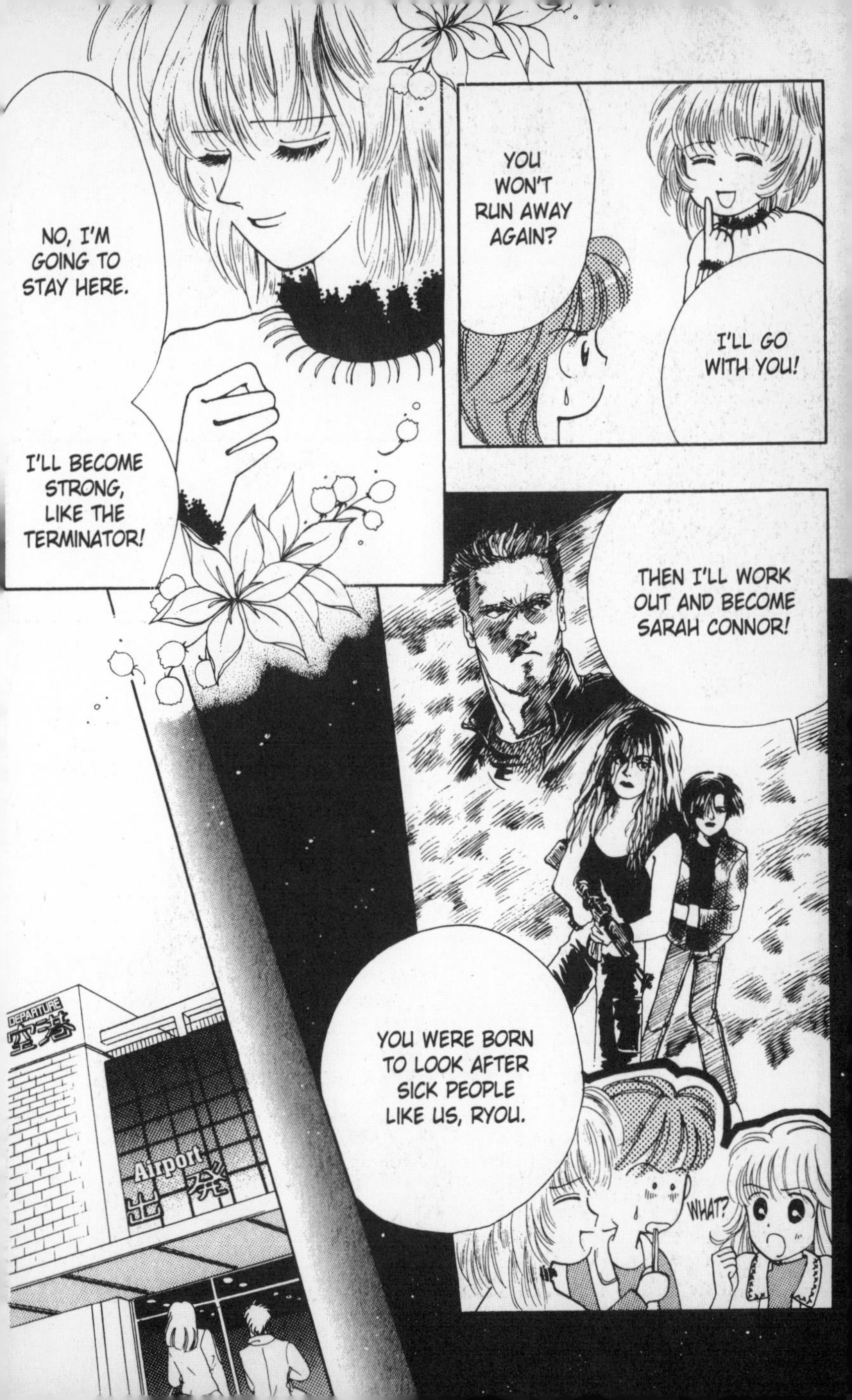
YOU WON'T RUN AWAY AGAIN?
I'LL GO WITH YOU!
NO, I'M GOING TO STAY HERE.
I'LL BECOME STRONG, LIKE THE TERMINATOR!
THEN I'LL WORK OUT AND BECOME SARAH CONNOR!
YOU WERE BORN TO LOOK AFTER SICK PEOPLE LIKE US, RYOU.
WHAT?
DEPARTURE
空港
Airport
出発

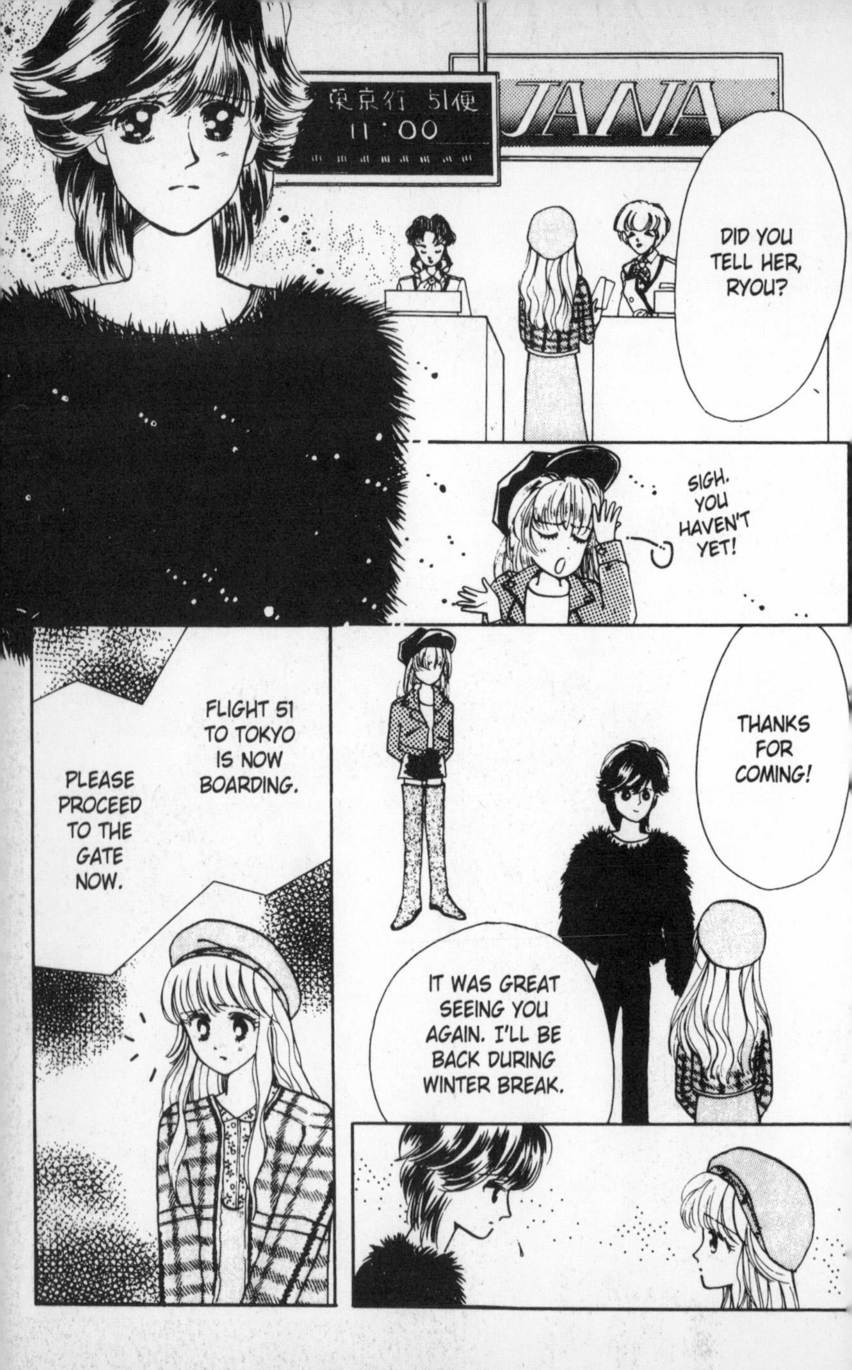
東京行 51便
11:00
JANA
DID YOU TELL HER, RYOU?
SIGH. YOU HAVEN'T YET!
THANKS FOR COMING!
IT WAS GREAT SEEING YOU AGAIN. I'LL BE BACK DURING WINTER BREAK.
FLIGHT 51 TO TOKYO IS NOW BOARDING.
PLEASE PROCEED TO THE GATE NOW.

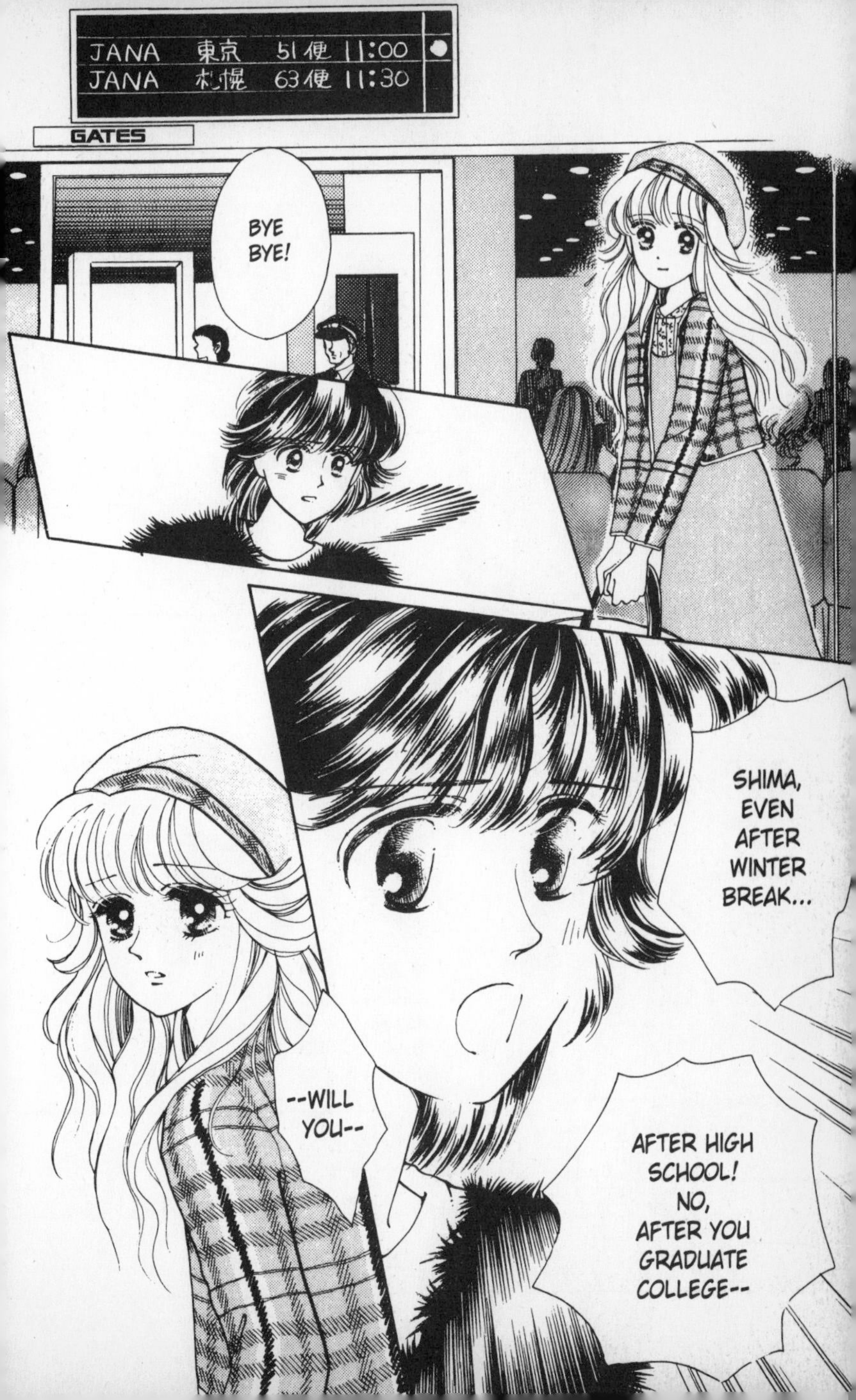
JANA 東京 51便 11:00
JANA 札幌 63便 11:30
GATES
BYE BYE!
SHIMA, EVEN AFTER WINTER BREAK...
AFTER HIGH SCHOOL! NO, AFTER YOU GRADUATE COLLEGE--
--WILL YOU--

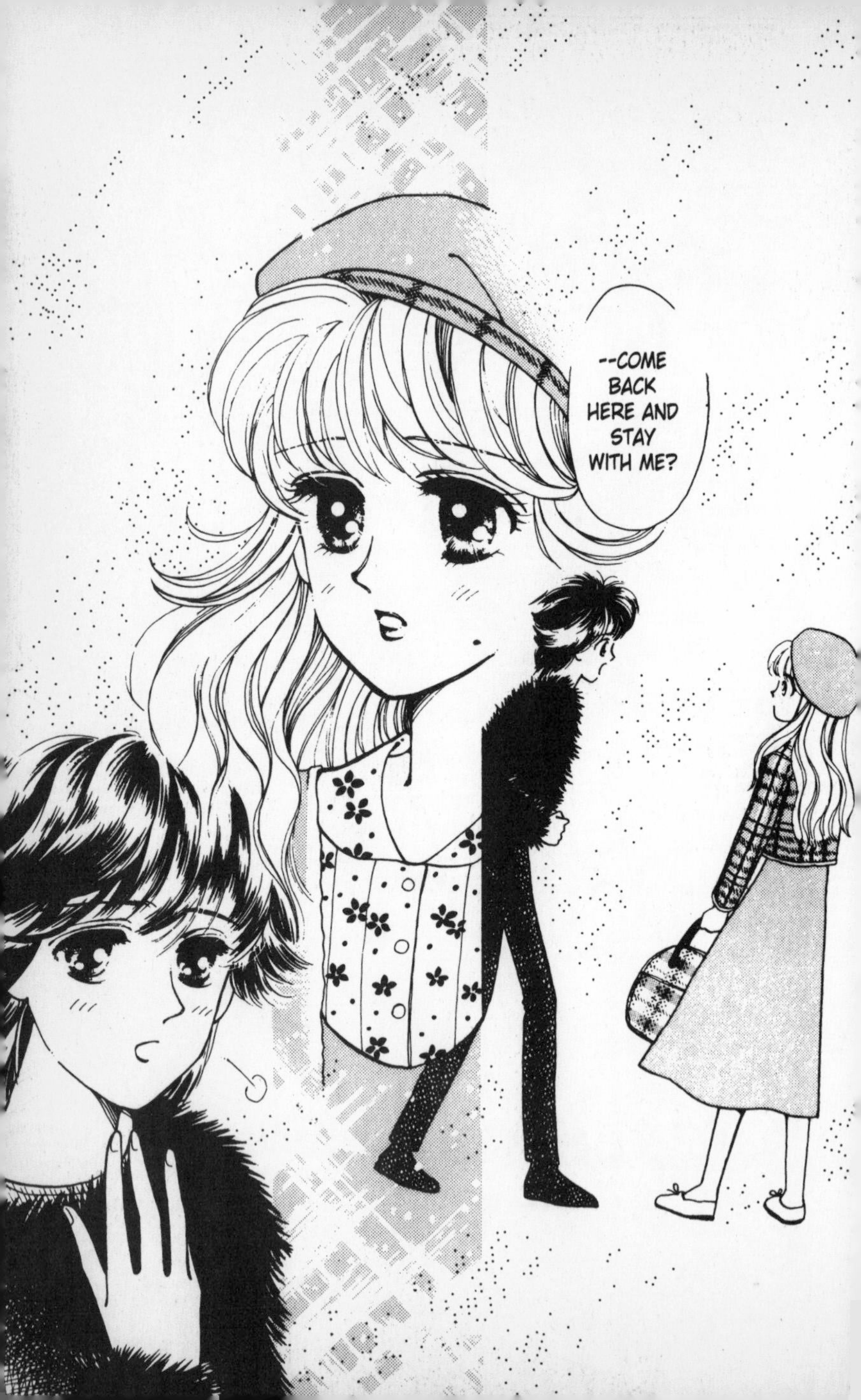
--COME BACK HERE AND STAY WITH ME?

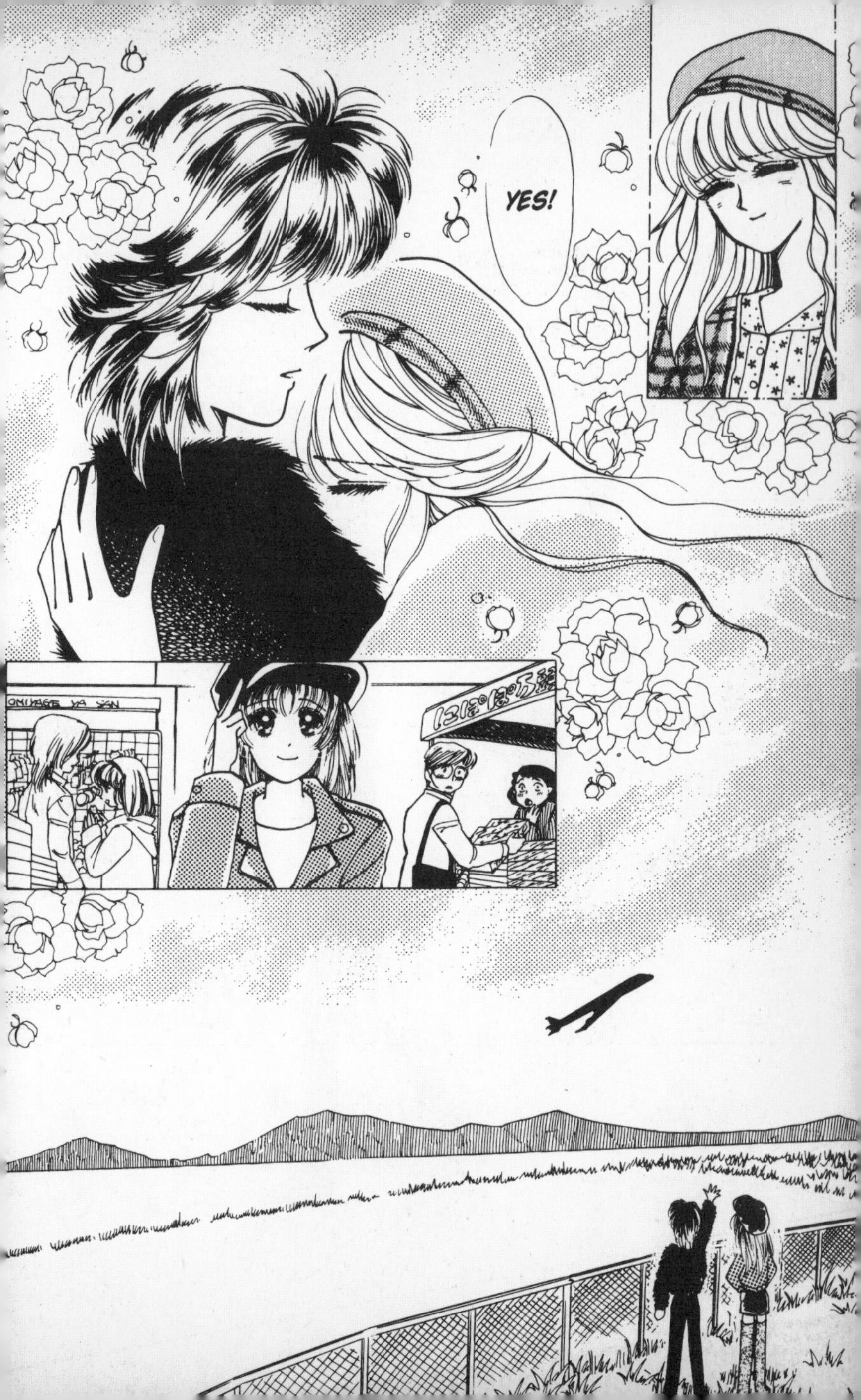
YES!
ONIYAGE YA SAN

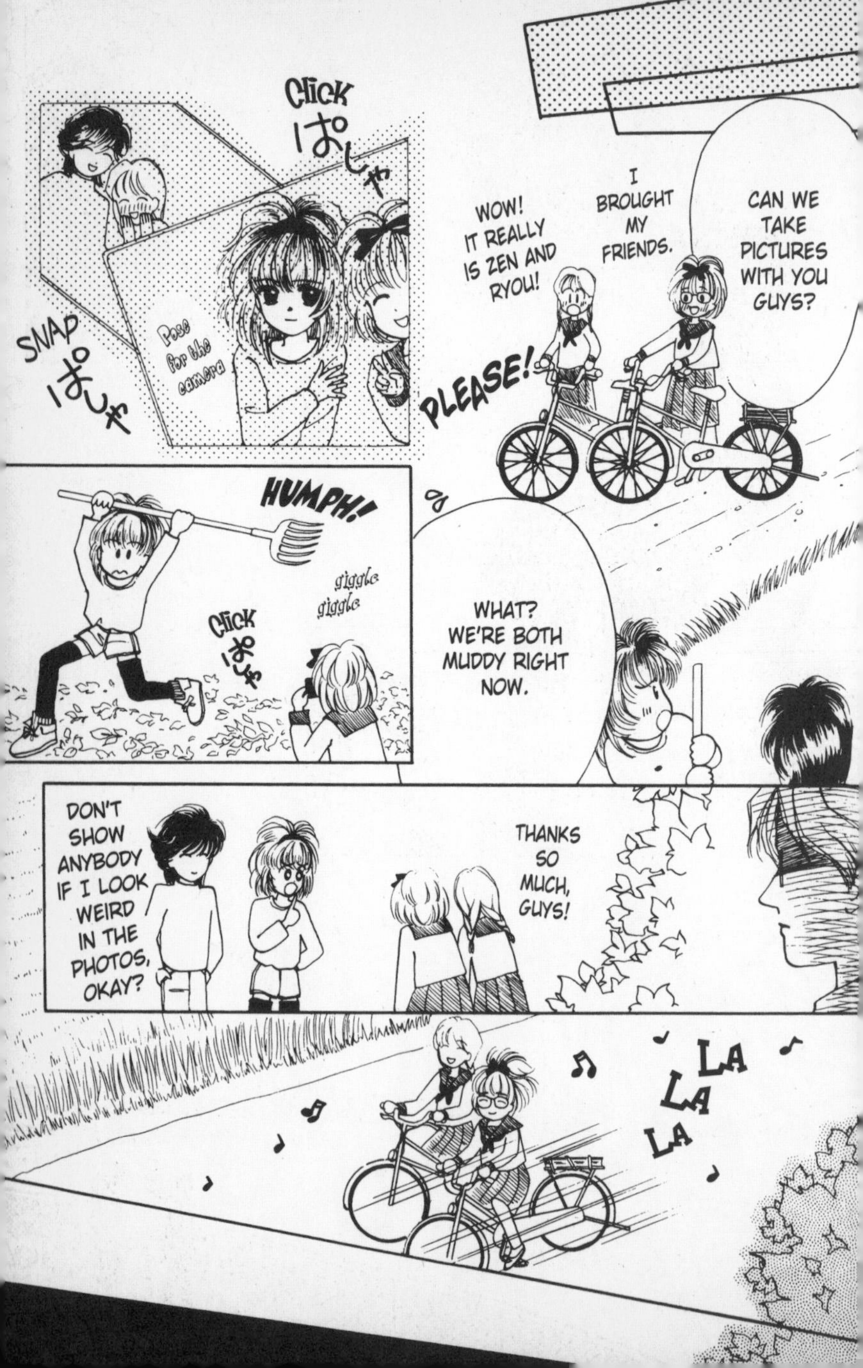

CAN WE TAKE PICTURES WITH YOU GUYS?
I BROUGHT MY FRIENDS.
WOW! IT REALLY IS ZEN AND RYOU!
PLEASE!
WHAT? WE'RE BOTH MUDDY RIGHT NOW.
Click ぱしゃ
Pose for the camera
SNAP ぱしゃ
HUMPH!
giggle giggle
Click ぱしゃ
THANKS SO MUCH, GUYS!
DON'T SHOW ANYBODY IF I LOOK WEIRD IN THE PHOTOS, OKAY?
LA LA LA

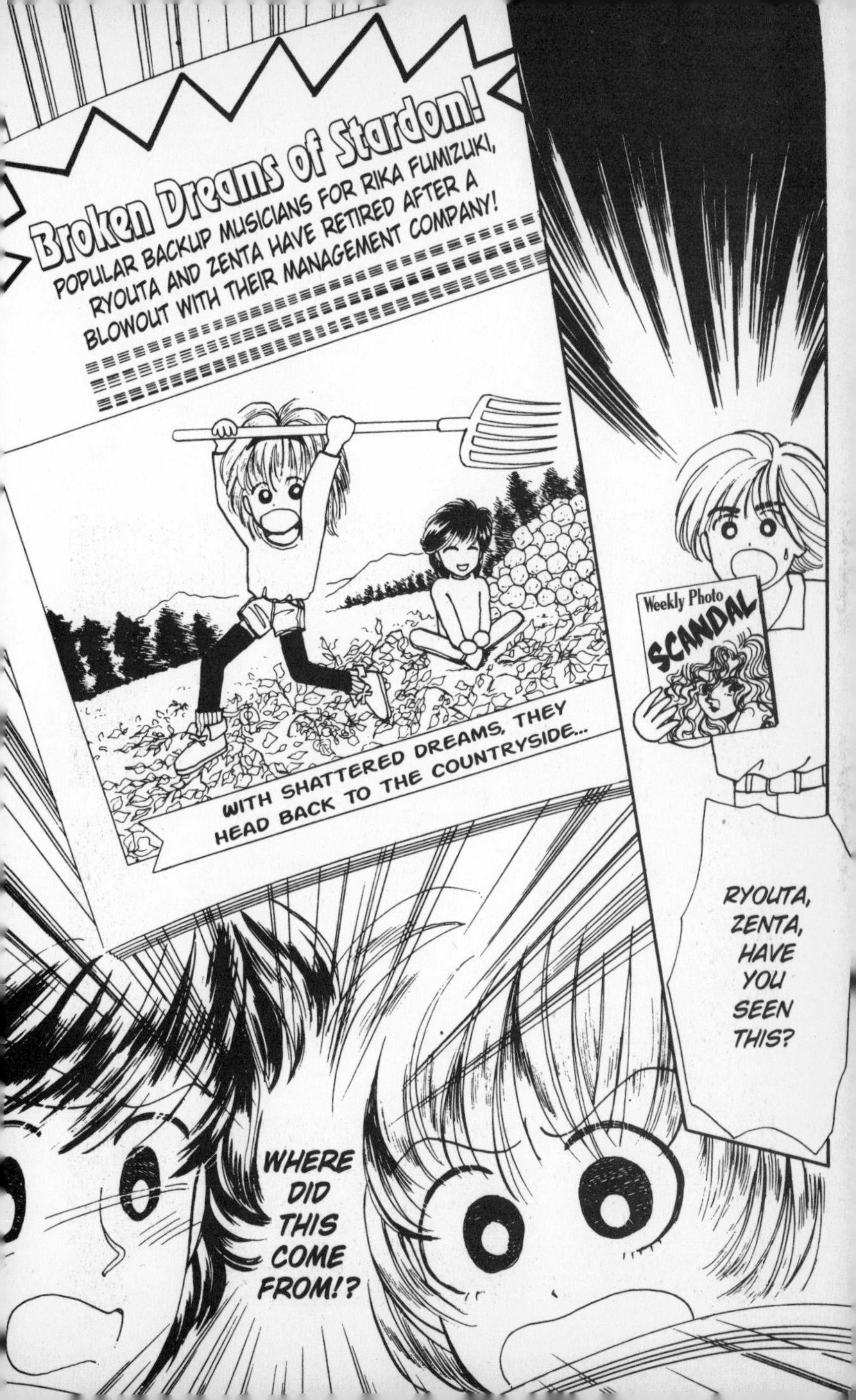
Weekly Photo
SCANDAL
RYOUTA, ZENTA, HAVE YOU SEEN THIS?
Broken Dreams of Stardom!
POPULAR BACKUP MUSICIANS FOR RIKA FUMIZUKI, RYOUTA AND ZENTA HAVE RETIRED AFTER A BLOWOUT WITH THEIR MANAGEMENT COMPANY!
WITH SHATTERED DREAMS, THEY HEAD BACK TO THE COUNTRYSIDE...
WHERE DID THIS COME FROM!?

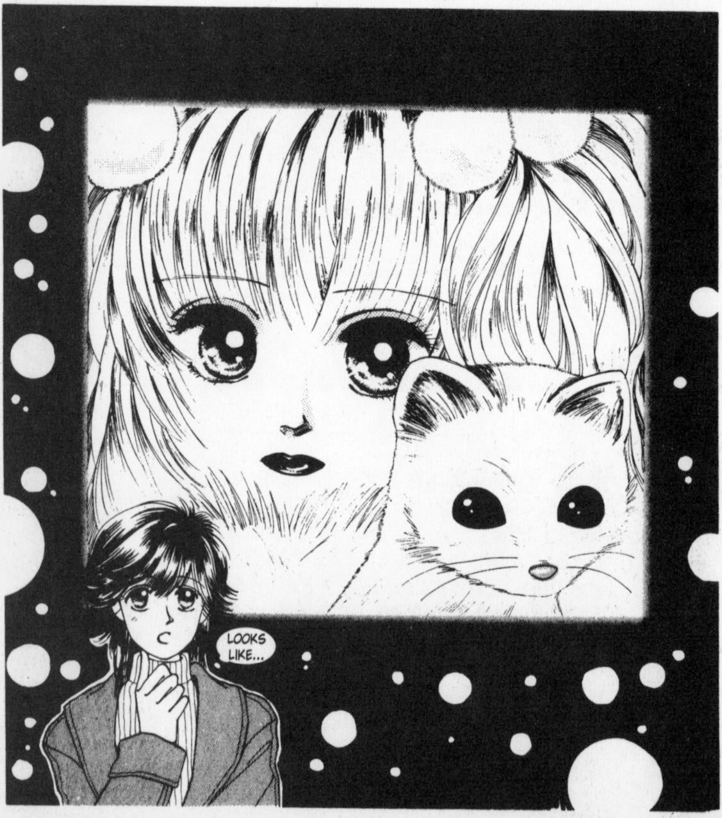
LOOKS LIKE...

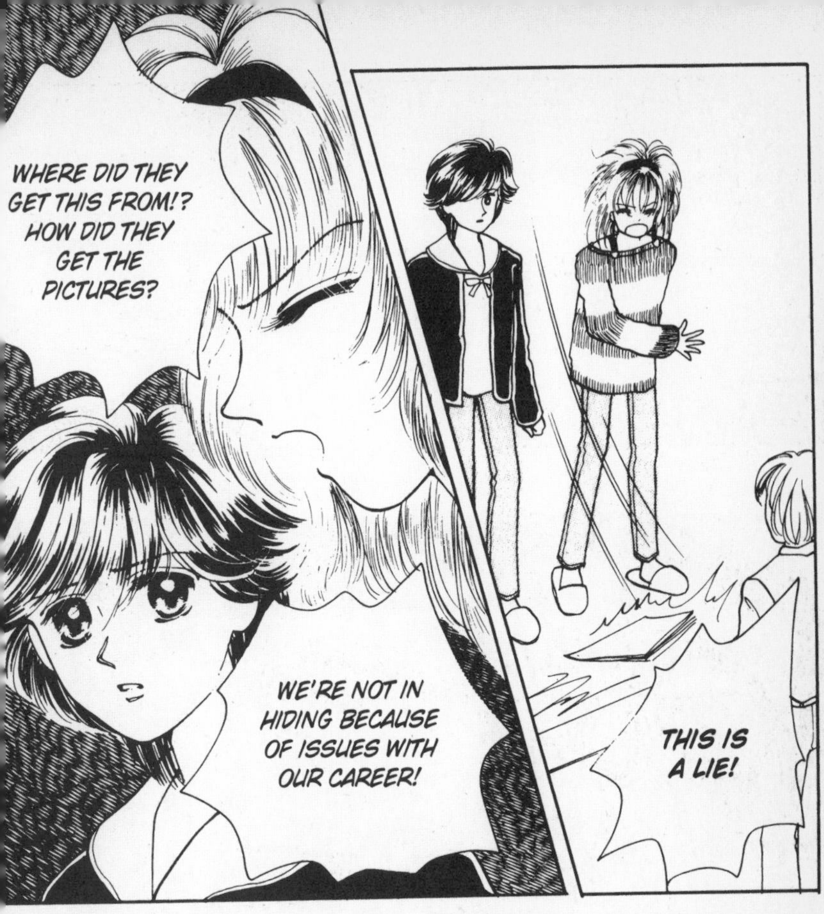
THIS IS A LIE!
WHERE DID THEY GET THIS FROM!? HOW DID THEY GET THE PICTURES?
WE'RE NOT IN HIDING BECAUSE OF ISSUES WITH OUR CAREER!

BONUS 4. IF I WAS OLDER BACK THEN, I WOULD HAVE BOUGHT THE FARM, AND IT WOULD NOT HAVE BEEN TURNED INTO A GOLF COURSE. THAT WAS TRAGIC. I WANTED TO AT LEAST GIVE MY STORY A HAPPY ENDING. MY FAMILY FARM WAS FULL OF WILD ANIMALS LIKE FOXES, SQUIRRELS, RABBITS, AND OCCASIONALLY A DEER (CITY FOLKS ARE REALLY SHOCKED WHEN I TALK ABOUT THIS)! ZENTA IS NAMED AFTER MY FRIEND'S YOUNGER BROTHER. I LOVE THAT NAME! (BY THE WAY, TO SHINICHI AND HIS BROTHER. PLEASE READ "MISS ME.") RYOUTA WAS THE NAME OF MY FRIEND'S TEDDY BEAR. I THOUGHT ZENTA AND RYOUTA SOUNDED GOOD TOGETHER, SO I USED IT! I MODELED ZENTA AFTER A CERTAIN MUSICIAN, BUT ZENTA ENDED UP LOOKING TOO CHILDISH, SO I WON'T TELL YOU WHO IT IS. MAYBE SOME OF YOU CAN GUESS. I HOPE HE'S STILL WORKING ON HIS MUSIC SINCE THE BAND SPLIT UP.

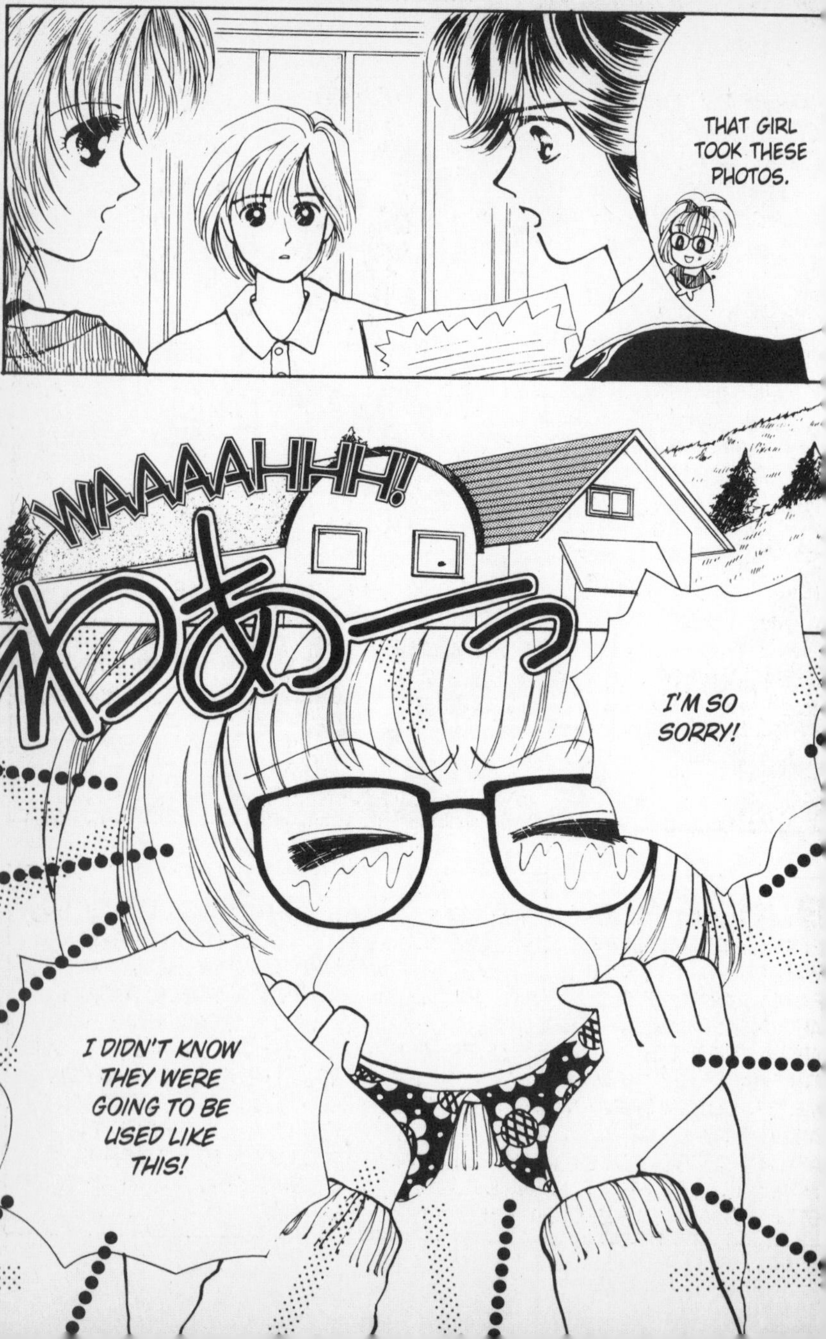
THAT GIRL TOOK THESE PHOTOS.
WAAAAHHH!
I'M SO SORRY!
I DIDN'T KNOW THEY WERE GOING TO BE USED LIKE THIS!

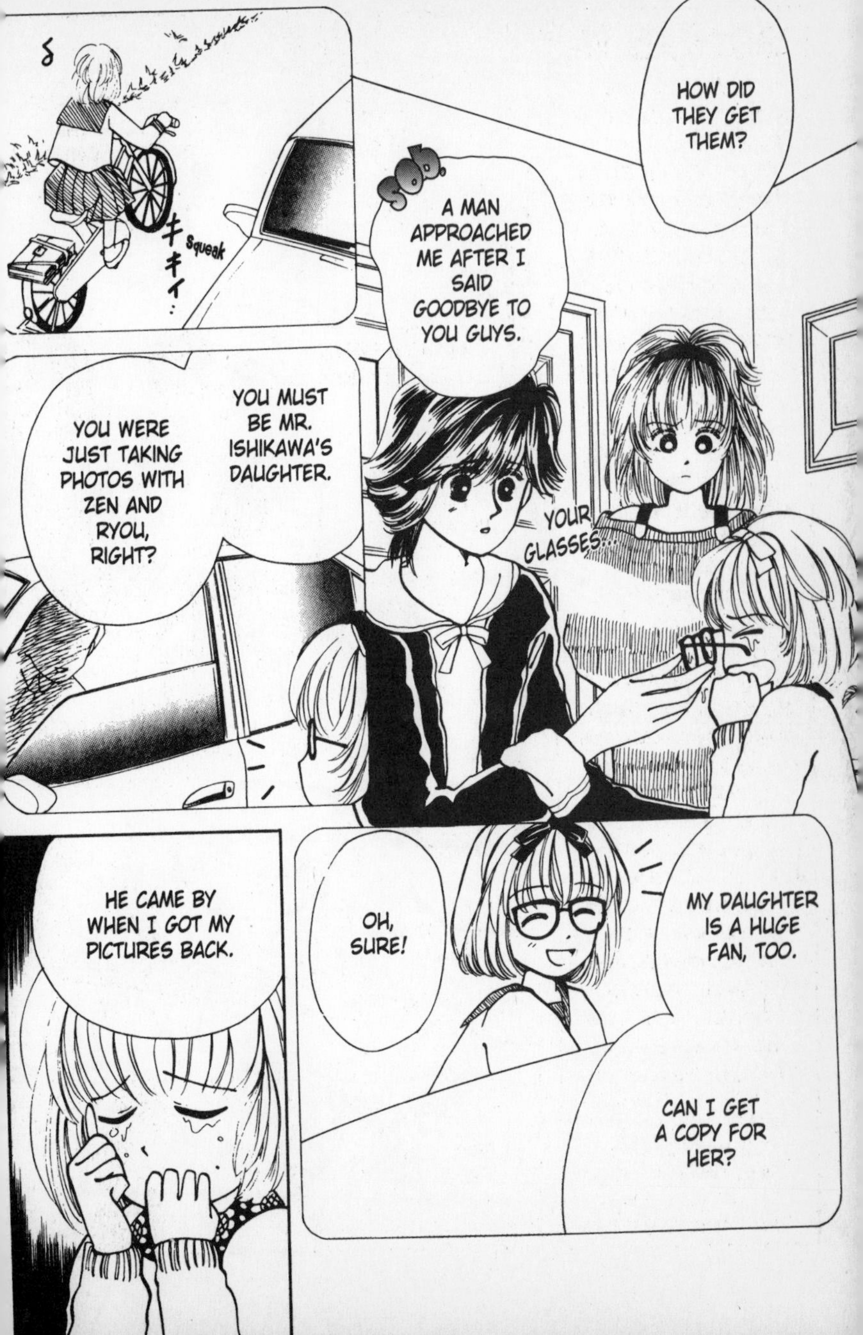
HOW DID THEY GET THEM?
sob
A MAN APPROACHED ME AFTER I SAID GOODBYE TO YOU GUYS.
YOUR GLASSES...
キキィ…
Squeak
YOU MUST BE MR. ISHIKAWA'S DAUGHTER.
YOU WERE JUST TAKING PHOTOS WITH ZEN AND RYOU, RIGHT?
MY DAUGHTER IS A HUGE FAN, TOO.
CAN I GET A COPY FOR HER?
OH, SURE!
HE CAME BY WHEN I GOT MY PICTURES BACK.

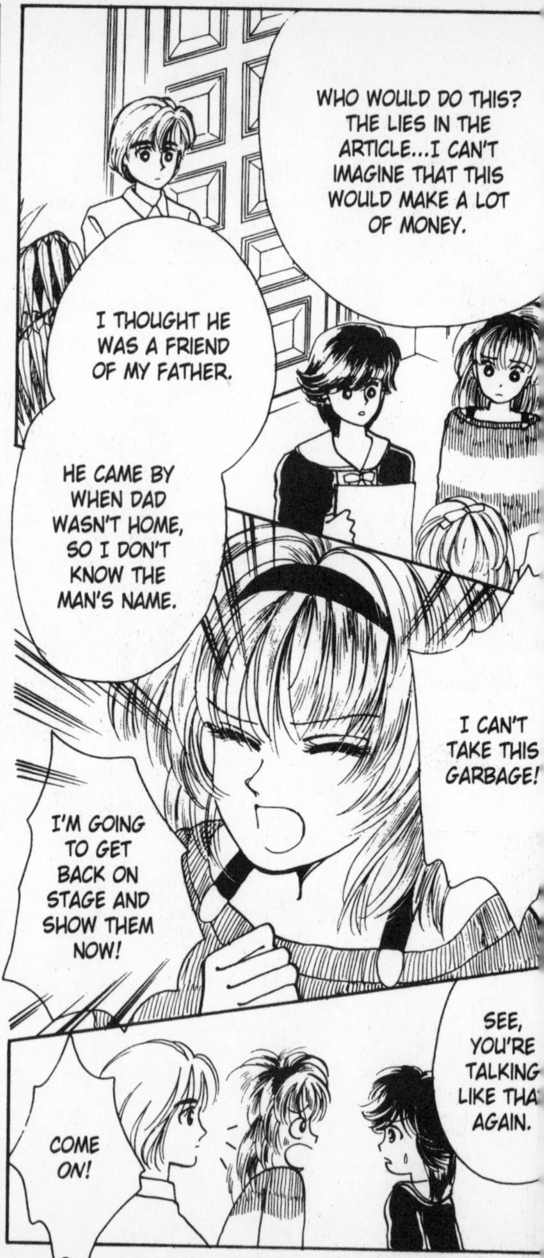
WHO WOULD DO THIS? THE LIES IN THE ARTICLE...I CAN'T IMAGINE THAT THIS WOULD MAKE A LOT OF MONEY.
I THOUGHT HE WAS A FRIEND OF MY FATHER.
HE CAME BY WHEN DAD WASN'T HOME, SO I DON'T KNOW THE MAN'S NAME.
I CAN'T TAKE THIS GARBAGE!
I'M GOING TO GET BACK ON STAGE AND SHOW THEM NOW!
SEE, YOU'RE TALKING LIKE THA AGAIN.
COME ON!

BONUS 5.

♡ RECENTLY, I HAD THE OPPORTUNITY TO HANG OUT WITH ROCKER GUYS AND GALS. (I HAVE NOT SEEN A LIVE METAL SHOW IN AGES...) WE WERE LAUGHING BECAUSE THE CONVERSATION TURNED INTO HOW "A METAL BAND SHOULD LOOK UNHEALTHY AND BE SKINNY." IT'S FUNNY, BECAUSE FOREIGN METAL BANDS TEND TO BE VERY SOLID AND HEALTHY (LAUGH).

(NOTE: METAL MUSICIANS IN JAPAN ARE USUALLY PALE, SKINNY FRAIL LOOKING GUYS. KIND OF LIKE THE GOTH MUSICIANS HERE IN THE STATES.)

A DEVIL'S HALO IS A TERM COINED BY MY PRETTY HAIR-STYLIST. IT'S THE OPPOSITE OF AN ANGEL'S HALO. I THOUGHT IT WAS A GREAT DESCRIPTION, SO I USED IT IN THIS PROJECT. I PERSONALLY LIKE THE DEVIL'S HALO! (LAUGH)

♡ THE NAMES FOR THE CHARACTERS IN "THE MAGIC OF LOVE" WERE NAMED AFTER MY FAVORITE MUSICIANS (I CHANGED THE KANJI). FOR EXAMPLE, I NAMED YUME'S NAME AFTER YUME SUZUKI. SHIMA OBATA FROM "LOVE AND PEACE IN A CORNFIELD," KAZU TERANISHI FROM "THE MAGIC OF LOVE." THESE NAMES ARE FROM "SKANCHI." (LAUGH) I HOPE THEY'RE NOT MAD.

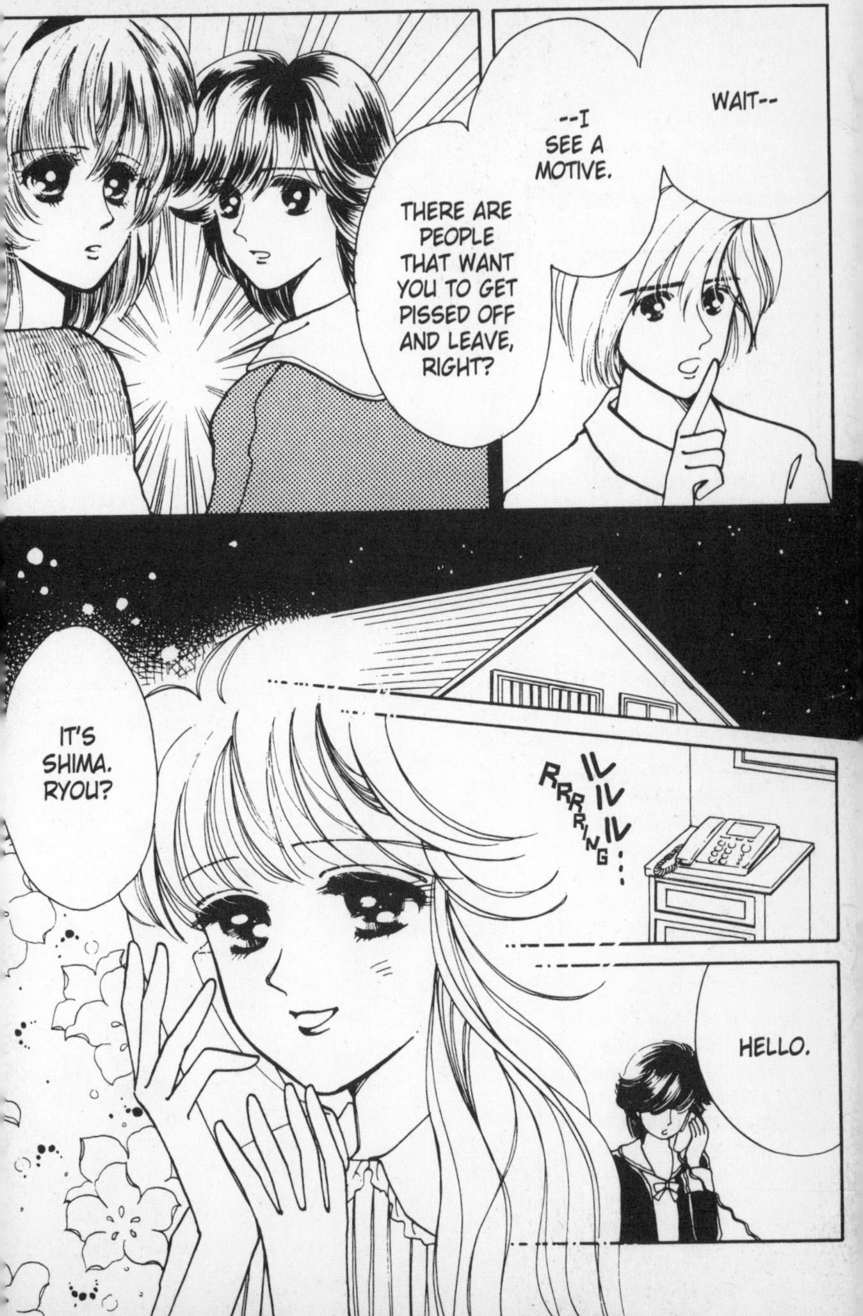
WAIT--
--I SEE A MOTIVE.
THERE ARE PEOPLE THAT WANT YOU TO GET PISSED OFF AND LEAVE, RIGHT?
RRRRING
HELLO.
IT'S SHIMA. RYOU?

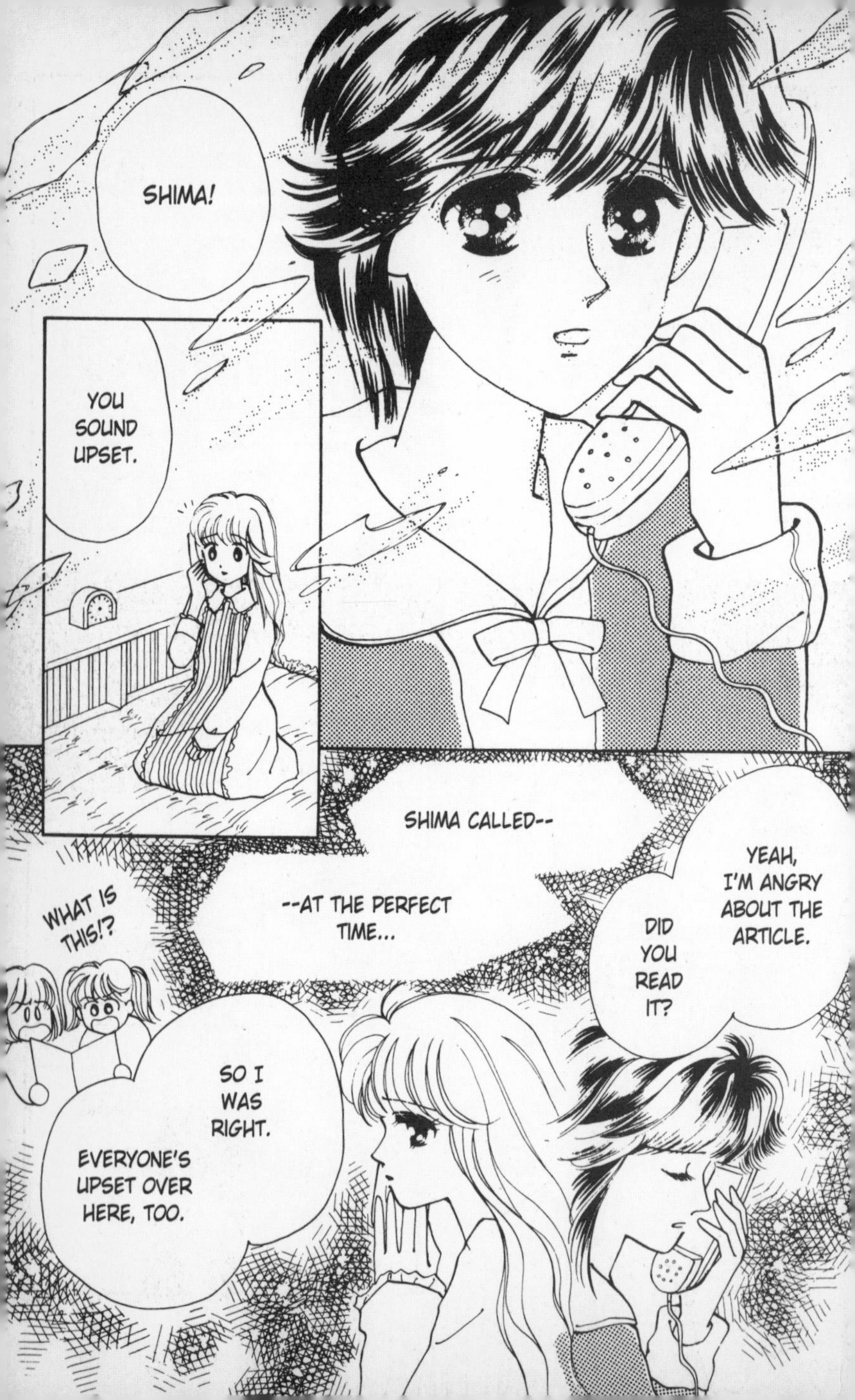
SHIMA!
YOU SOUND UPSET.
YEAH, I'M ANGRY ABOUT THE ARTICLE.
DID YOU READ IT?
SHIMA CALLED--
--AT THE PERFECT TIME...
WHAT IS THIS!?
SO I WAS RIGHT.
EVERYONE'S UPSET OVER HERE, TOO.

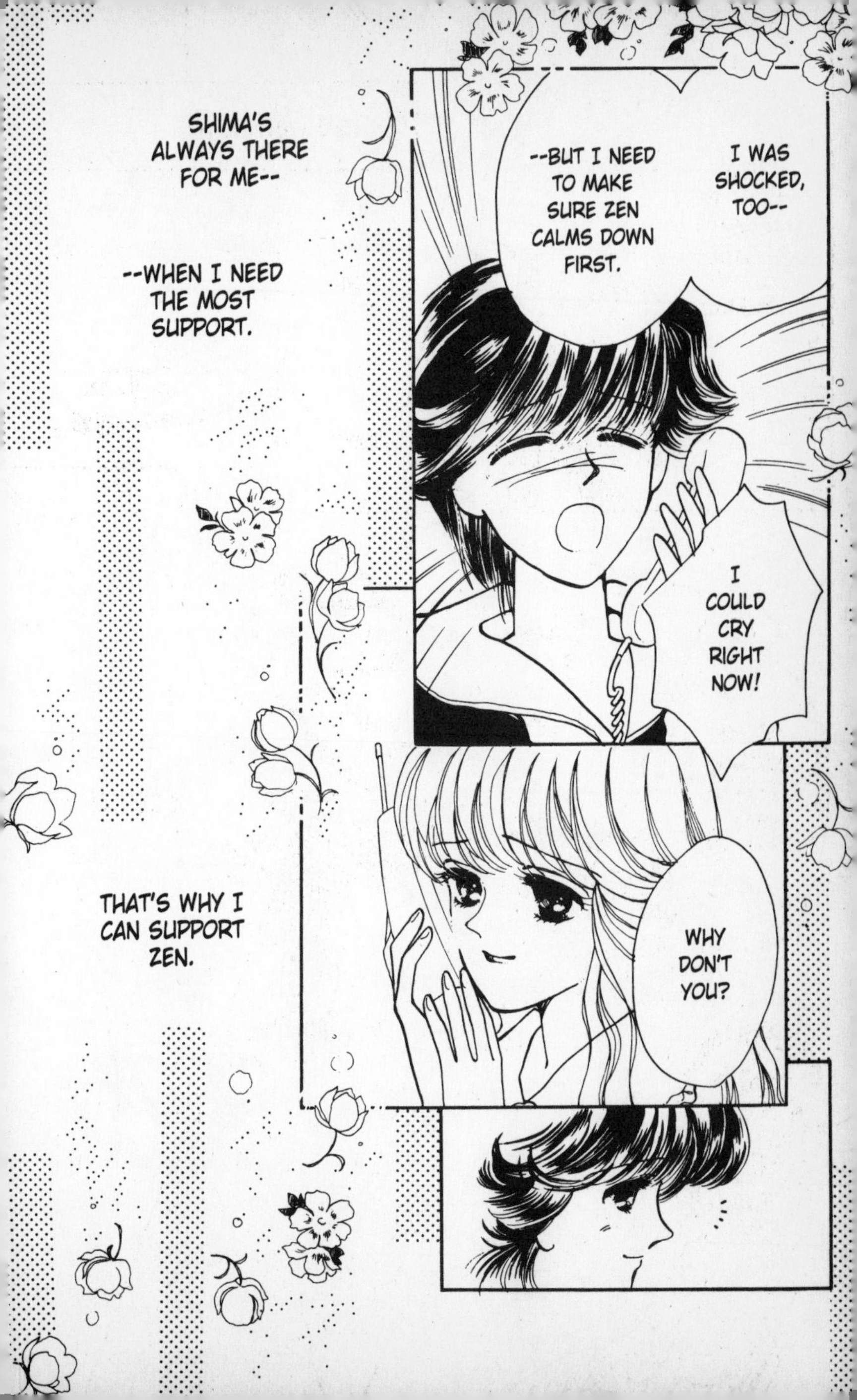
I WAS SHOCKED, TOO--
--BUT I NEED TO MAKE SURE ZEN CALMS DOWN FIRST.
SHIMA'S ALWAYS THERE FOR ME--
--WHEN I NEED THE MOST SUPPORT.
I COULD CRY RIGHT NOW!
WHY DON'T YOU?
THAT'S WHY I CAN SUPPORT ZEN.
...

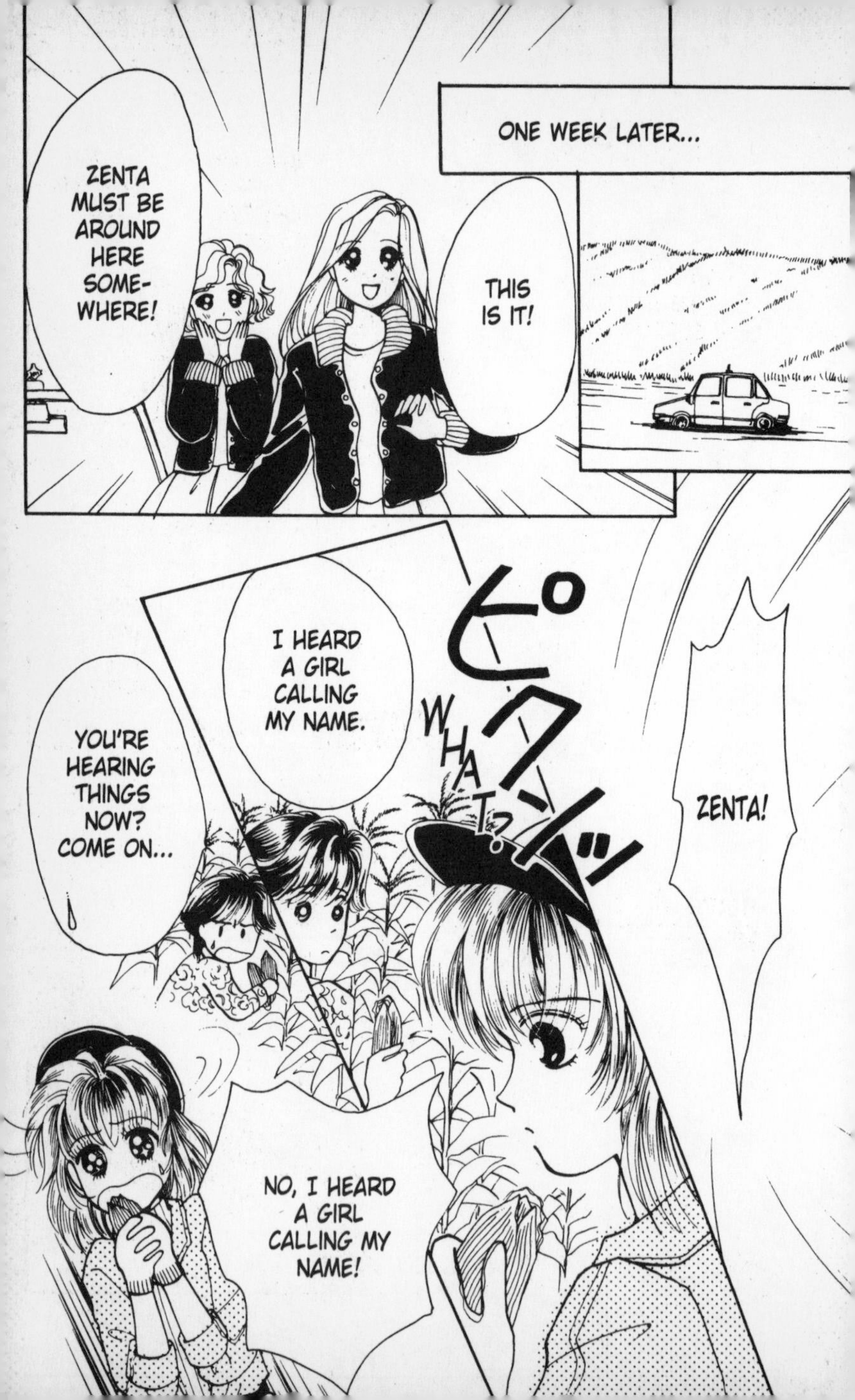
ONE WEEK LATER...
THIS IS IT!
ZENTA MUST BE AROUND HERE SOMEWHERE!
ZENTA!
ピクッ
WHAT?
I HEARD A GIRL CALLING MY NAME.
YOU'RE HEARING THINGS NOW? COME ON...
NO, I HEARD A GIRL CALLING MY NAME!

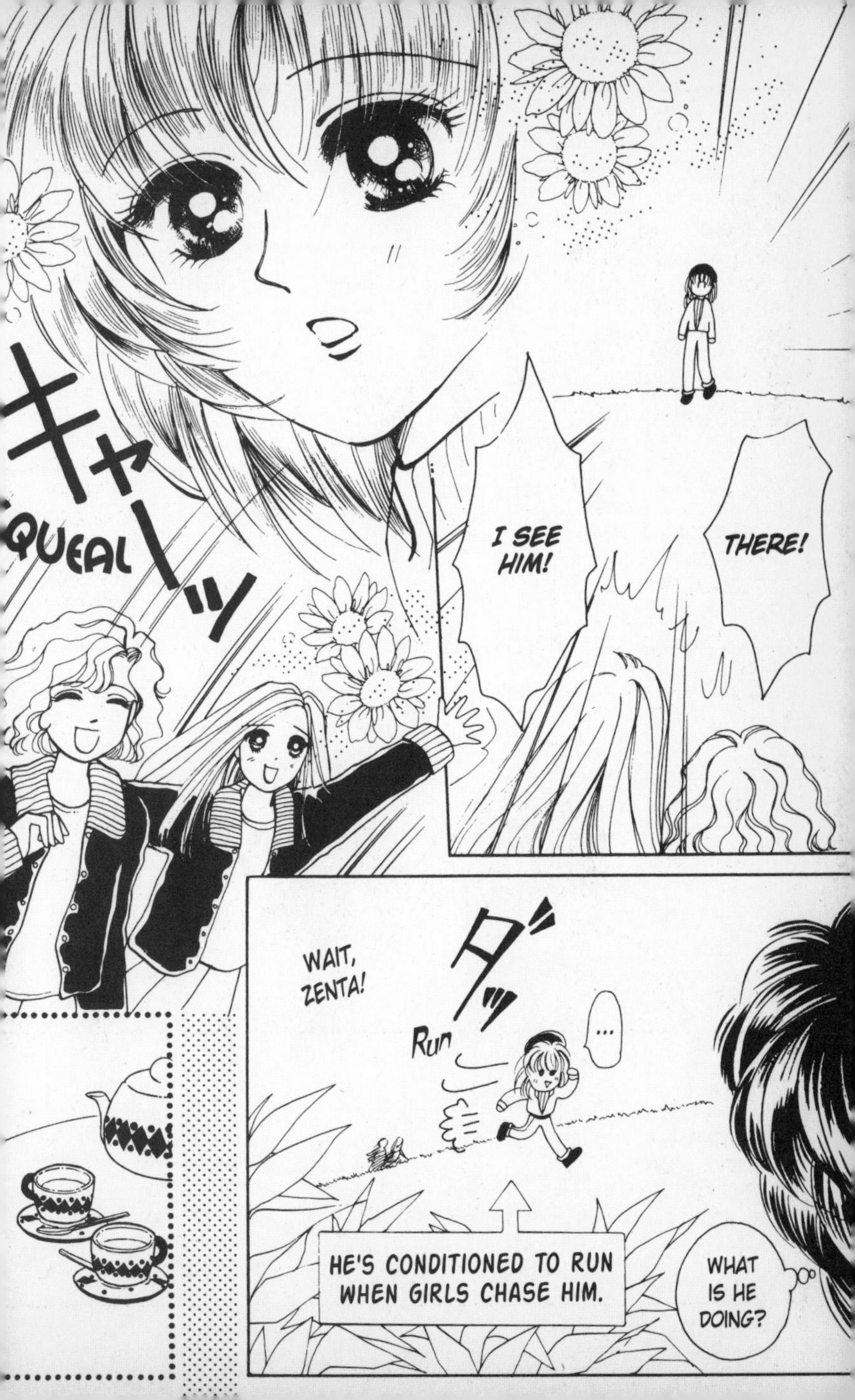
THERE!
I SEE HIM!
キャーッ
SQUEAL
WAIT, ZENTA!
ダッ
Run
...
HE'S CONDITIONED TO RUN WHEN GIRLS CHASE HIM.
WHAT IS HE DOING?

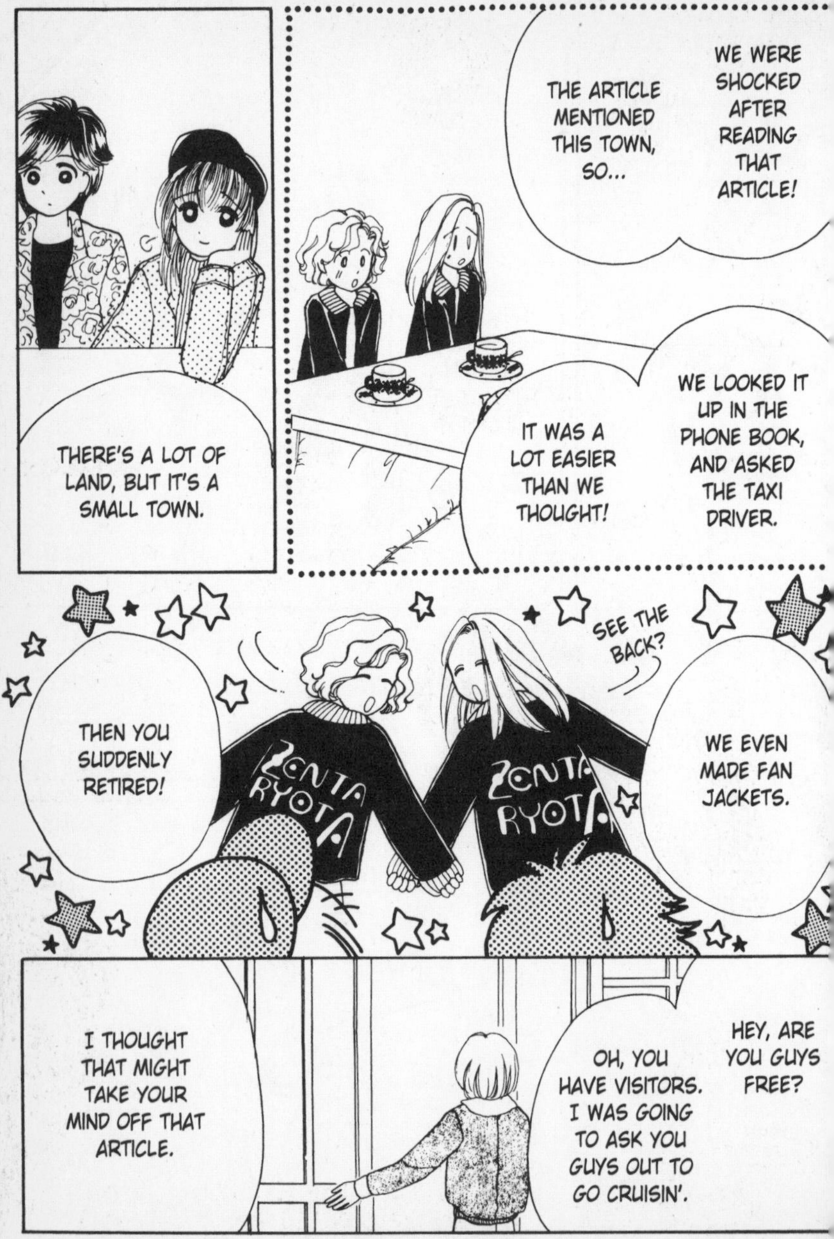
WE WERE SHOCKED AFTER READING THAT ARTICLE!
THE ARTICLE MENTIONED THIS TOWN, SO...
WE LOOKED IT UP IN THE PHONE BOOK, AND ASKED THE TAXI DRIVER.
IT WAS A LOT EASIER THAN WE THOUGHT!
THERE'S A LOT OF LAND, BUT IT'S A SMALL TOWN.
SEE THE BACK?
WE EVEN MADE FAN JACKETS.
ZENTA RYOTA
ZENTA RYOTA
THEN YOU SUDDENLY RETIRED!
HEY, ARE YOU GUYS FREE?
OH, YOU HAVE VISITORS. I WAS GOING TO ASK YOU GUYS OUT TO GO CRUISIN'.
I THOUGHT THAT MIGHT TAKE YOUR MIND OFF THAT ARTICLE.

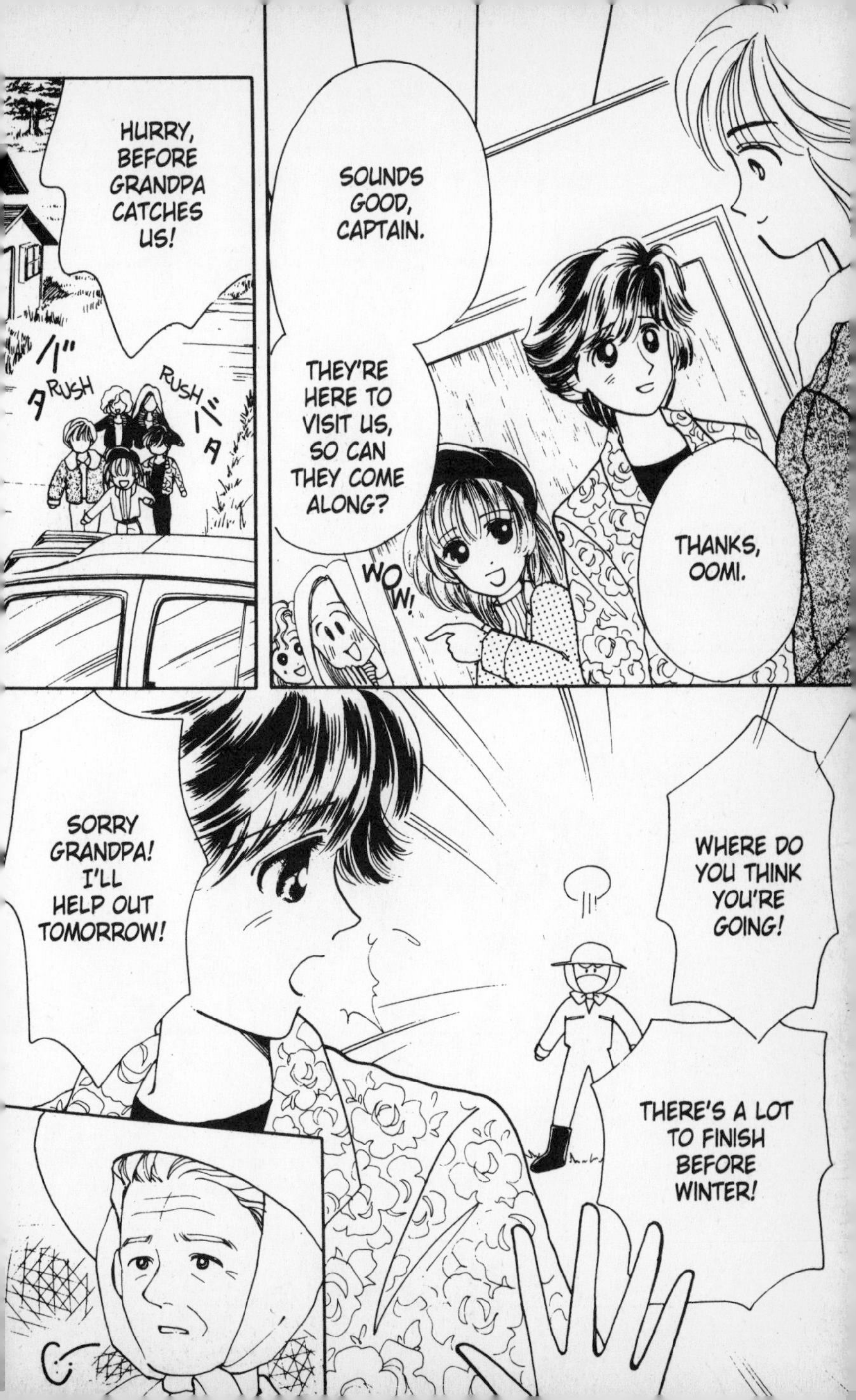
SOUNDS GOOD, CAPTAIN.
THEY'RE HERE TO VISIT US, SO CAN THEY COME ALONG?
THANKS, OOMI.
WOW!
HURRY, BEFORE GRANDPA CATCHES US!
RUSH
RUSH
WHERE DO YOU THINK YOU'RE GOING!
THERE'S A LOT TO FINISH BEFORE WINTER!
SORRY GRANDPA! I'LL HELP OUT TOMORROW!

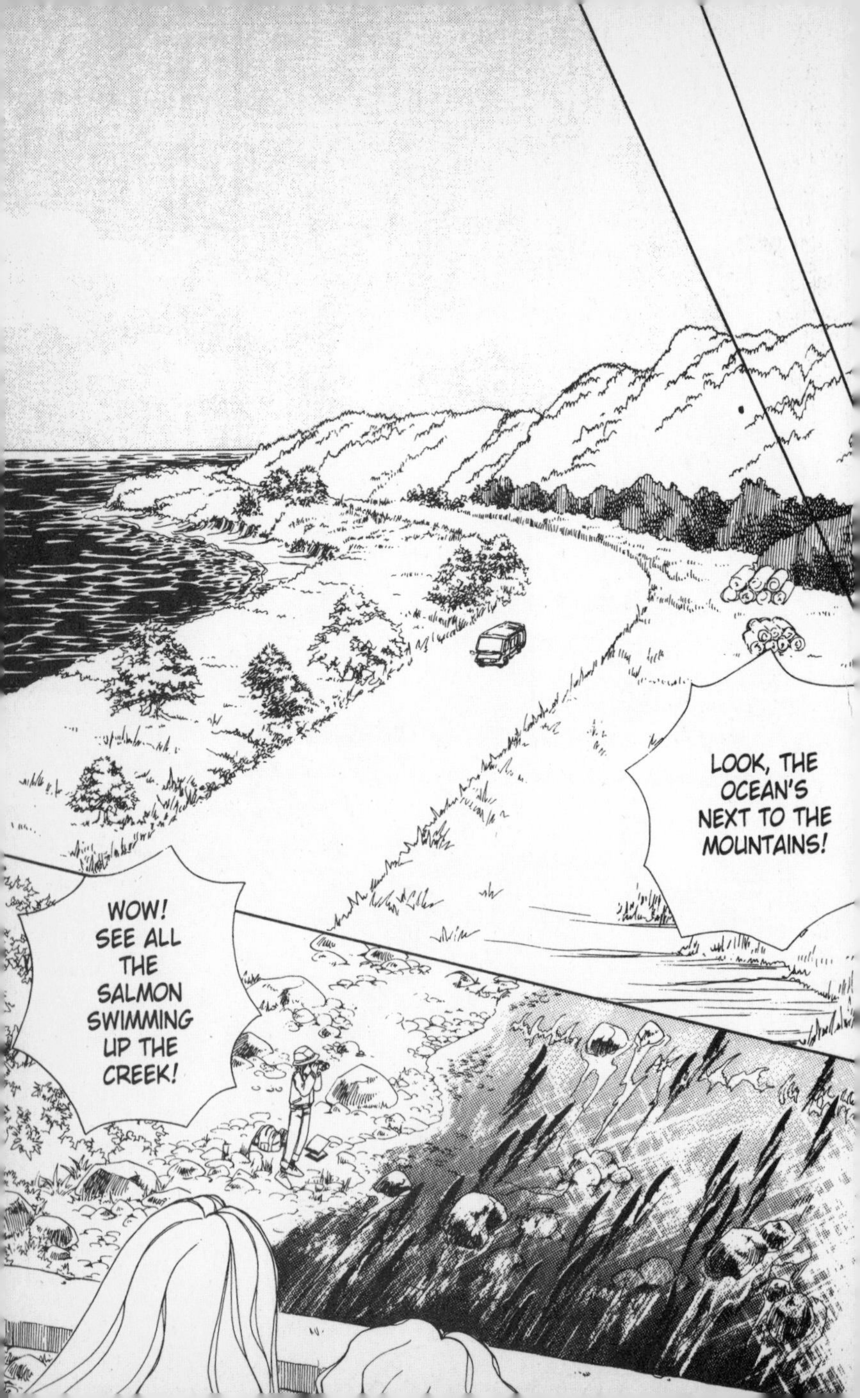
LOOK, THE OCEAN'S NEXT TO THE MOUNTAINS!
WOW! SEE ALL THE SALMON SWIMMING UP THE CREEK!

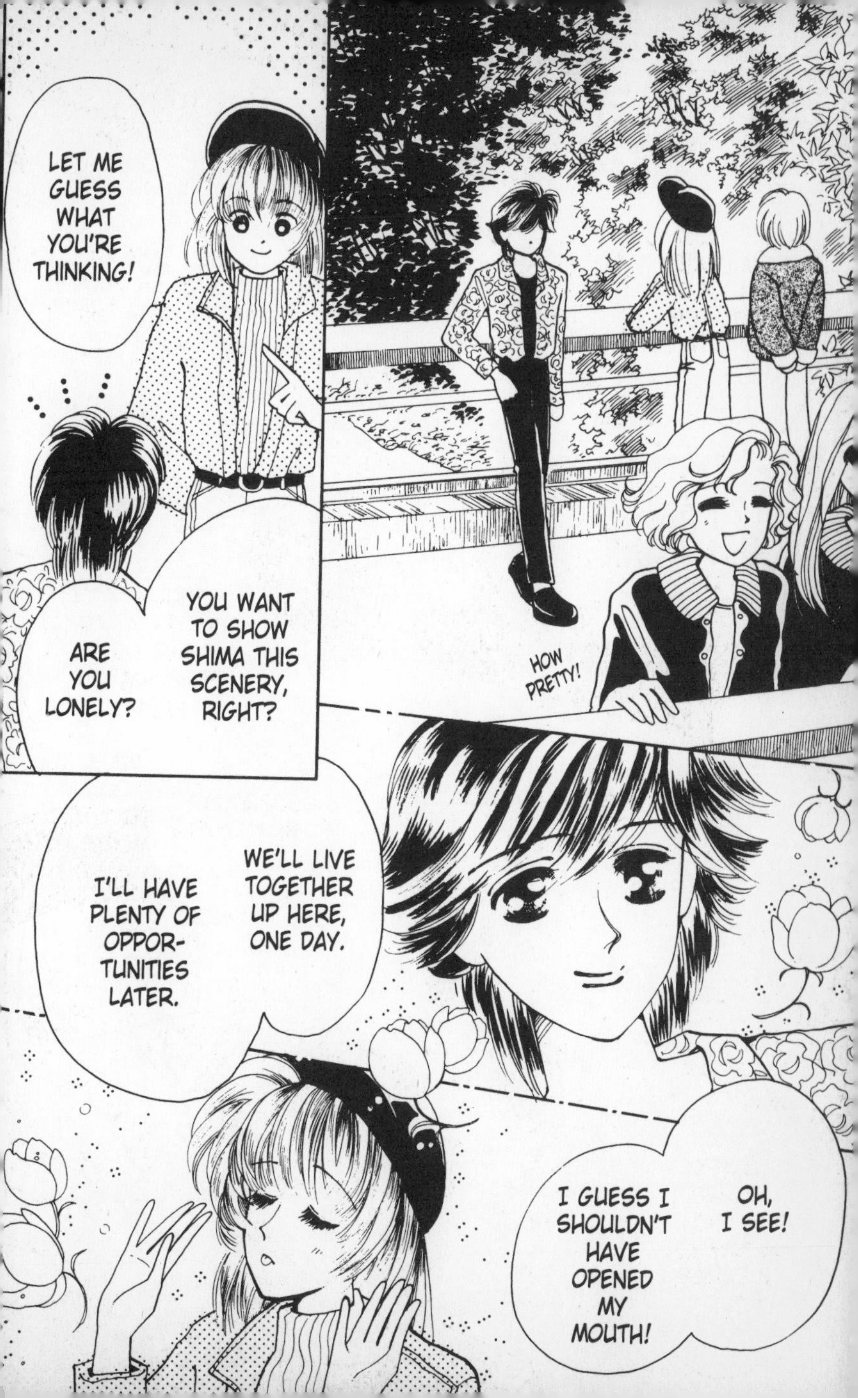
HOW PRETTY!
LET ME GUESS WHAT YOU'RE THINKING!
YOU WANT TO SHOW SHIMA THIS SCENERY, RIGHT?
ARE YOU LONELY?
WE'LL LIVE TOGETHER UP HERE, ONE DAY.
I'LL HAVE PLENTY OF OPPOR- TUNITIES LATER.
OH, I SEE!
I GUESS I SHOULDN'T HAVE OPENED MY MOUTH!

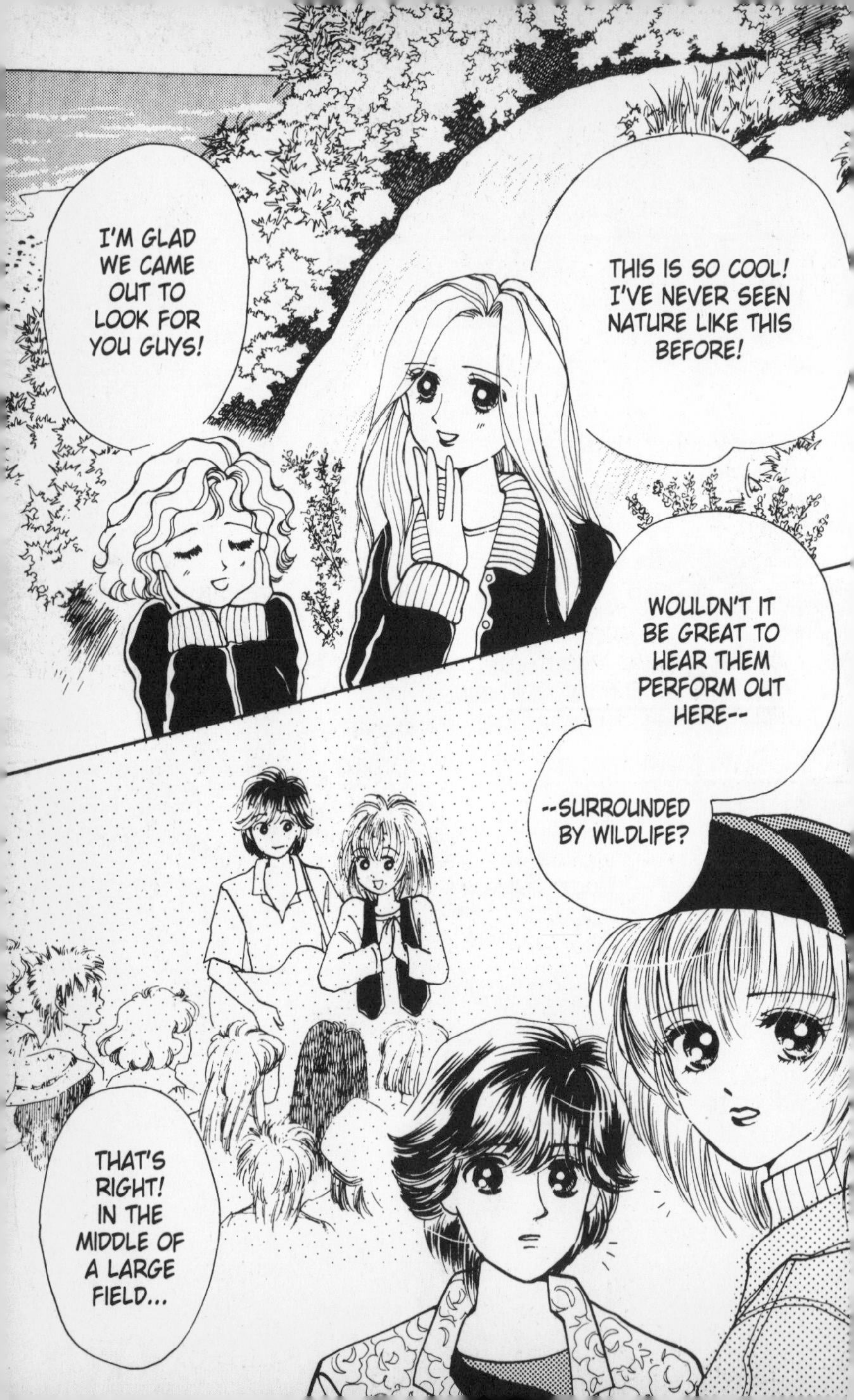
THIS IS SO COOL! I'VE NEVER SEEN NATURE LIKE THIS BEFORE!
I'M GLAD WE CAME OUT TO LOOK FOR YOU GUYS!
WOULDN'T IT BE GREAT TO HEAR THEM PERFORM OUT HERE--
--SURROUNDED BY WILDLIFE?
THAT'S RIGHT! IN THE MIDDLE OF A LARGE FIELD...

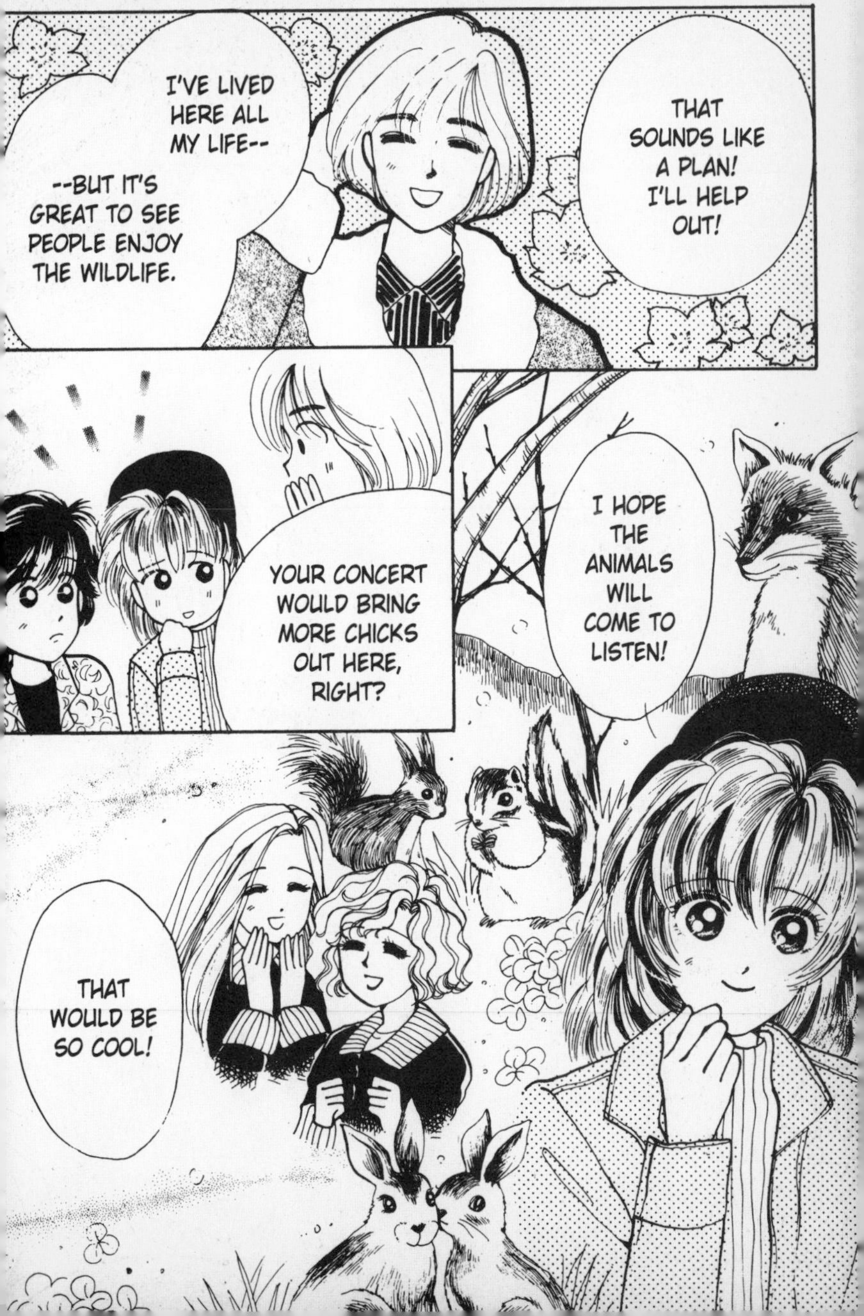
THAT SOUNDS LIKE A PLAN! I'LL HELP OUT!
I'VE LIVED HERE ALL MY LIFE--
--BUT IT'S GREAT TO SEE PEOPLE ENJOY THE WILDLIFE.
I HOPE THE ANIMALS WILL COME TO LISTEN!
THAT WOULD BE SO COOL!
YOUR CONCERT WOULD BRING MORE CHICKS OUT HERE, RIGHT?

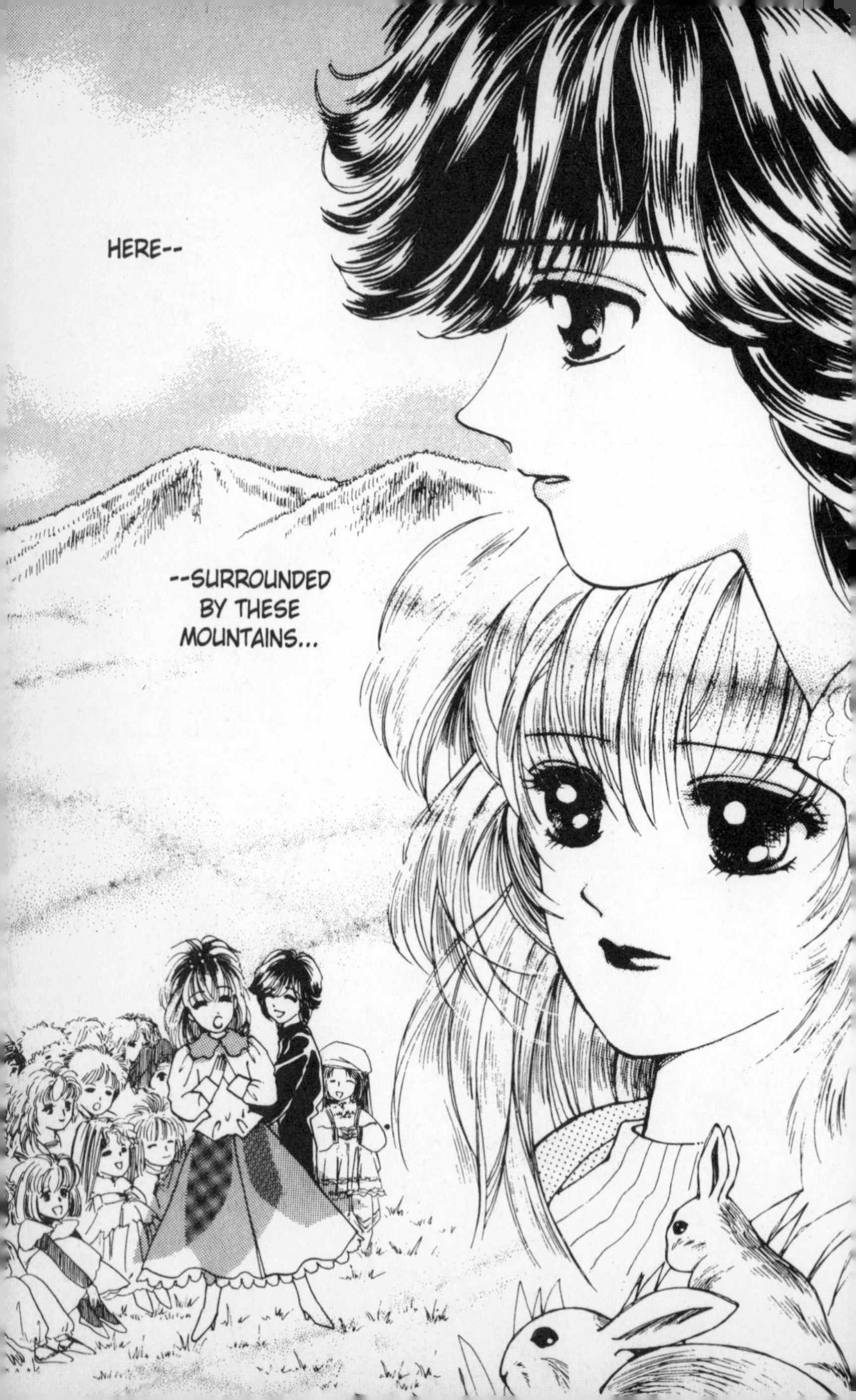
HERE--
--SURROUNDED BY THESE MOUNTAINS...

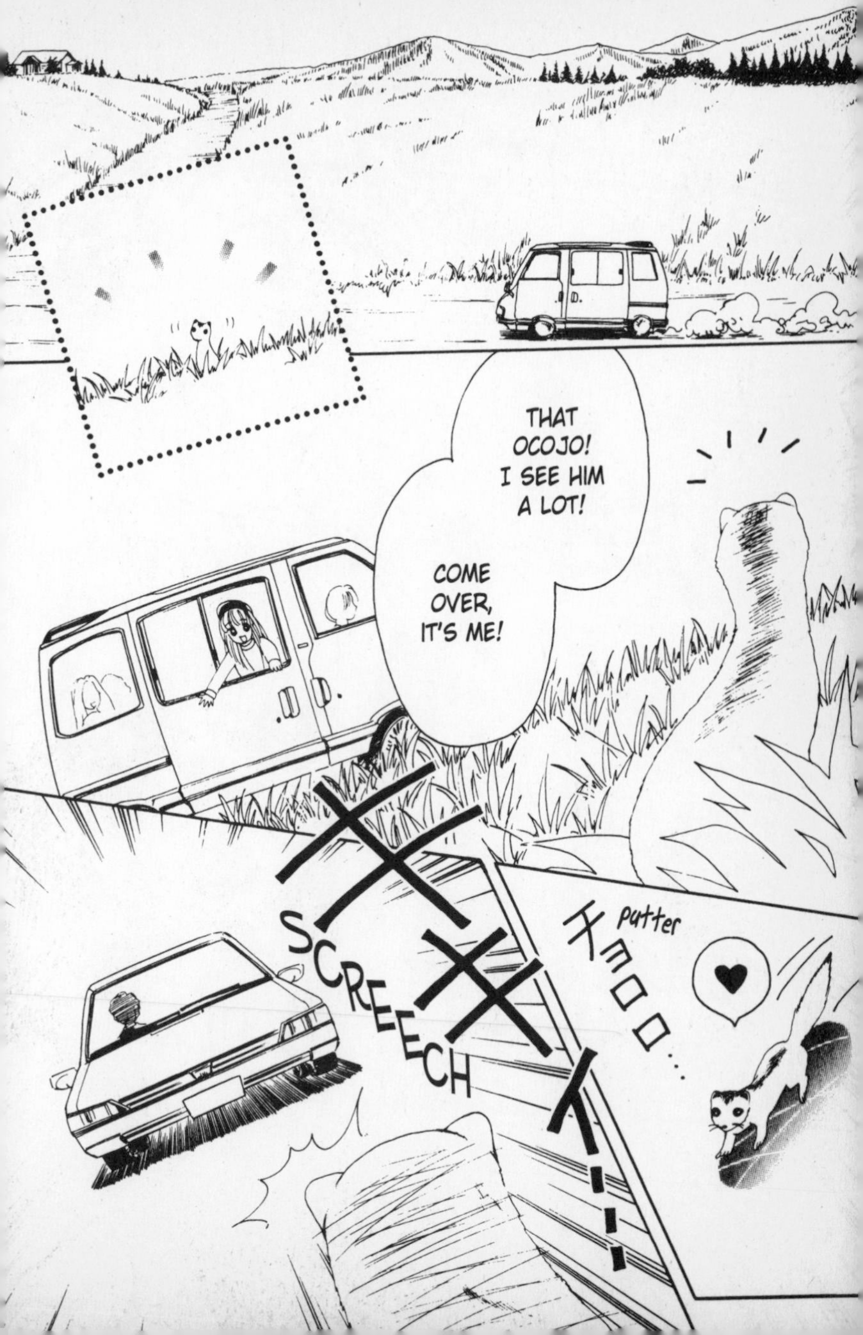
THAT OCOJO! I SEE HIM A LOT!
COME OVER, IT'S ME!
putter
チョロロ…
SCREEECH
キキ
ィーーー

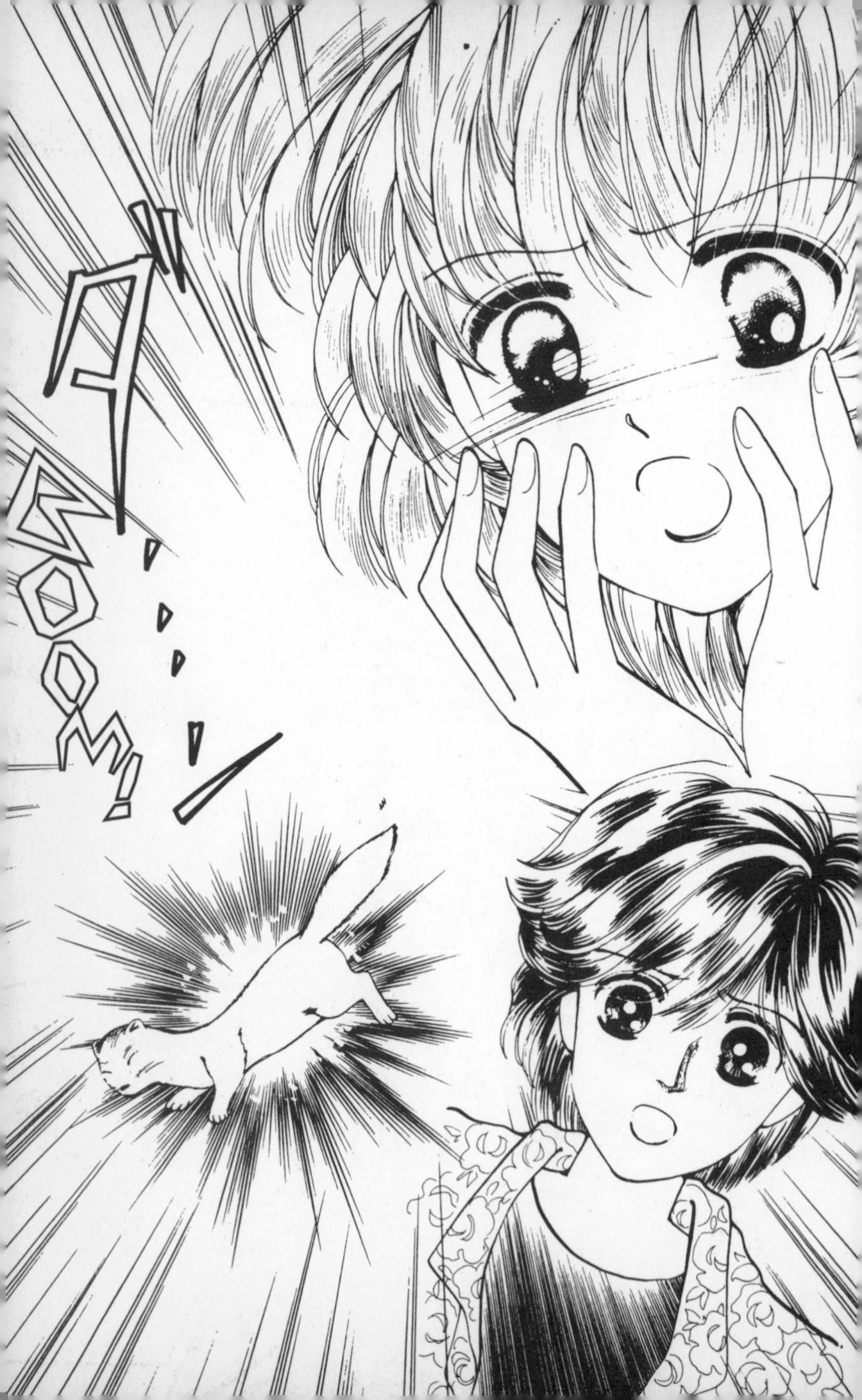
BOOM!

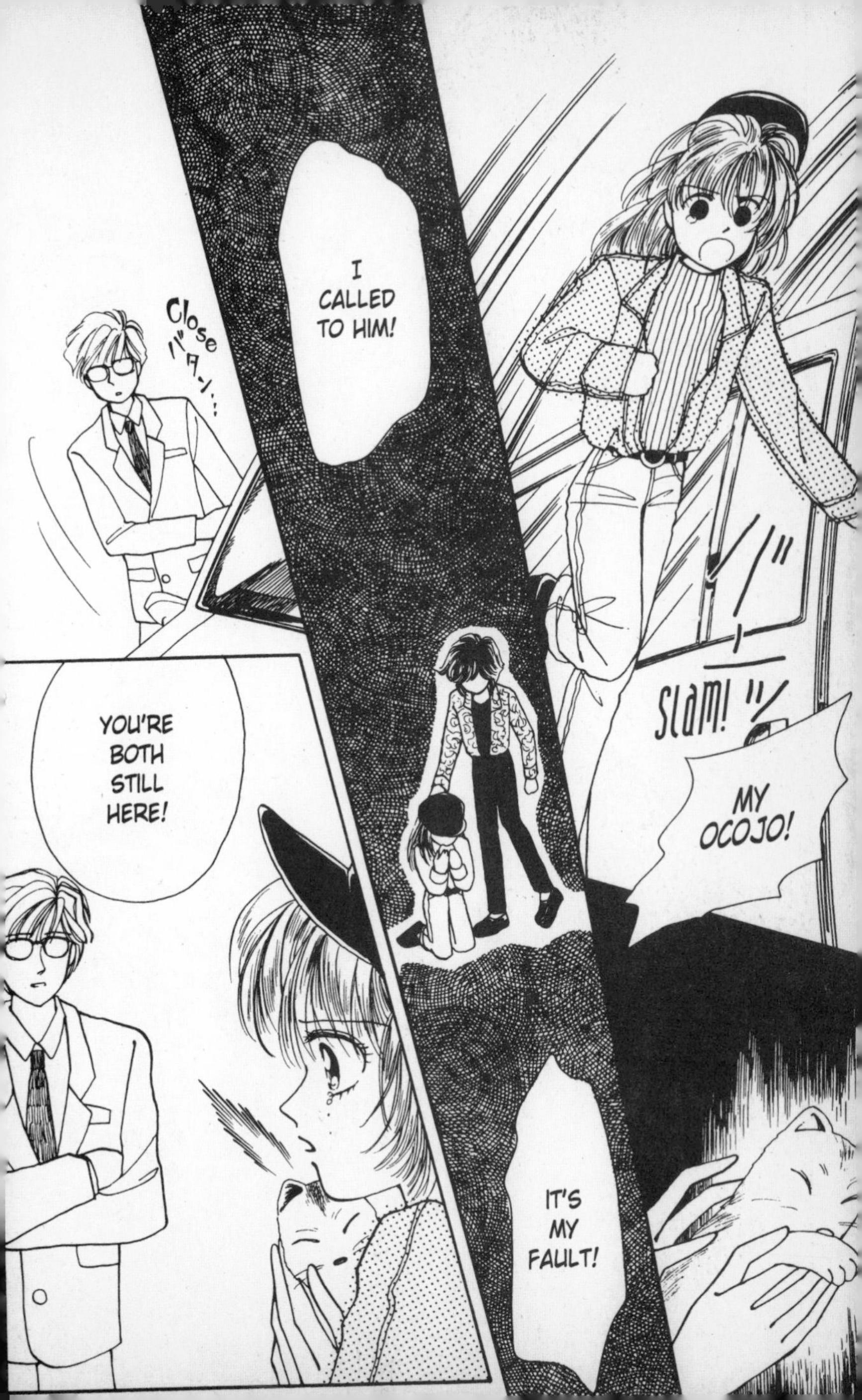
SLAM!
I CALLED TO HIM!
Close
バタン…
MY OCOJO!
IT'S MY FAULT!
YOU'RE BOTH STILL HERE!

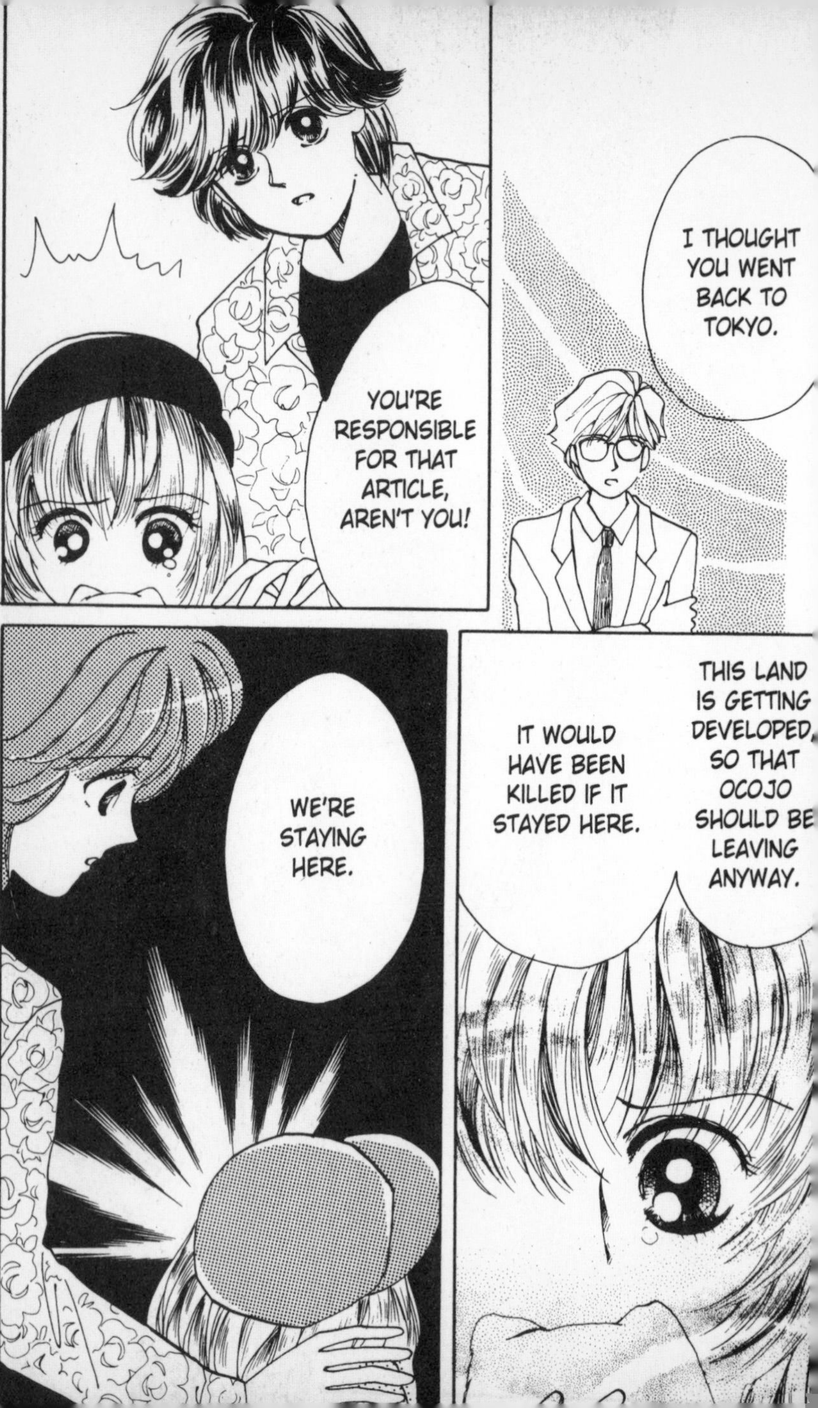
I THOUGHT YOU WENT BACK TO TOKYO.
YOU'RE RESPONSIBLE FOR THAT ARTICLE, AREN'T YOU!
THIS LAND IS GETTING DEVELOPED, SO THAT OCOJO SHOULD BE LEAVING ANYWAY.
IT WOULD HAVE BEEN KILLED IF IT STAYED HERE.
WE'RE STAYING HERE.

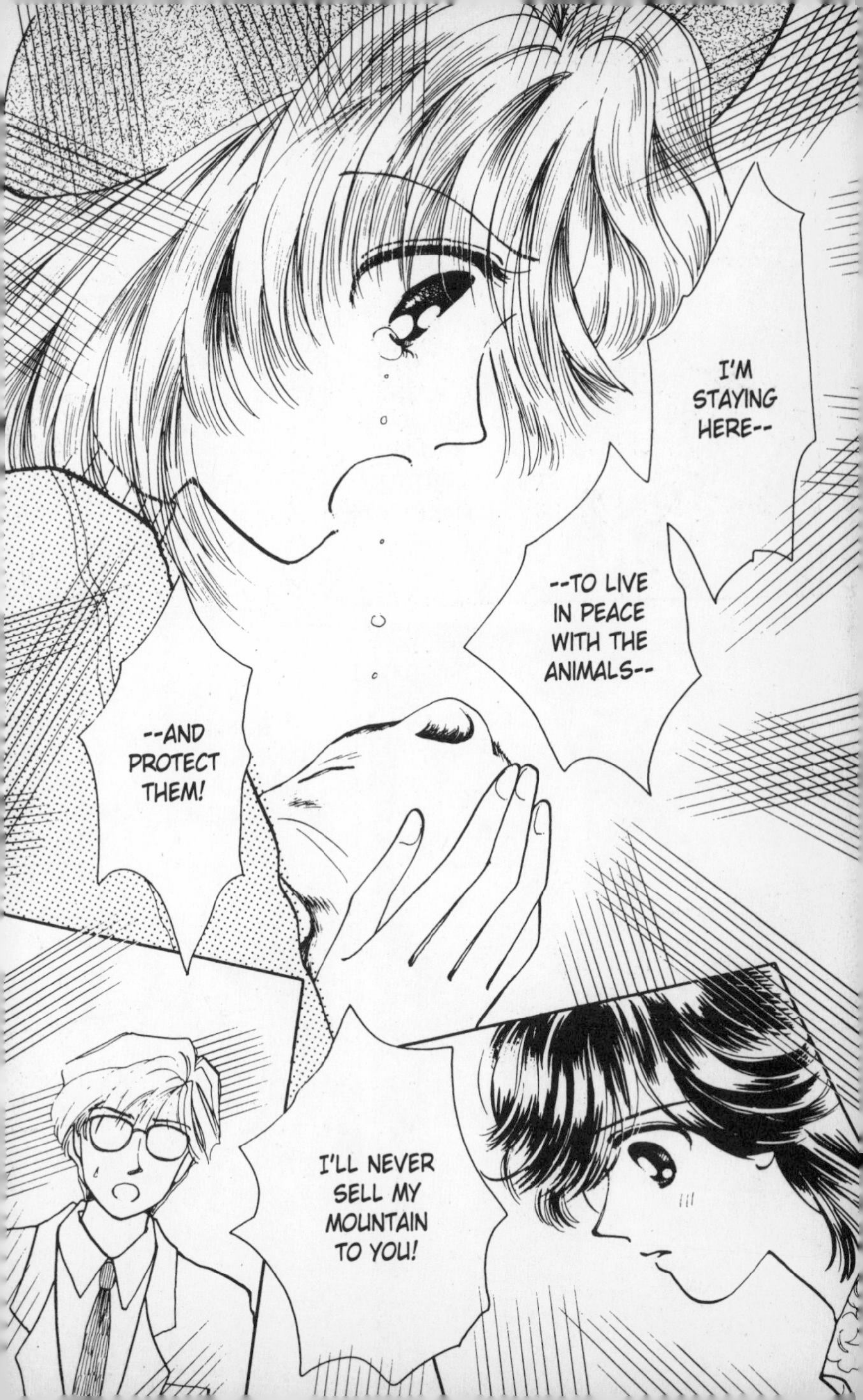
I'M STAYING HERE--
--TO LIVE IN PEACE WITH THE ANIMALS--
--AND PROTECT THEM!
I'LL NEVER SELL MY MOUNTAIN TO YOU!

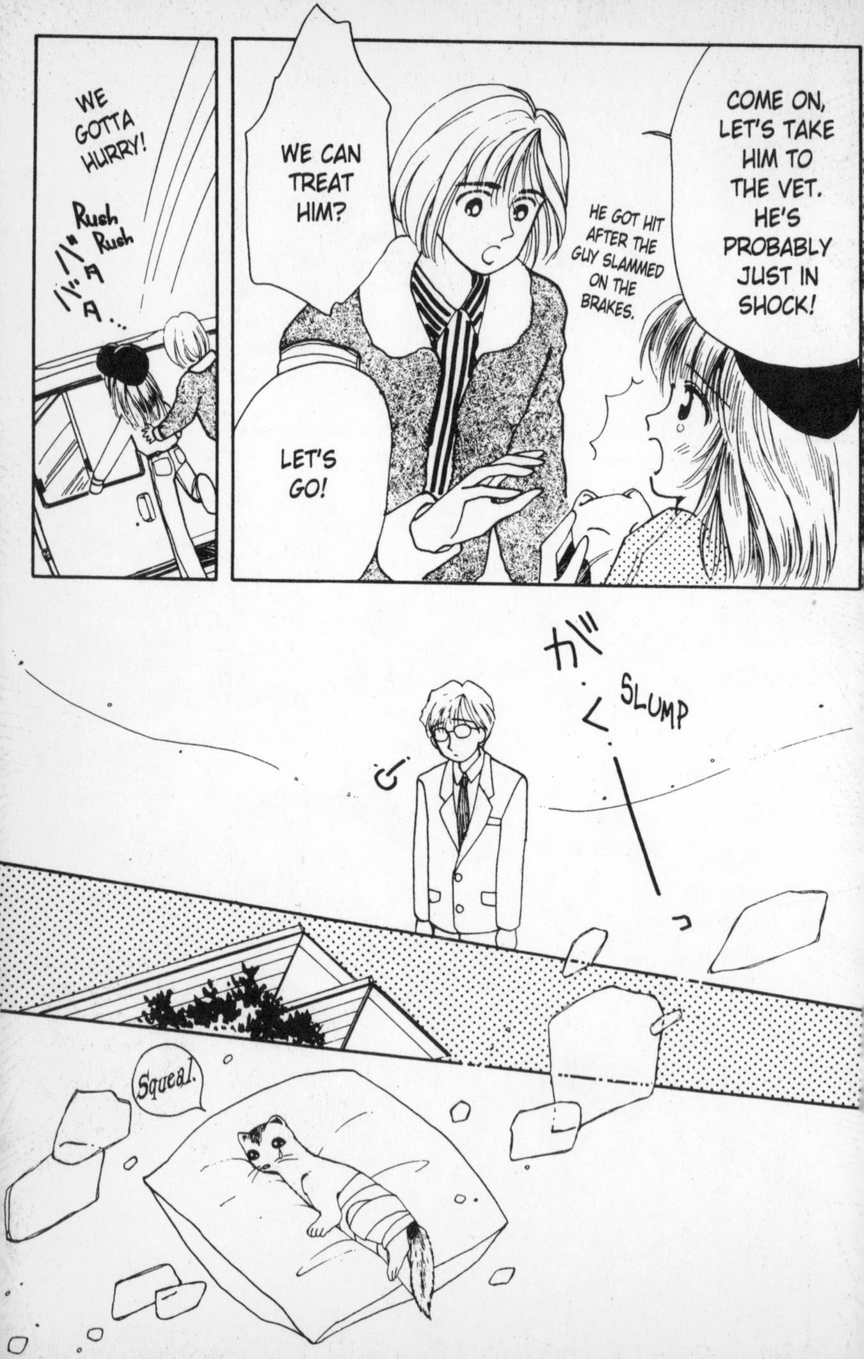

COME ON, LET'S TAKE HIM TO THE VET. HE'S PROBABLY JUST IN SHOCK!
HE GOT HIT AFTER THE GUY SLAMMED ON THE BRAKES.
WE CAN TREAT HIM?
LET'S GO!
WE GOTTA HURRY!
Rush Rush
SLUMP
Squeal.

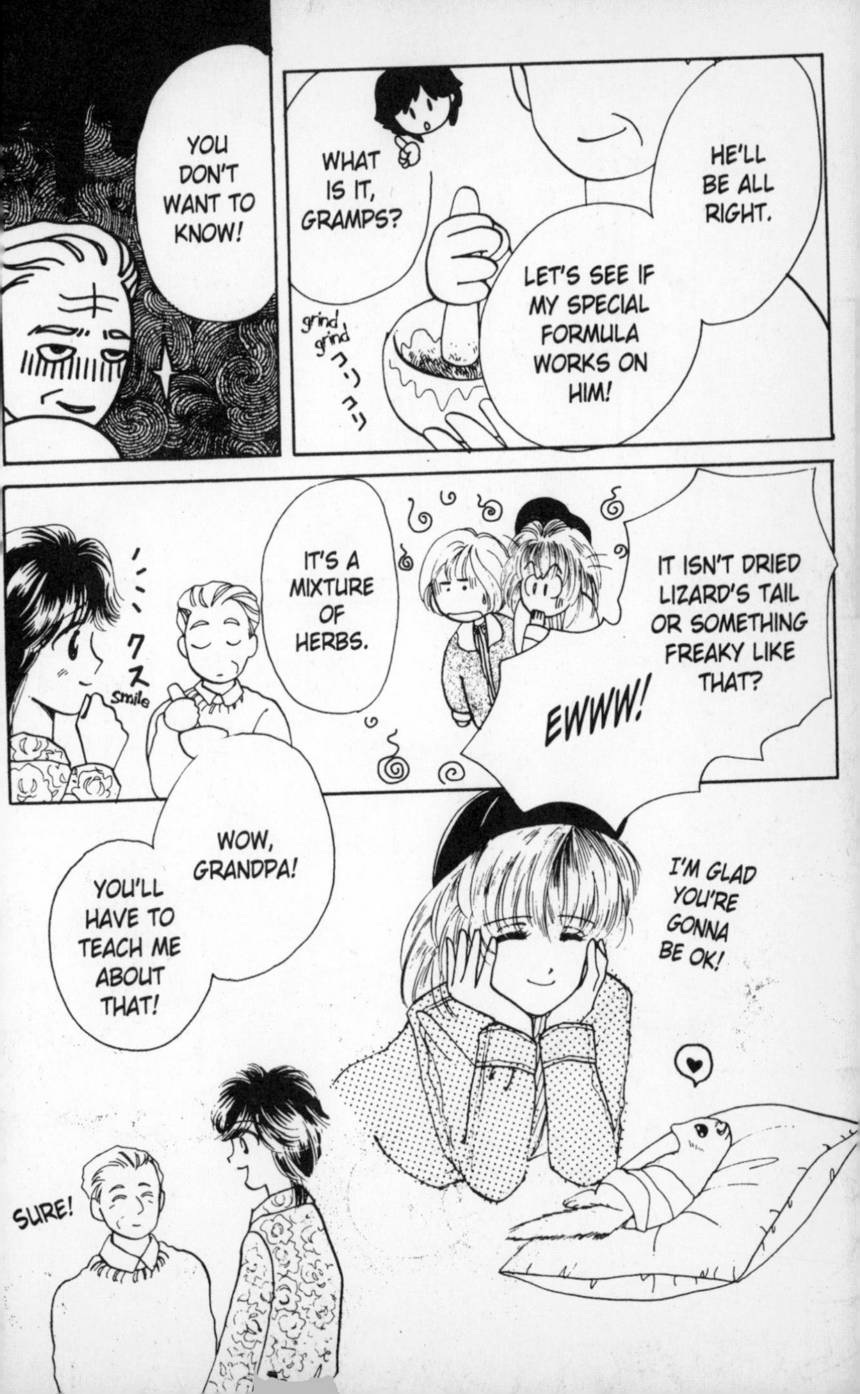
HE'LL BE ALL RIGHT.
LET'S SEE IF MY SPECIAL FORMULA WORKS ON HIM!
WHAT IS IT, GRAMPS?
grind grind
コリコリ
YOU DON'T WANT TO KNOW!
IT ISN'T DRIED LIZARD'S TAIL OR SOMETHING FREAKY LIKE THAT?
EWWW!
IT'S A MIXTURE OF HERBS.
クス
smile
I'M GLAD YOU'RE GONNA BE OK!
WOW, GRANDPA!
YOU'LL HAVE TO TEACH ME ABOUT THAT!
SURE!

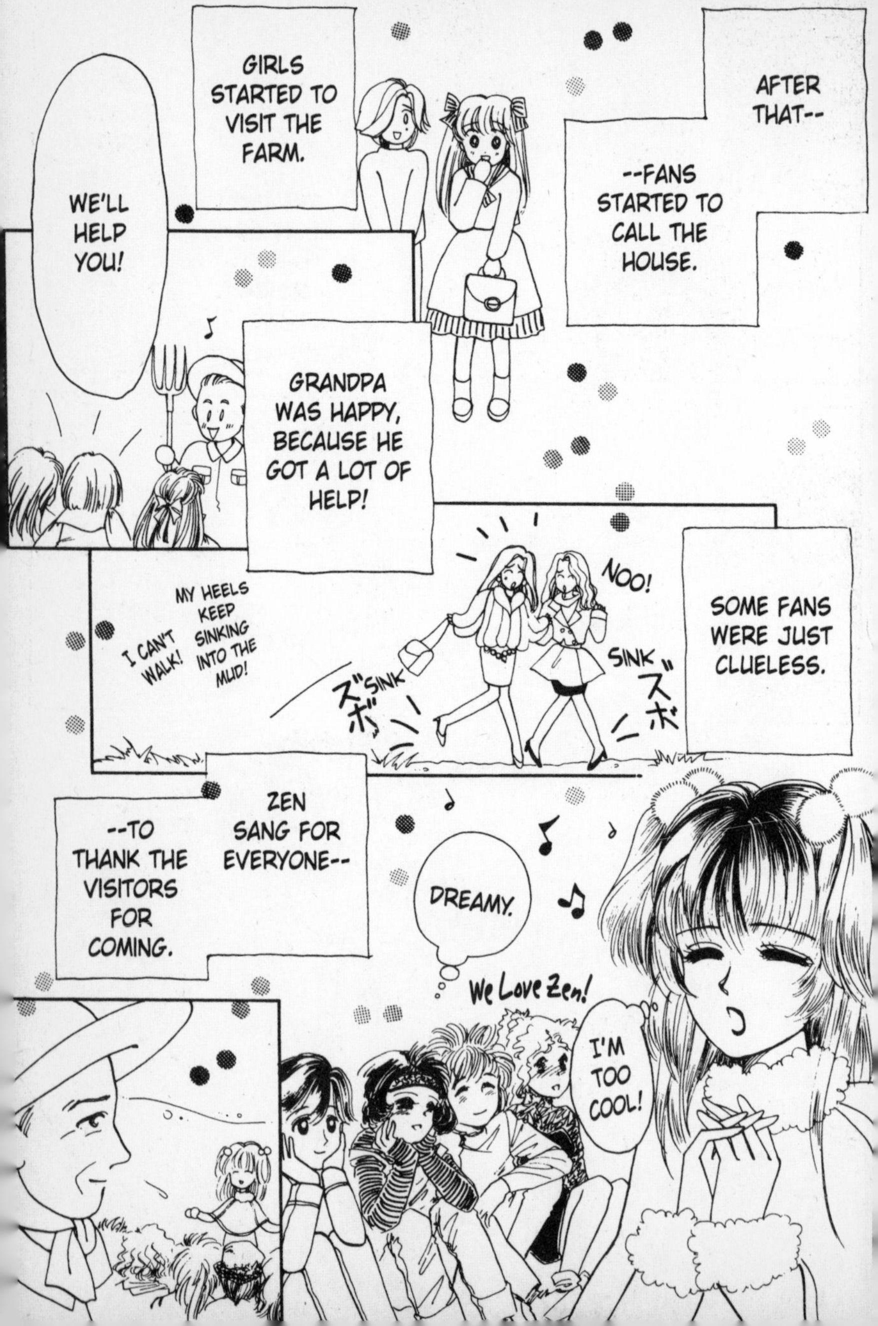
AFTER THAT--
--FANS STARTED TO CALL THE HOUSE.
GIRLS STARTED TO VISIT THE FARM.
GRANDPA WAS HAPPY, BECAUSE HE GOT A LOT OF HELP!
WE'LL HELP YOU!
SOME FANS WERE JUST CLUELESS.
NOO!
SINK ズボ
SINK ズボ
MY HEELS KEEP SINKING INTO THE MUD!
I CAN'T WALK!
ZEN SANG FOR EVERYONE--
--TO THANK THE VISITORS FOR COMING.
I'M TOO COOL!
We Love Zen!
DREAMY.

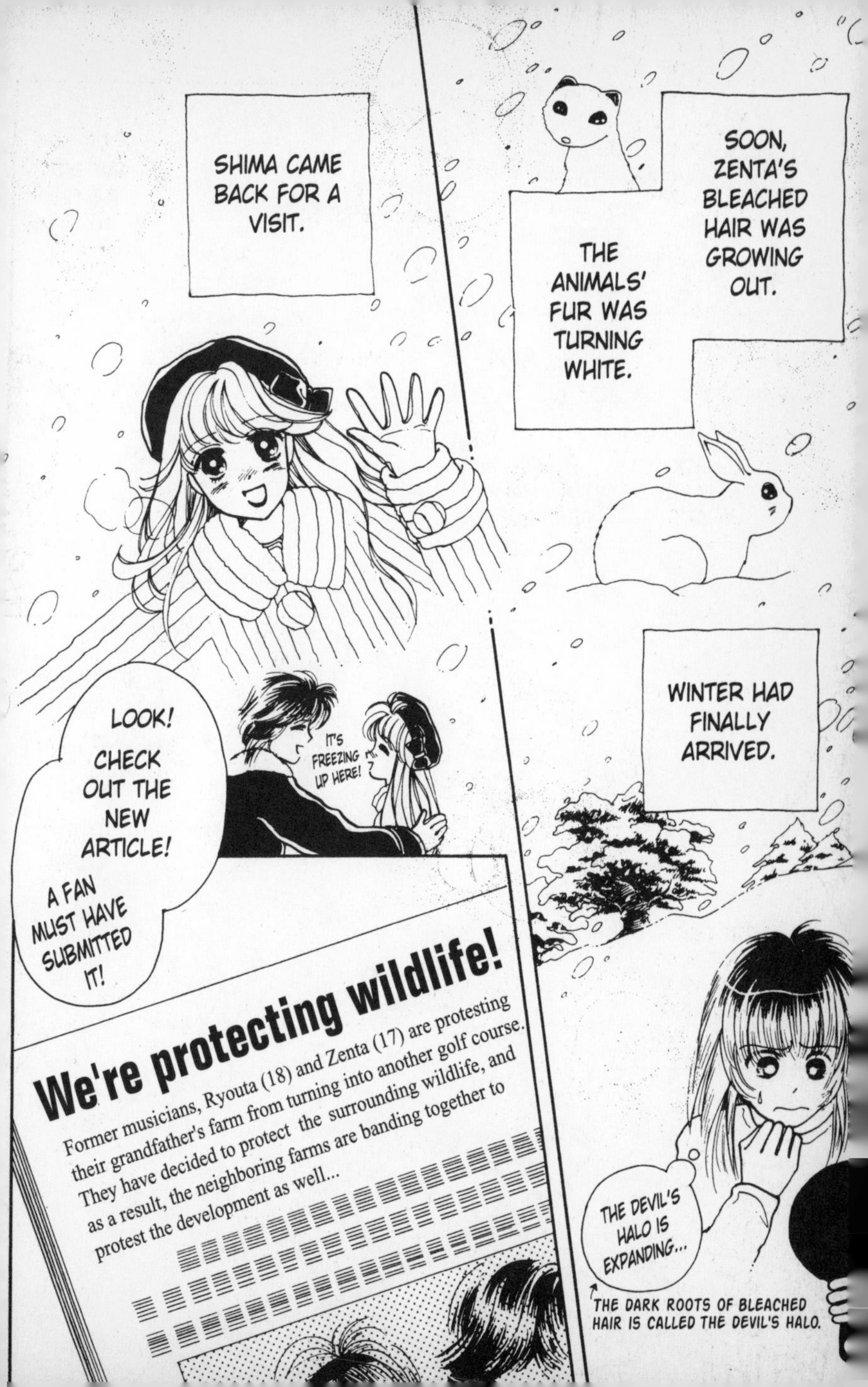
SOON, ZENTA'S BLEACHED HAIR WAS GROWING OUT.
THE ANIMALS' FUR WAS TURNING WHITE.
WINTER HAD FINALLY ARRIVED.
THE DEVIL'S HALO IS EXPANDING...
THE DARK ROOTS OF BLEACHED HAIR IS CALLED THE DEVIL'S HALO.
SHIMA CAME BACK FOR A VISIT.
IT'S FREEZING UP HERE!
LOOK! CHECK OUT THE NEW ARTICLE!
A FAN MUST HAVE SUBMITTED IT!
We're protecting wildlife!
Former musicians, Ryouta (18) and Zenta (17) are protesting their grandfather's farm from turning into another golf course. They have decided to protect the surrounding wildlife, and as a result, the neighboring farms are banding together to protest the development as well...

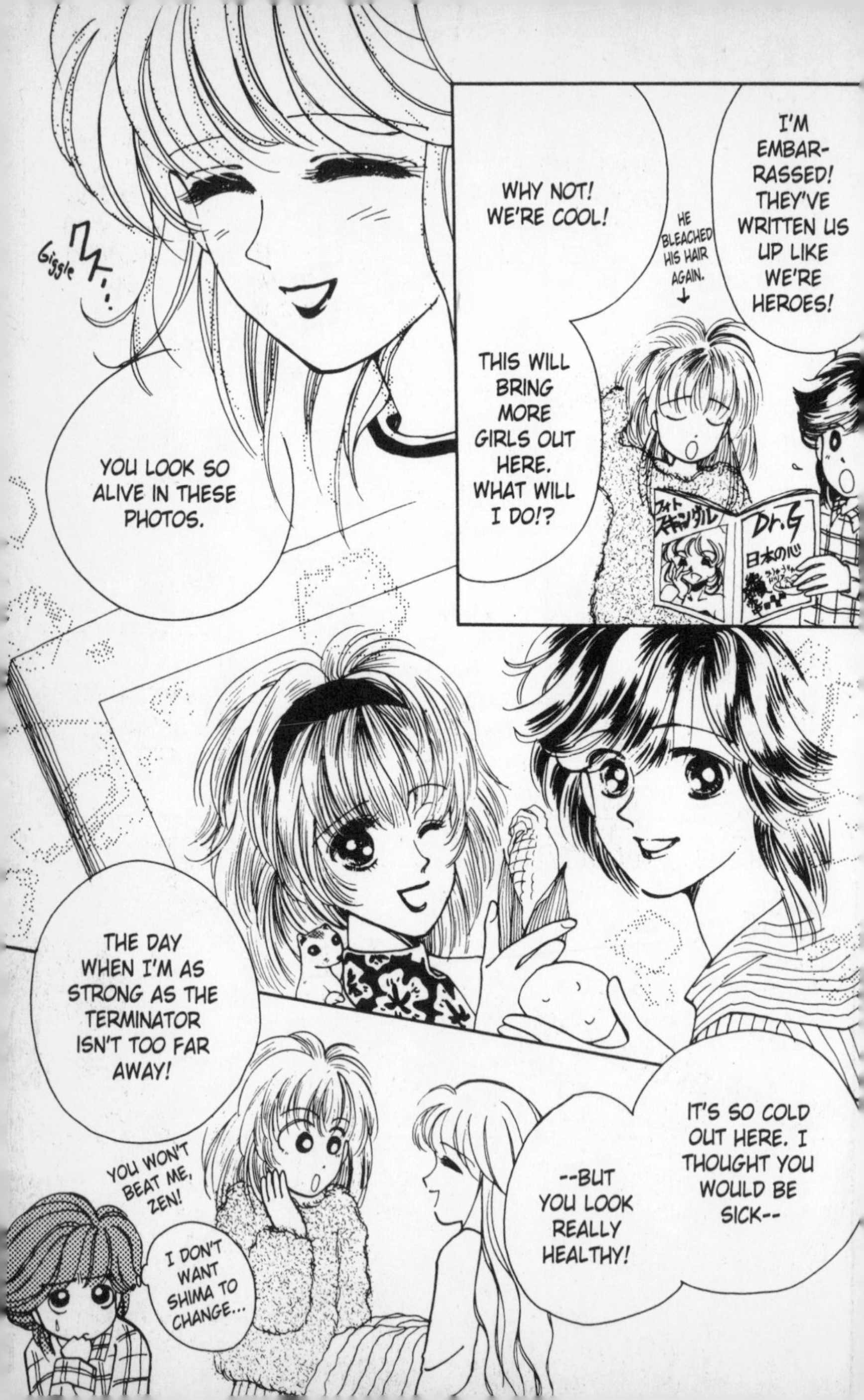
I'M EMBARRASSED! THEY'VE WRITTEN US UP LIKE WE'RE HEROES!
HE BLEACHED HIS HAIR AGAIN.
WHY NOT! WE'RE COOL!
THIS WILL BRING MORE GIRLS OUT HERE. WHAT WILL I DO!?
Dr.G
日本の心
Giggle
YOU LOOK SO ALIVE IN THESE PHOTOS.
THE DAY WHEN I'M AS STRONG AS THE TERMINATOR ISN'T TOO FAR AWAY!
IT'S SO COLD OUT HERE. I THOUGHT YOU WOULD BE SICK--
--BUT YOU LOOK REALLY HEALTHY!
YOU WON'T BEAT ME, ZEN!
I DON'T WANT SHIMA TO CHANGE...

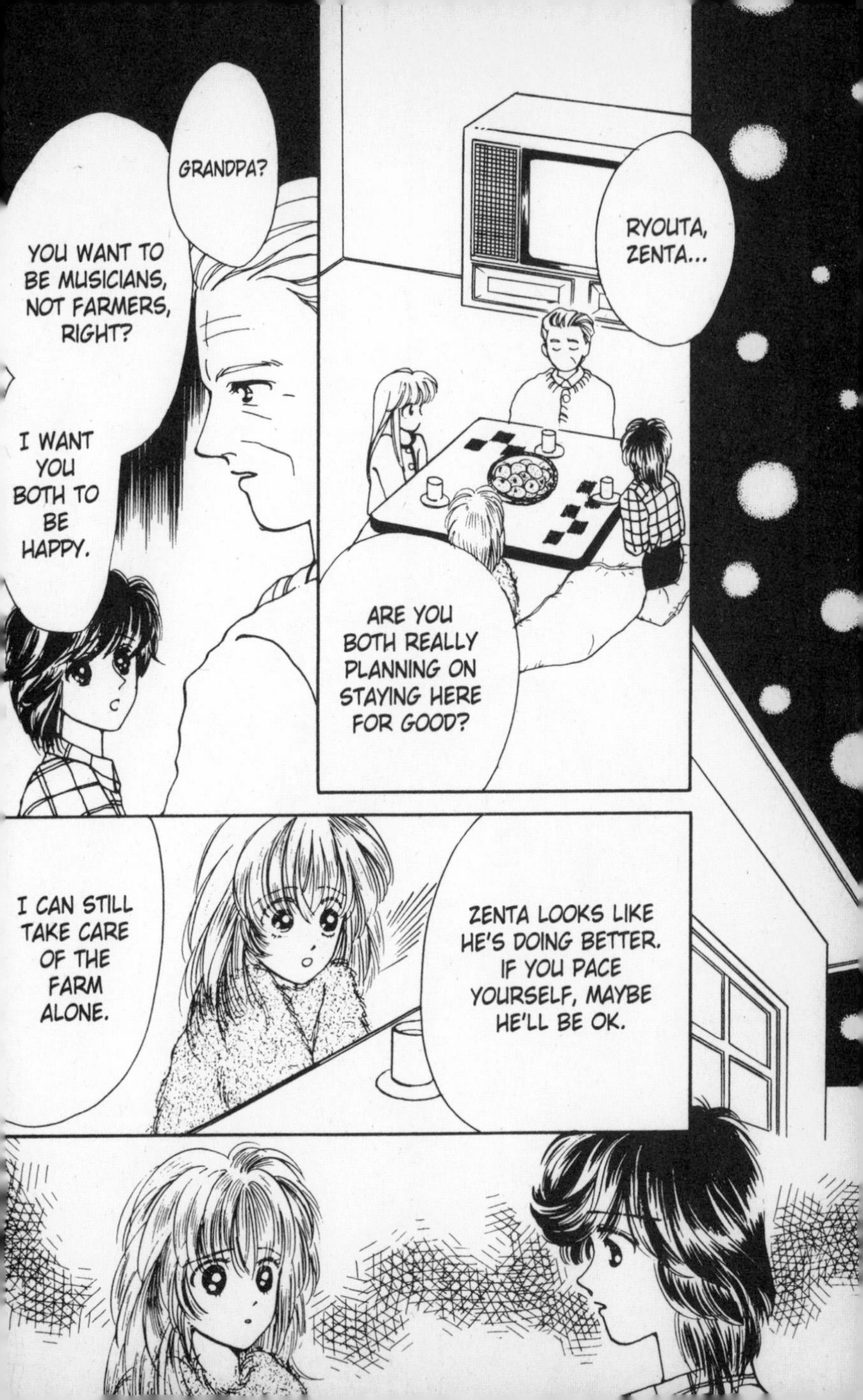
RYOUTA, ZENTA...
ARE YOU BOTH REALLY PLANNING ON STAYING HERE FOR GOOD?
GRANDPA?
YOU WANT TO BE MUSICIANS, NOT FARMERS, RIGHT?
I WANT YOU BOTH TO BE HAPPY.
ZENTA LOOKS LIKE HE'S DOING BETTER. IF YOU PACE YOURSELF, MAYBE HE'LL BE OK.
I CAN STILL TAKE CARE OF THE FARM ALONE.

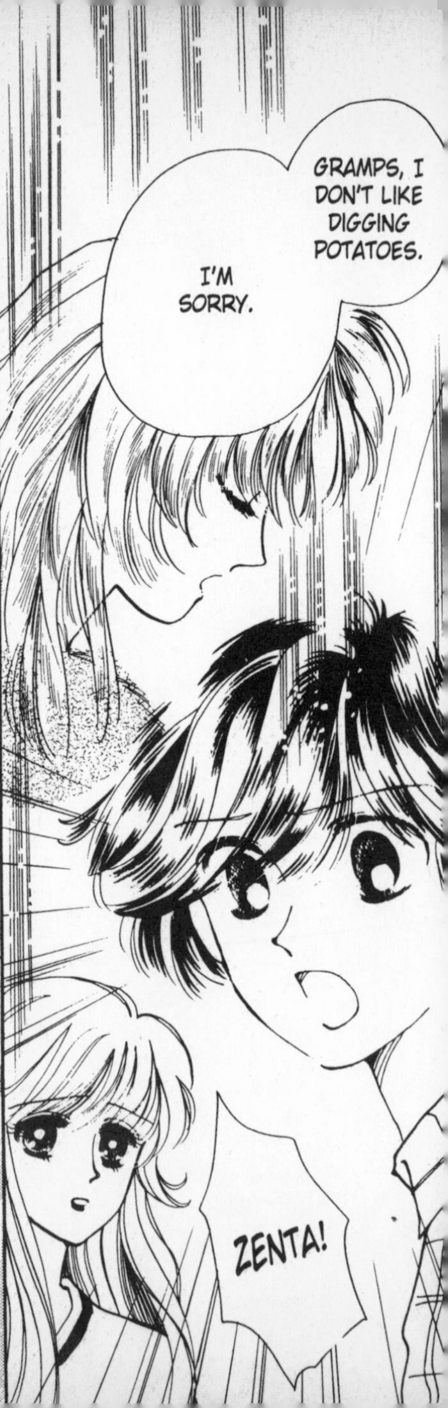
GRAMPS, I DON'T LIKE DIGGING POTATOES.
I'M SORRY.
ZENTA!
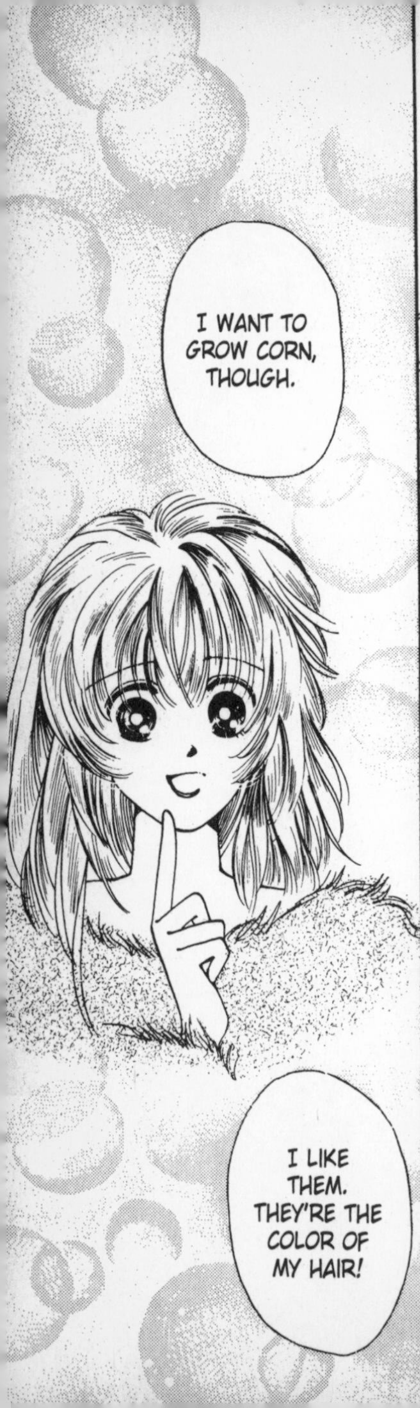
I WANT TO GROW CORN, THOUGH.
I LIKE THEM. THEY'RE THE COLOR OF MY HAIR!

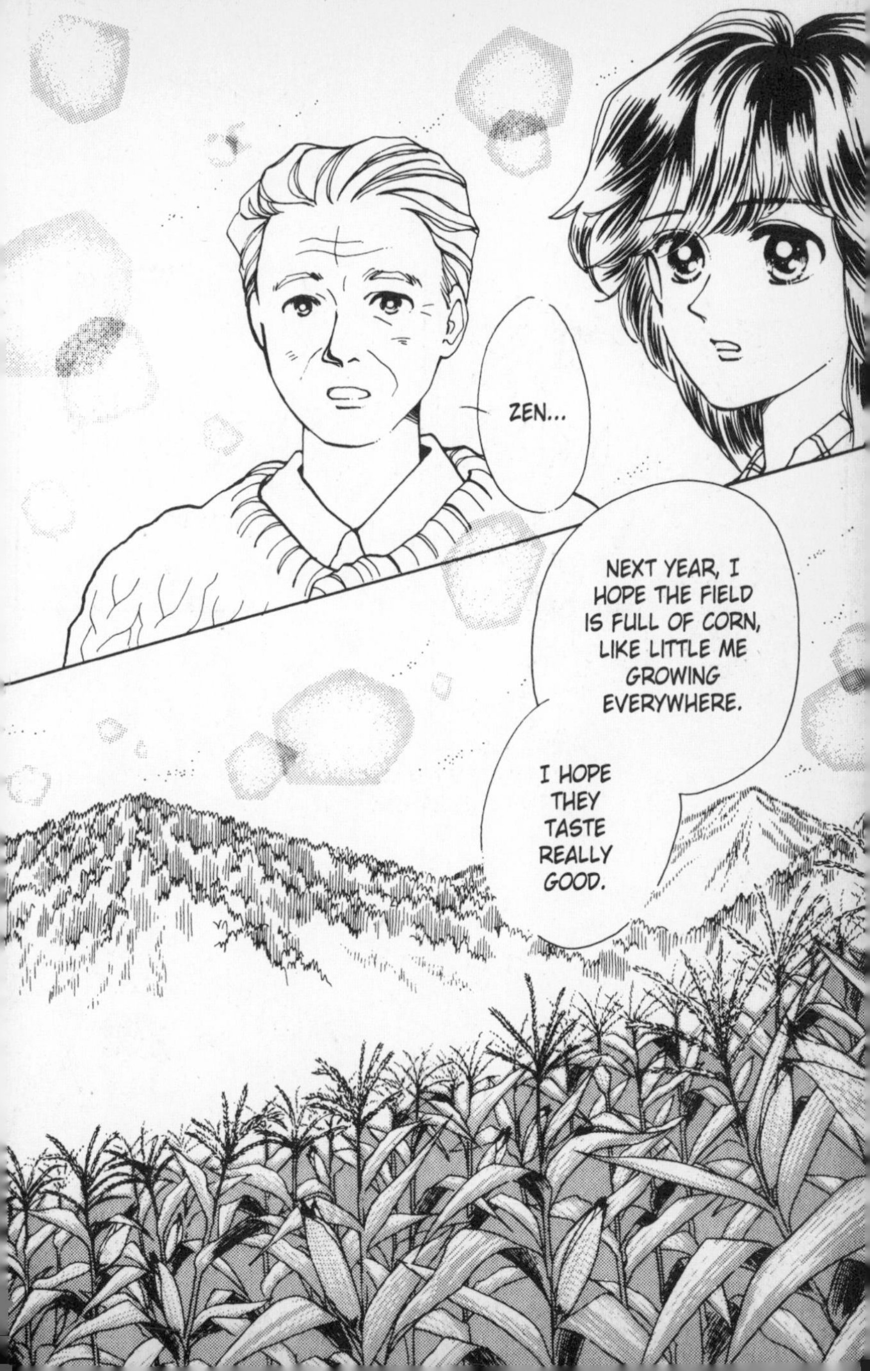
ZEN...
NEXT YEAR, I HOPE THE FIELD IS FULL OF CORN, LIKE LITTLE ME GROWING EVERYWHERE.
I HOPE THEY TASTE REALLY GOOD.

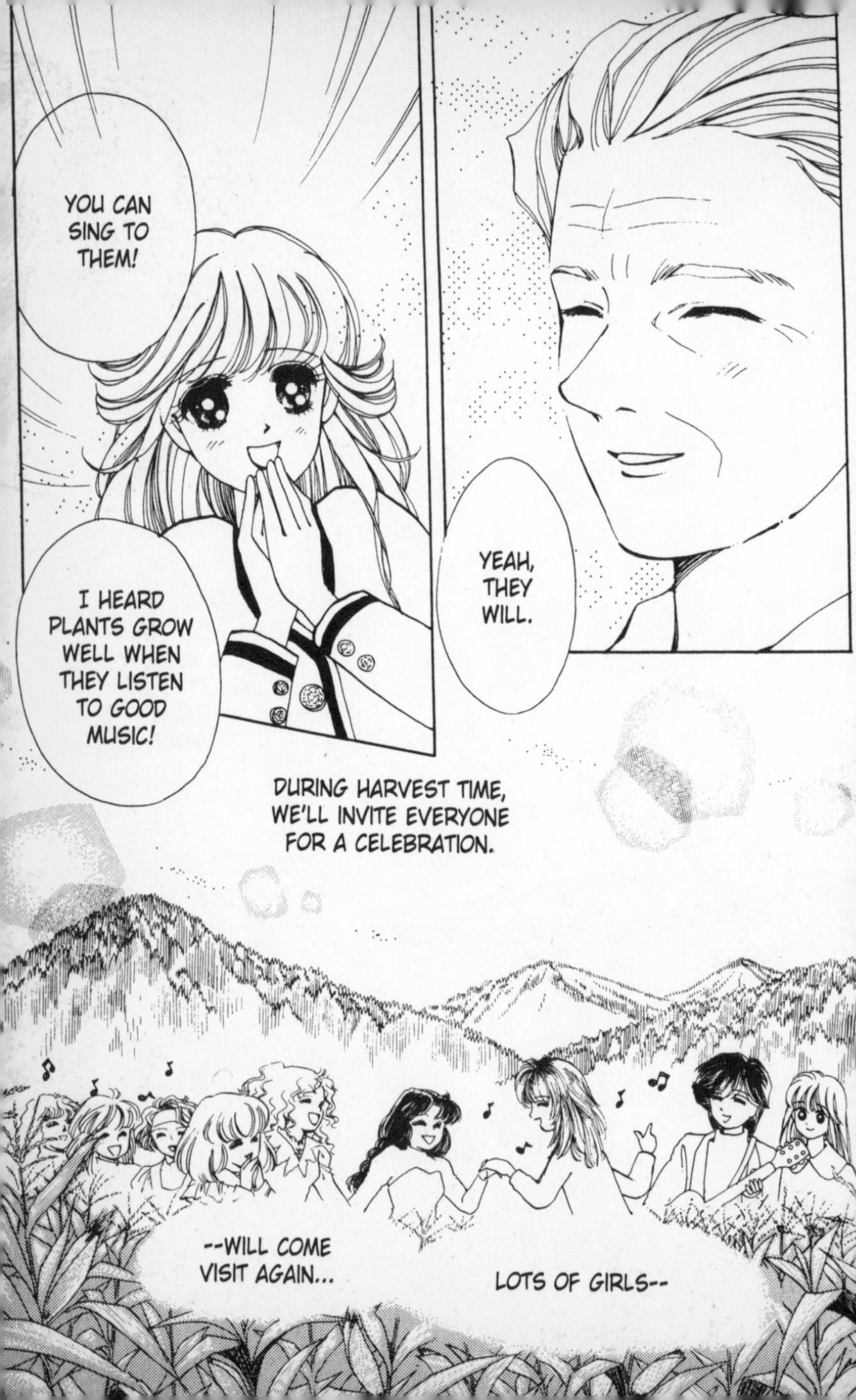
YEAH, THEY WILL.
YOU CAN SING TO THEM!
I HEARD PLANTS GROW WELL WHEN THEY LISTEN TO GOOD MUSIC!
DURING HARVEST TIME, WE'LL INVITE EVERYONE FOR A CELEBRATION.
LOTS OF GIRLS--
--WILL COME VISIT AGAIN...

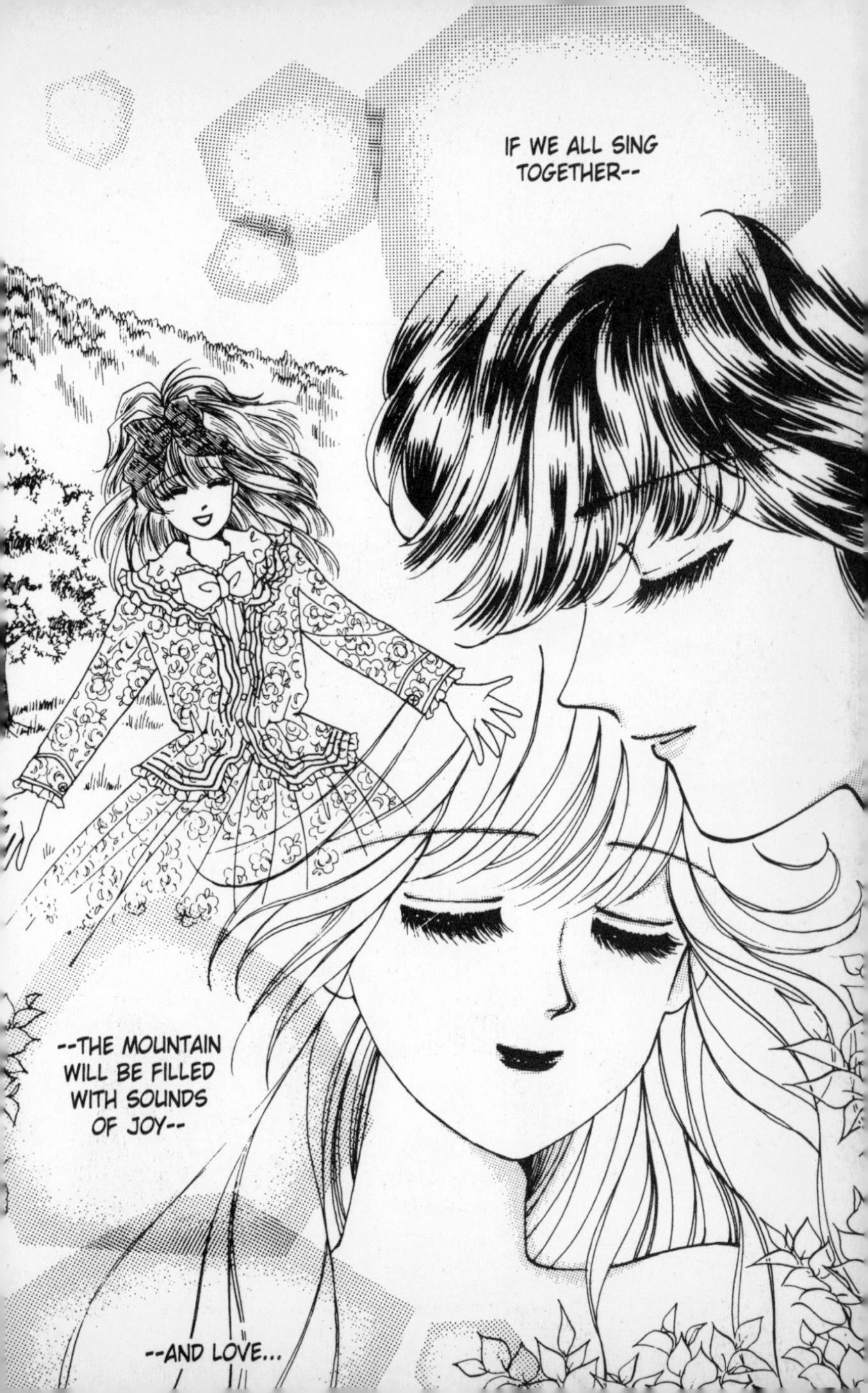
IF WE ALL SING TOGETHER--
--THE MOUNTAIN WILL BE FILLED WITH SOUNDS OF JOY--
--AND LOVE...

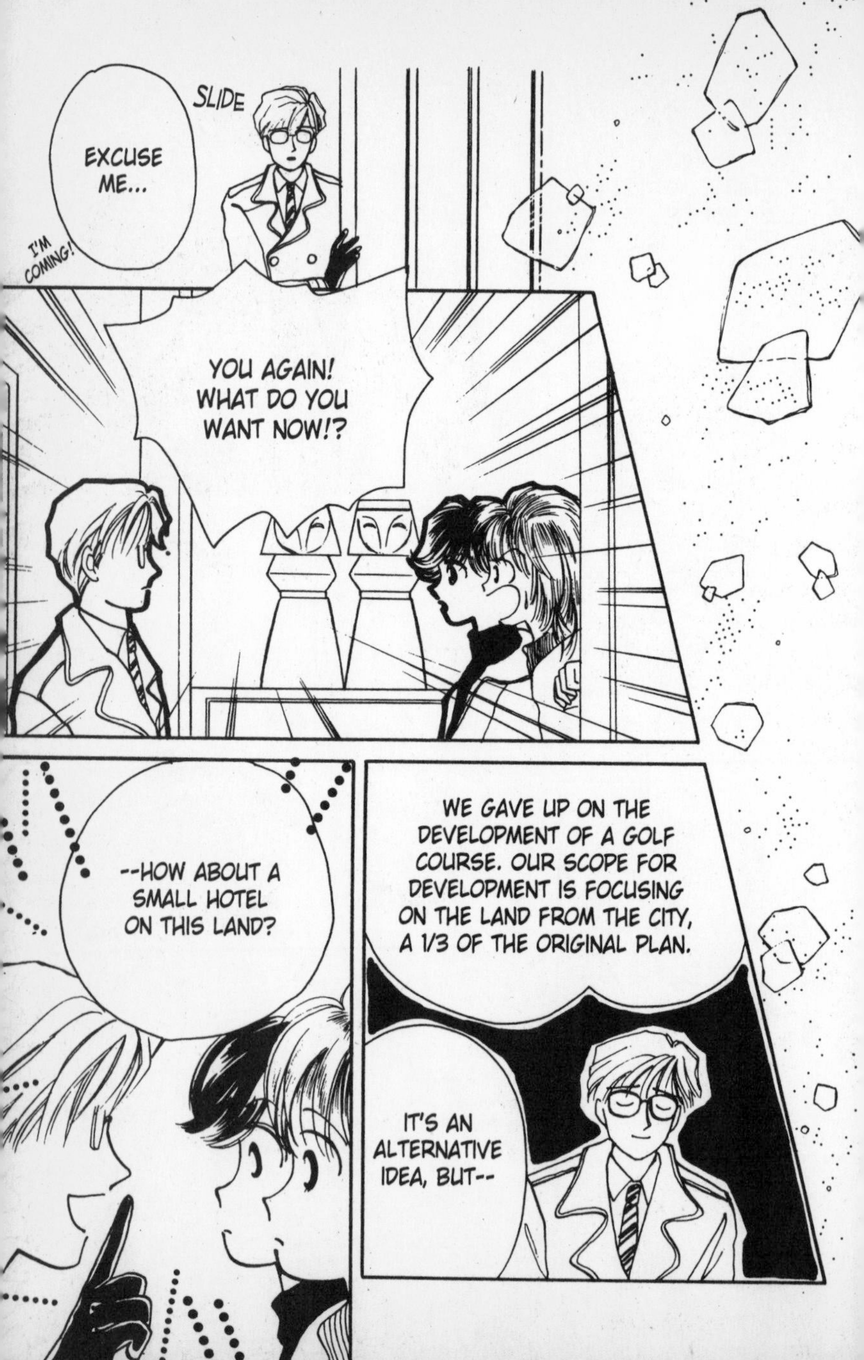
SLIDE
EXCUSE ME...
I'M COMING!
YOU AGAIN! WHAT DO YOU WANT NOW!?
WE GAVE UP ON THE DEVELOPMENT OF A GOLF COURSE. OUR SCOPE FOR DEVELOPMENT IS FOCUSING ON THE LAND FROM THE CITY, A 1/3 OF THE ORIGINAL PLAN.
IT'S AN ALTERNATIVE IDEA, BUT--
--HOW ABOUT A SMALL HOTEL ON THIS LAND?

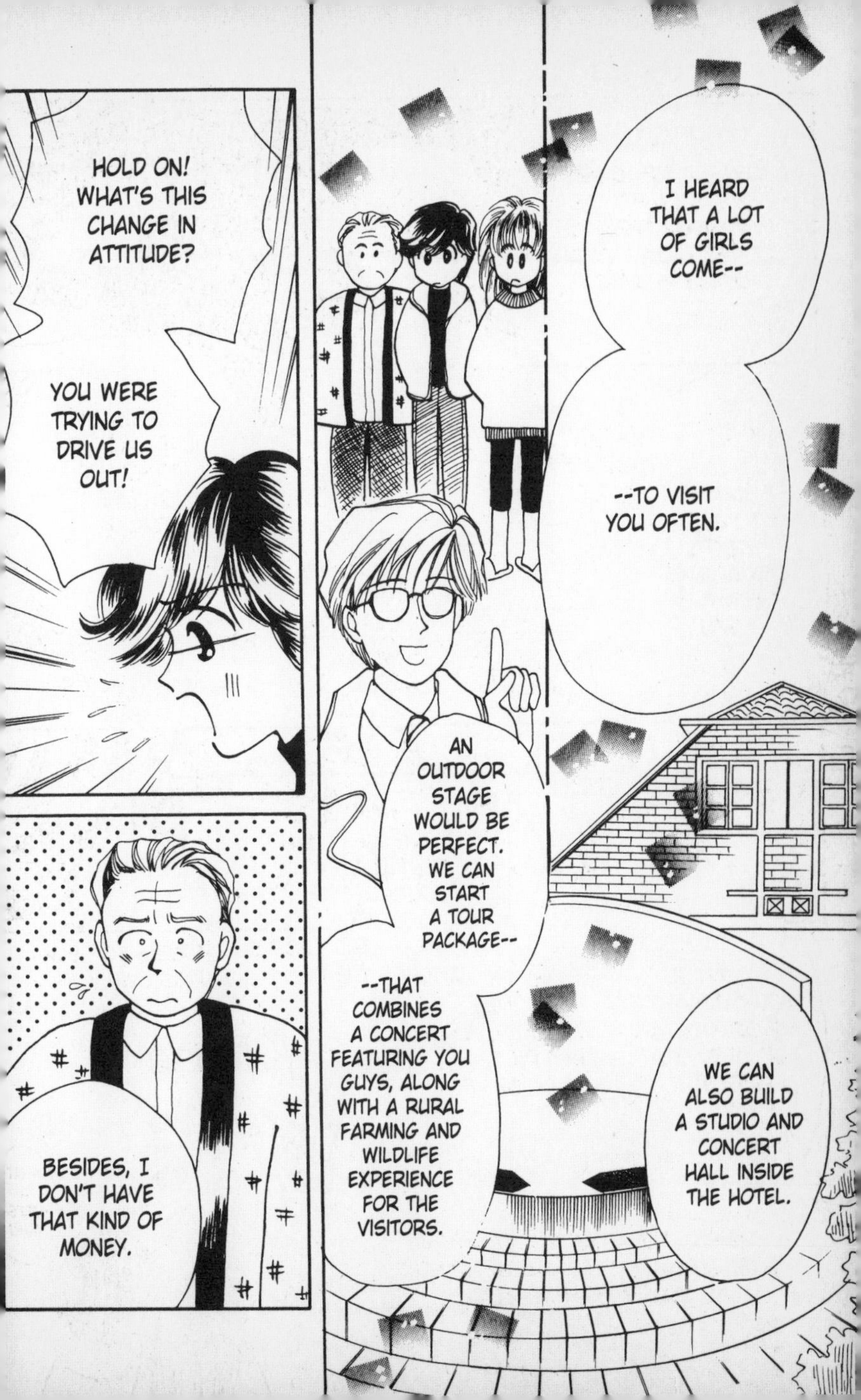

I HEARD THAT A LOT OF GIRLS COME--
--TO VISIT YOU OFTEN.
AN OUTDOOR STAGE WOULD BE PERFECT. WE CAN START A TOUR PACKAGE--
--THAT COMBINES A CONCERT FEATURING YOU GUYS, ALONG WITH A RURAL FARMING AND WILDLIFE EXPERIENCE FOR THE VISITORS.
WE CAN ALSO BUILD A STUDIO AND CONCERT HALL INSIDE THE HOTEL.
HOLD ON! WHAT'S THIS CHANGE IN ATTITUDE?
YOU WERE TRYING TO DRIVE US OUT!
BESIDES, I DON'T HAVE THAT KIND OF MONEY.

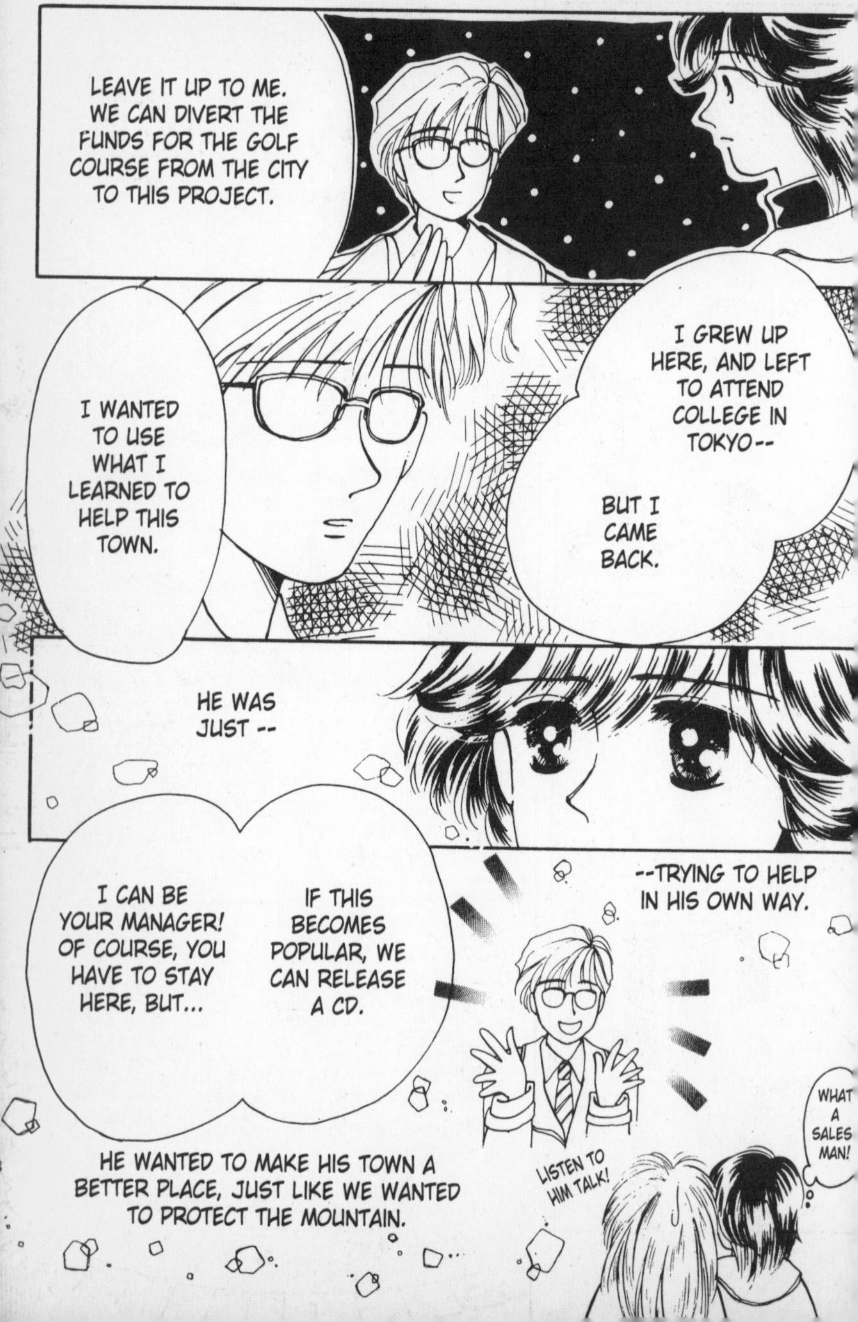
LEAVE IT UP TO ME. WE CAN DIVERT THE FUNDS FOR THE GOLF COURSE FROM THE CITY TO THIS PROJECT.
I GREW UP HERE, AND LEFT TO ATTEND COLLEGE IN TOKYO--
BUT I CAME BACK.
I WANTED TO USE WHAT I LEARNED TO HELP THIS TOWN.
HE WAS JUST --
--TRYING TO HELP IN HIS OWN WAY.
IF THIS BECOMES POPULAR, WE CAN RELEASE A CD.
I CAN BE YOUR MANAGER! OF COURSE, YOU HAVE TO STAY HERE, BUT...
WHAT A SALES MAN!
LISTEN TO HIM TALK!
HE WANTED TO MAKE HIS TOWN A BETTER PLACE, JUST LIKE WE WANTED TO PROTECT THE MOUNTAIN.

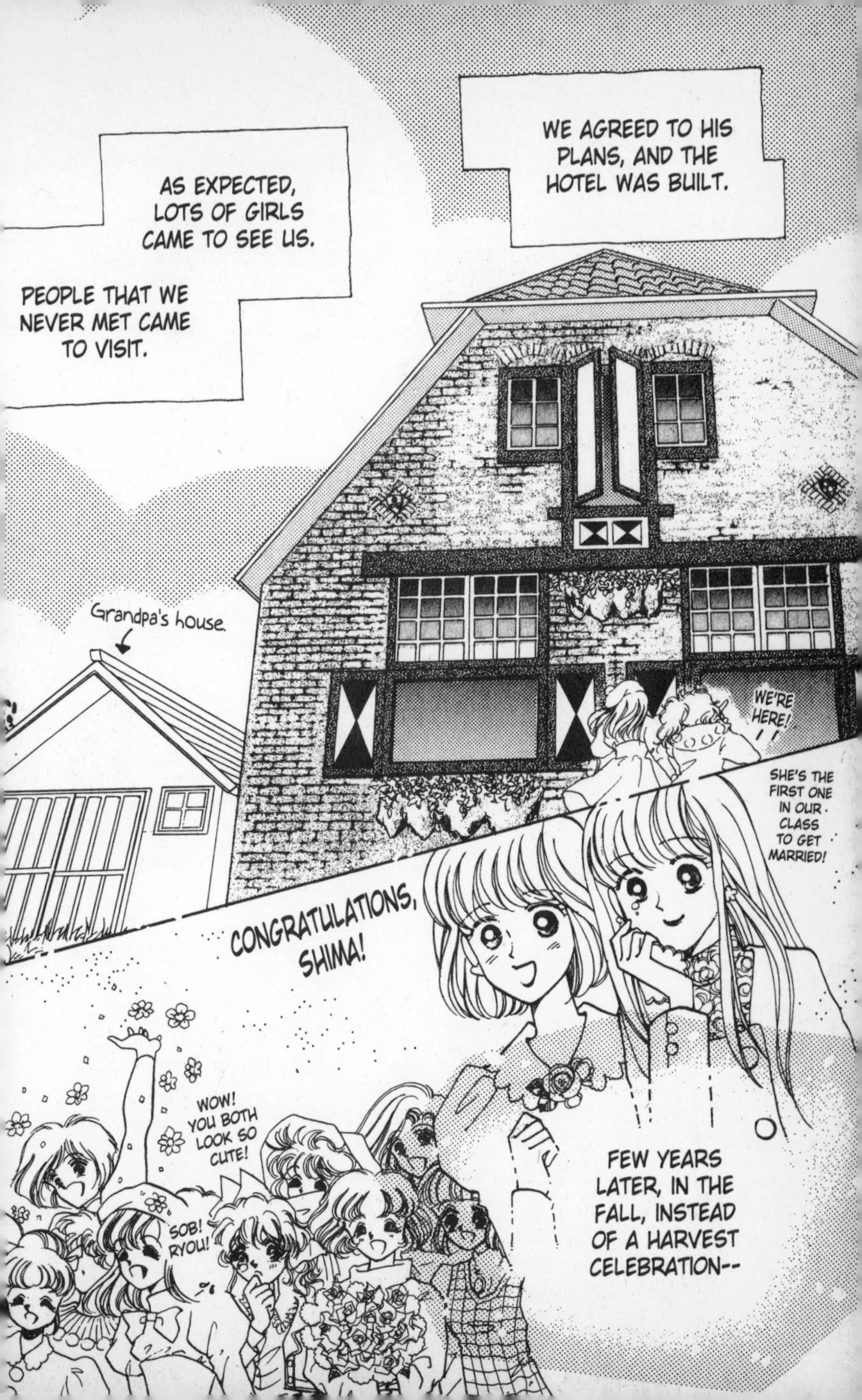
WE AGREED TO HIS PLANS, AND THE HOTEL WAS BUILT.
AS EXPECTED, LOTS OF GIRLS CAME TO SEE US.
PEOPLE THAT WE NEVER MET CAME TO VISIT.
WE'RE HERE!
Grandpa's house.
SHE'S THE FIRST ONE IN OUR CLASS TO GET MARRIED!
CONGRATULATIONS, SHIMA!
FEW YEARS LATER, IN THE FALL, INSTEAD OF A HARVEST CELEBRATION--
WOW! YOU BOTH LOOK SO CUTE!
SOB! RYOU!

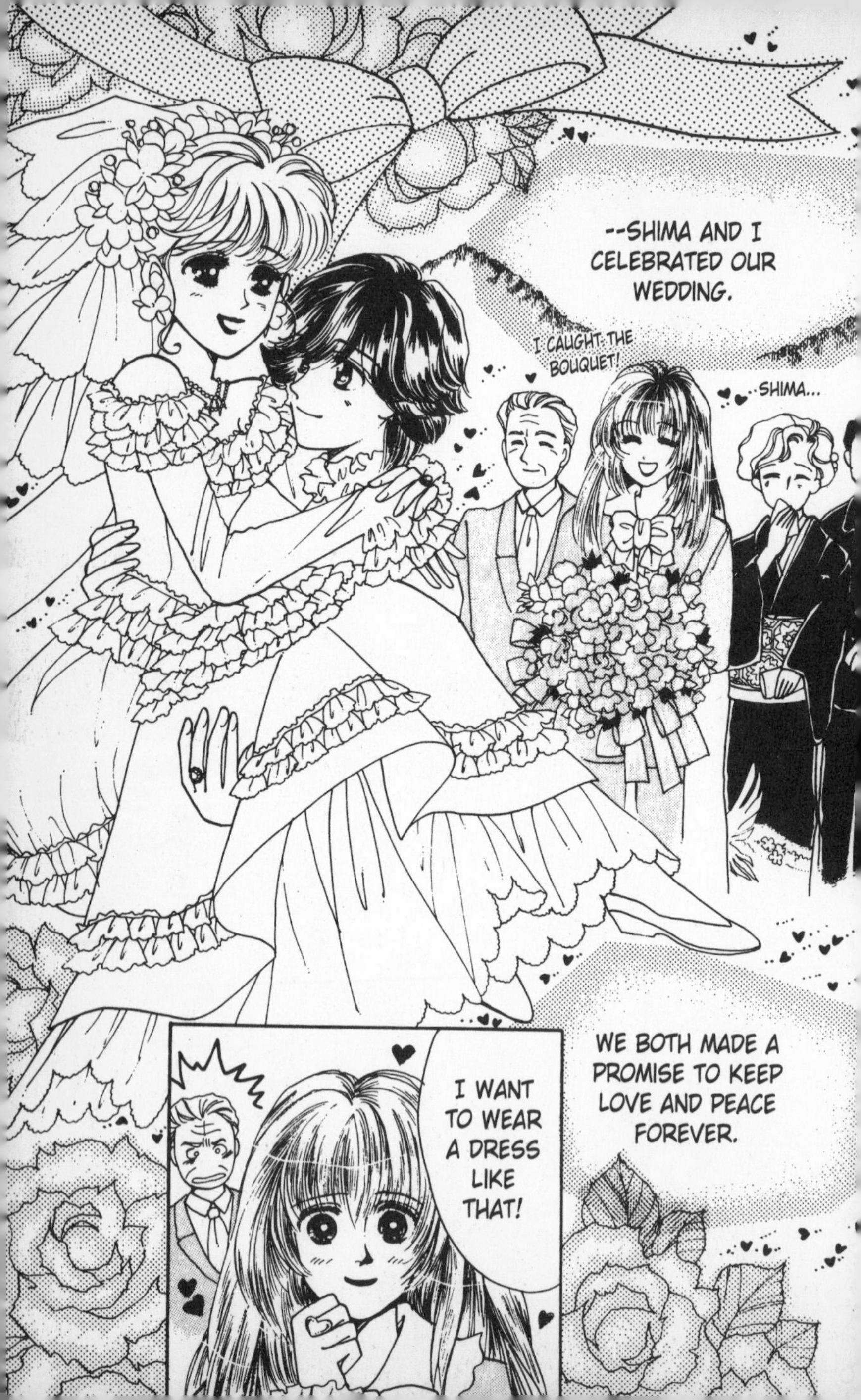
--SHIMA AND I CELEBRATED OUR WEDDING.
SHIMA...
I CAUGHT THE BOUQUET!
WE BOTH MADE A PROMISE TO KEEP LOVE AND PEACE FOREVER.
I WANT TO WEAR A DRESS LIKE THAT!

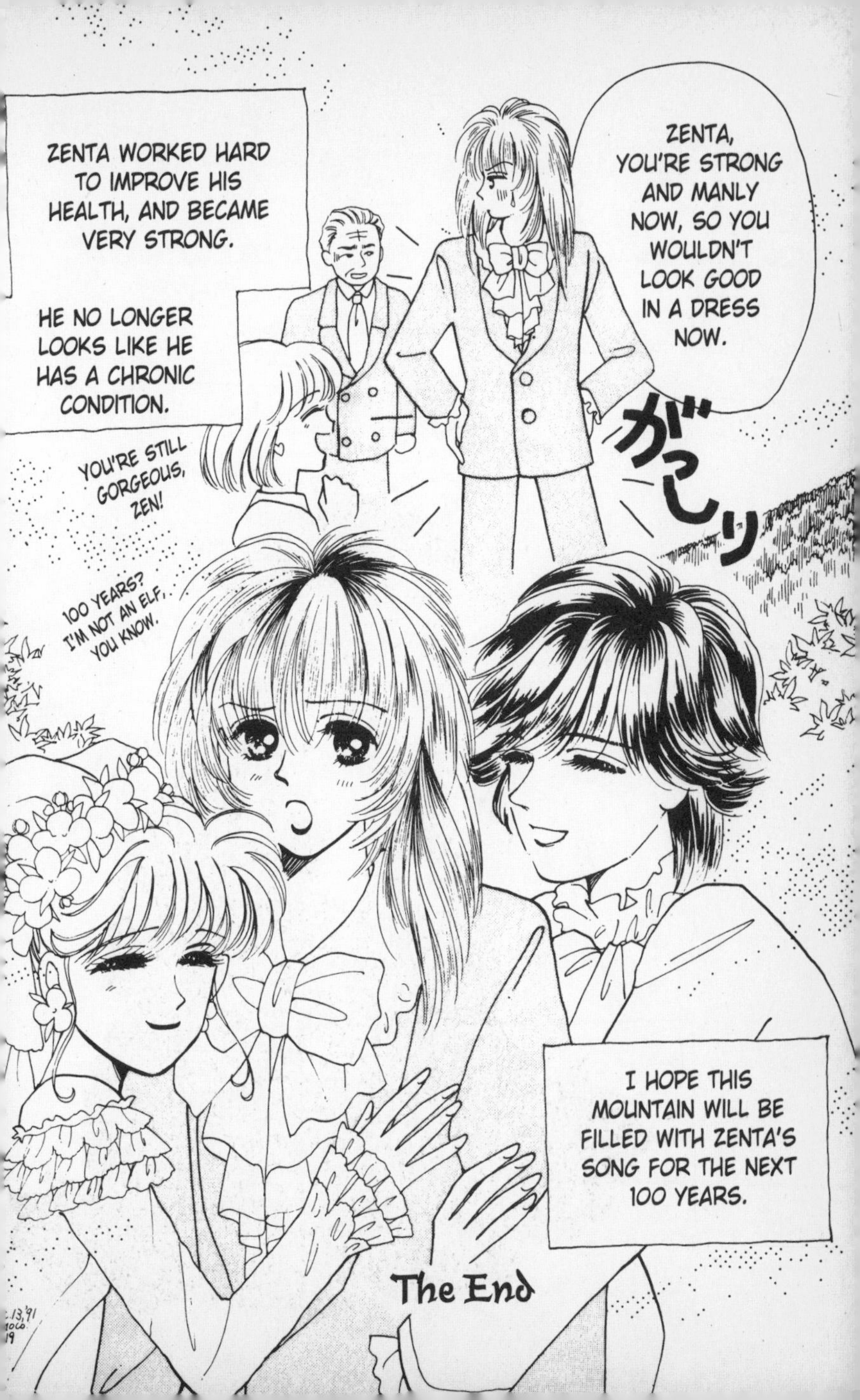
ZENTA, YOU'RE STRONG AND MANLY NOW, SO YOU WOULDN'T LOOK GOOD IN A DRESS NOW.
ZENTA WORKED HARD TO IMPROVE HIS HEALTH, AND BECAME VERY STRONG.
HE NO LONGER LOOKS LIKE HE HAS A CHRONIC CONDITION.
がっしり
YOU'RE STILL GORGEOUS, ZEN!
100 YEARS? I'M NOT AN ELF, YOU KNOW.
I HOPE THIS MOUNTAIN WILL BE FILLED WITH ZENTA'S SONG FOR THE NEXT 100 YEARS.
The End

BONUS 6.

FANS HAVE GUESSED CORRECTLY, IN SEVERAL LETTERS, THE IDENTITY OF THE PERSON THAT INSPIRED YOSHIEH'S CHARACTER. SHE'S ACTUALLY BASED ON A MAN (LAUGH). I WAS THRILLED BECAUSE I THOUGHT SHE DID LOOK LIKE HIM! I TURNED YOSHIEH'S CHARACTER INTO A GIRL BECAUSE I COULDN'T FIT A LONG-HAIRED, ANDROGYNOUS, MYSTERIOUS MALE CHARACTER IN THE STORY. BY THE WAY, MY CD AS A SINGER IS OUT! IT'S HILARIOUS! I SANG THE TITLE SONG FOR "DATTE ONNANOKO NANOYO" ON THE BONUS CD FOR VOL. 2. I PREVIOUSLY SANG A DUET WITH IZUMIHIGASHI ON TWO SONGS. HOWEVER, THE STAFF CONVINCED ME INTO SINGING SOLO, SO I DID IT! ALL MY READERS THAT HAVE WRITTEN TO ME, THANK YOU FOR BEING KIND AND ENJOYING MY SONG! I REALLY APPRECIATE THE COMPLIMENTS AND SUPPORT! I'VE ALSO WRITTEN LYRICS FOR SEVERAL PROJECTS. ONE IS A CD SINGLE CALLED "ZUTTO ISHONI IYOUNE." MY FRIEND, REIKO UDO, IS THE LEAD VOCALIST. THE OTHERS ARE "ANATAMO HAPPY END" AND "ANATAMO HAPPY END 2." PLEASE LOOK FOR THEM AT YOUR LOCAL MUSIC STORE!

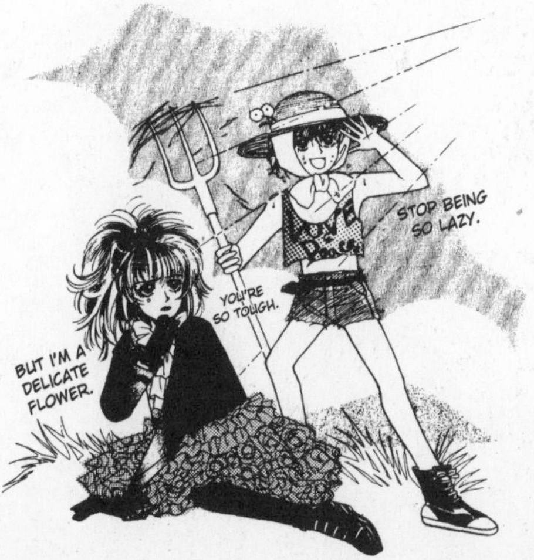
STOP BEING SO LAZY.
YOU'RE SO TOUGH.
BUT I'M A DELICATE FLOWER.

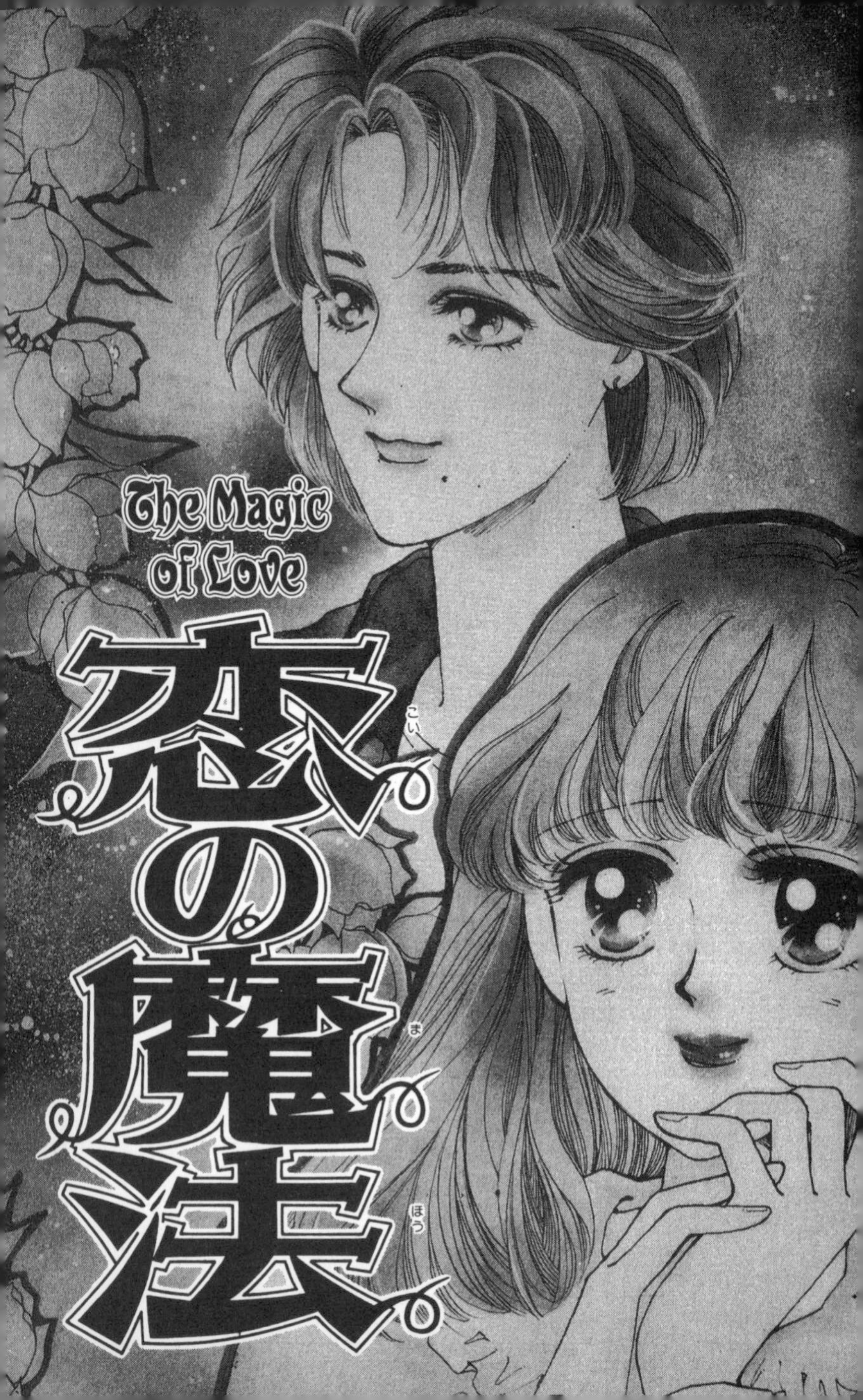
The Magic of Love
恋の魔法

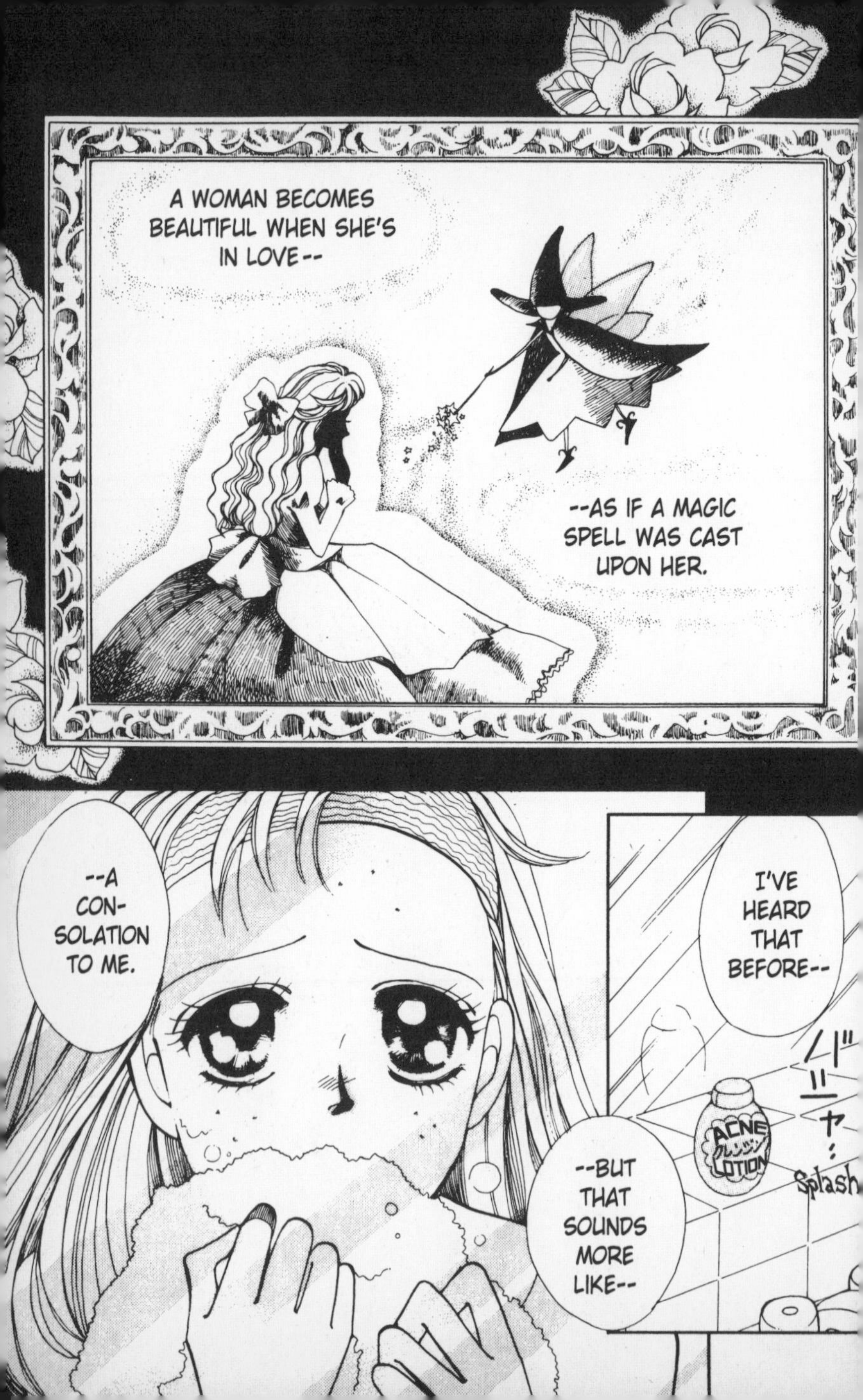
A WOMAN BECOMES BEAUTIFUL WHEN SHE'S IN LOVE--
--AS IF A MAGIC SPELL WAS CAST UPON HER.
I'VE HEARD THAT BEFORE--
--BUT THAT SOUNDS MORE LIKE--
ACNE LOTION
Splash
--A CON-SOLATION TO ME.

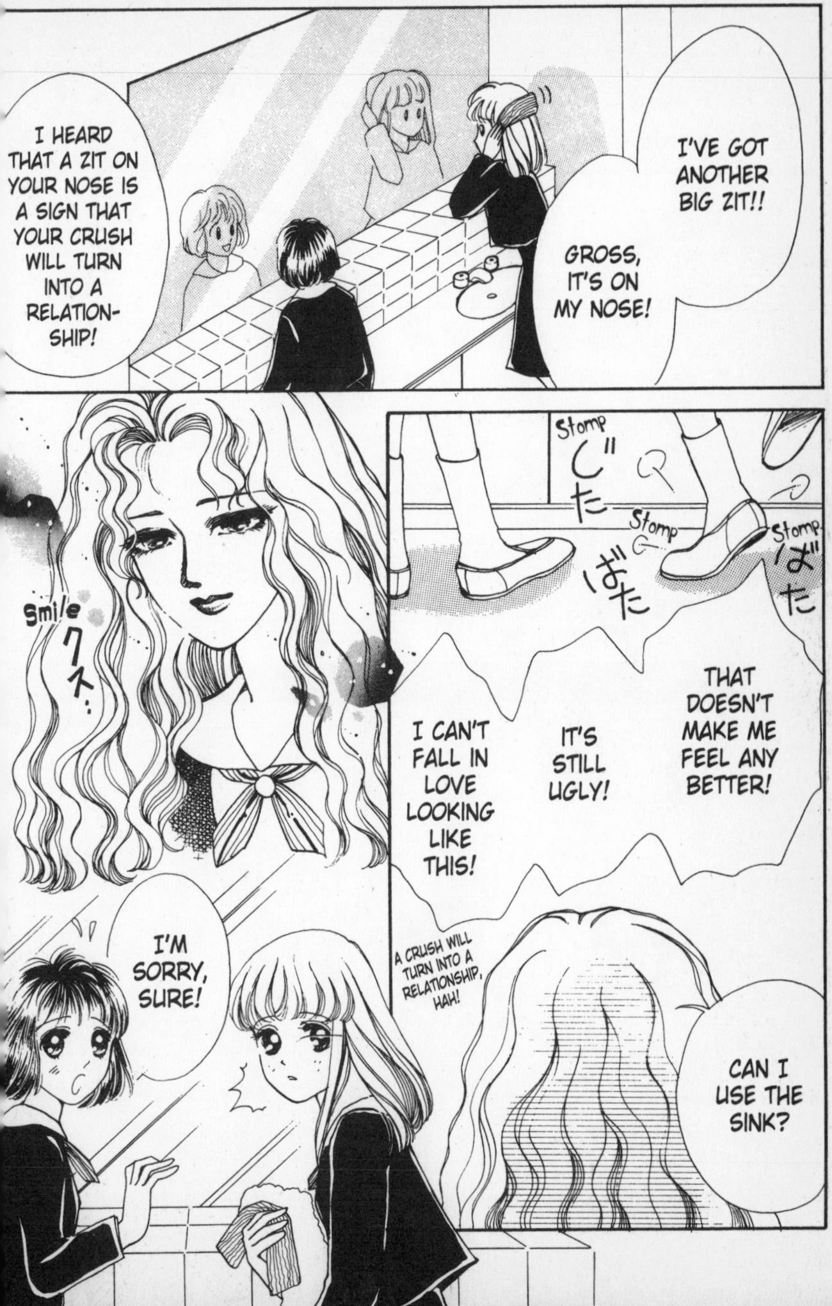
I'VE GOT ANOTHER BIG ZIT!!
GROSS, IT'S ON MY NOSE!
I HEARD THAT A ZIT ON YOUR NOSE IS A SIGN THAT YOUR CRUSH WILL TURN INTO A RELATION-SHIP!
Stomp じた
Stomp ばた
Stomp ばた
THAT DOESN'T MAKE ME FEEL ANY BETTER!
IT'S STILL UGLY!
I CAN'T FALL IN LOVE LOOKING LIKE THIS!
Smile クス…
CAN I USE THE SINK?
A CRUSH WILL TURN INTO A RELATIONSHIP, HAH!
I'M SORRY, SURE!

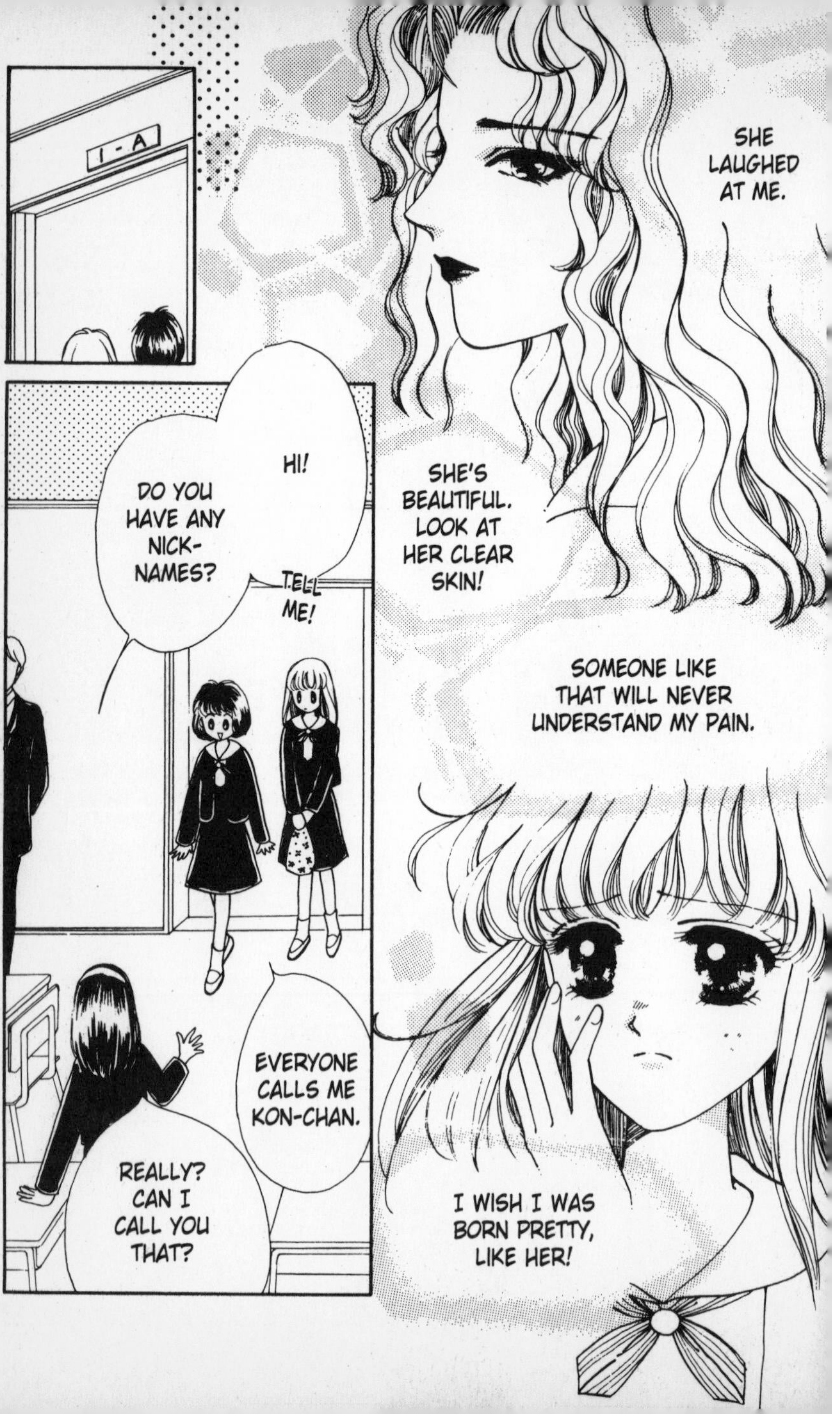
SHE LAUGHED AT ME.
SHE'S BEAUTIFUL. LOOK AT HER CLEAR SKIN!
SOMEONE LIKE THAT WILL NEVER UNDERSTAND MY PAIN.
I WISH I WAS BORN PRETTY, LIKE HER!
I-A
HI!
TELL ME!
DO YOU HAVE ANY NICK-NAMES?
EVERYONE CALLS ME KON-CHAN.
REALLY? CAN I CALL YOU THAT?

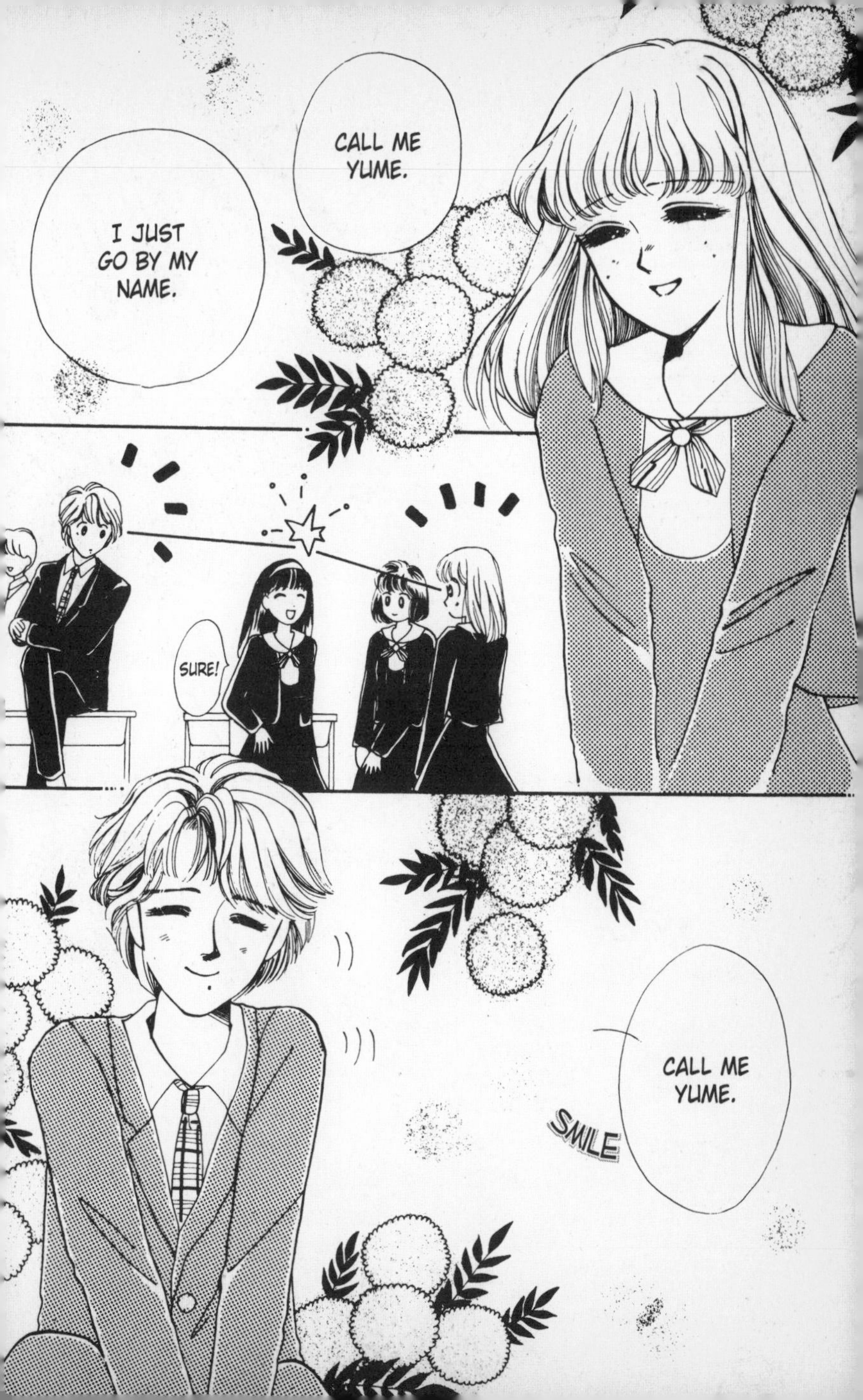
CALL ME YUME.
I JUST GO BY MY NAME.
SURE!
CALL ME YUME.
SMILE

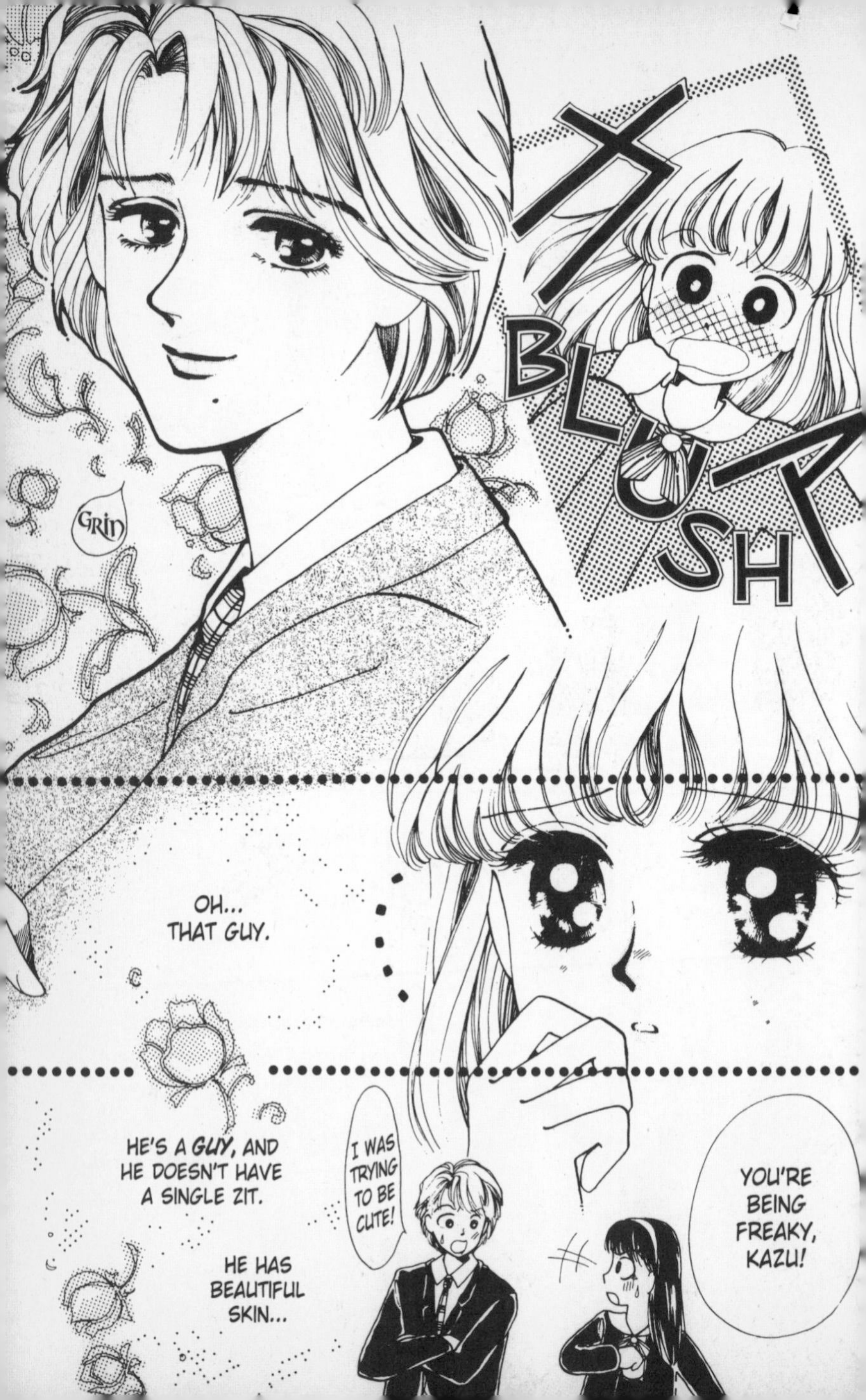

BLUSH
GRIN
OH... THAT GUY.
HE'S A ***GUY***, AND HE DOESN'T HAVE A SINGLE ZIT.
HE HAS BEAUTIFUL SKIN...
YOU'RE BEING FREAKY, KAZU!
I WAS TRYING TO BE CUTE!

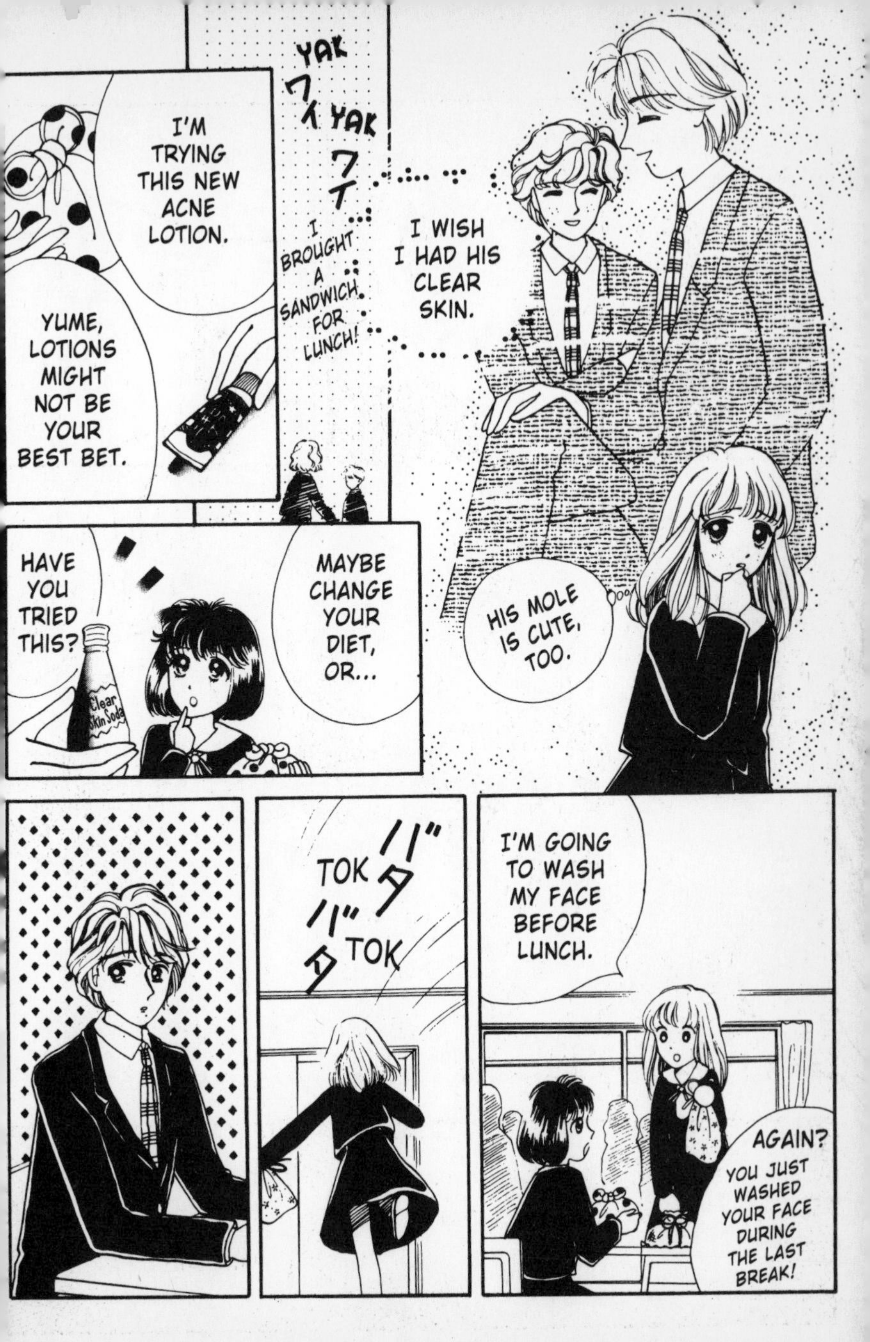
I WISH I HAD HIS CLEAR SKIN.
HIS MOLE IS CUTE, TOO.
YAK ワイ YAK ワイ
I BROUGHT A SANDWICH FOR LUNCH!
I'M TRYING THIS NEW ACNE LOTION.
YUME, LOTIONS MIGHT NOT BE YOUR BEST BET.
MAYBE CHANGE YOUR DIET, OR...
HAVE YOU TRIED THIS?
Clear Skin Soda
I'M GOING TO WASH MY FACE BEFORE LUNCH.
AGAIN? YOU JUST WASHED YOUR FACE DURING THE LAST BREAK!
TOK バタ TOK バタ

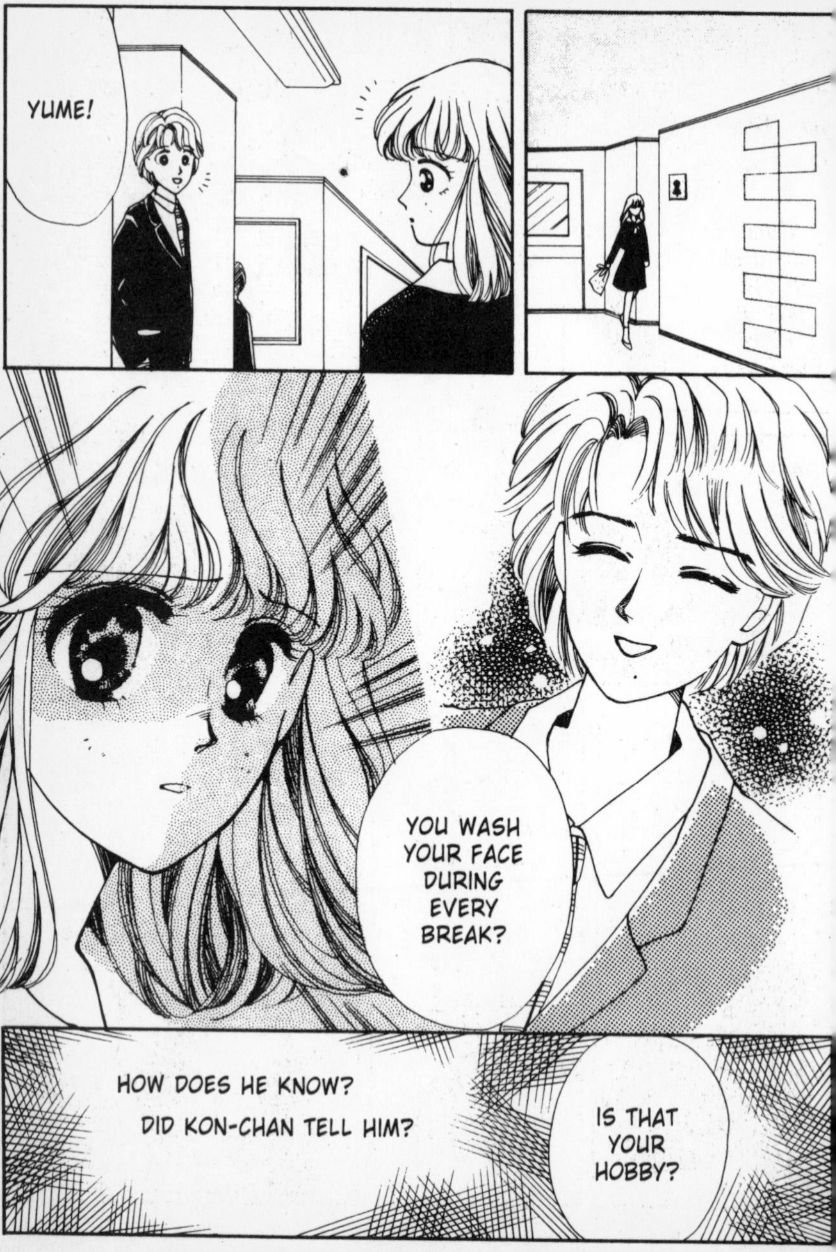
YUME!
YOU WASH YOUR FACE DURING EVERY BREAK?
IS THAT YOUR HOBBY?
HOW DOES HE KNOW?
DID KON-CHAN TELL HIM?

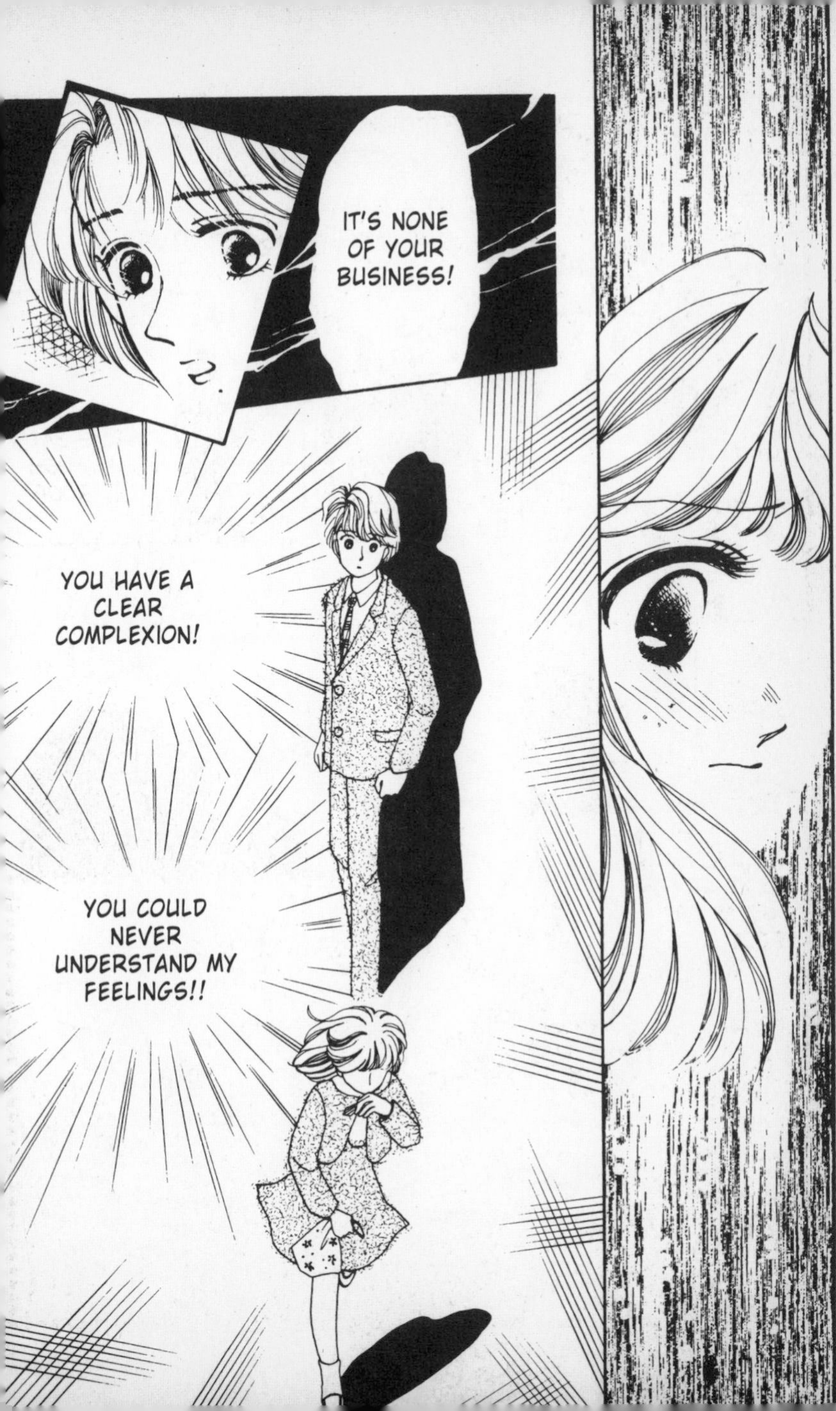
IT'S NONE OF YOUR BUSINESS!
YOU HAVE A CLEAR COMPLEXION!
YOU COULD NEVER UNDERSTAND MY FEELINGS!!

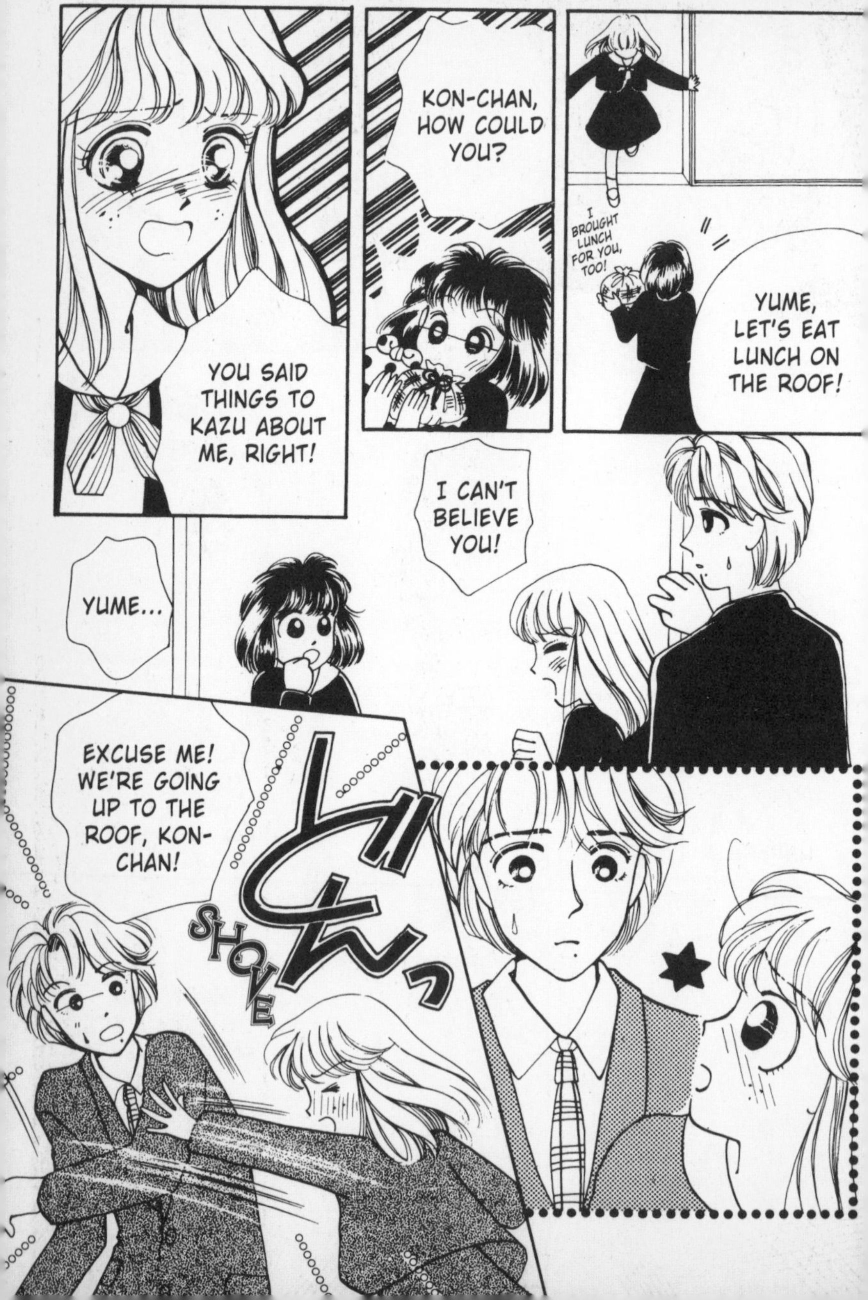
YUME, LET'S EAT LUNCH ON THE ROOF!
I BROUGHT LUNCH FOR YOU, TOO!
KON-CHAN, HOW COULD YOU?
YOU SAID THINGS TO KAZU ABOUT ME, RIGHT!
I CAN'T BELIEVE YOU!
YUME...
EXCUSE ME! WE'RE GOING UP TO THE ROOF, KON-CHAN!
SHOVE

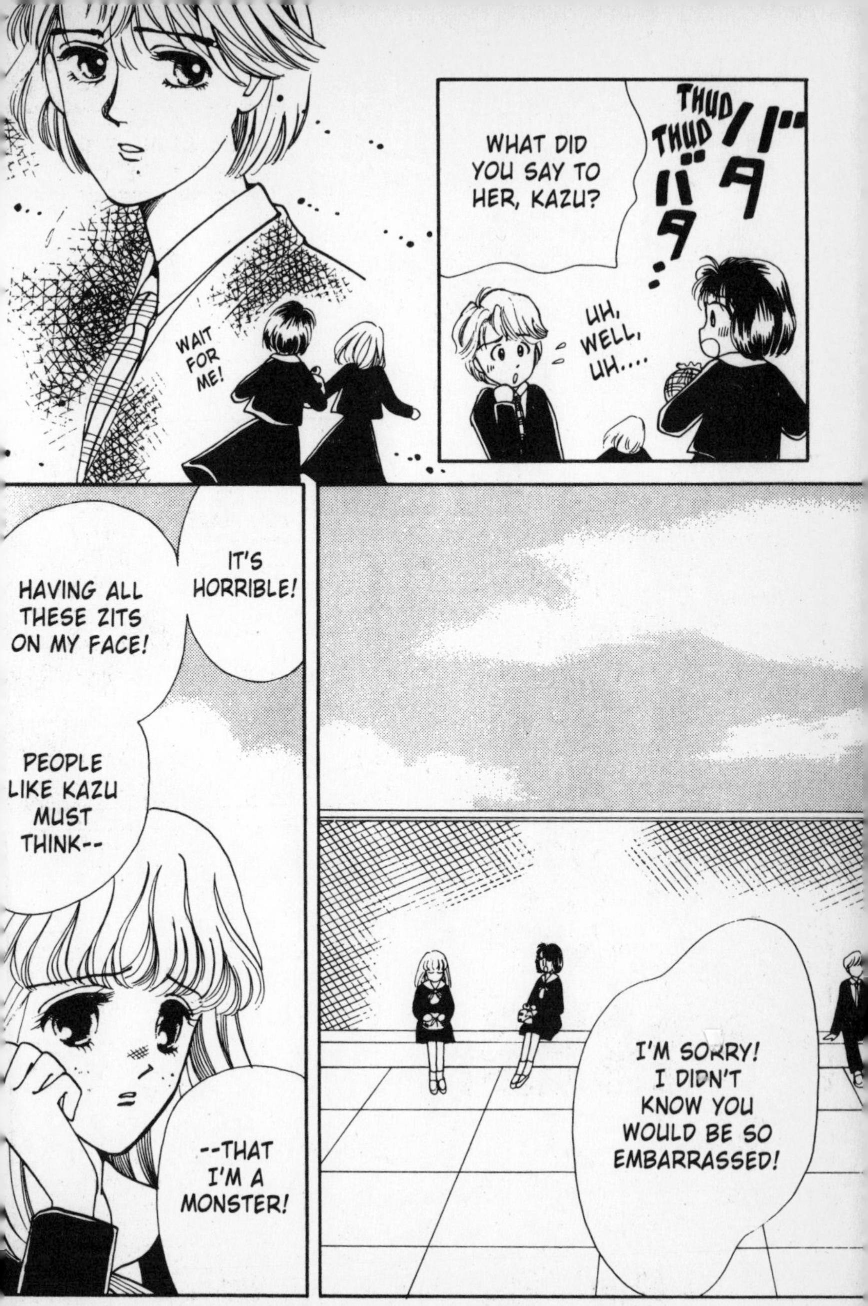

THUD THUD
バタバタ
WHAT DID YOU SAY TO HER, KAZU?
UH, WELL, UH....
WAIT FOR ME!
I'M SORRY! I DIDN'T KNOW YOU WOULD BE SO EMBARRASSED!
IT'S HORRIBLE!
HAVING ALL THESE ZITS ON MY FACE!
PEOPLE LIKE KAZU MUST THINK--
--THAT I'M A MONSTER!

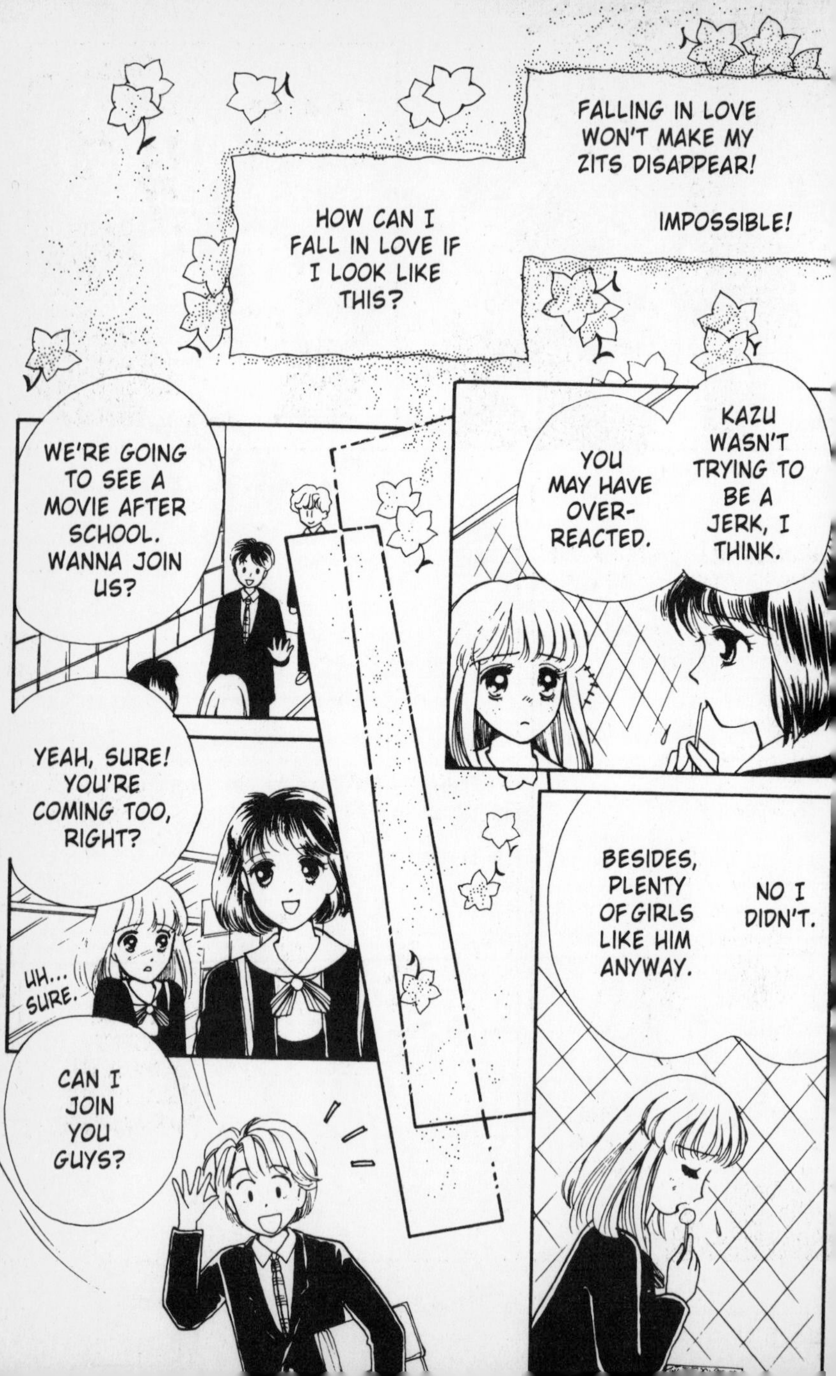
FALLING IN LOVE WON'T MAKE MY ZITS DISAPPEAR!
IMPOSSIBLE!
HOW CAN I FALL IN LOVE IF I LOOK LIKE THIS?
KAZU WASN'T TRYING TO BE A JERK, I THINK.
YOU MAY HAVE OVER-REACTED.
NO I DIDN'T.
BESIDES, PLENTY OF GIRLS LIKE HIM ANYWAY.
WE'RE GOING TO SEE A MOVIE AFTER SCHOOL. WANNA JOIN US?
YEAH, SURE! YOU'RE COMING TOO, RIGHT?
UH... SURE.
CAN I JOIN YOU GUYS?

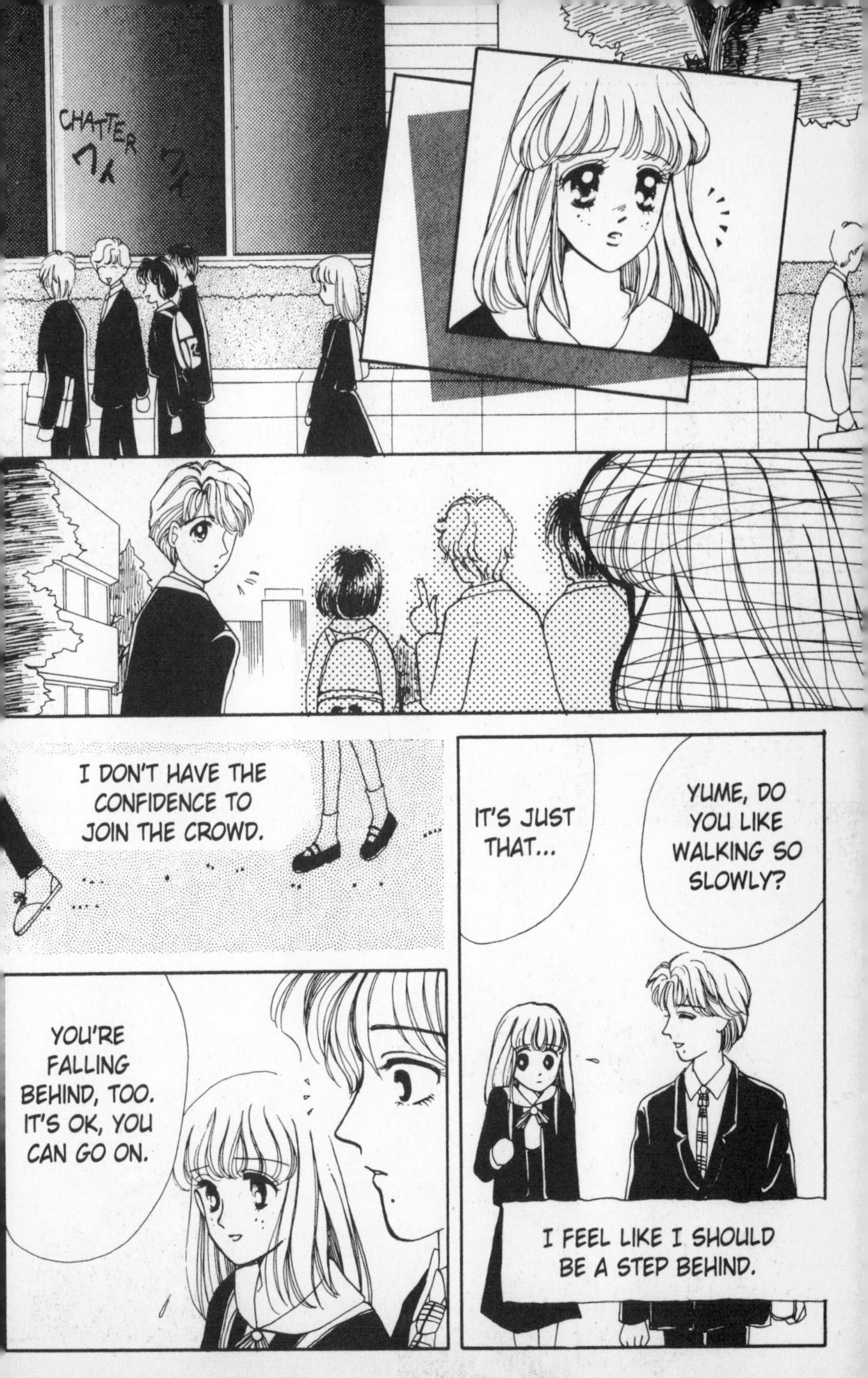
CHATTER
YUME, DO YOU LIKE WALKING SO SLOWLY?
IT'S JUST THAT...
I FEEL LIKE I SHOULD BE A STEP BEHIND.
I DON'T HAVE THE CONFIDENCE TO JOIN THE CROWD.
YOU'RE FALLING BEHIND, TOO. IT'S OK, YOU CAN GO ON.

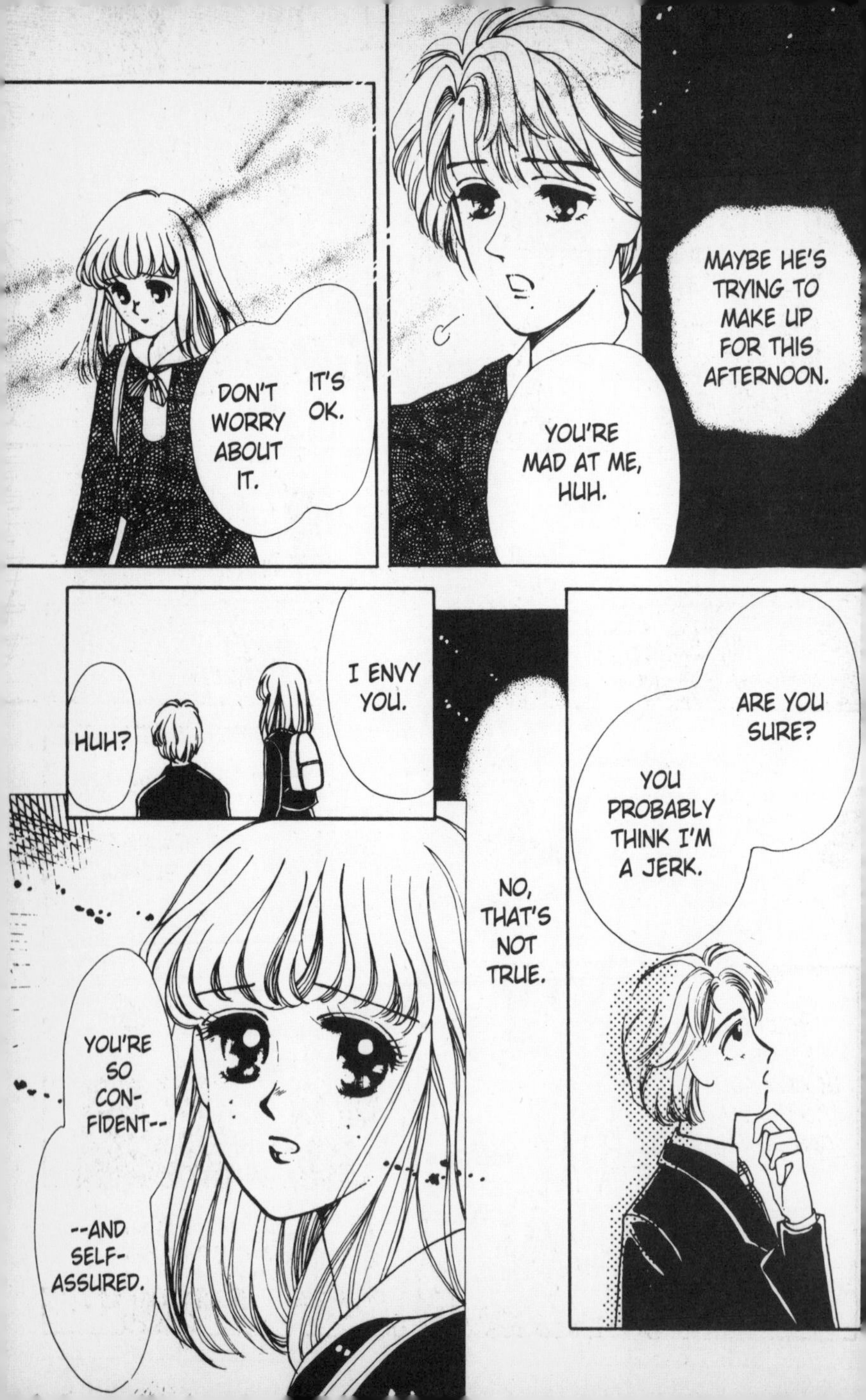
MAYBE HE'S TRYING TO MAKE UP FOR THIS AFTERNOON.
YOU'RE MAD AT ME, HUH.
IT'S OK.
DON'T WORRY ABOUT IT.
ARE YOU SURE?
YOU PROBABLY THINK I'M A JERK.
NO, THAT'S NOT TRUE.
I ENVY YOU.
HUH?
YOU'RE SO CON-FIDENT--
--AND SELF-ASSURED.

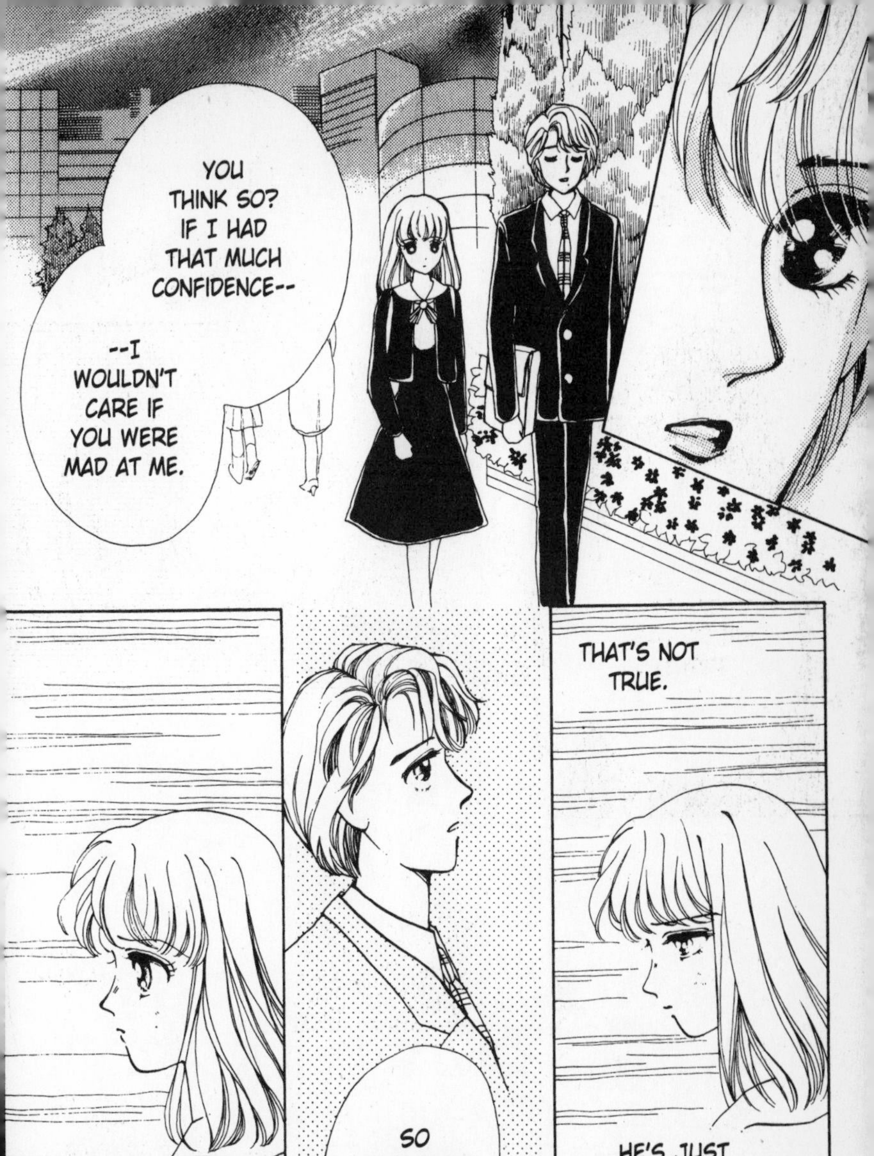
YOU THINK SO? IF I HAD THAT MUCH CONFIDENCE--
--I WOULDN'T CARE IF YOU WERE MAD AT ME.
THAT'S NOT TRUE.
HE'S JUST AMUSED THAT--
--A GIRL WOULD AVOID HIM.
SO YOU'RE NOT CONFIDENT, YUME?

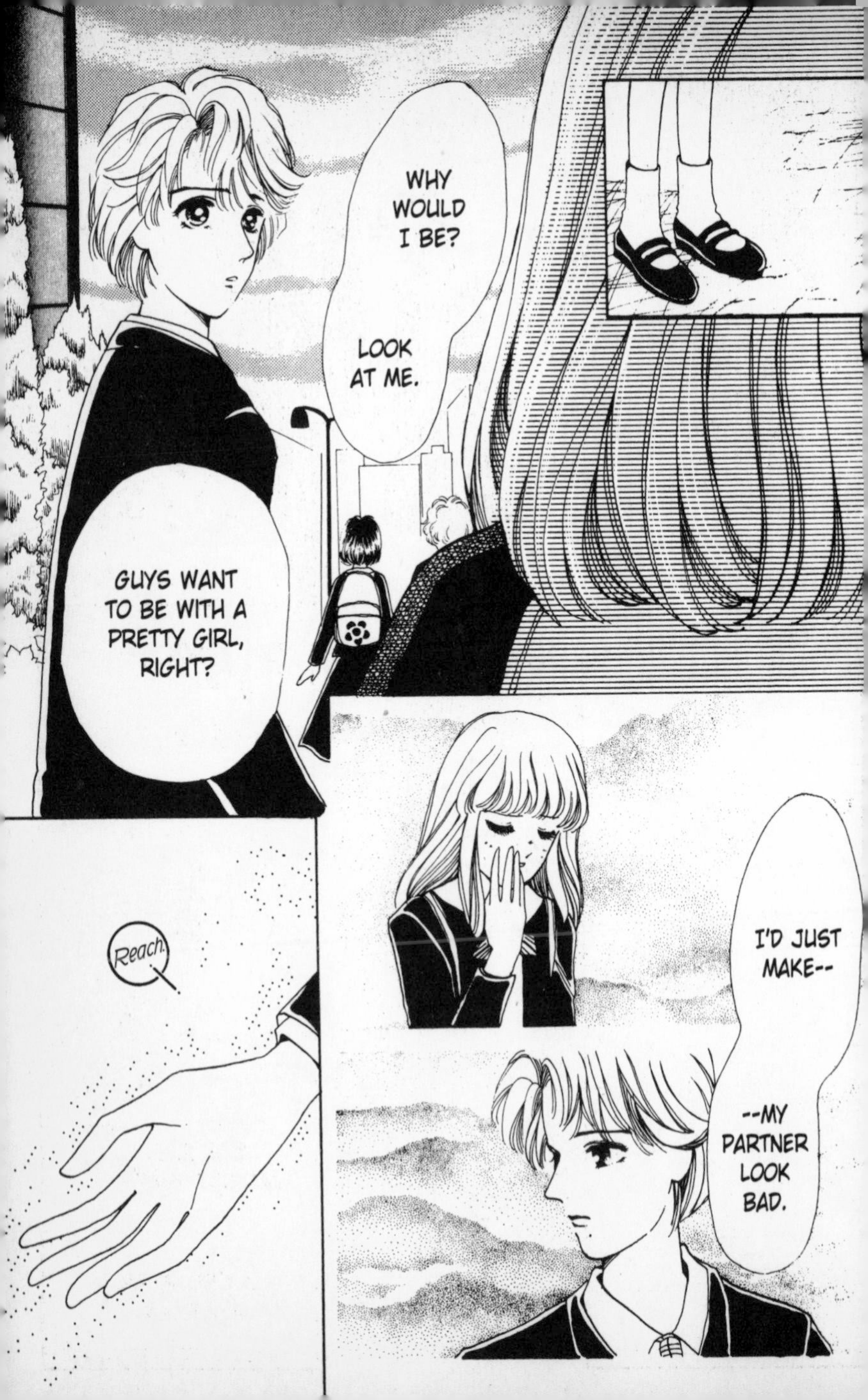
WHY WOULD I BE?
LOOK AT ME.
GUYS WANT TO BE WITH A PRETTY GIRL, RIGHT?
I'D JUST MAKE--
--MY PARTNER LOOK BAD.
Reach.

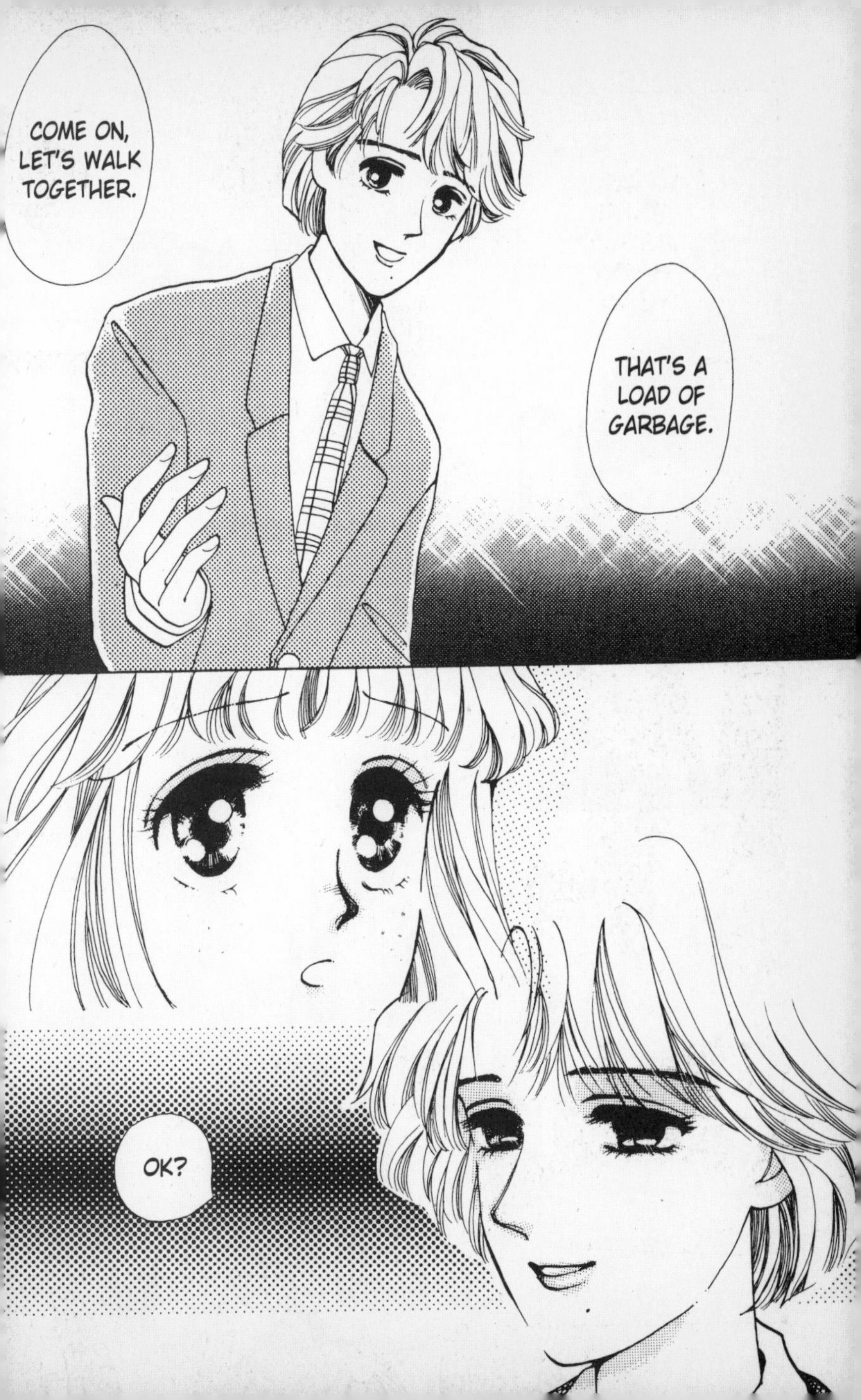
THAT'S A LOAD OF GARBAGE.
COME ON, LET'S WALK TOGETHER.
OK?

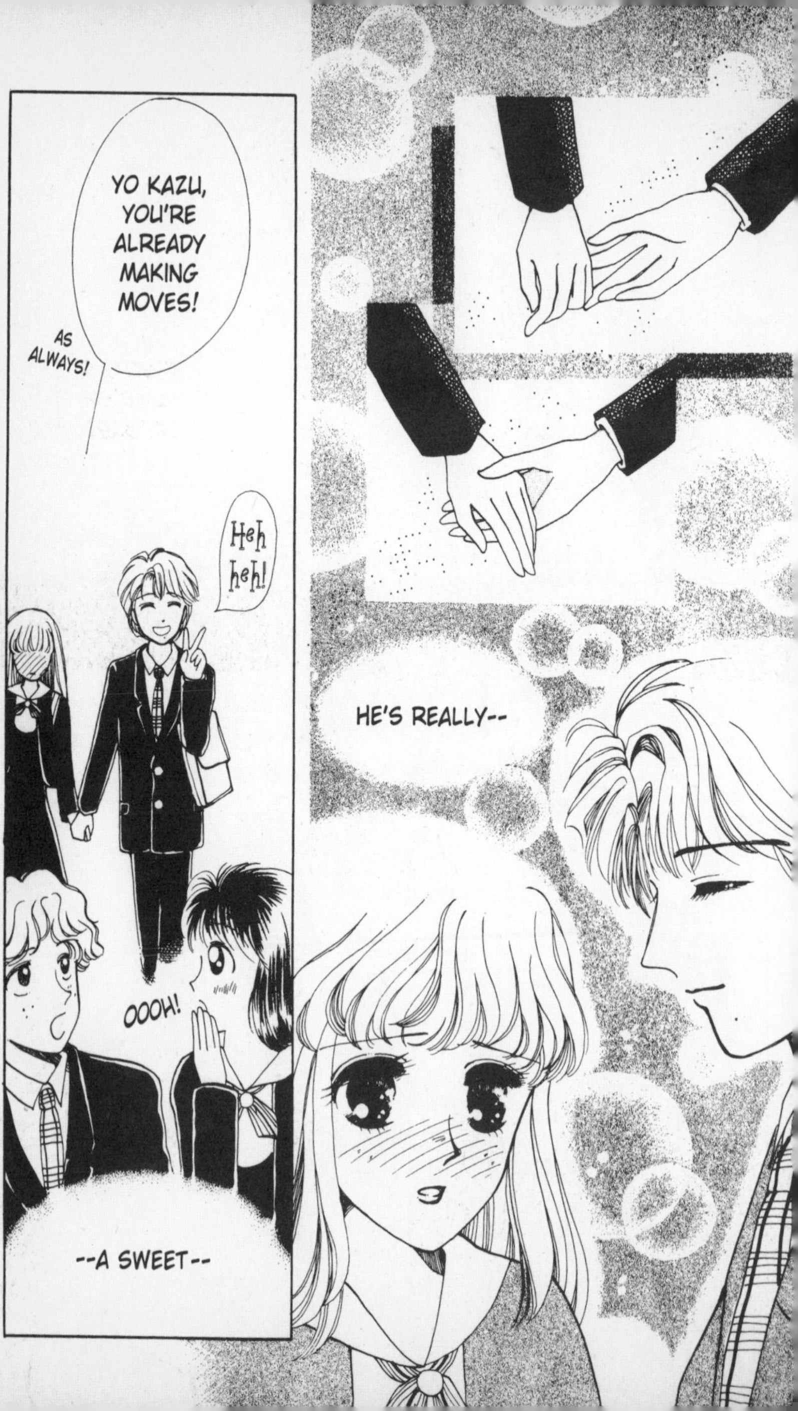
HE'S REALLY--
YO KAZU, YOU'RE ALREADY MAKING MOVES!
AS ALWAYS!
Heh heh!
OOOH!
--A SWEET--

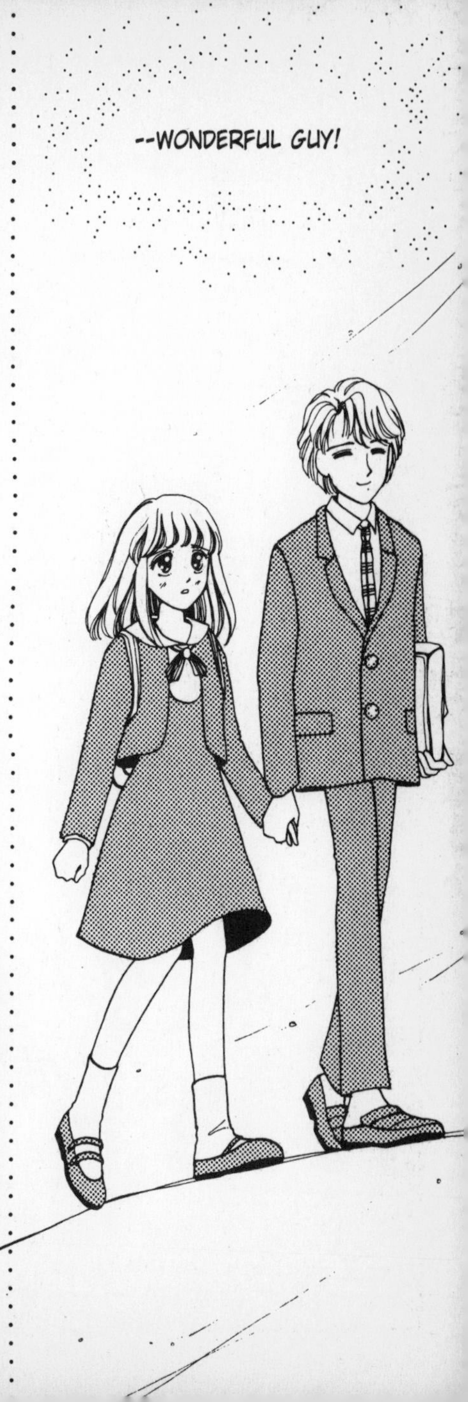
--WONDERFUL GUY!

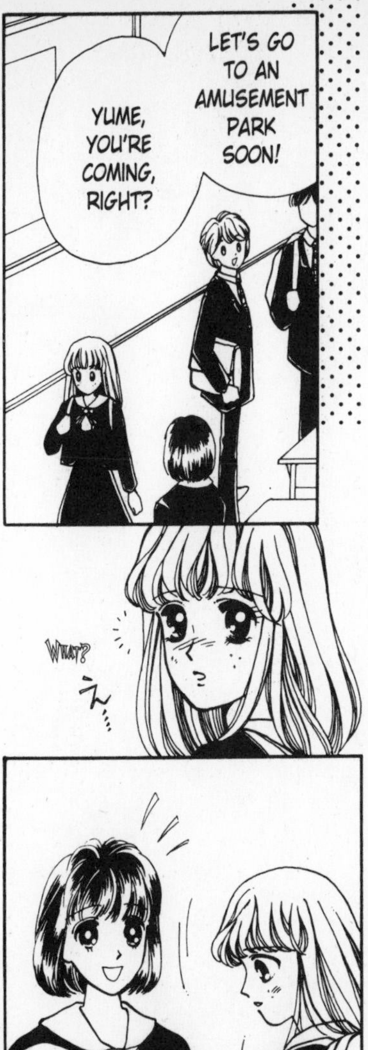
LET'S GO TO AN AMUSEMENT PARK SOON!
YUME, YOU'RE COMING, RIGHT?
WHAT?
IF KON-CHAN'S COMES WITH ME...
YEAH, OF COURSE! WHEN!?

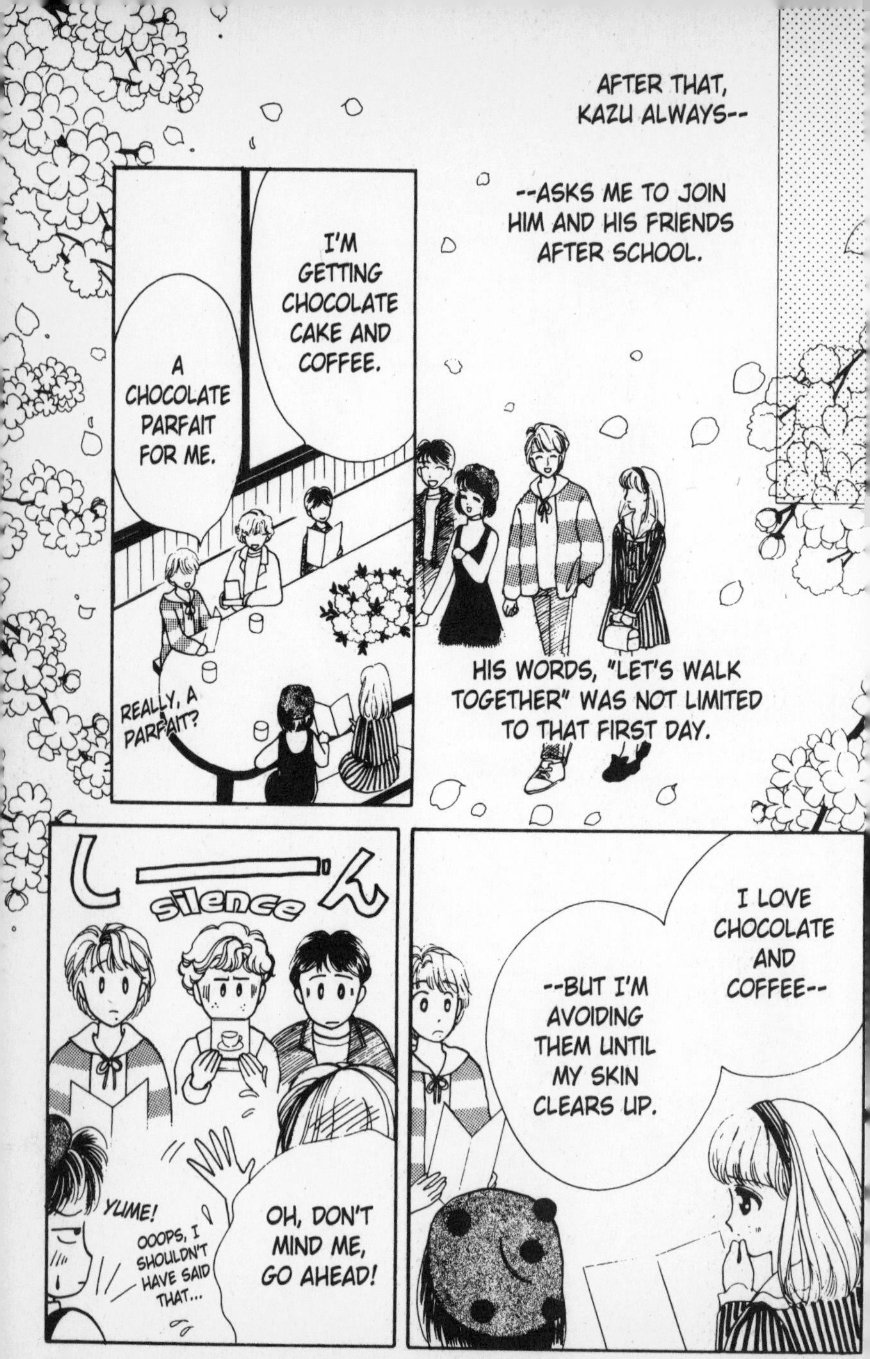

AFTER THAT, KAZU ALWAYS--
--ASKS ME TO JOIN HIM AND HIS FRIENDS AFTER SCHOOL.
HIS WORDS, "LET'S WALK TOGETHER" WAS NOT LIMITED TO THAT FIRST DAY.
I'M GETTING CHOCOLATE CAKE AND COFFEE.
A CHOCOLATE PARFAIT FOR ME.
REALLY, A PARFAIT?
I LOVE CHOCOLATE AND COFFEE--
--BUT I'M AVOIDING THEM UNTIL MY SKIN CLEARS UP.
silence
OH, DON'T MIND ME, GO AHEAD!
YUME!
OOOPS, I SHOULDN'T HAVE SAID THAT...

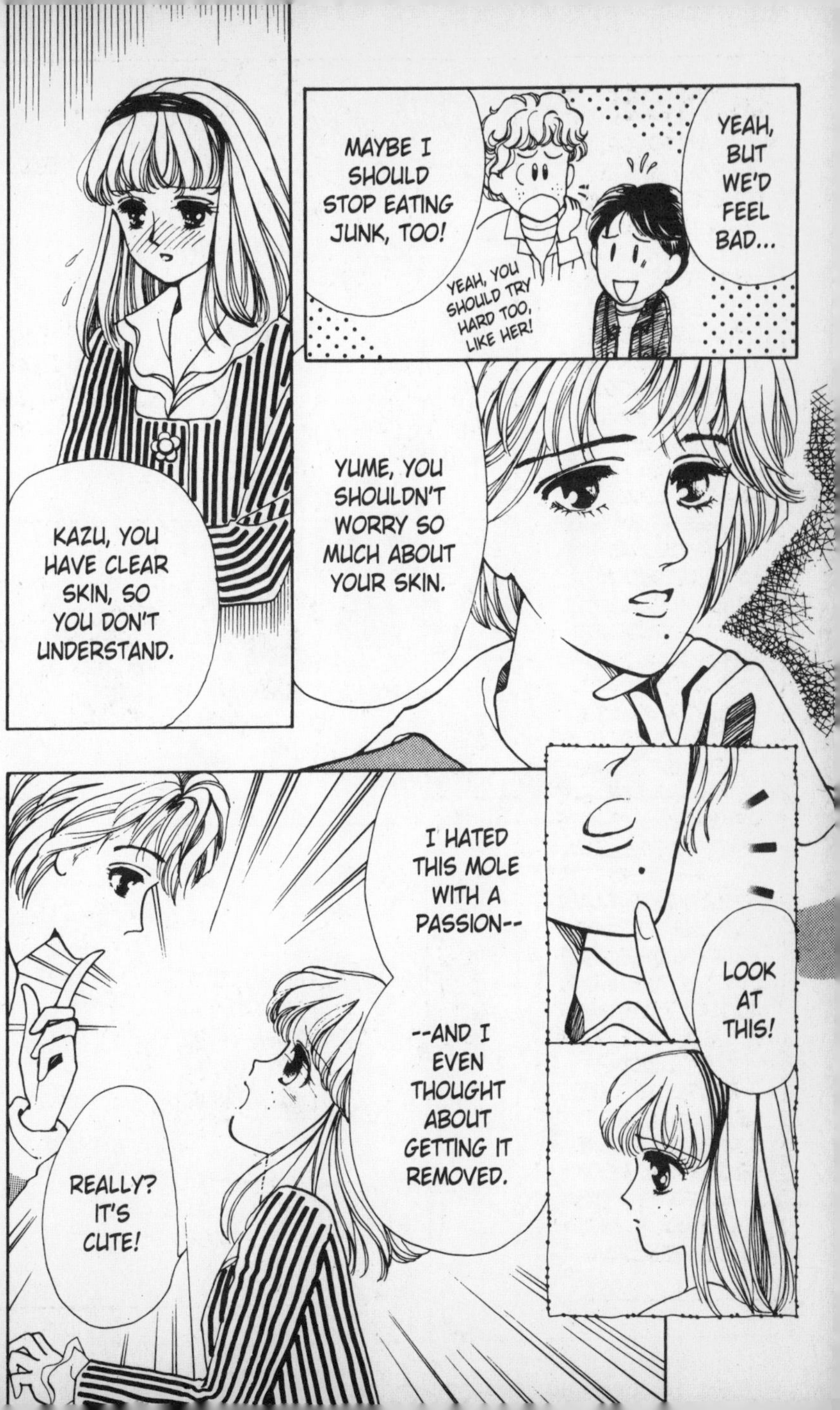
YEAH, BUT WE'D FEEL BAD...
MAYBE I SHOULD STOP EATING JUNK, TOO!
YEAH, YOU SHOULD TRY HARD TOO, LIKE HER!
YUME, YOU SHOULDN'T WORRY SO MUCH ABOUT YOUR SKIN.
KAZU, YOU HAVE CLEAR SKIN, SO YOU DON'T UNDERSTAND.
LOOK AT THIS!
I HATED THIS MOLE WITH A PASSION--
--AND I EVEN THOUGHT ABOUT GETTING IT REMOVED.
REALLY? IT'S CUTE!

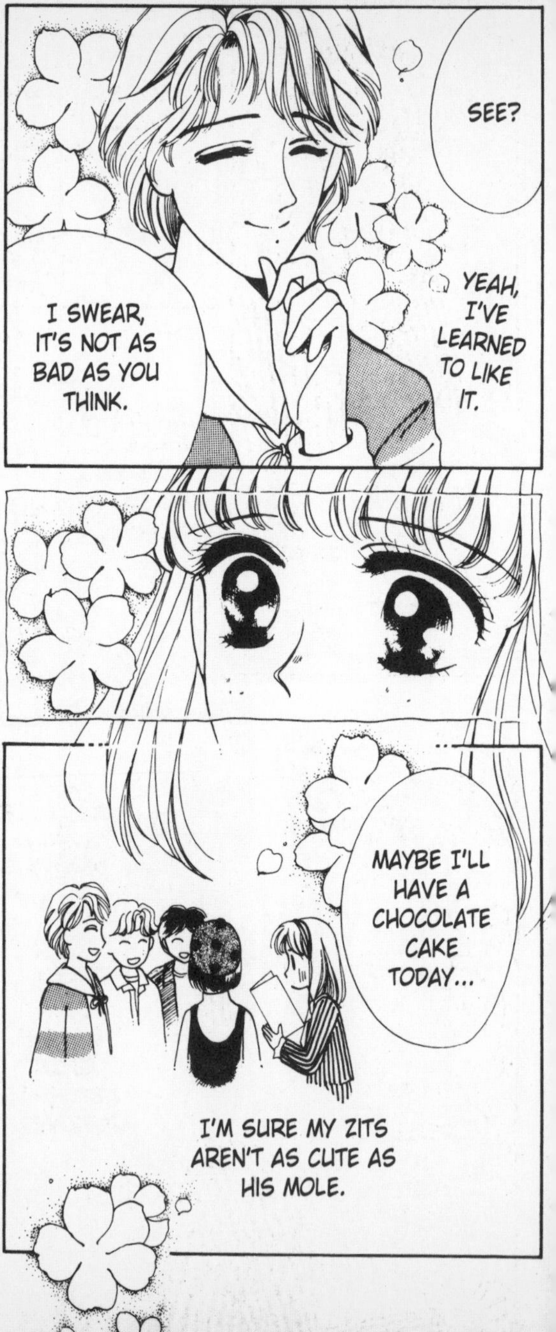
SEE?
YEAH, I'VE LEARNED TO LIKE IT.
I SWEAR, IT'S NOT AS BAD AS YOU THINK.
MAYBE I'LL HAVE A CHOCOLATE CAKE TODAY...
I'M SURE MY ZITS AREN'T AS CUTE AS HIS MOLE.

BONUS 7.

♥ MY FAVORITE BAND AT THE MOMENT IS SKANCHI-SAN. I STILL LIKE PRI2 AND MANABU MIYABARA. I WANT TO GO SEE "ALUCARD," BUT I HAVEN'T BEEN ABLE TO! BOO HOO!

FANS HAVE WRITTEN LETTERS ♡ASKING ME IF "THE MAGIC OF LOVE" WAS BASED ON MY OWN PERSONAL EXPERIENCE WITH ACNE. YES, IT WAS. I WAS PLAGUED WITH ACNE FOR A LONG TIME, UNTIL JUST RECENTLY (I THOUGHT IT WAS BECAUSE I WAS GETTING OLDER, BUT APPARENTLY, THAT'S NOT NECESSARILY THE CASE). IT TOTALLY CLEARED UP ONE DAY, LIKE SUDDENLY FIGURING OUT THE ANSWER TO A HARD PROBLEM! I DO TAKE CARE OF MY SKIN, USING PRODUCTS THAT KEEP THEM HEALTHY. ALSO, THE CLEAR SKIN DRINK REALLY HELPED, TOO (AYA SUGIYAMA IS IN THE COMMERCIAL)!

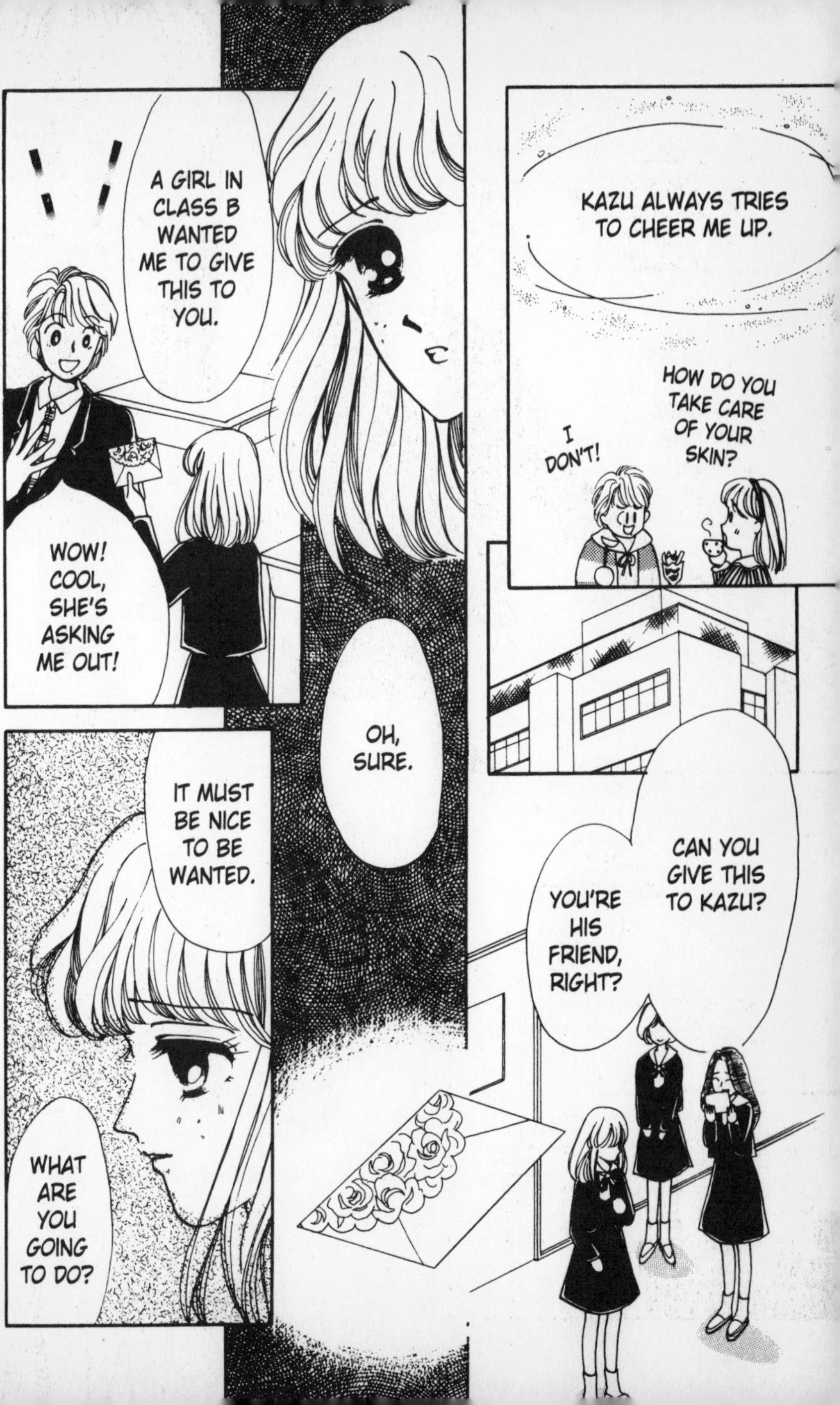
KAZU ALWAYS TRIES TO CHEER ME UP.
HOW DO YOU TAKE CARE OF YOUR SKIN?
I DON'T!
CAN YOU GIVE THIS TO KAZU?
YOU'RE HIS FRIEND, RIGHT?
OH, SURE.
A GIRL IN CLASS B WANTED ME TO GIVE THIS TO YOU.
WOW! COOL, SHE'S ASKING ME OUT!
IT MUST BE NICE TO BE WANTED.
WHAT ARE YOU GOING TO DO?

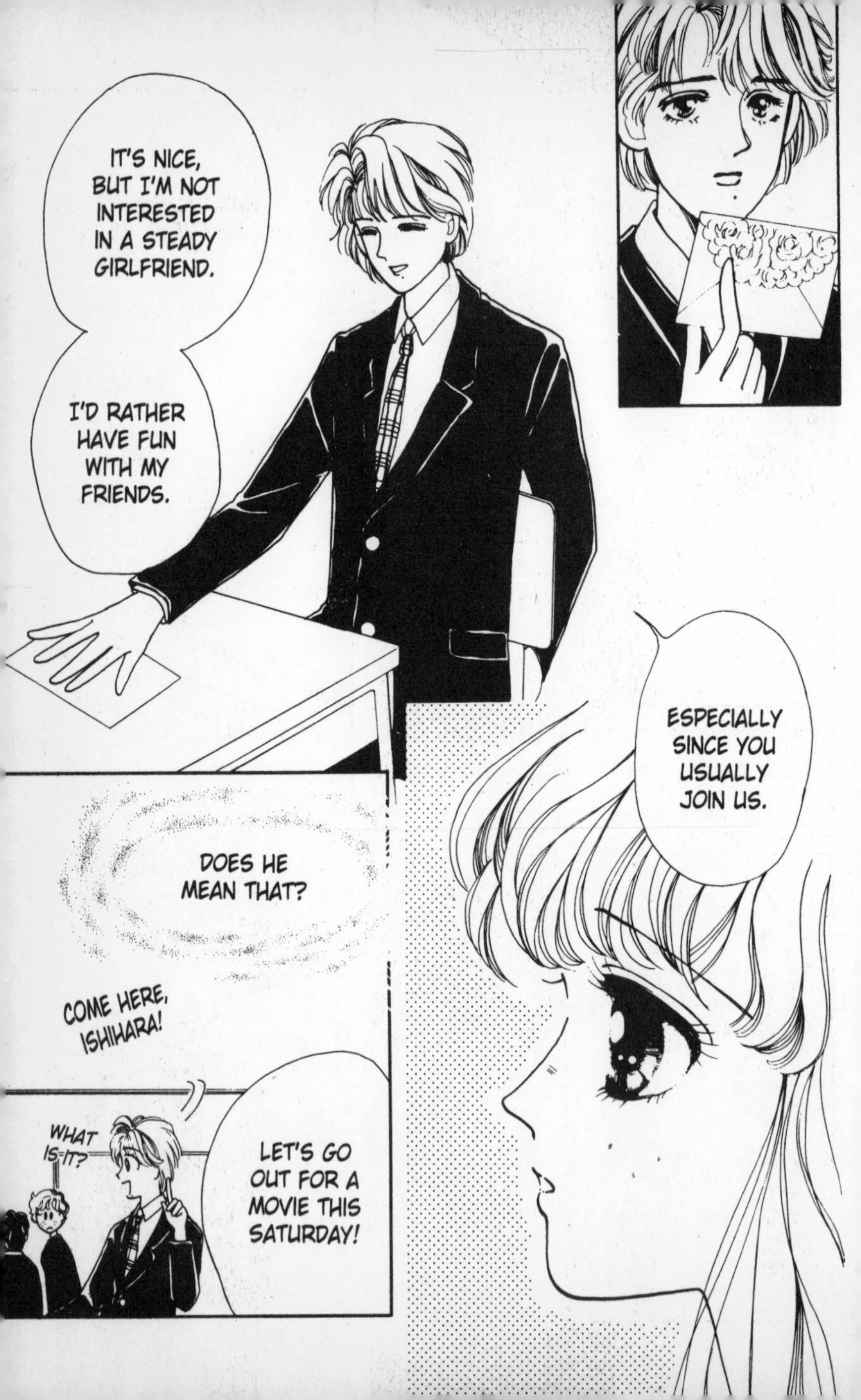
IT'S NICE, BUT I'M NOT INTERESTED IN A STEADY GIRLFRIEND.
I'D RATHER HAVE FUN WITH MY FRIENDS.
ESPECIALLY SINCE YOU USUALLY JOIN US.
DOES HE MEAN THAT?
COME HERE, ISHIHARA!
WHAT IS IT?
LET'S GO OUT FOR A MOVIE THIS SATURDAY!

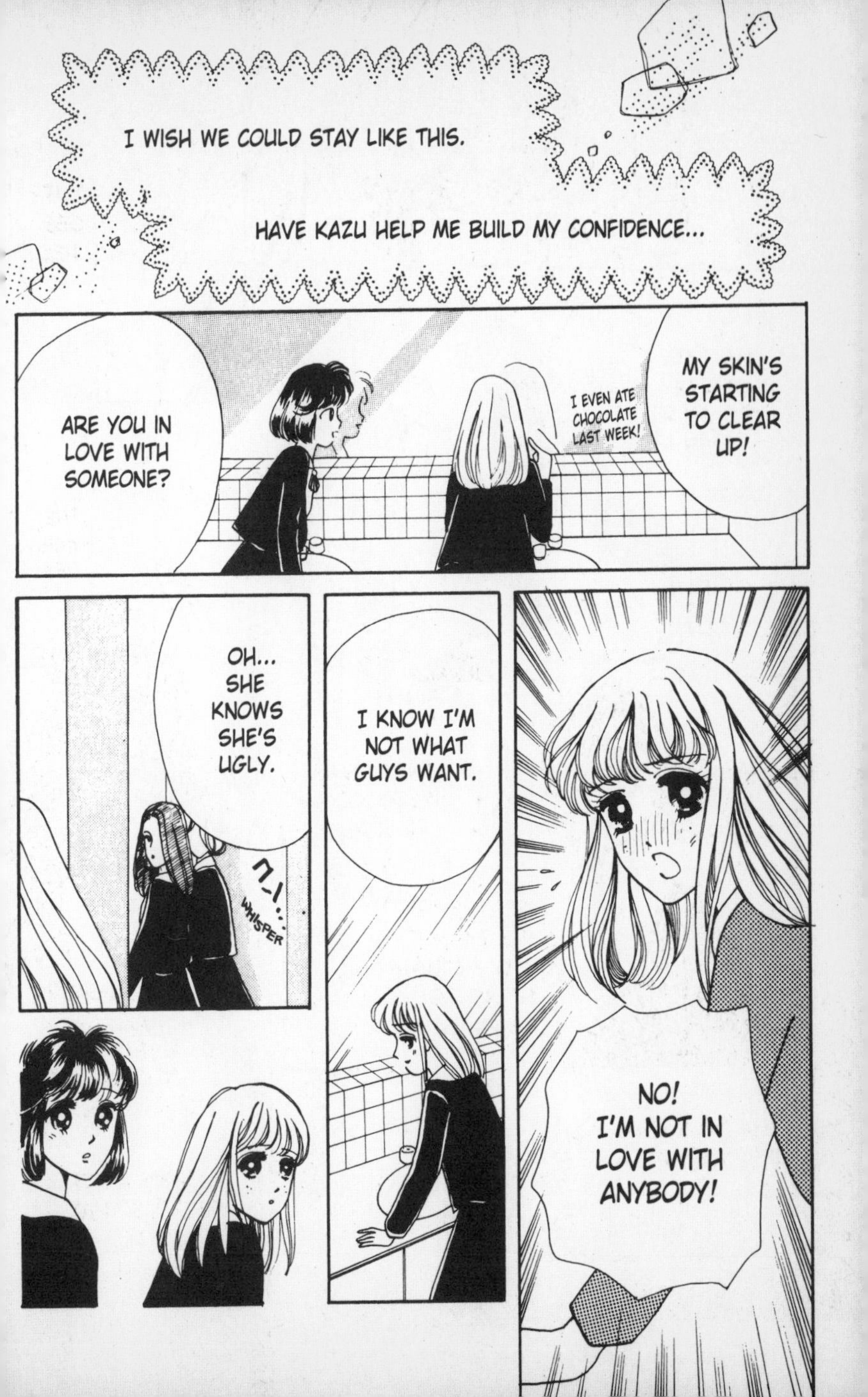
I WISH WE COULD STAY LIKE THIS.
HAVE KAZU HELP ME BUILD MY CONFIDENCE...
MY SKIN'S STARTING TO CLEAR UP!
I EVEN ATE CHOCOLATE LAST WEEK!
ARE YOU IN LOVE WITH SOMEONE?
NO! I'M NOT IN LOVE WITH ANYBODY!
I KNOW I'M NOT WHAT GUYS WANT.
OH... SHE KNOWS SHE'S UGLY.
WHISPER

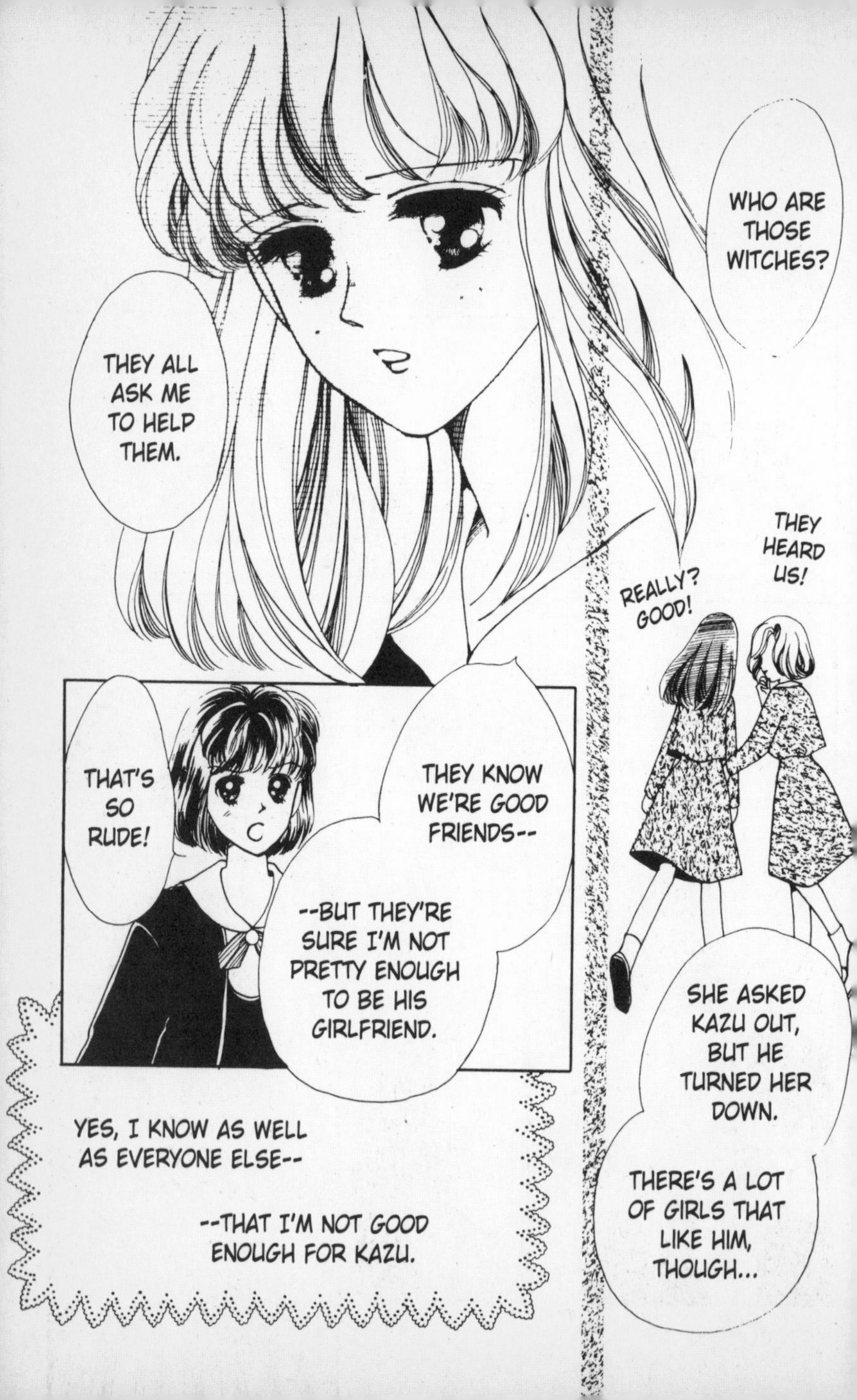
WHO ARE THOSE WITCHES?
THEY HEARD US!
REALLY? GOOD!
SHE ASKED KAZU OUT, BUT HE TURNED HER DOWN.
THERE'S A LOT OF GIRLS THAT LIKE HIM, THOUGH...
THEY ALL ASK ME TO HELP THEM.
THEY KNOW WE'RE GOOD FRIENDS--
--BUT THEY'RE SURE I'M NOT PRETTY ENOUGH TO BE HIS GIRLFRIEND.
THAT'S SO RUDE!
YES, I KNOW AS WELL AS EVERYONE ELSE--
--THAT I'M NOT GOOD ENOUGH FOR KAZU.

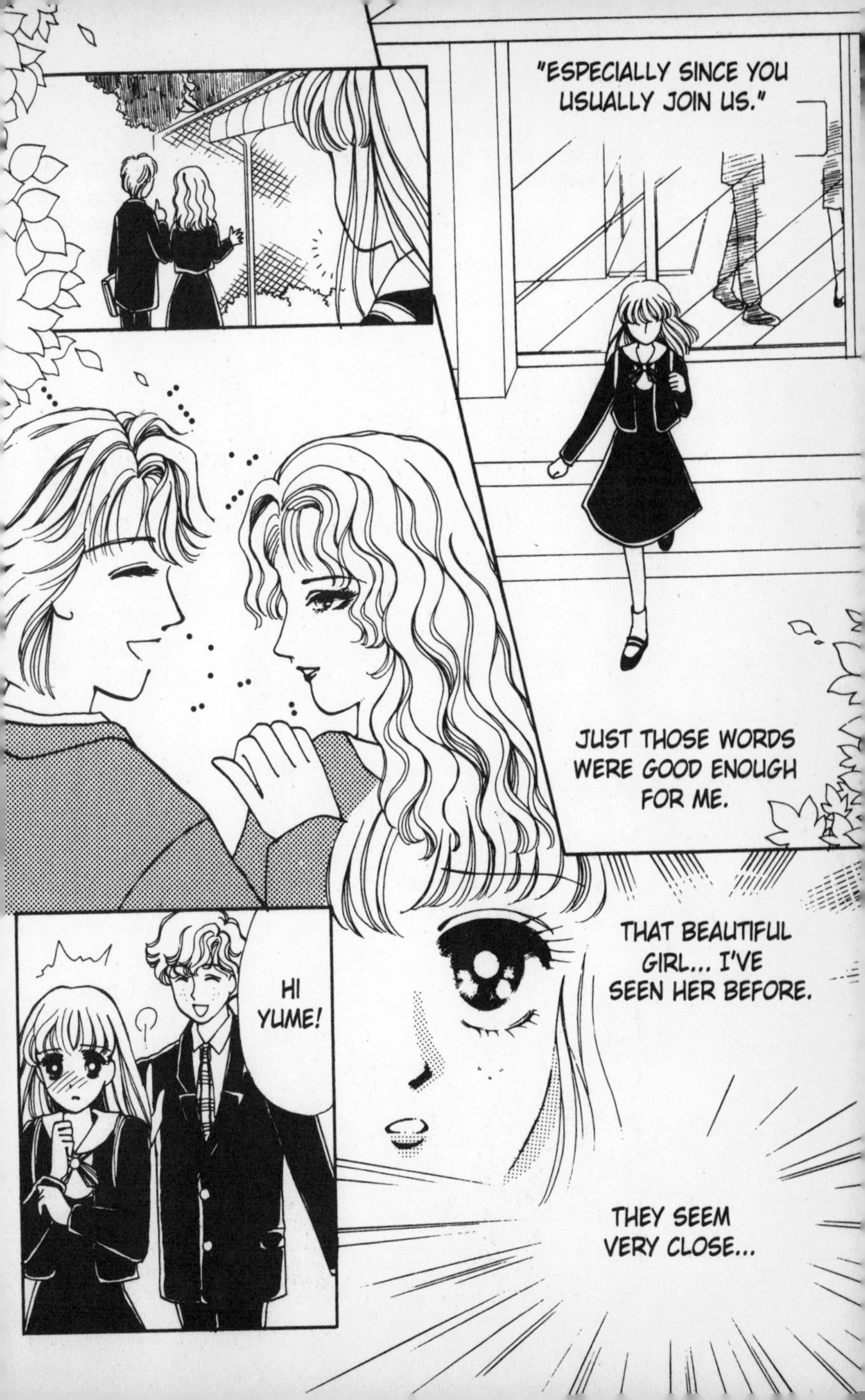
"ESPECIALLY SINCE YOU USUALLY JOIN US."
JUST THOSE WORDS WERE GOOD ENOUGH FOR ME.
THAT BEAUTIFUL GIRL... I'VE SEEN HER BEFORE.
THEY SEEM VERY CLOSE...
HI YUME!

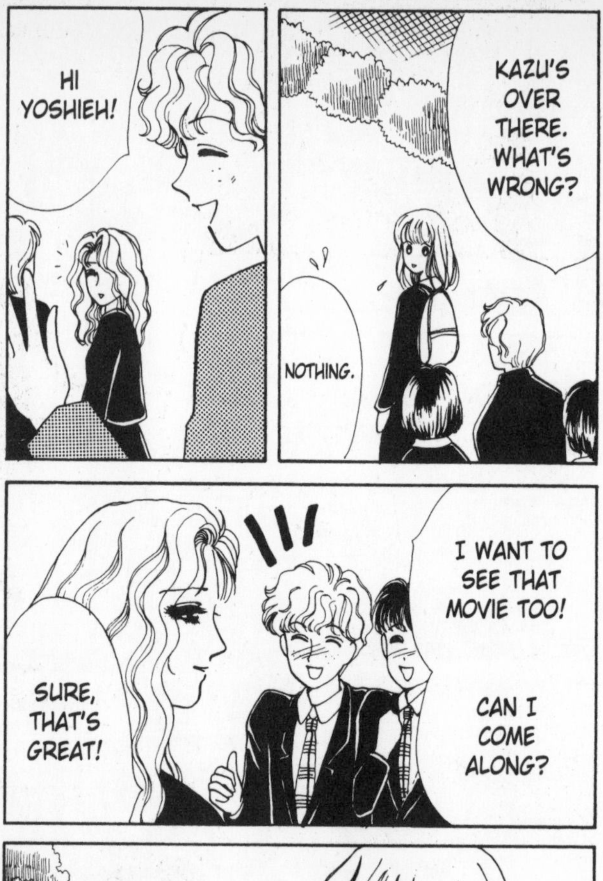
KAZU'S OVER THERE. WHAT'S WRONG?
NOTHING.
HI YOSHIEH!
I WANT TO SEE THAT MOVIE TOO!
CAN I COME ALONG?
SURE, THAT'S GREAT!
YUME, YOSHIEH AND KAZU ARE COUSINS.
COUSINS?

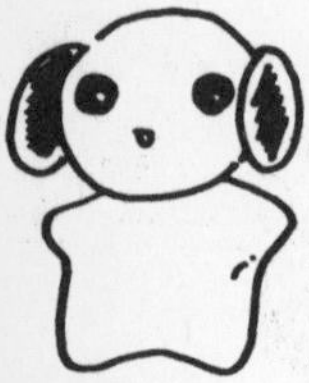

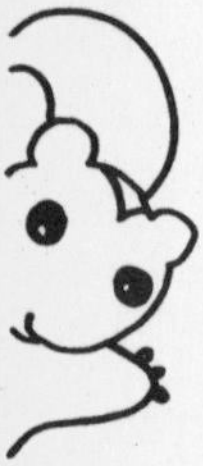

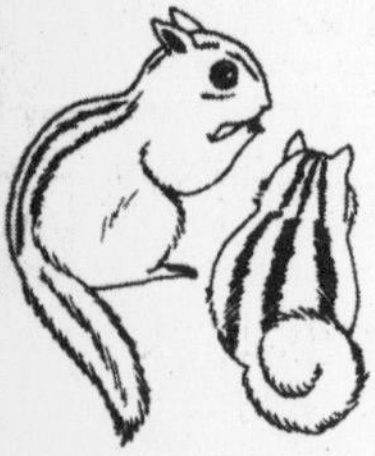

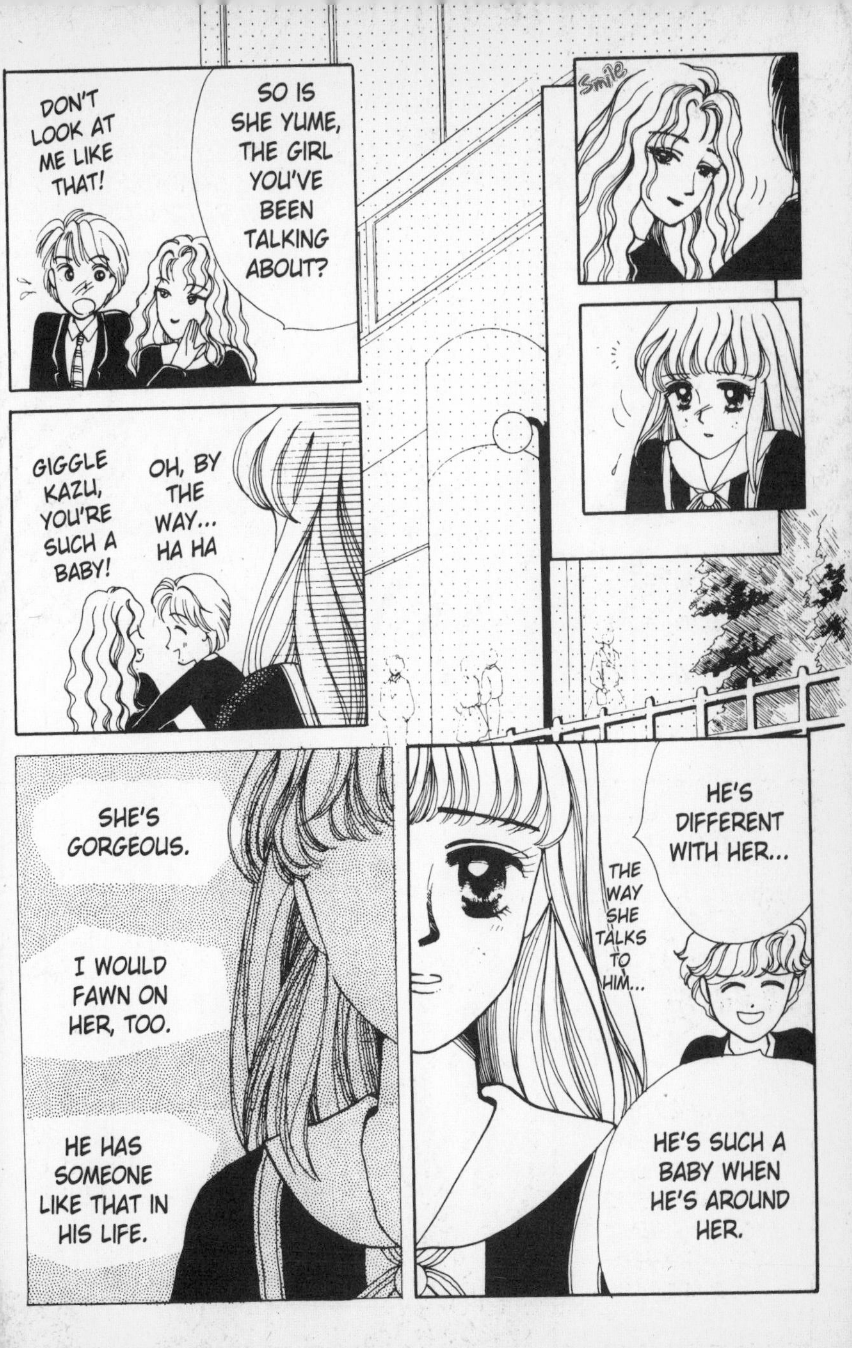
Smile
SO IS SHE YUME, THE GIRL YOU'VE BEEN TALKING ABOUT?
DON'T LOOK AT ME LIKE THAT!
OH, BY THE WAY... HA HA
GIGGLE KAZU, YOU'RE SUCH A BABY!
HE'S DIFFERENT WITH HER...
THE WAY SHE TALKS TO HIM...
HE'S SUCH A BABY WHEN HE'S AROUND HER.
SHE'S GORGEOUS.
I WOULD FAWN ON HER, TOO.
HE HAS SOMEONE LIKE THAT IN HIS LIFE.

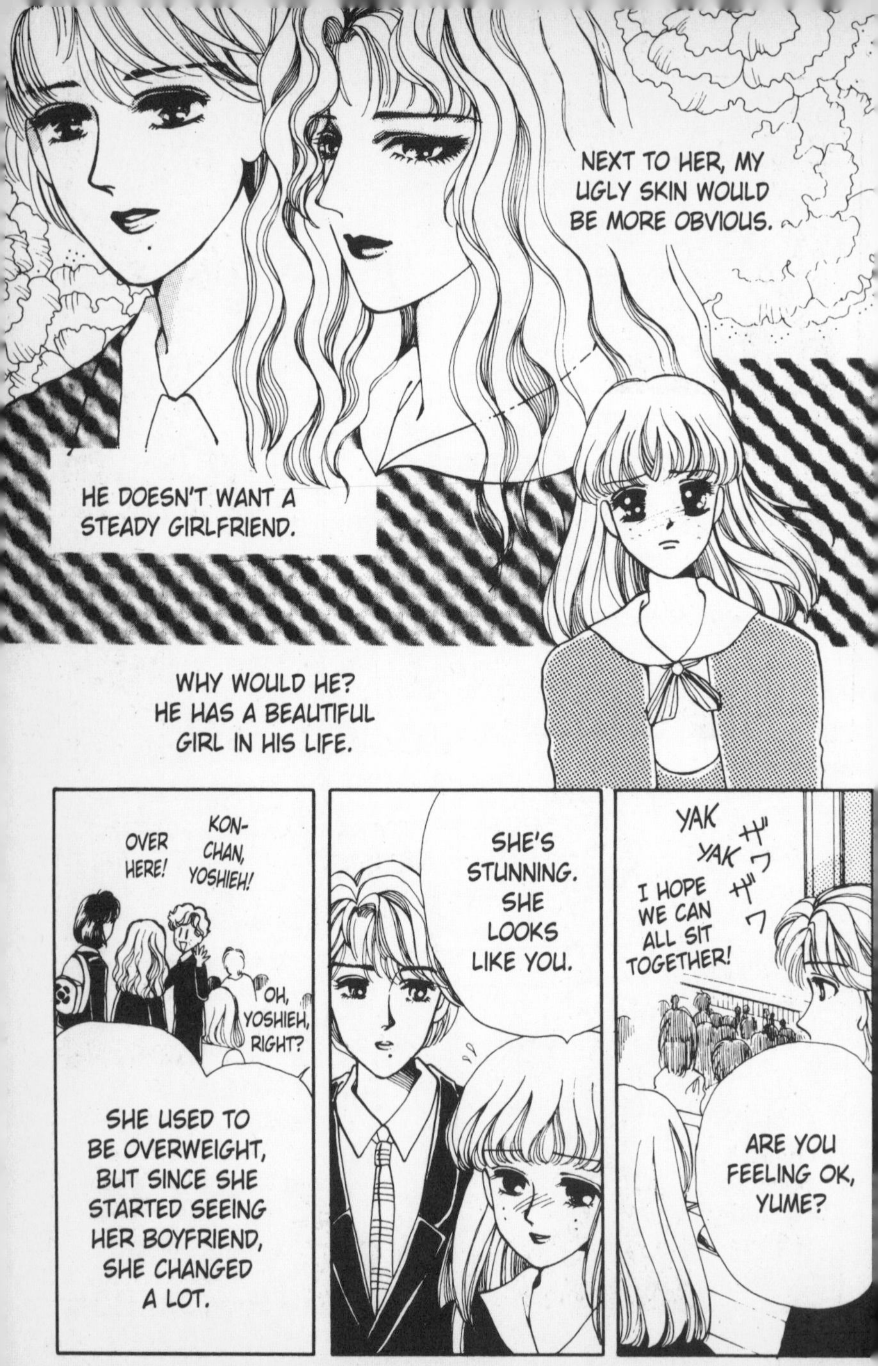
NEXT TO HER, MY UGLY SKIN WOULD BE MORE OBVIOUS.
HE DOESN'T WANT A STEADY GIRLFRIEND.
WHY WOULD HE? HE HAS A BEAUTIFUL GIRL IN HIS LIFE.
YAK YAK
ザワ ザワ
I HOPE WE CAN ALL SIT TOGETHER!
ARE YOU FEELING OK, YUME?
SHE'S STUNNING. SHE LOOKS LIKE YOU.
KON-CHAN, YOSHIEH!
OVER HERE!
OH, YOSHIEH, RIGHT?
SHE USED TO BE OVERWEIGHT, BUT SINCE SHE STARTED SEEING HER BOYFRIEND, SHE CHANGED A LOT.

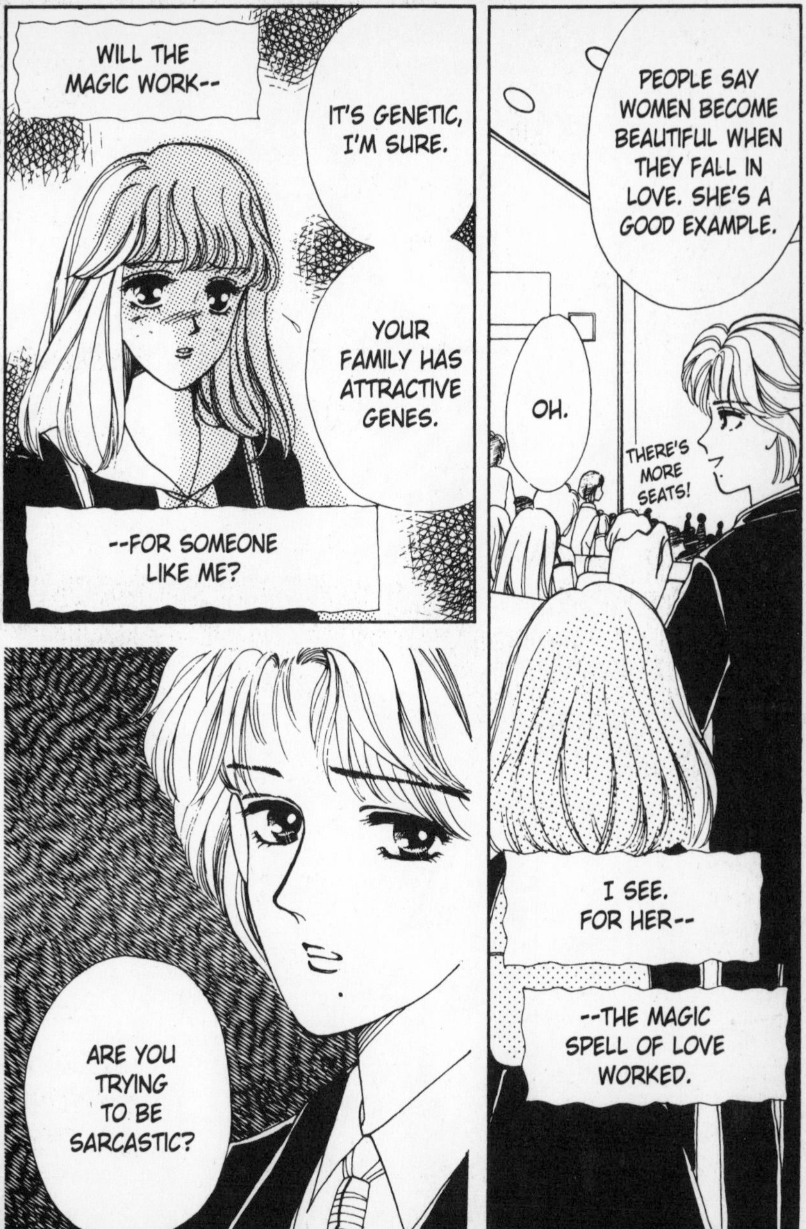
PEOPLE SAY WOMEN BECOME BEAUTIFUL WHEN THEY FALL IN LOVE. SHE'S A GOOD EXAMPLE.
OH.
THERE'S MORE SEATS!
I SEE. FOR HER--
--THE MAGIC SPELL OF LOVE WORKED.
IT'S GENETIC, I'M SURE.
YOUR FAMILY HAS ATTRACTIVE GENES.
WILL THE MAGIC WORK--
--FOR SOMEONE LIKE ME?
ARE YOU TRYING TO BE SARCASTIC?

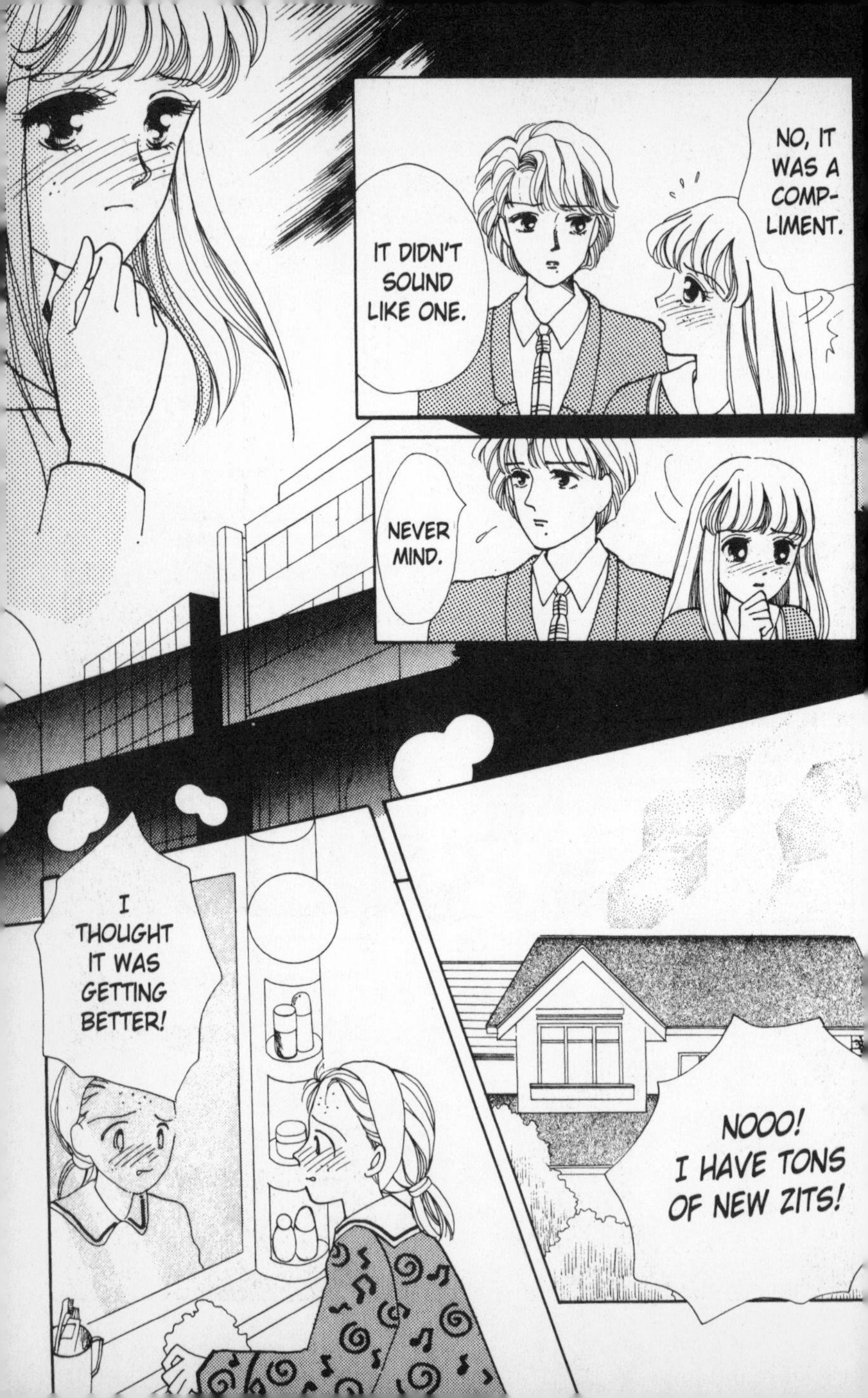
NO, IT WAS A COMP-LIMENT.
IT DIDN'T SOUND LIKE ONE.
NEVER MIND.
NOOO! I HAVE TONS OF NEW ZITS!
I THOUGHT IT WAS GETTING BETTER!

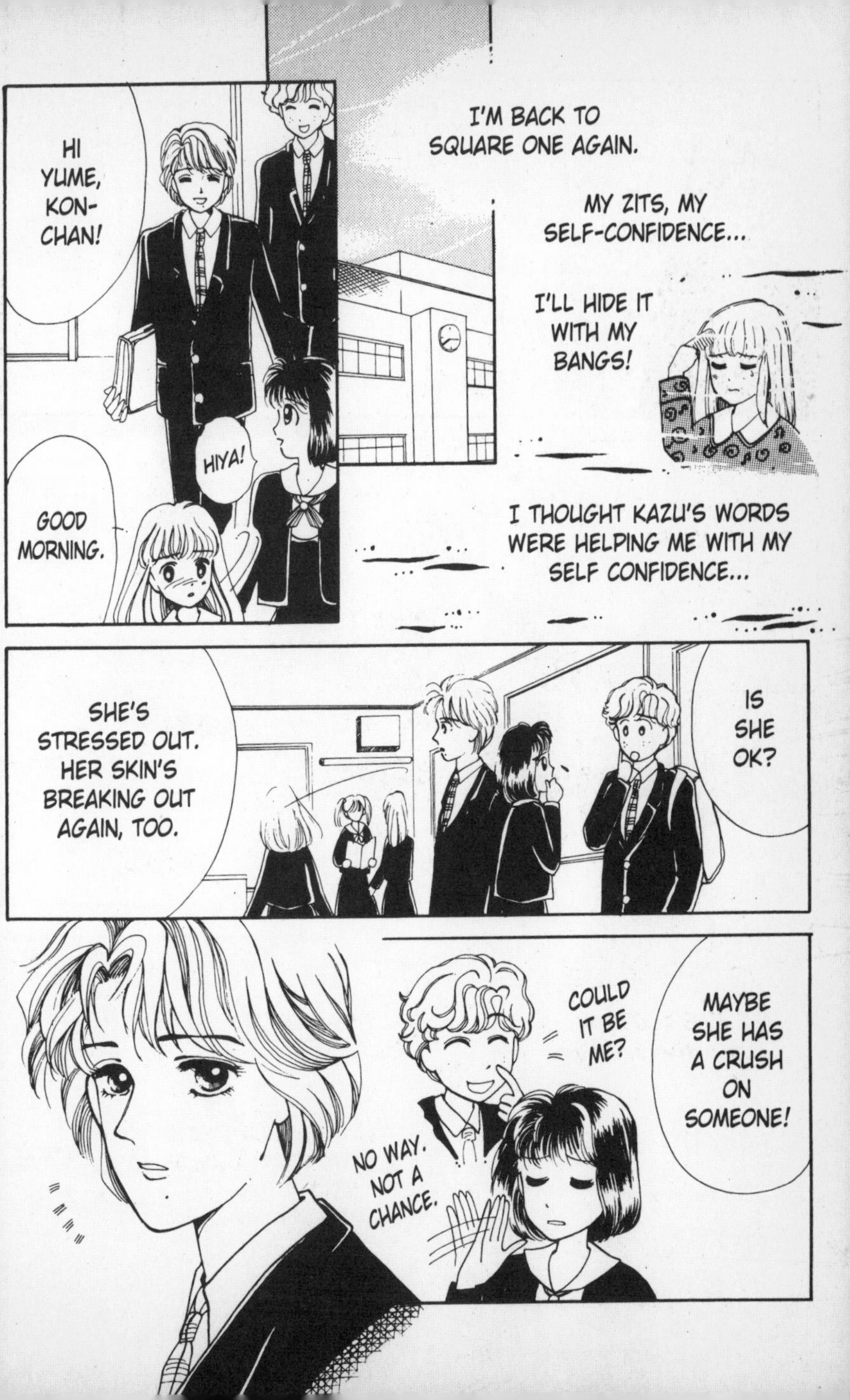
I'M BACK TO SQUARE ONE AGAIN.
MY ZITS, MY SELF-CONFIDENCE...
I'LL HIDE IT WITH MY BANGS!
I THOUGHT KAZU'S WORDS WERE HELPING ME WITH MY SELF CONFIDENCE...
HI YUME, KON-CHAN!
HIYA!
GOOD MORNING.
IS SHE OK?
SHE'S STRESSED OUT. HER SKIN'S BREAKING OUT AGAIN, TOO.
MAYBE SHE HAS A CRUSH ON SOMEONE!
COULD IT BE ME?
NO WAY. NOT A CHANCE.

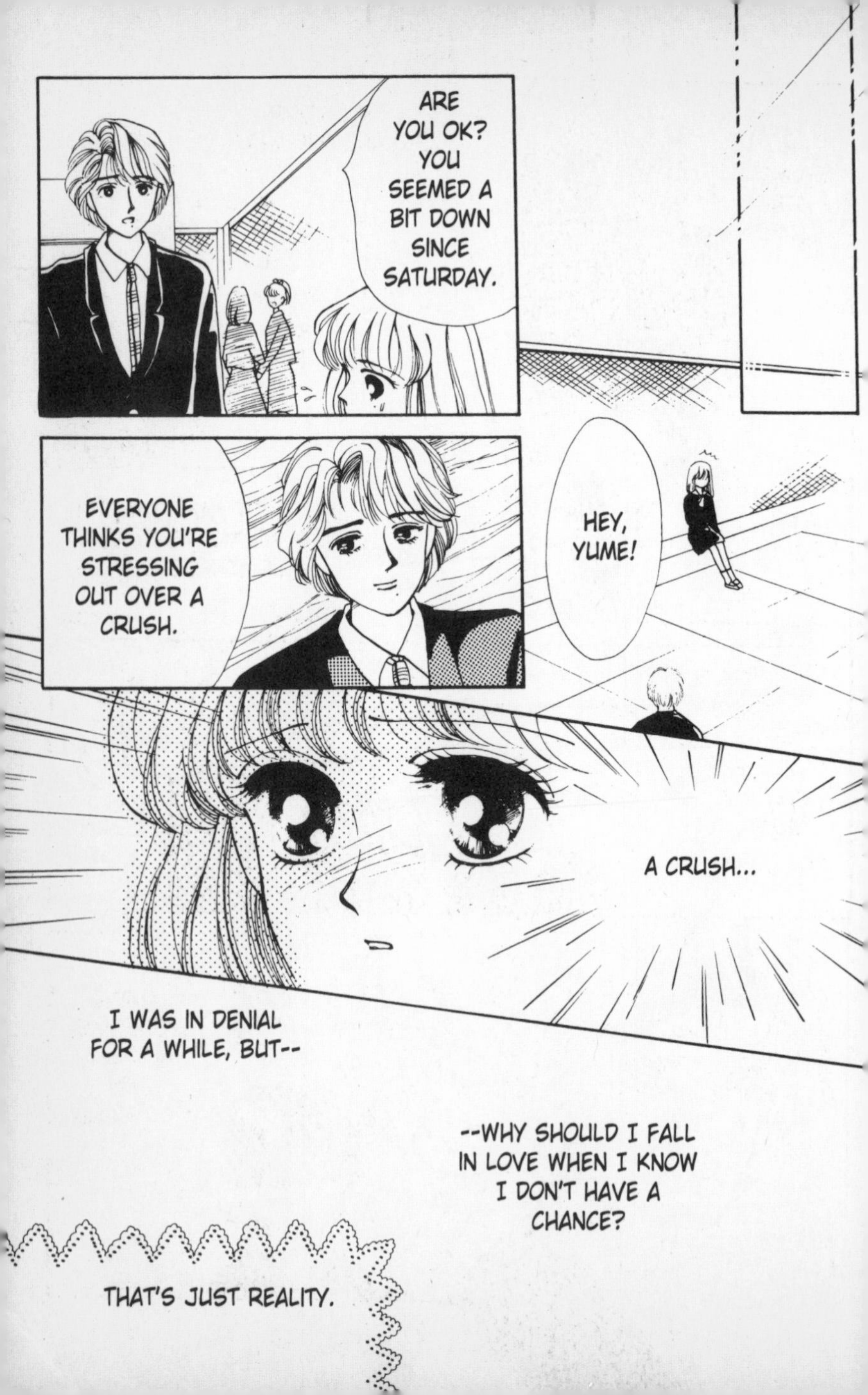
HEY, YUME!
ARE YOU OK? YOU SEEMED A BIT DOWN SINCE SATURDAY.
EVERYONE THINKS YOU'RE STRESSING OUT OVER A CRUSH.
A CRUSH...
I WAS IN DENIAL FOR A WHILE, BUT--
--WHY SHOULD I FALL IN LOVE WHEN I KNOW I DON'T HAVE A CHANCE?
THAT'S JUST REALITY.

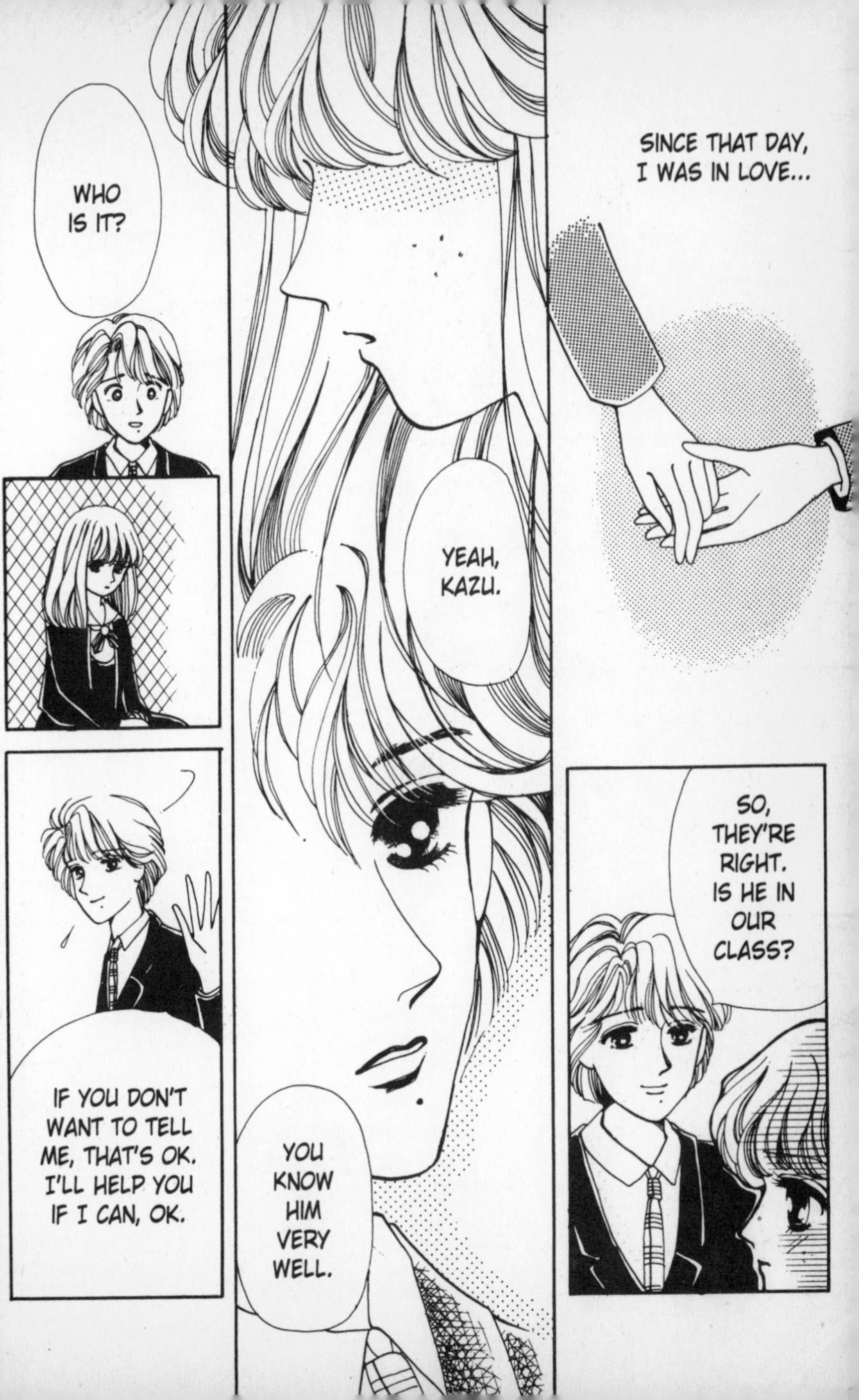
SINCE THAT DAY, I WAS IN LOVE...
SO, THEY'RE RIGHT. IS HE IN OUR CLASS?
YEAH, KAZU.
YOU KNOW HIM VERY WELL.
WHO IS IT?
IF YOU DON'T WANT TO TELL ME, THAT'S OK. I'LL HELP YOU IF I CAN, OK.

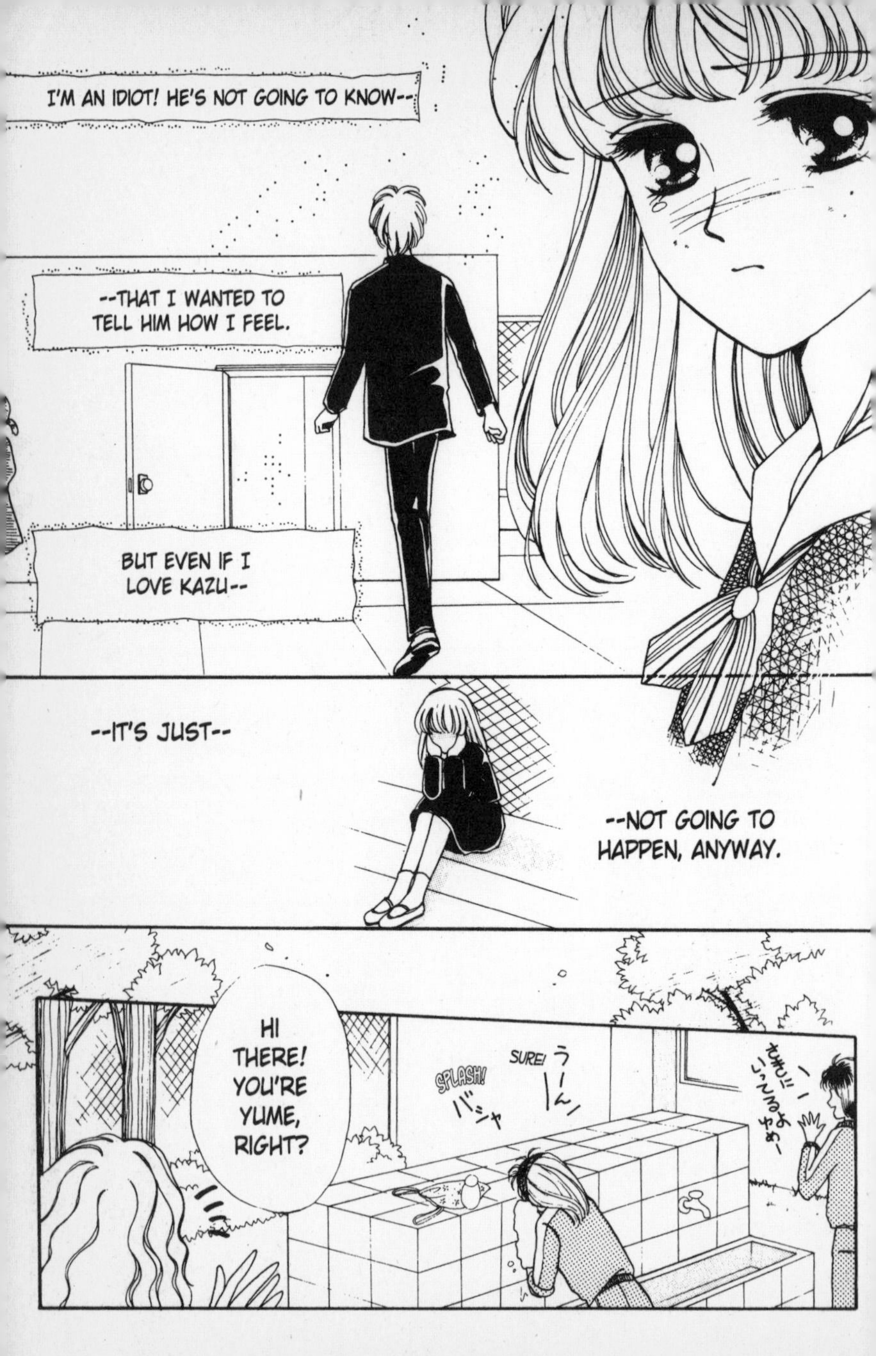
I'M AN IDIOT! HE'S NOT GOING TO KNOW--
--THAT I WANTED TO TELL HIM HOW I FEEL.
BUT EVEN IF I LOVE KAZU--
--IT'S JUST--
--NOT GOING TO HAPPEN, ANYWAY.
さきにいってるよゆめー
SURE! うーん
SPLASH! バシャ
HI THERE! YOU'RE YUME, RIGHT?

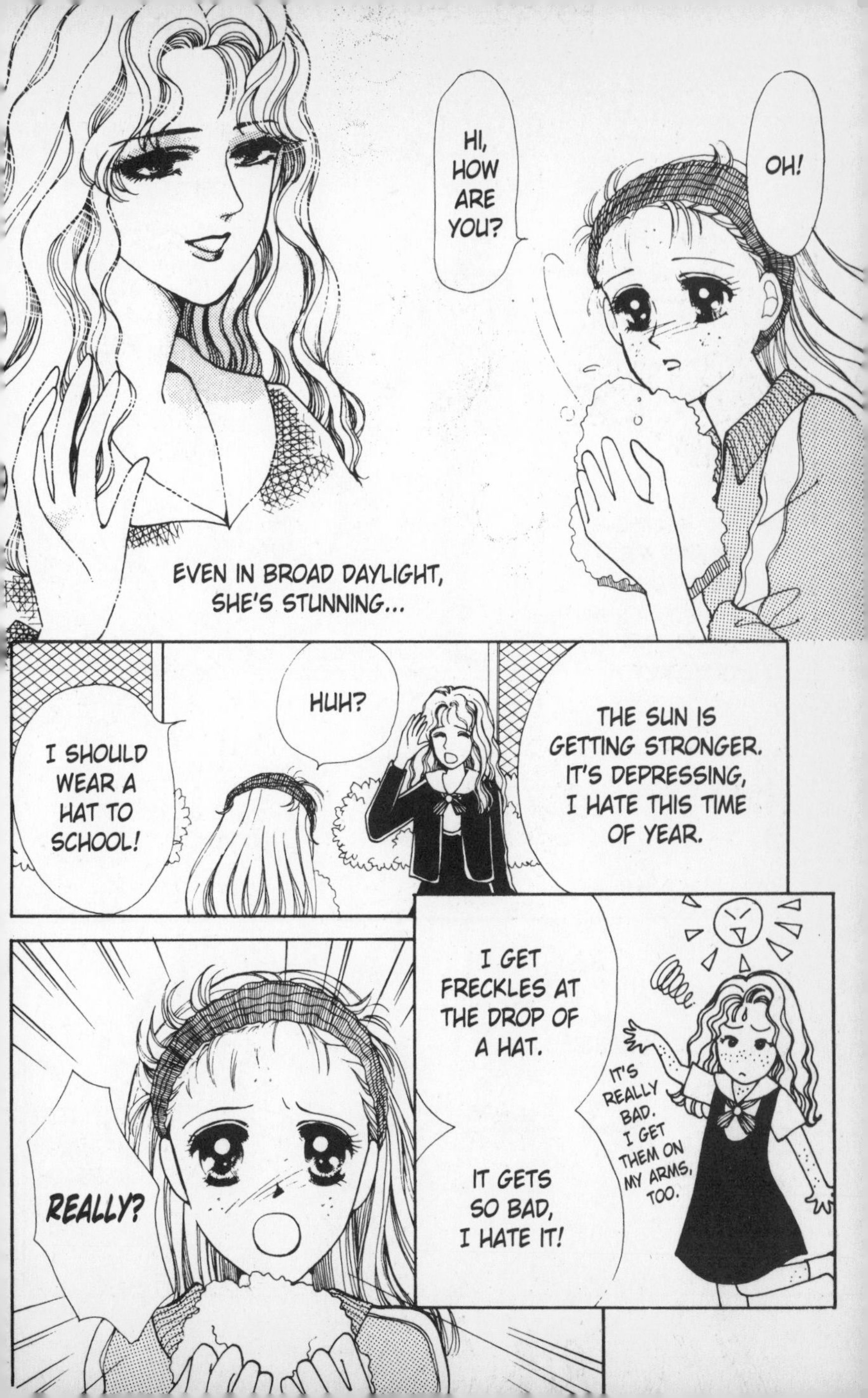
OH!
HI, HOW ARE YOU?
EVEN IN BROAD DAYLIGHT, SHE'S STUNNING...
THE SUN IS GETTING STRONGER. IT'S DEPRESSING, I HATE THIS TIME OF YEAR.
HUH?
I SHOULD WEAR A HAT TO SCHOOL!
I GET FRECKLES AT THE DROP OF A HAT.
IT'S REALLY BAD. I GET THEM ON MY ARMS, TOO.
IT GETS SO BAD, I HATE IT!
REALLY?

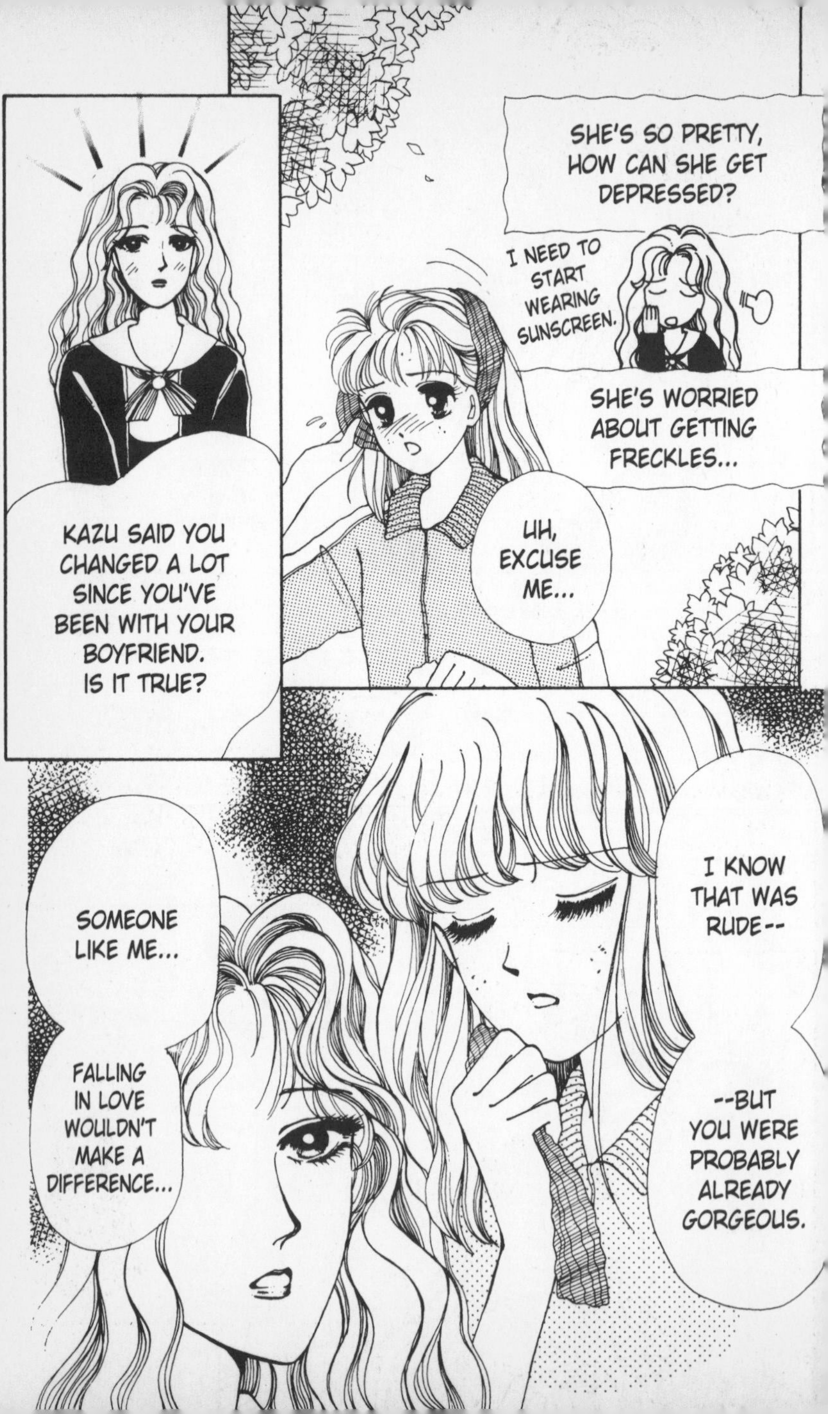
SHE'S SO PRETTY, HOW CAN SHE GET DEPRESSED?
I NEED TO START WEARING SUNSCREEN.
SHE'S WORRIED ABOUT GETTING FRECKLES...
UH, EXCUSE ME...
KAZU SAID YOU CHANGED A LOT SINCE YOU'VE BEEN WITH YOUR BOYFRIEND. IS IT TRUE?
I KNOW THAT WAS RUDE--
--BUT YOU WERE PROBABLY ALREADY GORGEOUS.
SOMEONE LIKE ME...
FALLING IN LOVE WOULDN'T MAKE A DIFFERENCE...

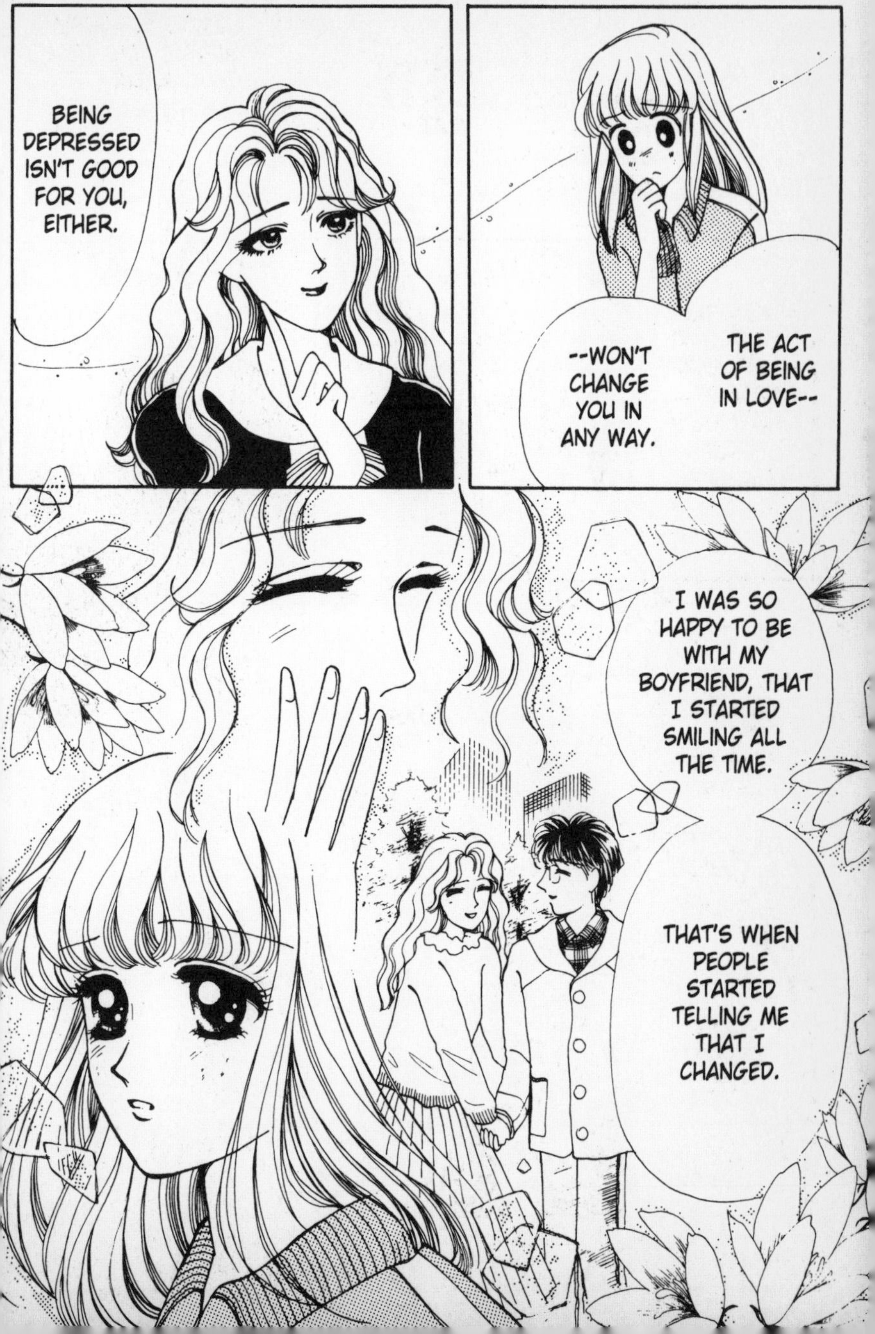
THE ACT OF BEING IN LOVE--
--WON'T CHANGE YOU IN ANY WAY.
BEING DEPRESSED ISN'T GOOD FOR YOU, EITHER.
I WAS SO HAPPY TO BE WITH MY BOYFRIEND, THAT I STARTED SMILING ALL THE TIME.
THAT'S WHEN PEOPLE STARTED TELLING ME THAT I CHANGED.

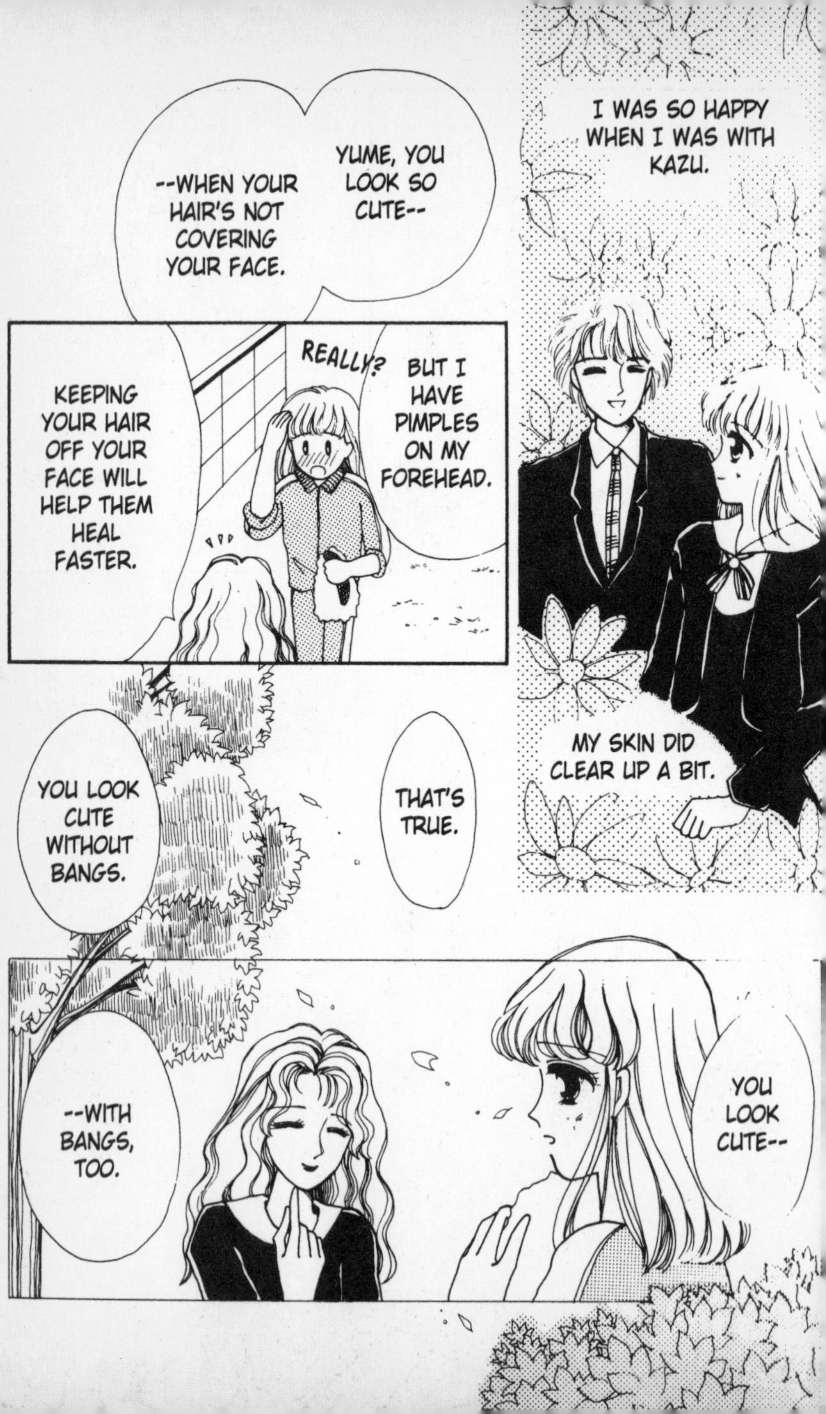
I WAS SO HAPPY WHEN I WAS WITH KAZU.
MY SKIN DID CLEAR UP A BIT.
YUME, YOU LOOK SO CUTE--
--WHEN YOUR HAIR'S NOT COVERING YOUR FACE.
REALLY?
BUT I HAVE PIMPLES ON MY FOREHEAD.
KEEPING YOUR HAIR OFF YOUR FACE WILL HELP THEM HEAL FASTER.
THAT'S TRUE.
YOU LOOK CUTE WITHOUT BANGS.
YOU LOOK CUTE--
--WITH BANGS, TOO.

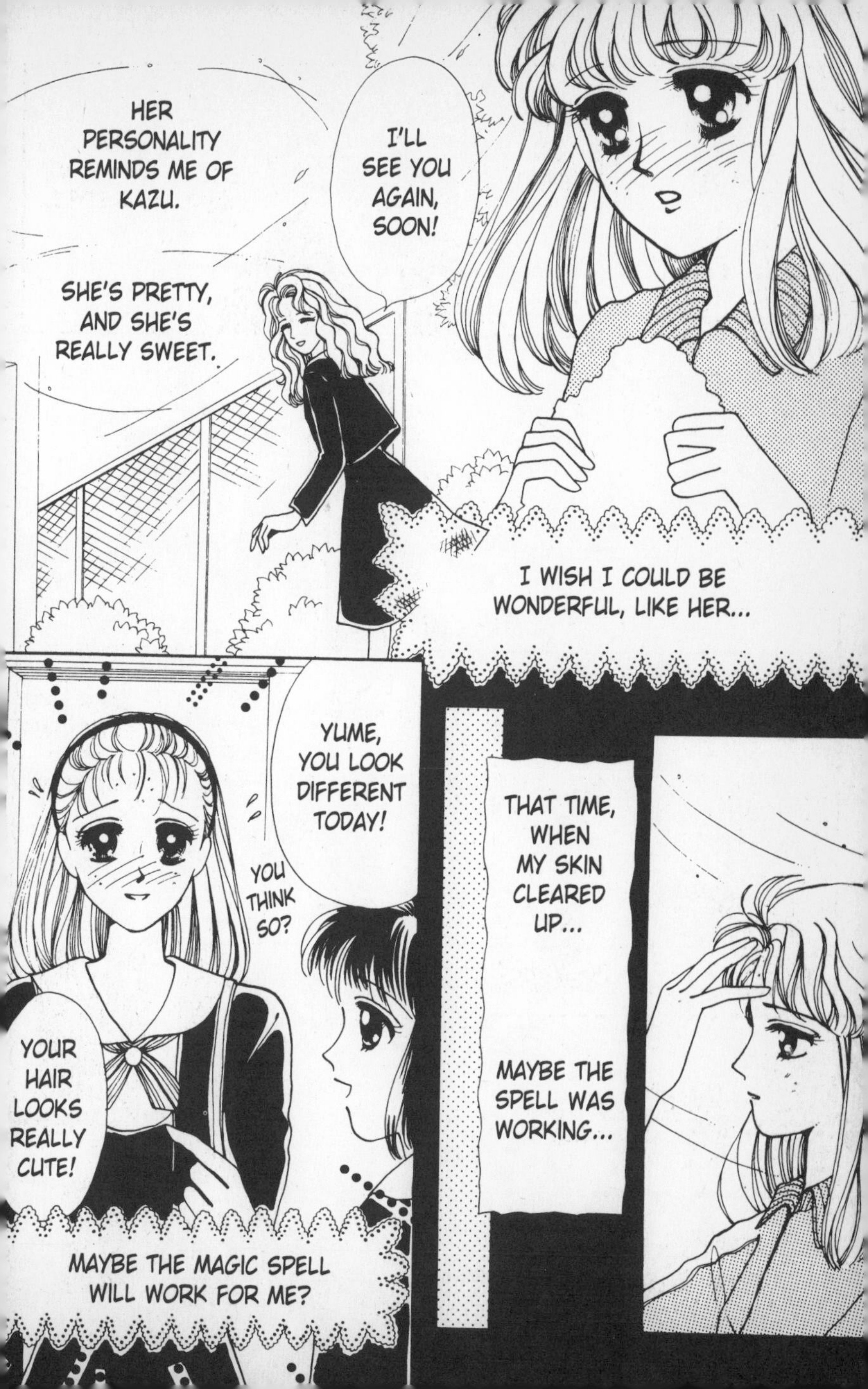
I WISH I COULD BE WONDERFUL, LIKE HER...
I'LL SEE YOU AGAIN, SOON!
HER PERSONALITY REMINDS ME OF KAZU.
SHE'S PRETTY, AND SHE'S REALLY SWEET.
THAT TIME, WHEN MY SKIN CLEARED UP...
MAYBE THE SPELL WAS WORKING...
YUME, YOU LOOK DIFFERENT TODAY!
YOU THINK SO?
YOUR HAIR LOOKS REALLY CUTE!
MAYBE THE MAGIC SPELL WILL WORK FOR ME?

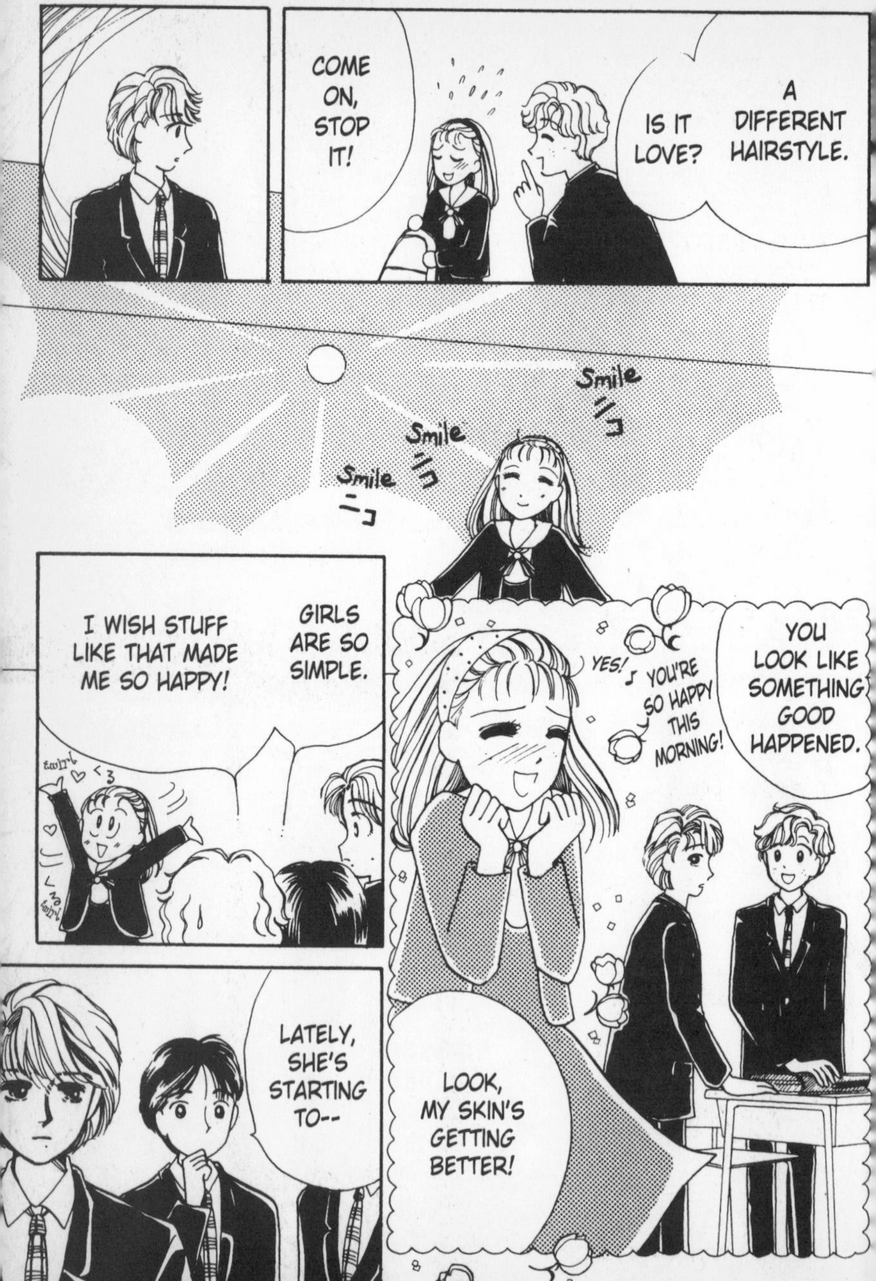
A DIFFERENT HAIRSTYLE.
IS IT LOVE?
COME ON, STOP IT!
Smile
ニコ
Smile
ニコ
Smile
ニコ
YOU LOOK LIKE SOMETHING GOOD HAPPENED.
YES! ♪ YOU'RE SO HAPPY THIS MORNING!
LOOK, MY SKIN'S GETTING BETTER!
GIRLS ARE SO SIMPLE.
I WISH STUFF LIKE THAT MADE ME SO HAPPY!
LATELY, SHE'S STARTING TO--

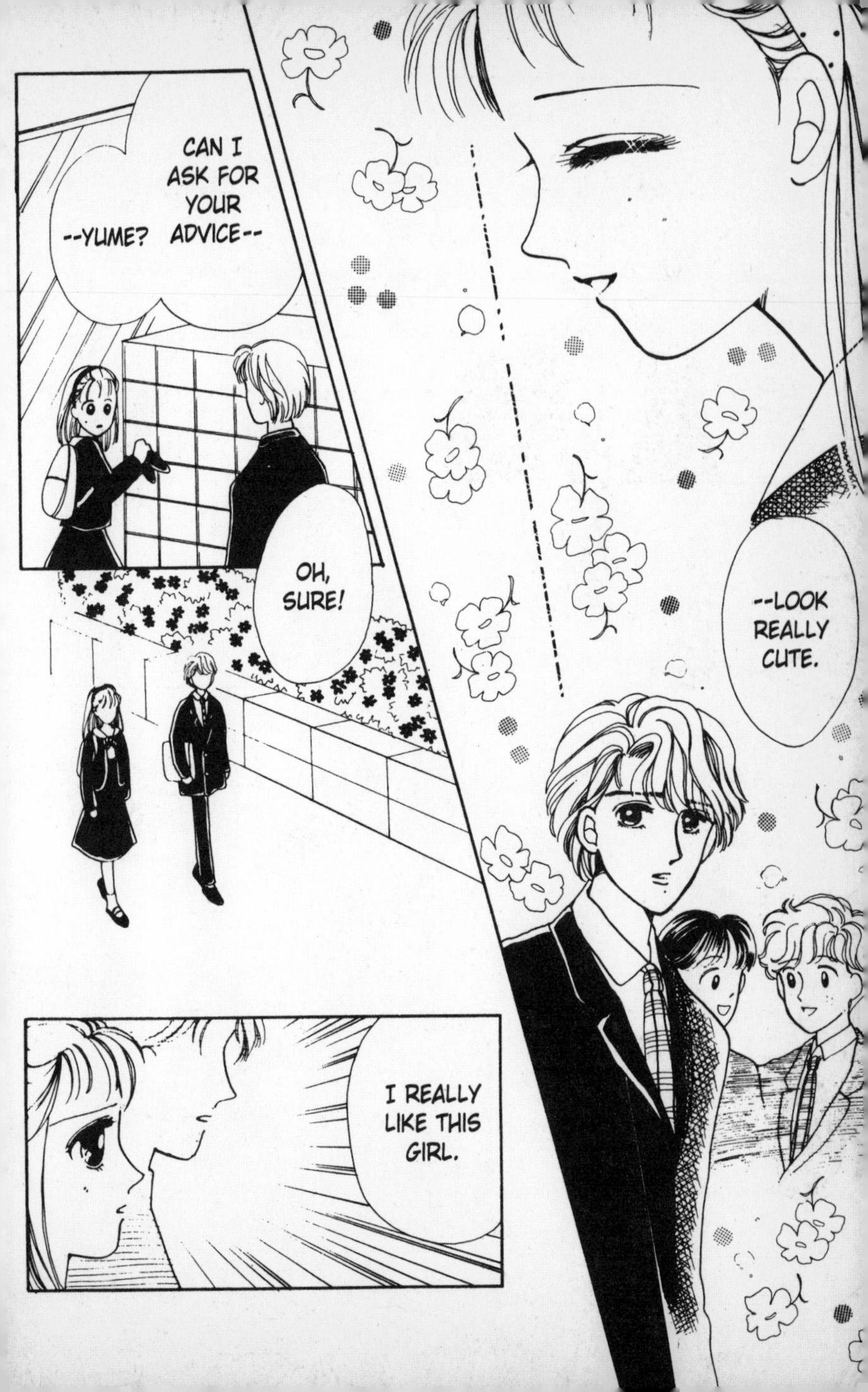
--LOOK REALLY CUTE.
CAN I ASK FOR YOUR ADVICE--
--YUME?
OH, SURE!
I REALLY LIKE THIS GIRL.

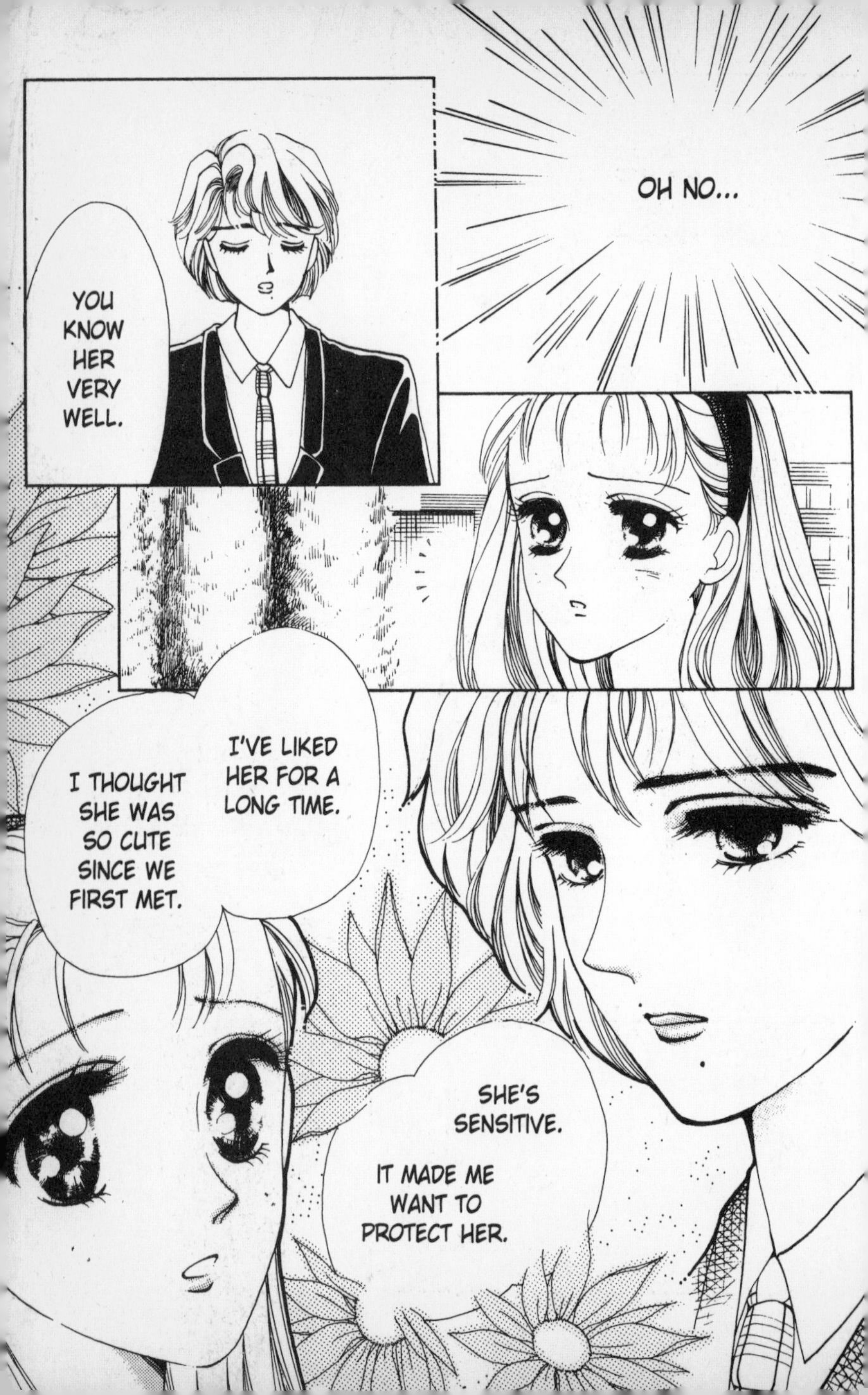
OH NO...
YOU KNOW HER VERY WELL.
I'VE LIKED HER FOR A LONG TIME.
I THOUGHT SHE WAS SO CUTE SINCE WE FIRST MET.
SHE'S SENSITIVE.
IT MADE ME WANT TO PROTECT HER.

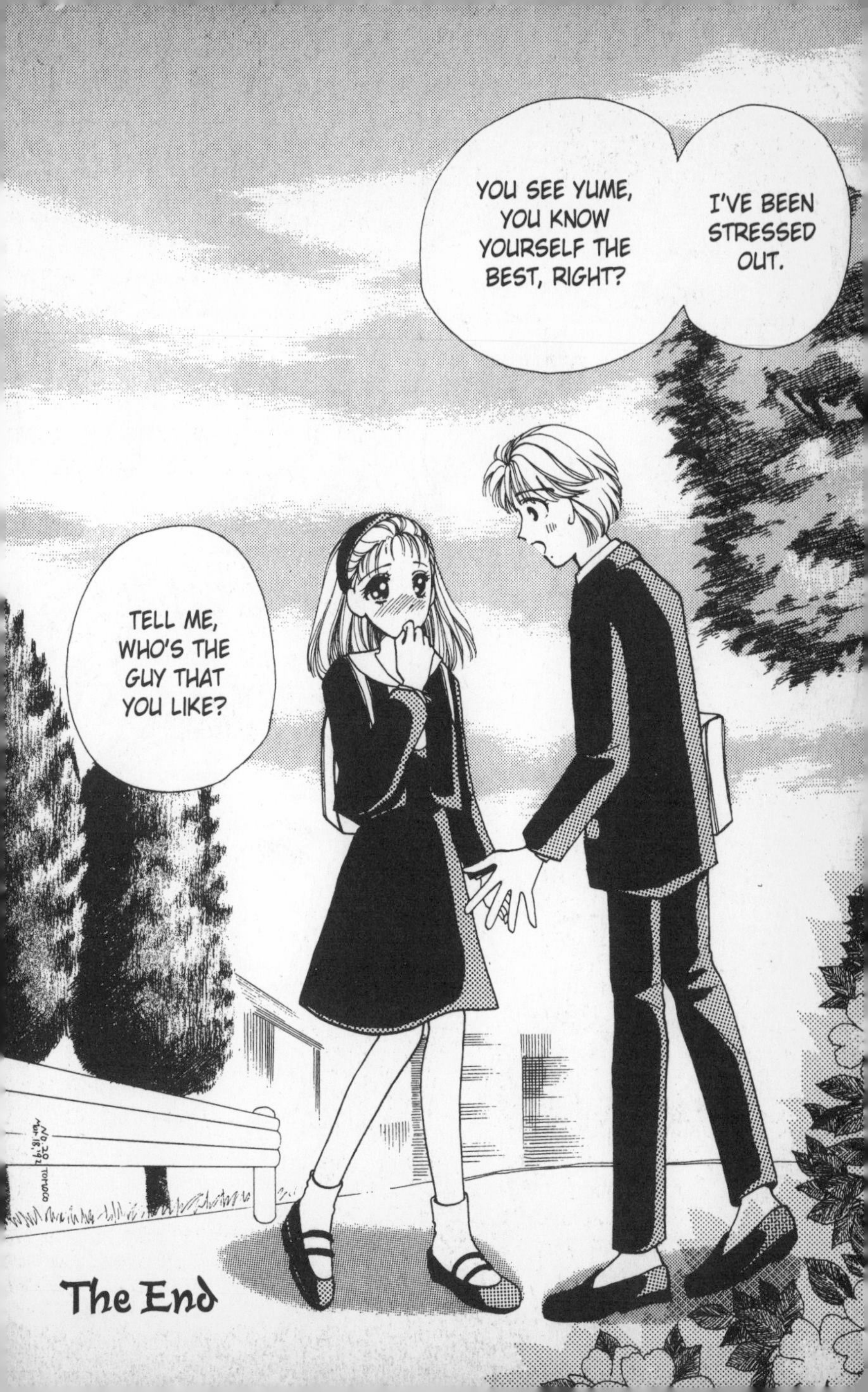
I'VE BEEN STRESSED OUT.
YOU SEE YUME, YOU KNOW YOURSELF THE BEST, RIGHT?
TELL ME, WHO'S THE GUY THAT YOU LIKE?
The End

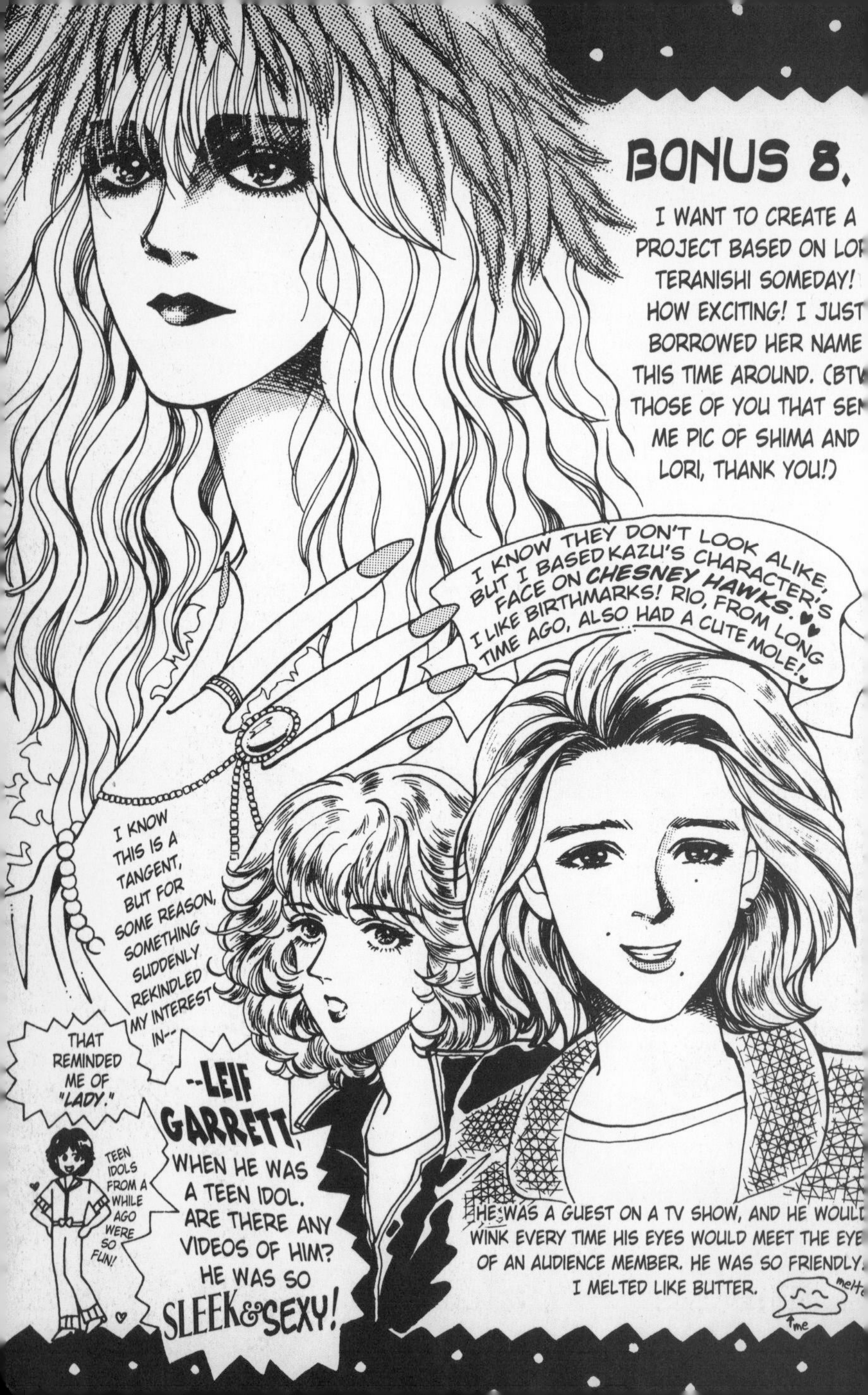
BONUS 8.
I WANT TO CREATE A PROJECT BASED ON LO
LOR TERANISHI SOMEDAY! HOW EXCITING! I JUST BORROWED HER NAME THIS TIME AROUND. (BT
THOSE OF YOU THAT SEN
ME PIC OF SHIMA AND LORI, THANK YOU!)
I KNOW THEY DON'T LOOK ALIKE, BUT I BASED KAZU'S CHARACTER'S FACE ON CHESNEY HAWKS. I LIKE BIRTHMARKS! RIO, FROM LONG TIME AGO, ALSO HAD A CUTE MOLE!
I KNOW THIS IS A TANGENT, BUT FOR SOME REASON, SOMETHING SUDDENLY REKINDLED MY INTEREST IN--
--LEIF GARRETT, WHEN HE WAS A TEEN IDOL. ARE THERE ANY VIDEOS OF HIM? HE WAS SO SLEEK&SEXY!
THAT REMINDED ME OF "LADY."
TEEN IDOLS FROM A WHILE AGO WERE SO FUN!
HE WAS A GUEST ON A TV SHOW, AND HE WOUL
WINK EVERY TIME HIS EYES WOULD MEET THE EYE
OF AN AUDIENCE MEMBER. HE WAS SO FRIENDLY.
I MELTED LIKE BUTTER.
melt
me

♡ THANK YOU TO ALL MY READERS! IF YOU BOTHERED TO READ THE BONUS COMMENTS, THANK YOU VERY MUCH! I WOULD LOVE TO HEAR FROM YOU! I HOPE LOVE AND PEACE COMES INTO YOUR LIFE, JUST LIKE RYOU AND ZEN!

♡ THANK YOU, TO EVERYONE THAT HELPED ME WITH THIS PROJECT! KUMI OKAMOTO AND HARUE MODEKI, THANK YOU FOR TAKING TIME OUT OF YOUR BUSY SCHEDULE TO HELP ME. MISAKO YAMADA, KEI MIZUKI, THANK YOU FOR THE GORGEOUS BACKGROUNDS!

♡ MY EDITOR, THANK YOU FOR YOUR HARD WORK DURING THE MANY YEARS WE WORKED TOGETHER!

♡ THANK YOU TO ALL MY FRIENDS THAT PROVIDE ME, THE PROBLEM-RIDDLED, IMMATURE ONE, WITH SUPPORT. I AM ABLE TO WORK SO HARD BECAUSE YOU ARE ALL A PART OF MY LIFE. I'VE ALWAYS FELT THIS WAY, BUT I'VE BEEN FEELING IT A LOT MORE LATELY. AGAIN, THANK YOU.

♡ LIVE LONG & PROSPER ♡ 🖖

May the Force be with You ✦

We'll meet again in my next project! ♡

Tomoco Taniguchi

June. 7, '92

D. LEE: HIS FANS WILL BE MAD! IT DOESN'T LOOK LIKE HIM!

I WANTED TO BASE RYOUTA'S CHARACTER ON HIM, BUT RYOUTA ENDED UP BEING COMPLETELY DIFFERENT. THANK YOU FOR LETTING ME KNOW ABOUT HIS LIVE CONCERT, "IRIMACHI, DEMACHI." YOU CAN HAVE FUN BEING A GROUPIE FOR ME (LAUGH)! PLEASE KEEP SENDING ME UPDATES! BOO HOO! I CAN'T GO SEE HIS SHOW!

TOMOKO'S OMAKE

I hesitate publishing old books because I am a little embarrassed by my early works, but I appreciate that American readers requested to see more books by me.

This story is one of my favorites because it's about my grandparents' farm in Hokkaido. After my grandparents passed away, my uncle took over the farm. He couldn't run it forever and wanted to pass it onto his children, but none of his children wanted to take it over, so my uncle thought about selling the huge farmyard to a golf course. I was shocked to hear that I might lose my homeland where I spent a lot of time communing with animals and nature. I wanted our family to keep the land natural, the way I remembered it, so I wrote this story. Then, after all that, the golf company did not build the golf course, so my wish came true and nobody took over the farm.

In Japan there is not much natural land left anymore, so people appreciate Hokkaido where it is still unspoiled. Hokkaido is the northernmost part of Japan and it gets lots of snow so many people think it's not the place to live in winter, but many tourists visit there in the summer and autumn. It is also known as a place to get delicious food like seafood, vegetables and dairy products. People in the city envy me because I have such a nice hometown.

The model of Zenta was a drummer who was in a visual punk band (I guess many Japanese manga fans know what a Japanese visual band is). He dressed like a girl and the band broke up because he was sick. Fans were really shocked about that. I added him to my hometown story to give it a little color.

I thought it might be confusing for American readers since all of the characters in this story looked like girls. Seeing these old drawings, I feel really embarrassed…but still, this is my favorite comic.

I hope you like this book as much as you liked my other books.

Thank you very much!!
Tomoko Taniguchi
May 2003

Classic Manga
The Right Size, The Right Price

$9⁹⁹ each

Call Me Princess
Available now

Popcorn Romance
All new romance from
Tomoko Taniguchi
Available now

Aquarium
Available
November 2003

Nadesico
Book 1
As seen on
Cartoon Network!
Available now

Dark Angel
Book 1: The Path To Destiny
By **Kia Asamiya**:
*Batman Child of Dreams,
Uncanny X-Men*

Available
November 2003

WORLD ANIME PARTY ®
BIG APPLE ANIME FEST ™

SHERWOOD

New York City

ANIME SCREENINGS

WORLD PREMIERES   **SPECIAL GUESTS**

LIVE EVENTS

BAAF MART DEALER ROOM

WORKSHOPS

THEATRICAL FILM FESTIVAL

AUTOGRAPH SIGNINGS

COSPLAY ON BROADWAY™   and **MUCH MUCH MORE!**

Guests and Friends of BAAF 2001-2002

YOKO KANNO

Music Composer
(Cowboy Bebop)

ERIC STUART & VERONICA TAYLOR

Voice Actors
(Pokémon)

AKITAROH DAICHI

Director
(Now & Then,
Here & There)

RUDY GIULIANI

Former Mayor
of New York

bigappleanimefest.com

This sign reads "Tomare" and it means:

STOP!

THIS IS THE LAST PAGE OF THE BOOK! DON'T RUIN THE ENDING FOR YOURSELF.
This book is printed in the original Japanese format, which means that it reads from right to left (example on right).

You'll find that all CPM Manga books that are part of our Original Manga line are published in this format. The original artwork and sound effects are presented just like they were in Japan with minimal sound-effect translation so that you can see and enjoy the comic like the creators intended.

The format we have decided to use to present our ___ books was chosen by YOU, the fans. We conducted ___ and found that the overwhelming ___ their manga sound effects transla___ ___using.